T0214690

Algorithms and Data Structures

Helmut Knebl

Algorithms and Data Structures

Foundations and Probabilistic Methods for Design and Analysis

 Springer

Helmut Knebl
Fakultät Informatik
Technische Hochschule Nürnberg
Nürnberg, Germany

Ursprünglich veröffentlicht in deutscher Sprache:
Algorithmen und Datenstrukturen von Prof. Dr. Helmut Knebl
Copyright © Springer Fachmedien Wiesbaden GmbH, ein Teil von Springer Nature 2019.
Alle Rechte vorbehalten.

ISBN 978-3-030-59760-3   ISBN 978-3-030-59758-0 (eBook)
https://doi.org/10.1007/978-3-030-59758-0

This Springer imprint is published by the registered company Springer Nature Switzerland AG
The registered company address is: Gewerbestrasse 11, 6330 Cham, Switzerland

Preface

Many practical problems can be solved by algorithms. For this reason, computer algorithms are diverse and ubiquitous today. The spectrum ranges from one of the oldest recorded algorithms, the algorithm of Euclid from the third century B.C., to algorithms for the investigation of large amounts of data, algorithms for communication and searching on the Internet, algorithms for imaging procedures and for diagnostics in medical technology, and algorithms for assistance systems in cars, engine control or the control of household appliances. Algorithms are the subject of intensive research and belong to the fundamental concepts of computer science. The design of efficient algorithms and their analysis with regard to resource requirements are fundamental for the development of computer programs. Therefore, the subject Algorithms and Data Structures is a central component of any computer science curriculum.

This book originates from lectures on algorithms and data structures for students of computer science, media and business informatics at the Technische Hochschule Nürnberg Georg Simon Ohm. The basic topics of the book are covered in the bachelor's courses. Advanced parts, such as randomized algorithms, are reserved for master's courses.

The algorithms of the first chapter, all of which are popular algorithms, are studied to introduce common design principles for the development of algorithms. The following Chapters 2 to 6 are organized by problem areas. We consider the problem of storing and retrieving elements of a set and problems that can be formulated with graphs. For the first problem, we use three techniques to efficiently implement these operations: Sorting with binary search, search trees and hashing. The first two methods require ordered sets, the last method requires that the elements of the set are uniquely identified by keys.

The sorting methods quicksort and heapsort, binary search and searching for the kth-smallest element are the subject of Chapter 2. Special attention is paid to the analysis of the running time of the algorithms. Throughout all chapters, the aim is to develop explicit formulas or precise estimates for the running time. Difference equations are used as a solution method. This allows exact and not only asymptotic statements to be made about the running times of algorithms. We use a standardized method for the running time calculation: First, establish a difference equation for the running time and then solve the equation with known methods.

Hash functions, in particular universal families of hash functions, methods for the treatment of collisions and a detailed analysis of hash procedures are the subject of Chapter 3.

Chapter 4 deals with binary search trees, AVL trees and randomized binary search trees. B-trees are used to store data on secondary storage. Code trees for the graphical representation of codes for data compression complete the chapter.

Graphs play a fundamental role in many areas of computer science. For many graph problems, solutions exist in the form of efficient algorithms. In Chapter 5 breadth-first search and depth-first search for graphs are studied and as an application topological sorting and the calculation of the strongly connected components. Fundamental optimization problems, such as the construction of minimum spanning trees and shortest paths as well as the flow problem in networks, are the contents of Chapter 6.

Probabilistic methods are fundamental for the construction of simple and efficient algorithms. In each chapter at least one problem is solved by using a randomized algorithm. In detail, it is about the verification of the identity of polynomials, the randomized version of quicksort and quickselect, universal families of hash functions and randomized binary search trees. Randomized algorithms for the computation of a minimal section in a graph and for the construction of a minimum spanning tree for a weighted graph are among the advanced topics.

The book focuses on algorithms. Data structures are discussed as far as they are needed for the implementation of the algorithms. The selection of the topics is mainly based on the aim to treat elementary algorithms which have a wide field of application. The aim is a detailed and in-depth study.

The text assumes experience in programming algorithms, especially with elementary data structures – such as chained lists, queues and stacks – in the scope of the contents of the programming lectures of the first year of computer science studies. Familiarity with mathematical methods covered in the first year is also desirable. For the convenience of the reader, the mathematical methods necessary for understanding, in particular elementary solution methods for difference equations and special probability distributions, are repeated in the first chapter and in the appendix.

The formulation of the algorithms by using pseudo-code focuses on the essentials and thus makes the idea of the algorithm clear. It is sufficiently precise to allow considerations on the correctness and calculations of the running time to be carried out. More than 100 figures illustrate the algorithms. Many examples help the reader to understand the individual steps of the algorithms. Numerous exercises complete each chapter and help the reader to practice and deepen the material. Answers to the exercises are provided on the webpage for this book: www.in.th-nuernberg.de/Knebl/Algorithms.

This book stems from lectures on algorithms and data structures that I taught at the Technische Hochschule Nürnberg Georg Simon Ohm for many years. During this time, the university changed its name twice and still remained the same. During the preparation of the lecture I used the textbooks listed in Section 1.8.

I received a lot of support for the completion of the book. My colleagues Jens Albrecht, Christian Schiedermeier and especially Alexander Kröner have carefully looked through parts of it, which has led to the correction of mistakes and ambiguities. I owe Harald Stieber valuable suggestions and discussions, which have contributed to the improvement of the book. I would like to express my sincere thanks to all those who have supported me, including those not mentioned. I would especially like to thank my students, who have attended the lecture with dedication in the past years, worked diligently on exercises and helped to track down mistakes.

The book is essentially the translation of [Knebl19]

Algorithmen und Datenstrukturen
Grundlagen und probabilistische
Methoden für den Entwurf und die Analyse

The content and structure of the text is the same as that of the German edition. During the translation, the book was also thoroughly reviewed and the presentation improved in many places. Inaccuracies of the German edition have been corrected.

I am grateful to Patricia Brockmann and Sebastian Knebl for their support in proofreading, and I thank Ronan Nugent and Sybille Thelen at Springer for their pleasant and valuable cooperation.

Nürnberg, September 2020   Helmut Knebl

Contents

1. Introduction

An algorithm provides a solution to a computational problem. An example of a computational problem is the computation of the product of two numbers. The most important feature of an algorithm is that it works correctly. A mathematical proof that shows the correctness of an algorithm gives complete confidence in its correctness. The method of verification goes one step further. It not only proves that an algorithm is correct; it even proves that an implementation of the algorithm in a given programming language is correct.

Following correctness, running time is the second most important feature of an algorithm. Although it is often easy to count the number of operations for a fixed input, the calculation of the running time in the worst case and the average running time requires considerable effort. The average is calculated over all inputs of a fixed size. We treat mathematical methods such as linear difference equations, which are necessary for the running time analysis of the algorithms.

Orthogonal to the classification of algorithms according to problems – as done in this book in the Chapters 2-6 – you can classify algorithms according to algorithm types or design methods for algorithms. In this chapter, we discuss the design methods respectively algorithm types recursion, greedy algorithms, divide and conquer, dynamic programming and branch and bound. Subsequently, randomized algorithms will be introduced. Randomized algorithms, introduced in recent years, capture a wide field of applications. We study a Monte Carlo algorithm for the comparison of polynomials and in each of the following Chapters 2-6 we also solve a problem by a randomized algorithm.

The book covers many concrete algorithms. Theoretical concepts that are indispensable for the formal definition of the concept of algorithm, e.g., Turing machines, are not necessary here. The algorithms are formulated by using pseudo-code, which is based on common programming languages such as Java, and contains the most important elements of a high-level programming language. The representation by pseudo-code abstracts from the details of a programming language. But it is sufficiently precise to allow consideration of the correctness and calculation of the running time. We introduce the notation towards the end of the chapter (see Section 1.7).

© Springer Nature Switzerland AG 2020
H. Knebl, *Algorithms and Data Structures*, https://doi.org/10.1007/978-3-030-59758-0_1

1.1 Correctness of Algorithms

An algorithm is referred to as *correct* if, with respect to a given specification, it works correctly. Algorithms operate on data. The specification must therefore sufficiently and precisely reflect these data before executing the algorithm – the *precondition* – and the desired state after execution of the algorithm – the *postcondition*.

We now explain this method in more detail using the algorithm *sorting by selection* – SelectionSort.

SelectionSort should sort an array $a[1..n]$. The precondition is that the $<$-operator can be applied to the elements in $a[1..n]$. The postcondition is $a[1..n]$ is sorted, i.e., $a[1] \leq a[2] \leq \ldots \leq a[n]$.

The idea of sorting by selection, as the name suggests, is to search for the smallest item in $a[1..n]$. Assuming it is at the kth position, we then swap $a[1]$ with $a[k]$ and continue the procedure recursively with $a[2..n]$.

Algorithm 1.1.
SelectionSort(item $a[1..n]$)
1   index i, j, k; item m
2   for $i \leftarrow 1$ to $n - 1$ do
3        $k \leftarrow i; m \leftarrow a[i]$
4   for $j \leftarrow i + 1$ to n do
5   if $a[j] < m$
6   then $k \leftarrow j; m \leftarrow a[j]$
7   exchange $a[i]$ and $a[k]$

The algorithm SelectionSort implements the idea from above iteratively using two for loops.[1] We now show by induction on the loop parameters that the algorithm is correct. The task of the inner loop is to calculate the minimum of $a[i..n]$. More precisely, after each iteration of the loop we obtain:

$$m = \min a[i..j] \text{ for } j = i + 1, \ldots, n \text{ and } a[k] = m.$$

This condition is called an *invariant of the loop*. The condition must be checked after the last statement of the loop is executed. In the above algorithm, this is line 6. By induction on j, we see immediately that the statement is true. After each iteration of the outer loop, we get

$$a[1..i] \text{ is sorted, } i = 1, \ldots, n - 1, \text{ and } a[i] \leq a[k] \text{ for } k \geq i + 1.$$

This statement can be shown by induction on i. Since our algorithm terminates and the loop variable i has the value $n - 1$ after termination, $a[1..n-1]$ is sorted. Since $a[n] \geq a[n - 1]$, the assertion is proven.

In our proof, which shows that the algorithm is correct, the variables of the algorithm occur. It thus refers to a concrete implementation. Such a proof,

---

[1] The notation for the formulation of algorithms is described in more detail in Section 1.7.

which shows that the implementation of an algorithm A is correct, is called *program verification*. Preconditions and postconditions are specified as *predicates* V and N of the program variables. A mathematical proof that shows that if the predicate V is valid before executing A then the predicate N is valid after executing A proves the correctness of A, provided that A terminates. The technique of program verification was developed, among others, by Hoare[2] and Dijkstra[3]. Textbooks on program verification are [Gries81] and [Backhouse86].

The procedure to show, with specified pre- and postconditions, that a code segment transfers the precondition into the postcondition can be formalized. The proof can be done with computer support. A theorem prover goes one step further. It is an algorithm that finds a proof that shows that a precondition implies a particular postcondition. The proof found is constructive. It transforms the precondition into the postcondition and provides the coding of the algorithm.

We provide evidence which shows that algorithms are correct. Thereby the concrete implementation is not considered, with a few exceptions.

Our example SelectionSort terminates for each input. An algorithm which contains not only for loops, but also while loops or recursive calls, does not have to terminate for each input. The problem to decide for any algorithm whether it terminates or not is called the *halting problem*. The question of termination cannot be answered by an algorithm, i.e., the halting problem is not *decidable*. Similarly, it is not possible to specify an algorithm that decides for any algorithm A whether A is correct, or which calculates the running time of A. Therefore, these questions must be answered individually for each algorithm.

The following example shows that it is not even easy to decide for a given concrete algorithm whether the algorithm terminates for each admissible input.

Algorithm 1.2.
   int Col(int n)
  1   while $n \neq 1$ do
  2   if $n \bmod 2 = 0$
  3   then $n \leftarrow n \operatorname{div} 2$
  4   else $n \leftarrow (3n + 1) \operatorname{div} 2$
  5   return 1

It is assumed that Col terminates for each call parameter $n \in \mathbb{N}$. This assumption is called the Collatz[4] conjecture and has been unsolved for over 60 years.

---

[2] Tony Hoare (1934 –) is a British computer scientist and Turing Award winner.
[3] Edsger W. Dijkstra (1930 – 2002) was a Dutch Turing Award winner and made fundamental contributions to several areas of computer science.
[4] Lothar Collatz (1910 – 1990) was a German mathematician.

Recursion is a powerful design and programming method. We will study two interesting recursive functions.

McCarthy's[5] function, known as McCarthy's 91 function, has a complex recursive structure. We call this function M. For $n > 100$, M terminates with return value $n - 10$. For $n < 100$ the termination is not so obvious.

Algorithm 1.3.
```
int M(int n)
  1   if n > 100
  2     then return n − 10
  3     else  return M(M(n + 11))
```

Proposition 1.4. M *terminates for all* $n \leq 101$ *with the return value 91.*

Proof. First we show the statement of the proposition for n with $90 \leq n \leq 100$. For $n \geq 90$ we have $n + 11 \geq 101$. Hence, we have

$$M(M(n + 11)) = M(n + 1).$$

For n with $90 \leq n \leq 100$ follows

$$M(n) = M(M(n + 11)) = M(n + 1) = M(M(n + 12)) =$$

$$M(n + 2) = \ldots = M(101) = 91.$$

Now let $n \leq 89$ and $k = \max\{j \mid n + 11j \leq 100\}$. Then $90 \leq n + 11k \leq 100$ and because

$$M(n) = M^2(n + 11) = \ldots$$
$$= M^{k+1}(n + 11k) = M^k(M(n + 11k)) = M^k(91) = 91,$$

the assertion is shown. □

Our second example, the Ackermann function[6], has interesting properties which are relevant for theoretical computer science. It shows that Turing[7] computable functions exist that are not *primitive recursive*. Ackermann published his function in 1928 and thus refuted a conjecture of Hilbert[8] that every computable function is primitive recursive. Ackermann's function increases faster than is possible for primitive recursive functions. Primitive recursive functions are the result of a limited computation model that only allows for

---

[5] John McCarthy (1927 – 2011) was an American mathematician.

[6] Wilhelm Friedrich Ackermann (1896 – 1962) was a German mathematician. He was a student of Hilbert and studied the foundations of mathematics.

[7] Alan Mathison Turing (1912 – 1954) was an English mathematician and computer scientist. He made fundamental contributions to theoretical computer science and practical cryptanalysis (Enigma).

[8] David Hilbert (1862 – 1943) was a German mathematician. He is considered one of the most important mathematicians of the late 19th and the 20th century.

loops, but no while loops (loop programs). Ackermann's function[9] is an extremely fast increasing function that depends on two parameters $m, n \in \mathbb{N}_0$.

Algorithm 1.5.
   int A(int m, n)
    1 if $m = 0$
    2   then return $n + 1$
    3 if $n = 0$
    4   then return A$(m - 1, 1)$
    5 return A$(m - 1, \mathrm{A}(m, n - 1))$

For $m = 0$, A terminates immediately. In order to show that A terminates for all inputs, we consider the lexicographical order on $\mathbb{N}_0 \times \mathbb{N}_0$:

$$(m, n) < (m', n') \text{ if and only if } \begin{cases} m < m' \text{ or if} \\ m = m' \text{ and } n < n'. \end{cases}$$

Since

$$(m - 1, 1) < (m, 0), (m, n - 1) < (m, n) \text{ and } (m - 1, \mathrm{A}(m, n - 1)) < (m, n)$$

the recursive call is made with a smaller parameter regarding the lexicographical order. According to the following Lemma 1.6 there are only finite descending sequences starting with (m, n). Therefore, the function A terminates for all inputs (m, n) with a return value in $\mathbb{N}_0$.

The Ackermann function is used to analyze the union-find data type (Section 6.1.2).

Lemma 1.6. *Regarding the lexicographical order on $\mathbb{N}_0 \times \mathbb{N}_0$, there are only finite descending sequences.*

Proof. Suppose there is an infinite strictly descending sequence

$$(m_1, n_1) > (m_2, n_2) > (m_3, n_3) > \dots$$

The set $\{m_1, m_2, m_3, \dots\} \subset \mathbb{N}_0$ possesses a smallest element m_ℓ[10]. Hence, $m_\ell = m_{\ell+1} = m_{\ell+2} = \dots$. Then the set $\{n_\ell, n_{\ell+1}, n_{\ell+2}, \dots\}$ has no smallest element, a contradiction. $\square$

1.2 Running Time of Algorithms

The running time analysis – or analysis for short – of algorithms plays an important role in the study of algorithms. Often several algorithms are available

---

[9] The following function is called the Ackermann function. However, it is a simplified version of the original function that was introduced in 1955 by the Hungarian mathematician Rózsa Péter (1905 – 1977).

[10] The following property of natural numbers is used here: Let $M \subset \mathbb{N}_0$, $M \neq \emptyset$. Then M has a smallest element.

to solve a problem. Only due to analysis can you decide which of the algorithms is the most appropriate for a particular application. In the analysis, we strive for formulas that are as explicit as possible. We now demonstrate this with Algorithm 1.1 – SelectionSort.

1.2.1 Explicit Formulas

We analyze how often the individual lines of SelectionSort (Algorithm 1.1) are executed. We count the number of executions in the worst case and on average. The average is calculated over all possible arrangements of the elements in the array a. For the analysis we assume that all elements in a are pairwise distinct.

Let a_i be the number of executions of line i in the worst case and $\tilde{a}_i$ the number of executions of line i on average – each depending on n.

Line i	a_i	$\tilde{a}_i$
3, 7	$n - 1$	$n - 1$
5	$n(n-1)/2$	$n(n-1)/2$
6	$\leq n^2/4$	?

a_3, a_5 and a_7 do not depend on the arrangement of the elements in a. Therefore, $a_i = \tilde{a}_i$ for $i = 3, 5, 7$. The number a_6 of executions in the worst case of line 6 is limited by $n(n-1)/2$. However, this bound is not reached by any input instance. The specified bound $n^2/4$ is complicated to determine, see [Knuth98a, section 5.2.3][11]. In lines 4, 5 and 6 the minimum is determined in a subarray. To calculate $\tilde{a}_6$, we first consider the search for the minimum in an array.

Algorithm 1.7.
   item Min(item $a[1..n]$)
   1   index i; item m
   2    $m \leftarrow a[1]$
   3   for $i \leftarrow 2$ to n do
   4   if $a[i] < m$
   5   then $m \leftarrow a[i]$
   6   return m

We are now interested in the average number a_n of executions of line 5. An element $a[i]$ for which line 5 is executed is called an *intermediate minimum*.

Often recursive algorithms are easier to analyze. A recursive algorithm implies a recursive equation for the running time of the algorithm. Therefore, we program the minimum search recursively.

---

[11] Donald E. Knuth (1938 –) is an American computer scientist. He is the author of TEX and Metafont and of "The Art of Computer Programming", a standard work on basic algorithms and data structures that now comprises four volumes, was started almost 50 years ago and has not yet been completed ([Knuth97], [Knuth98], [Knuth98a] and [Knuth11]).

Algorithm 1.8.
  item MinRec(item $a[1..n]$)
  1 item m
  2 if $n > 1$
  3   then $m \leftarrow$ MinRec($a[1..n-1]$)
  4   if $m > a[n]$
  5   then $m \leftarrow a[n]$
  6   return m
  7 return $a[1]$

Let x_n be the average number of executions of line 5 in MinRec. We have $a_n = x_n$. Line 5 in MinRec is executed if and only if the smallest element is at position n. This case occurs with a probability of $1/n$, because there are $(n-1)!$ arrangements in which the smallest element is at position n and there are $n!$ arrangements in total. With a probability of $1/n$ the number of executions of line 5 is equal to the number of executions of line 5 in MinRec($a[1..n-1]$) plus 1, and with probability $1 - 1/n$ it is equal to the number of executions of line 5 in MinRec($a[1..n-1]$). The following equation holds for x_n.

$$x_1 = 0, \quad x_n = \frac{1}{n}(x_{n-1}+1) + \left(1 - \frac{1}{n}\right)x_{n-1} = x_{n-1} + \frac{1}{n}, \quad n \geq 2.$$

Equations of this kind are called *linear difference equations*. We discuss a general solution method for these equations in Section 1.3. The equation from above is easy to solve by repeatedly replacing x_j on the right-hand side by $x_{j-1} + 1/j$, $j = n-1, \ldots, 2$. We say the equation is solved by *expanding the right-hand side.*

$$x_n = x_{n-1} + \frac{1}{n} = x_{n-2} + \frac{1}{n-1} + \frac{1}{n} = \ldots$$
$$= x_1 + \frac{1}{2} + \ldots + \frac{1}{n-1} + \frac{1}{n}$$
$$= \sum_{i=2}^{n} \frac{1}{i} = \mathrm{H}_n - 1.$$

H_n is the nth harmonic number (Definition B.4).[12]
    We record the result of the previous calculation in the following lemma.

Lemma 1.9. *The mean value of the intermediate minima of the array $a[1..n]$ is $\mathrm{H}_n - 1$.*

Proposition 1.10. *The average number of executions of line 6 in Algorithm 1.1 is*

$$\tilde{a}_6 = (n+1)\mathrm{H}_n - 2n.$$

---

[12] The approximation of H_n by $\log_2(n)$ defines a closed form for H_n (Appendix B (F.1)).

Proof. The algorithm SelectionSort determines the minimum in the array $a[i \ldots n]$ for $i = 1, \ldots, n-1$. The length of this array is $n - (i-1)$. By Lemma B.6 we obtain

$$\tilde{a}_6 = \sum_{i=1}^{n-1}(\mathrm{H}_{n-i+1} - 1) = \sum_{i=2}^{n}\mathrm{H}_i - (n-1)$$
$$= (n+1)\mathrm{H}_n - n - 1 - (n-1) = (n+1)\mathrm{H}_n - 2n.$$

This shows the assertion.   □

During the analysis of Algorithm 1.1 we counted how often the individual lines were executed in the *worst case* and on average (*average case*).

The total number of operations is obtained by multiplying the operations of a line with the number of executions of the line and summing up all lines. By an *operation* we mean an elementary operation of a computer on which the algorithm is to be executed. If each operation is weighted with the running time of the operation in time units, the *running time* for the algorithm is calculated in time units.

The calculation of the running time of an algorithm is based on the basic constructs sequence, loop and branch, which make up an algorithm.

The running time of a sequence of statements is the sum of the running times of the statements that occur in the sequence.

When calculating the running time for a loop, we add the running times for the individual loop passes and the running time for the last check of the termination condition. The running time for a loop pass is calculated by adding together the running time to check the termination condition and the running time required for the loop body. If the running time is the same for all loop passes, we multiply the running time for a loop pass by the number of iterations of the loop.

The running time for an if-then-else statement results from the running time for checking the condition, the running time for the if-part and the running time for the else-part. When calculating the running time of the statement in the worst case, it is the maximum of the running times for the if- and the else-part. In the average case, it is the term specified by the weighted sum of the terms for the if- and else-part.

Definition 1.11. Let $\mathcal{P}$ be a computational problem, A an algorithm for $\mathcal{P}$ and J the set of instances of $\mathcal{P}$. Let $l : J \longrightarrow \mathbb{N}$ be a map that defines the size of an instance. Let $J_n := \{I \in J \mid l(I) = n\}$ be the *set of instances of size n*.[13] We define

$$S : J \longrightarrow \mathbb{N},$$

$S(I) = $ number of operations (or the number of time units) that A needs to solve I.

---

[13] For our applications, J_n can be assumed to be finite.

1. The *running time* or *(time) complexity* of A (in the worst case) is defined by

$$T : \mathbb{N} \longrightarrow \mathbb{N}, \ T(n) := \max_{I \in J_n} S(I).$$

2. If a probability distribution $(\mathrm{p}(I))_{I \in J_n}$ is given on J_n (Definition A.1), then $S_n : J_n \longrightarrow \mathbb{N}$, $S_n(I) := S(I)$ is a random variable (Definition A.5). The expected value $\mathrm{E}(S_n) = \sum_{I \in J_n} \mathrm{p}(I)S(I)$ of S_n is called the *average running time* or *average (time) complexity* of A

$$\tilde{T} : \mathbb{N} \longrightarrow \mathbb{N}, \ \tilde{T}(n) := \mathrm{E}(S_n).$$

In this text, the uniform distribution is always assumed for all calculations, i.e., all elements from J_n occur with the same probability. Then the expected value is the mean value.

Remark. Let the input of Algorithm 1.7, used to calculate the minimum, be an array of integers. The inputs of size n are arrays of length n. We assume the elements to be pairwise distinct. For each set $\{a_1, \ldots, a_n\}$ of integers, there are $n!$ different arrays.

The number of digits of an integer is determined by the architecture of the computer used. The representable integers form a finite subset $I \subset \mathbb{Z}$ of the integers. If the number of digits of the integers is limited only by the available memory of the computer, the effort for an operation with integers depends on the length of the numbers and can no longer be assumed to be constant.

Although the definition of the running time and the average running time depend on all inputs of size n, it is possible to calculate the running time in the worst case and on the average.

With a computer, we can simply calculate the running time needed to compute an instance by executing the algorithm. However, it is not possible to determine the running time in the worst case or the average running time in this way.

Remark. Analogous to the time complexity one can define the *memory complexity* of A. Memory complexity does not play a major role in the algorithms we are investigating. The algorithms in Chapters 2 – 4 essentially get along with constant memory. The memory consumption of the algorithms for graphs is linear in the size of the input.

1.2.2 O-Notation

Let A_1 and A_2 be algorithms for the same computational problem, and let $T_1(n)$ and $T_2(n)$ be the running times of A_1 and A_2. We now want to compare $T_1(n)$ and $T_2(n)$ for large n, which means we are interested in the running time for large inputs. Suppose $T_2(n) \leq T_1(n)$ for large n. This difference is insignificant[14] if there is a constant c such that we obtain $T_1(n) \leq cT_2(n)$ for large n. If the inequality is satisfied for no constant c, the running time of A_2 is much better than the running time of A_1 for large inputs. This is captured by the O-notation, which is one of the Landau symbols[15].

Definition 1.12 *(order of growth).* Let $f, g : \mathbb{N} \longrightarrow \mathbb{R}_{\geq 0}$ be functions. g is called *in the order of f*, or g is $O(f)$ for short, if there are constants $c, n_0 \in \mathbb{N}$ with:
$$g(n) \leq cf(n) \text{ for all } n \geq n_0.$$
This means g grows *asymptotically not faster than f*. We write $g(n) = O(f(n))$ or $g = O(f)$.

Example. Let $d > 0$, $\ell \geq 1$, $f(n) = n^\ell$ and $g(n) = n^\ell + dn^{\ell-1}$. Then
$$n^\ell + dn^{\ell-1} \leq n^\ell + n^\ell = 2n^\ell \text{ for } n \geq d.$$
For $c = 2$ and $n_0 = d$, we obtain $g(n) \leq cf(n)$ for $n \geq n_0$, i.e., $g(n) = O(f(n))$.
It is also valid that
$$n^\ell \leq n^\ell + dn^{\ell-1} \text{ for } n \geq 0,$$
so for $c = 1$ and $n_0 = 0$, $f(n) \leq cg(n)$ holds for $n \geq n_0$, i.e., $f(n) = O(g(n))$.

Remarks:

1. Directly from the definition of the O-notation follows transitivity: $f(n) = O(g(n))$ and $g(n) = O(h(n))$ implies $f(n) = O(h(n))$.
2. $g(n) = O(f(n))$ compares f and g with respect to their asymptotic growth (g does not grow asymptotically faster than f).
3. $g(n) = O(f(n))$ and $f(n) = O(g(n))$ means f and g have the same asymptotic growth. Then there are constants $c_1 > 0$, $c_2 > 0$ and $n_0 \in \mathbb{N}$, so that $c_1 g(n) \leq f(n) \leq c_2 g(n)$ for all $n \geq n_0$.
4. We extend the O-notation to functions depending on two parameters n, m. Let
$$f, g : D \longrightarrow \mathbb{R}_{\geq 0}, D \subset \mathbb{N}_0 \times \mathbb{N}_0,$$
be functions. We say $g(n, m) = O(f(n, m))$ if there are constants $c, n_0, m_0 \in \mathbb{N}$ with:
$$g(n, m) \leq cf(n, m) \text{ for all } (n, m) \in D, n \geq n_0 \text{ or } m \geq m_0.$$

This means that there are only finitely many pairs $(m, n) \in D$ which do not satisfy the inequality.
Note that $1 = O(nm)$ if $D = \mathbb{N} \times \mathbb{N}$, and $1 \neq O(nm)$ if $D = \mathbb{N}_0 \times \mathbb{N}_0$.
We will use this generalization in Chapters 5 and 6. The running time $T(n, m)$ of graph algorithms depends on n, the number of nodes, and on m, the number of edges of a graph.

---

[14] In the sense of the O-notation, but not in the practical use of algorithms.
[15] Edmund Georg Hermann Landau (1877 – 1938) was a German mathematician who worked in the field of analytic number theory. Landau made the O-notation known.

Proposition 1.13. *Let $f(n) \neq 0$, $n \in \mathbb{N}$. Then*

$$g(n) = O(f(n)) \text{ if and only if} \left(\frac{g(n)}{f(n)} \right)_{n \in \mathbb{N}} \text{ is bounded.}$$

Proof. We have $g(n) = O(f(n))$ if and only if there is a $c \in \mathbb{N}$ with $\frac{g(n)}{f(n)} \leq c$ for almost all $n \in \mathbb{N}$. This is equivalent to the fact that $\left(\frac{g(n)}{f(n)} \right)_{n \in \mathbb{N}}$ is bounded. □

Remark. To decide the convergence of a sequence, analysis provides assistance. Convergence of a sequence implies that the sequence is bounded (see [AmannEscher05, Chapter II.1]). So we conclude $g(n) = O(f(n))$ if the sequence $\left(\frac{g(n)}{f(n)} \right)_{n \in \mathbb{N}}$ converges. In particular,

$$g(n) = O(f(n)) \text{ and } f(n) = O(g(n)) \text{ if } \lim_{n \to \infty} \frac{g(n)}{f(n)} = c, c \neq 0.$$

$$g(n) = O(f(n)) \text{ and } f(n) \neq O(g(n)) \text{ if } \lim_{n \to \infty} \frac{g(n)}{f(n)} = 0.$$

$$f(n) = O(g(n)) \text{ and } g(n) \neq O(f(n)) \text{ if } \lim_{n \to \infty} \frac{g(n)}{f(n)} = \infty.$$

Example. Figure 1.1 shows graphs of elementary functions that occur as running times of algorithms.

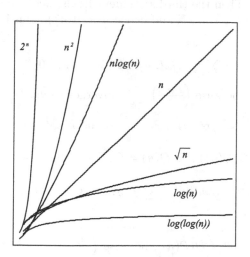

Fig. 1.1: Elementary functions.

Proposition 1.14 *(asymptotic growth of elementary functions). Let $n \in \mathbb{N}$.*

1. *Let $k \geq 0$ and $a > 1$. Then $\lim_{n \to \infty} \frac{n^k}{a^n} = 0$. In particular, $n^k = O(a^n)$ follows.*

2. Let $k \geq 0$, $\ell > 0$ and $a > 1$. Then $\lim_{n \to \infty} \frac{\log_a(n)^k}{n^\ell} = 0$. Consequently, $\log_a(n)^k = O(n^\ell)$.
3. Let $a > 1$. Then $a^n = O(n!)$.
4. $n! = O(n^n)$.

Proof.

1. The general exponential function is defined by $a^n := e^{\ln(a)n}$. Applying the chain rule, we get $\frac{da^n}{dn} = \ln(a)a^n$. We show that $\lim_{n \to \infty} n^k/a^n = 0$. By the rule of L'Hôpital[16] for "$\frac{\infty}{\infty}$", a quotient of sequences converges if the quotient of the derivatives of the numerator and denominator converge (see [AmannEscher05, Chapter IV.2]). Then the limit values are the same. We consider

$$\frac{n^k}{a^n}, \frac{kn^{k-1}}{\ln(a)a^n}, \frac{k(k-1)n^{k-2}}{\ln(a)^2 a^n}, \ldots, \frac{k(k-1) \cdot \ldots \cdot 1}{\ln(a)^k a^n}.$$

The last quotient converges to 0. Thus, all quotients converge to 0. This shows the first assertion.

2. We set $\log_a(n) = m$. Then $n = a^m$ and

$$\lim_{n \to \infty} \frac{\log_a(n)^k}{n^\ell} = \lim_{m \to \infty} \frac{m^k}{((a^\ell)^m)} = 0 \text{ (following point 1).}$$

The second assertion is shown.

3. Let $n_0 := \lceil a \rceil$. Then the third statement holds, because $a^n \leq a^{n_0} n!$.
4. We have $n! \leq n^n$ for $n \in \mathbb{N}$ and hence $n! = 0(n^n)$. This is statement four.

$\square$

Examples: Let $P(x) = \sum_{j=0}^{k} a_j x^j$, $a_j \in \mathbb{R}$, and $a_k > 0$.

1. $P(n) = O(n^k)$, because $\left(\frac{P(n)}{n^k}\right)_{n \in \mathbb{N}}$ converges to a_k.

2. Let $Q(x) = \sum_{j=0}^{l} a_j x^j$, $a_j \in \mathbb{R}$, $a_l > 0$ and $k < l$.

   Then $P(n) = O(Q(n))$ and $Q(n) \neq O(P(n))$, because

   $$P(n)/Q(n) = n^{k-l} \sum_{j=0}^{k} a_j n^{j-k} / \sum_{j=0}^{l} a_j n^{j-l} \text{ converges to 0.}$$

3. Let $a \in \mathbb{R}$, $a > 1$.

   $$P(n) = O(a^n), \ a^n \neq O(P(n)), \text{ because } \left(\frac{P(n)}{a^n}\right)_{n \in \mathbb{N}} \text{ converges to 0.}$$

4. Let $P(x) = a_i x^i + \ldots + a_k x^k$, $a_i > 0$, $i \leq k$.

   $$P\left(\tfrac{1}{n}\right) = O\left(\tfrac{1}{n^i}\right), \text{ because } \left(n^i P\left(\tfrac{1}{n}\right)\right)_{n \in \mathbb{N}} \text{ converges to } a_i.$$

---

[16] Guillaume François Antoine Marquis de L'Hôpital (1661 – 1704) was a French mathematician.

5. Let

$$f(n) = \begin{cases} \frac{1}{n} & \text{if } n \text{ is odd and} \\ n & \text{if } n \text{ is even.} \end{cases} \qquad g(n) = \begin{cases} \frac{1}{n} & \text{if } n \text{ is even and} \\ n & \text{if } n \text{ is odd.} \end{cases}$$

Then neither $\frac{f(n)}{g(n)}$ nor $\frac{g(n)}{f(n)}$ is bounded. Thus, $f \neq O(g)$ and $g \neq O(f)$.

Calculating the asymptotic growth of the running time of an algorithm, we can follow its construction from sequences, branches and loops (page 8). In particular, the following rules can be helpful: Let $g_i = O(f_i)$, $i = 1, 2$. Then

$$g_1 + g_2 = O(max(f_1, f_2)),$$
$$g_1 \cdot g_2 = O(f_1 \cdot f_2).$$

These rules follow directly from the definition of the O-notation (Definition 1.12).

If an analysis reveals that the running time $T(n)$ of an algorithm is of the order $O(f(n))$, this statement is likely to be of mainly theoretical interest. For an application, a precise specification of the constants c and n_0 would be very helpful, and if the size of the input is $< n_0$, of course also the behavior of $T(n)$ for small n. Therefore, an exact determination of $T(n)$ should be the aim of the running time analysis.

Sometimes, we use the O-notation as a convenient notation to specify the running time of an algorithm. For example, we write $T(n) = O(n^2)$, although we could accurately determine the polynomial $T(n)$ of degree 2. So we do not need to specify the coefficients of the polynomial.

An important class of algorithms are the algorithms with *polynomial running time* $T(n)$. With the introduced O-notation, this means $T(n) = O(n^k)$ for a $k \in \mathbb{N}$. An algorithm with a polynomial running time is also called an *efficient algorithm*. If the degree of the polynomial indicating the running time is large, even a polynomial running time algorithm is not applicable for practical applications. Algorithms of exponential running time are not efficient. We say $T(n)$ grows *exponentially* if $T(n)$ grows at least as fast as $f(n) = 2^{n^\varepsilon}$, $\varepsilon > 0$.

When specifying the asymptotic growth of the running time of algorithms, the functions $\log(n), n, n\log(n), n^2$ and 2^n appear many times. Then we say that the algorithm has *logarithmic, linear, super-linear, quadratic* or *exponential running time*.

1.3 Linear Difference Equations

The calculation of the running times of algorithms can often be done using linear difference equations. We therefore discuss methods for solving linear difference equations, which we will later use to calculate the running times of algorithms. There is an exhaustive theory about difference equations, the discrete analogues to differential equations (see for example [KelPet91] or [Elaydi03]).

1.3.1 First-Order Linear Difference Equations

Given are sequences of real numbers $(a_n)_{n \in \mathbb{N}}$ and $(b_n)_{n \in \mathbb{N}}$ and a real number b. A *first-order linear difference equation* is defined by

$$x_1 = b,$$
$$x_n = a_n x_{n-1} + b_n, \ n \geq 2.$$

The sequence x_n is searched for. The sequences a_n and b_n are called coefficients of the equation and are assumed to be known. The equation is of first order because x_n depends only on x_{n-1}, the predecessor of x_n. The number b is called the *initial condition* of the equation.

The sequence $x_1, x_2, \ldots$ can be calculated with a computer. However, we are interested in a formula for x_n that allows us to calculate x_n by inserting n. Such a formula is called a *closed solution* of the difference equation.

The two cases $b_n = 0$ and $a_n = 1$ can simply be solved by *expanding the right-hand side* of the equation. We obtain

$$x_n = a_n x_{n-1} = a_n a_{n-1} x_{n-2} = \ldots = b \prod_{i=2}^{n} a_i, \text{ and}$$

$$x_n = x_{n-1} + b_n = x_{n-2} + b_{n-1} + b_n = \ldots = b + \sum_{i=2}^{n} b_i.$$

In the general case, we first consider the *assigned homogeneous equation*

$$x_1 = b, \ x_n = a_n x_{n-1}, \ n \geq 2.$$

A solution of the homogeneous equation is obtained as above:

$$x_n = \pi_n b, \text{ where } \pi_n = \prod_{i=2}^{n} a_i, \ n \geq 2, \ \pi_1 = 1.$$

Let $\pi_n \neq 0$ for all $n \in \mathbb{N}$. The solution of the inhomogeneous equation is obtained by the approach:

$$x_n = \pi_n c_n, n \geq 1.$$

We substitute $x_n = \pi_n c_n$ into the equation and get

$$\pi_n c_n = a_n \pi_{n-1} c_{n-1} + b_n = \pi_n c_{n-1} + b_n.$$

Division by π_n yields a difference equation for c_n

$$c_n = c_{n-1} + \frac{b_n}{\pi_n}.$$

We solve this equation by expanding the right-hand side:

$$c_n = c_{n-1} + \frac{b_n}{\pi_n} = c_{n-2} + \frac{b_n}{\pi_n} + \frac{b_{n-1}}{\pi_{n-1}} = \ldots = b + \sum_{i=2}^{n} \frac{b_i}{\pi_i}.$$

We obtain

$$x_n = \pi_n \left(b + \sum_{i=2}^{n} \frac{b_i}{\pi_i} \right), n \geq 1,$$

as solution of the original equation.

The discussed method for solving linear difference equations of the first order is described as the *method of variation of constants*. Summarizing yields the following proposition.

Proposition 1.15. *The solution of the linear difference equation*

$$x_1 = b, \ x_n = a_n x_{n-1} + b_n, \ n \geq 2,$$

is given by

$$x_n = \pi_n \left(b + \sum_{i=2}^{n} \frac{b_i}{\pi_i} \right), \ n \geq 1,$$

where $\pi_i = \prod_{j=2}^{i} a_j$ for $2 \leq i \leq n$ and $\pi_1 = 1$.

A solution can be given in closed form if this succeeds for the product and the sum which occur in the general solution.

Corollary 1.16. *The linear difference equation with constant coefficients a and b*

$$x_1 = c, \ x_n = a x_{n-1} + b \text{ for } n \geq 2$$

has the solution

$$x_n = \begin{cases} a^{n-1}c + b\frac{a^{n-1}-1}{a-1} & \text{if } a \neq 1, \\ \\ c + (n-1)b & \text{if } a = 1. \end{cases}$$

Proof.

$$x_n = a^{n-1} \left(c + \sum_{i=2}^{n} \frac{b}{a^{i-1}} \right) = a^{n-1}c + b\sum_{i=2}^{n} a^{n-i} = a^{n-1}c + b\sum_{i=0}^{n-2} a^i$$

$$= \begin{cases} a^{n-1}c + b\frac{a^{n-1}-1}{a-1} & \text{if } a \neq 1 \text{ (Appendix B (F.5))}, \\ \\ c + (n-1)b & \text{if } a = 1. \end{cases}$$

$\square$

Examples:

1. The equation

$$x_1 = 2, \ x_n = 2x_{n-1} + 2^{n-2}, \ n \geq 2,$$

has the solution

$$\pi_n = \prod_{i=2}^{n} 2 = 2^{n-1}.$$

$$x_n = 2^{n-1}\left(2 + \sum_{i=2}^{n} \frac{2^{i-2}}{2^{i-1}}\right) = 2^{n-1}\left(2 + \sum_{i=2}^{n} \frac{1}{2}\right) = 2^{n-2}(n+3).$$

2. Consider the equation

(d) $$x_1 = c, \ x_n = \frac{n+2}{n}x_{n-1} + (an + b), \ n \geq 2,$$

where a, b, c are constant. Solving the equation we compute

$$\pi_n = \prod_{i=2}^{n} \frac{i+2}{i} = \frac{(n+1)(n+2)}{6}.$$

$$x_n = \frac{(n+1)(n+2)}{6}\left(c + \sum_{i=2}^{n} \frac{6(ai+b)}{(i+1)(i+2)}\right)$$

$$= (n+1)(n+2)\left(\frac{c}{6} + \sum_{i=2}^{n}\left(\frac{2a-b}{(i+2)} - \frac{b-a}{(i+1)}\right)\right)$$

$$= (n+1)(n+2)\left(\frac{c}{6} + (2a-b)\sum_{i=4}^{n+2}\frac{1}{i} - (b-a)\sum_{i=3}^{n+1}\frac{1}{i}\right)$$

$$= (n+1)(n+2)\left(aH_{n+1} + \frac{2a-b}{n+2} - \frac{13a}{6} + \frac{b}{3} + \frac{c}{6}\right).$$

$H_n = \sum_{i=1}^{n} \frac{1}{i}$ is the nth harmonic number (Definition B.4).
Adding up rational functions is done by using the partial fraction decomposition (Appendix B (F.2)):

$$\frac{ai+b}{(i+1)(i+2)} = \frac{A}{(i+1)} + \frac{B}{(i+2)}.$$

Multiplying by the common denominator we obtain

$$ai + b = A(i+2) + B(i+1) = (A+B)i + 2A + B.$$

Comparison of coefficients yields the equations

$$A + B = a \text{ and } 2A + B = b.$$

These equations have the solutions $A = b - a$ and $B = 2a - b$.
We will apply this with $(a, b, c) = (1, -1, 0)$ and $(a, b, c) = (\frac{1}{6}, \frac{2}{3}, 0)$ when calculating the average number of comparisons and exchanges for the quicksort algorithm (proof of Proposition 2.5 and of Proposition 2.7) and with $(a, b, c) = (1, 0, 1)$ when calculating the average path length in a binary search tree (proof of Proposition 4.20).

3. We now apply linear difference equations in order to analyze the running time of algorithms. We compute the number of outputs of the following algorithm HelloWorld.[17]

Algorithm 1.17.
   HelloWorld(int n)
   1   if $n > 0$
   2   then for $i \leftarrow 1$ to 2 do
   3   HelloWorld($n - 1$)
   4   print(hello, world)

Let x_n denote the number of outputs of "hello, world", depending on n.

$$x_1 = 1, \ x_n = 2x_{n-1} + 1 \text{ for } n \geq 2.$$

Thus,

$$\pi_n = \prod_{i=2}^{n} 2 = 2^{n-1}.$$

$$x_n = 2^{n-1}\left(1 + \sum_{i=2}^{n} \frac{1}{2^{i-1}}\right) = 2^{n-1} + \sum_{i=2}^{n} 2^{n-i}$$

$$= 2^{n-1} + \sum_{i=0}^{n-2} 2^i = 2^{n-1} + 2^{n-1} - 1 = 2^n - 1.$$

4. We consider a modified algorithm.

Algorithm 1.18.
   HelloWorld2(int n)
   1   if $n >= 1$
   2   then print(hello, world)
   3   for $i \leftarrow 1$ to $n - 1$ do
   4   HelloWorld2(i)
   5   print(hello, world)

Again, x_n denotes the number of outputs of "hello, world".

$$x_1 = 1, \ x_n = \sum_{i=1}^{n-1}(x_i + n) \text{ for } n \geq 2.$$

---

[17] Referring to Kernighan and Ritchie's famous "hello, world" ([KerRit78]).

We obtain

$$x_n - x_{n-1} = x_{n-1} + 1, \text{ hence}$$
$$x_n = 2x_{n-1} + 1, \ x_1 = 1.$$

Thus, the solution of the difference equation is $x_n = 2^n - 1$.

1.3.2 Fibonacci Numbers

Fibonacci numbers are named after Fibonacci[18], who is regarded as the discoverer of these numbers. Fibonacci numbers have many interesting properties. Among other things they appear in the analysis of algorithms. We will use the Fibonacci numbers in Section 4.3 to find an upper bound for the height of a balanced binary search tree.

Definition 1.19. *Fibonacci numbers* are recursively defined by

$$f_0 = 0, \ f_1 = 1,$$
$$f_n = f_{n-1} + f_{n-2}, \ n \geq 2.$$

Figure 1.2 illustrates the development of the Fibonacci numbers through a growth process. An unfilled node becomes a filled node in the next level. From a filled node, an unfilled node and a filled node are created in the next level.

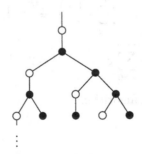

Fig. 1.2: Fibonacci numbers.

The number of nodes in the ith level is equal to the ith Fibonacci number f_i, because the nodes of the $(i-1)$th level also occur in the ith level (as filled nodes) and the nodes of the $(i-2)$th level are filled in the $(i-1)$th level.

The goal is to develop an algorithm to calculate the Fibonacci numbers and to derive a closed formula for the Fibonacci numbers. For this purpose

---

[18] Leonardo da Pisa, also called Fibonacci, was an Italian mathematician. He lived in Pisa in the second half of the 12th and first half of the 13th century.

we consider the somewhat more general *linear difference equation of second order*

$$x_0 = u_0, \; x_1 = u_1,$$
$$x_n = v_n x_{n-1} + w_n x_{n-2} + b_n, \; w_n \neq 0, \; n \geq 2.$$

The sequence x_n is wanted. The sequences v_n, w_n and b_n are called coefficients of the equation and are assumed to be known.

A second-order difference equation is converted to a system of first-order difference equations:

$$X_1 = B,$$
$$X_n = A_n X_{n-1} + B_n, \; n \geq 2,$$

where

$$B = \begin{pmatrix} u_0 \\ u_1 \end{pmatrix}, \; X_n = \begin{pmatrix} x_{n-1} \\ x_n \end{pmatrix}, \; n \geq 1,$$

$$A_n = \begin{pmatrix} 0 & 1 \\ w_n & v_n \end{pmatrix}, \; B_n = \begin{pmatrix} 0 \\ b_n \end{pmatrix}, \; n \geq 2.$$

This system has the solution

$$X_n = \pi_n \left(B + \sum_{i=2}^{n} \pi_i^{-1} B_i \right), \; n \geq 1, \text{ where}$$

$$\pi_i = A_i \cdot \ldots \cdot A_2, \; 2 \leq i \leq n, \; \pi_1 = \begin{pmatrix} 1 & 0 \\ 0 & 1 \end{pmatrix}.$$

In particular, the homogeneous equation

$$x_0 = u_0, x_1 = u_1,$$
$$x_n = v_n x_{n-1} + w_n x_{n-2}, \; w_n \neq 0, \; n \geq 2,$$

has the solution

$$X_n = \pi_n B, n \geq 1, \text{ where } \pi_n = A_n \cdot \ldots \cdot A_2, \; \pi_1 = \begin{pmatrix} 1 & 0 \\ 0 & 1 \end{pmatrix}.$$

The homogeneous difference equation with constant coefficients

$$x_0 = u_0, \; x_1 = u_1,$$
$$x_n = v x_{n-1} + w x_{n-2}, \; w \neq 0, \; n \geq 2$$

has the solution

$$X_n = A^{n-1} B, n \geq 1, \text{ where } A = \begin{pmatrix} 0 & 1 \\ w & v \end{pmatrix}.$$

Remarks:

1. The matrix A^n can be calculated by an efficient exponentiation algorithm in $\log_2(n)$ steps (see below).
2. The method for solving second-order difference equations can be generalized to kth-order difference equations.

Algorithm for Computing the nth Fibonacci Number. The Fibonacci numbers are defined by a homogeneous second-order linear difference equation with constant coefficients. With

$$X_n = \begin{pmatrix} f_{n-1} \\ f_n \end{pmatrix} \text{ and } A = \begin{pmatrix} 0 & 1 \\ 1 & 1 \end{pmatrix},$$

we get for $n \geq 1$

$$\begin{pmatrix} f_{n-1} & f_n \\ f_n & f_{n+1} \end{pmatrix} = \left(A^{n-1} \begin{pmatrix} 0 \\ 1 \end{pmatrix} A^n \begin{pmatrix} 0 \\ 1 \end{pmatrix} \right) = A^{n-1} \begin{pmatrix} 0 & 1 \\ 1 & 1 \end{pmatrix} = A^n.$$

We calculate $A^{n-1} = \begin{pmatrix} a_{11} & a_{12} \\ a_{21} & a_{22} \end{pmatrix}$ with the following Algorithm 1.20 and get $f_n = a_{22}$.

This algorithm calculates $(A^l)^2$ and possibly $A^l A$ in one step.

Calculating $(A^l)^2$, the terms $f_{l-1}^2 + f_l^2$, $f_{l-1}f_l + f_l f_{l+1}$ and $f_l^2 + f_{l+1}^2$ have to be used. If you replace f_{l+1} with $f_{l-1} + f_l$, you see that the squaring requires three multiplications (f_{l-1}^2, $f_{l-1}f_l$, f_l^2) and six additions due to the special shape of A^l. Multiplying A^l by A, the first line of $A^l A$ is the second line of A^l, and the second line of $A^l A$ is the sum of the two lines of A^l. Therefore, only two additions of integers are required.

Algorithm for Fast Exponentiation. Due to the formula

$$A^n = \begin{cases} (A^{n/2})^2 & \text{if } n \text{ is even,} \\ (A^{(n-1)/2})^2 A & \text{if } n \text{ is odd,} \end{cases}$$

the exponent n can be halved in one step, consisting of a squaring and at most one multiplication. This results in an algorithm that calculates A^n in time $O(\log_2(n))$.

To avoid recursion, we consider n in the binary numeral system,

$$n = 2^{l-1}n_{l-1} + 2^{l-2}n_{l-2} + \ldots + 2^1 n_1 + 2^0 n_0 \text{ (with } n_{l-1} = 1)$$
$$= (2^{l-2}n_{l-1} + 2^{l-3}n_{l-2} + \ldots + n_1) \cdot 2 + n_0$$
$$= (\ldots((2n_{l-1} + n_{l-2}) \cdot 2 + n_{l-3}) \cdot 2 + \ldots + n_1) \cdot 2 + n_0.$$

Then $l = \lfloor \log_2(n) \rfloor + 1$ and

$$A^{2^{l-1}+2^{l-2}n_{l-2}+\ldots+2n_1+n_0} = (\ldots(((A^2 \cdot A^{n_{l-2}})^2 \cdot A^{n_{l-3}})^2 \cdot \ldots)^2 \cdot A^{n_1})^2 \cdot A^{n_0}.$$

We also get this formula if we expand the recursive formula from above, i.e., by continually applying it on $A^{n/2}$ and $A^{(n-1)/2}$. We convert the formula into an algorithm:

Algorithm 1.20.
   matrix Power(int matrix A; bitString $n_{l-1} \dots n_0$)
   1   int i; matrix $B \leftarrow A$
   2   for $i \leftarrow l - 2$ downto 0 do
   3      $B \leftarrow B^2 \cdot A^{n_i}$
   4   return B

The number of iterations of the for loop is $\lfloor \log_2(n) \rfloor$, the bit length of n minus 1. The running time of the algorithm Power is logarithmic in the exponent n, hence linear in $|n|$, the bit length of n. This applies if the effort for the arithmetic operation of addition and multiplication is constant. However, note that the effort for large numbers depends on the length of the numbers and is therefore no longer constant. This increases the complexity if we use the algorithm to calculate very large Fibonacci numbers.

The iterative solution, which calculates f_n by adding f_{i-1} to f_{i-2} to get f_i for $i = 2 \dots n$, needs $n - 1$ additions. The running time of this algorithm is linear in n and therefore exponential in $|n|$. But it calculates the first n Fibonacci numbers.

The following is a closed solution for the Fibonacci numbers.

Proposition 1.21. *The Fibonacci number* f_n *can be calculated by*

$$f_n = \frac{1}{\sqrt{5}} (g^n - \hat{g}^n), \ n \geq 0,$$

where

$$g = \frac{1}{2} \left(1 + \sqrt{5} \right) \ \textit{and} \ \hat{g} = 1 - g = -\frac{1}{g} = \frac{1}{2} \left(1 - \sqrt{5} \right)$$

are the solutions of the equation $x^2 = x + 1$.

Definition 1.22. The number g is called the *ratio of the golden mean* or *golden ratio*.[19]

Proof. The solution approach with the exponential function

$$f_n = q^n,$$

inserted into the equation $x_n - x_{n-1} - x_{n-2} = 0$, yields

$$q^n - q^{n-1} - q^{n-2} = q^{n-2} \left(q^2 - q - 1 \right) = 0.$$

The base q of the exponential function is a zero of the quadratic polynomial $X^2 - X - 1$. This has the solutions g and $\hat{g}$. Thus,

---

[19] A line segment is divided in the ratio of the golden mean if the ratio of the whole to its greater part is equal to the ratio of the greater to the smaller part. In formulas: $(x + y)/x = x/y$. This ratio does not depend on x and y and is the solution of the equation $X^2 = X + 1$. In architecture, proportions satisfying the ratio of the golden mean are considered ideal.

$$g^n - g^{n-1} - g^{n-2} = 0 \text{ and } \hat{g}^n - \hat{g}^{n-1} - \hat{g}^{n-2} = 0$$

is valid, i.e., the functions g^n and $\hat{g}^n$ are solutions of the equation $x_n - x_{n-1} - x_{n-2} = 0$. Since the equation is linear,

$$\lambda_1 g^n + \lambda_2 \hat{g}^n, \lambda_1, \lambda_2 \in \mathbb{R}$$

is also a solution. It is called the *general solution* of the difference equation.

The initial condition $f_0 = 0$, $f_1 = 1$ implies

$$\lambda_1 g^0 + \lambda_2 \hat{g}^0 = 0,$$
$$\lambda_1 g^1 + \lambda_2 \hat{g}^1 = 1.$$

The solutions of the linear equations are $\lambda_1 = -\lambda_2 = \frac{1}{\sqrt{5}}$. Inserting $\lambda_1 = -\lambda_2 = \frac{1}{\sqrt{5}}$ into the solution yields

$$f_n = \frac{1}{\sqrt{5}}(g^n - \hat{g}^n),$$

the *solution for the initial condition* $f_0 = 0$, $f_1 = 1$. $\quad\square$

Remarks:

1. The proof method can be used to find a closed form for the solution of homogeneous difference equations with constant coefficients (not only for equations of order 2).
2. Since $|\frac{1}{\sqrt{5}}\hat{g}^n| < \frac{1}{2}$ for $n \geq 0$, we conclude that

$$f_n = \text{round}\left(\frac{g^n}{\sqrt{5}}\right),$$

   where $\text{round}(x)$ rounds to the nearest integer x. In particular, the formula shows that the Fibonacci numbers have exponential growth.
3. The calculation of Fibonacci numbers with the formula from Proposition 1.21 is done in the quadratic number field $\mathbb{Q}(\sqrt{5})$[20]. The arithmetic in $\mathbb{Q}(\sqrt{5})$ gives exact results. If this is not implemented, irrational numbers are usually approximated by floating-point numbers. However, these only offer limited precision and the computational effort is higher compared to integer arithmetic.
4. The quotient of two consecutive Fibonacci numbers converges to the golden ratio g. This follows because

$$\frac{f_{n+1}}{f_n} = \frac{g^{n+1} - \hat{g}^{n+1}}{g^n - \hat{g}^n} = g\frac{1 - \left(\frac{\hat{g}}{g}\right)^{n+1}}{1 - \left(\frac{\hat{g}}{g}\right)^n} = g\frac{1 - \left(\frac{-1}{g^2}\right)^{n+1}}{1 - \left(\frac{-1}{g^2}\right)^n}.$$

The last fraction converges to 1. This implies the assertion.

---

[20] Quadratic number fields are the subject of algebraic number theory and are also studied in [RemUll08].

We will discuss the solution of second-order linear difference equations with constant coefficients that are not homogeneous. For this purpose we consider the recursive calculation of Fibonacci numbers – as in the defining equation.

Algorithm 1.23.
  int Fib(int n)
   1   if $n = 0$ or $n = 1$
   2   then return n
   3   else return Fib$(n - 1)$ + Fib$(n - 2)$

Let x_n denote the number of calls to Fib to calculate the nth Fibonacci number. Then

$$x_0 = 1, \ x_1 = 1,$$
$$x_n = x_{n-1} + x_{n-2} + 1, \ n \geq 2.$$

We calculate a *special solution* of the equation by the approach $\varphi_n = c$, c constant, and get $c = 2c + 1$ or $c = -1$.
The general solution x_n results from the general solution of the homogeneous equation and the special solution $\varphi_n = -1$:

$$x_n = \lambda_1 g^n + \lambda_2 \hat{g}^n - 1, \ \lambda_1, \ \lambda_2 \in \mathbb{R}.$$

From the initial conditions $x_0 = x_1 = 1$ results $\lambda_1 g^0 + \lambda_2 \hat{g}^0 - 1 = 1$ and $\lambda_1 g^1 + \lambda_2 \hat{g}^1 - 1 = 1$. We get

$$\lambda_1 = \frac{2(1 - \hat{g})}{\sqrt{5}} = \frac{2g}{\sqrt{5}}, \lambda_2 = -\frac{2(g - \sqrt{5})}{\sqrt{5}} = -\frac{2\hat{g}}{\sqrt{5}}.$$

This results in the following solution:

$$x_n = \frac{2}{\sqrt{5}}\left(gg^n - \hat{g}\hat{g}^n\right) - 1 = \frac{2}{\sqrt{5}}\left(g^{n+1} - \hat{g}^{n+1}\right) - 1 = 2f_{n+1} - 1.$$

The term is therefore exponential in n. The algorithm from above, which uses the exponentiation method, has a logarithmic running time.

Remark. We consider an inhomogeneous linear difference equation of order k with constant coefficients:

(1.1) $x_n + a_{k-1}x_{n-1} + \ldots + a_1 x_{n-k+1} + a_0 x_{n-k} = r_n, \ a_0 \neq 0.$

We assign the *characteristic polynomial* to the equation.

$$P(X) := X^k + a_{k-1}X^{k-1} + \ldots + a_1 X^1 + a_0.$$

1. A general solution is computed as follows:
   If $P(X)$ has the zeros $x_1, \ldots, x_\mu$ with the multiples $\alpha_1, \ldots, \alpha_\mu$, then

$$x_n = \sum_{i=1}^{\mu} \sum_{j=1}^{\alpha_i} \lambda_{ij} n^{j-1} x_i^n, \ \lambda_{i,j} \in \mathbb{R}$$

   is a general solution of the assigned homogeneous equation.
2. The approach to the right-hand side provides a solution of the inhomogeneous equation: If the right-hand side r_n of equation (1.1) is of the form $r_n = p(n)a^n$, where $p(n)$ is a polynomial of degree ν, then the approach $n^\ell a^n \varphi(n)$ with a polynomial $\varphi(n)$ of degree ν with indeterminate coefficients delivers a special solution. ℓ is the multiplicity of the zero a of the characteristic polynomial.

The methods discussed in this section for solving recursive equations, especially first-order linear difference equations, are applied in the running time calculation of quicksort (Section 2.1.1) and quickselect (Section 2.31), for determining the average path length in binary search trees (Proposition 4.20) and in Section 4.4 for analyzing the running time of the access functions to randomized binary search trees (Proposition 4.24), and in the analysis of a randomized algorithm for calculating a minimal cut in a graph (Section 5.7). An upper bound for the height of an AVL tree can be specified using a second-order difference equation (Proposition 4.14).

1.4 The Master Method for Recurrences

In the literature the following proposition is called the "master theorem". It is applicable to algorithms that follow the divide and conquer strategy (see Section 1.5.2). The running time $T(n)$ of such algorithms fulfills a recurrence equation, i.e., the value $T(n)$ is defined by the values of arguments preceding n.

We consider the case that only one smaller value occurs, which is determined by a contraction. If only integer input variables are considered, the contraction must be supplemented by rounding up or down.

The method we are using to solve recurrences allows precise statements and provides a simple proof. First, we formulate the concept of the contraction and two preparatory lemmas.

Definition 1.24. Let $g : \mathbb{R}_{\geq 0} \longrightarrow \mathbb{R}_{\geq 0}$ be a function and $0 \leq q < 1$. g is said to be a *contraction* if $g(x) \leq qx$ for all $x \in \mathbb{R}_{\geq 0}$.

Lemma 1.25. *Let* $g : \mathbb{R}_{\geq 0} \longrightarrow \mathbb{R}_{\geq 0}$ *be a contraction,* $r : \mathbb{R}_{\geq 0} \longrightarrow \mathbb{R}_{\geq 0}$ *a function and* $b \in \mathbb{N}$. *We consider for* $x \in \mathbb{R}_{\geq 0}$ *the recurrence*

(R0) $T_g(x) = d$ *for* $x < b$, *and* $T_g(x) = aT_g(g(x)) + r(x)$ *for* $x \geq b$, where $a \geq 1$ and d are constants from $\mathbb{R}_{\geq 0}$. Let k be the recursion depth of g with respect to x and b, i.e., k is the smallest exponent with $g^k(x) < b$. Then

$$(S0) \qquad T_g(x) = a^k d + \sum_{i=0}^{k-1} a^i r(g^i(x)).$$

In particular, if r is an increasing function[21] and h and g are contractions with $h(x) \leq g(x)$ for all $x \in \mathbb{R}_{\geq 0}$, then $T_h(x) \leq T_g(x)$ for all $x \in \mathbb{R}_{\geq 0}$.

Proof. We get the formula by expanding the right-hand side.

$$\begin{aligned}
T_g(x) &= aT_g(g(x)) + r(x) \\
&= a(aT_g(g^2(x)) + r(g(x))) + r(x) \\
&= a^2 T_g(g^2(x)) + ar(g(x)) + r(x) \\
&\vdots \\
&= a^k T_g(g^k(x)) + a^{k-1} r(g^{k-1}(x)) + \ldots + ar(g(x)) + r(x) \\
&= a^k d + \sum_{i=0}^{k-1} a^i r(g^i(x)).
\end{aligned}$$

The solution formula (S0) implies the statement about monotonicity. □

Lemma 1.26. *Let $n \in \mathbb{R}_{\geq 0}$. We consider the recurrence*

$$(R1) \qquad T_{(\bar{5})}(n) = d \text{ for } n < b, \text{ and } T_{(\bar{5})}(n) = aT_{(\bar{5})}\left(\frac{n}{b}\right) + cn^l \text{ for } n \geq b,$$

where $a \geq 1$, c, d are constants from $\mathbb{R}_{\geq 0}$, $b > 1$ and l are constants from $\mathbb{N}_0$. Let $q = a/b^l$. Then

$$(S1) \qquad T_{(\bar{5})}(n) = \begin{cases} da^{\lfloor \log_b(\lfloor n \rfloor) \rfloor} + cn^l \, \dfrac{q^{\lfloor \log_b(\lfloor n \rfloor) \rfloor}-1}{q-1} & \text{if } b^l \neq a, \\[3mm] da^{\lfloor \log_b(\lfloor n \rfloor) \rfloor} + cn^l \lfloor \log_b(\lfloor n \rfloor) \rfloor & \text{if } b^l = a. \end{cases}$$

The order of $T_{(\bar{5})}(n)$ satisfies

$$T_{(\bar{5})}(n) = \begin{cases} O(n^l) & \text{if } l > \log_b(a), \\ O(n^l \log_b(n)) & \text{if } l = \log_b(a), \\ O(n^{\log_b(a)}) & \text{if } l < \log_b(a). \end{cases}$$

Proof. Let $n = \sum_{i=-\infty}^{k-1} n_i b^i = n_{k-1} \ldots n_1 n_0 . n_{-1} \ldots$ with $n_{k-1} \neq 0$ in the base-b numeral system. Then $k = \lfloor \log_b(\lfloor n \rfloor) \rfloor + 1 = \lfloor \log_b(n) \rfloor + 1$, and $\frac{n}{b^i} = n_{k-1} \ldots n_i . n_{i-1} \ldots n_0 n_{-1} \ldots$. With Lemma 1.25 and $g(n) = n/b$, $r(n) = cn^l$ and $g^i(n) = n/b^i$ we conclude

---

[21] A function f is said to be *increasing* if $f(x) \leq f(y)$ for all arguments $x \leq y$ and *strictly increasing* if we require "<" instead of "≤".

$$T_{(\overline{b})}(n) = a^{k-1}d + c\sum_{i=0}^{k-2} a^i \left(\frac{n}{b^i}\right)^l = a^{k-1}d + cn^l \sum_{i=0}^{k-2}\left(\frac{a}{b^l}\right)^i$$

$$= \begin{cases} da^{k-1} + cn^l \frac{q^{k-1}-1}{q-1} & \text{if } b^l \neq a, \\ da^{k-1} + cn^l(k-1) & \text{if } b^l = a \end{cases}$$

(Appendix B (F.5)). Replacing k with $\lfloor \log_b(n)\rfloor + 1^{22}$, we obtain the formula for $T_{(\overline{b})}(n)$.

It remains to show the statements about the order of $T_{(\overline{b})}(n)$.

If $q > 1$, i.e., $\log_b(a) > l$, then $O\left(\frac{q^{k-1}-1}{q-1}\right) = O(q^{k-1})$, and
$O(a^{k-1} + n^l q^{k-1}) = O\left(a^{\log_b(n)} + n^l q^{\log_b(n)}\right) =^{23} O\left(n^{\log_b(a)} + n^l n^{\log_b(q)}\right) = O(n^{\log_b(a)} + n^l n^{\log_b(a)-l}) = O(n^{\log_b(a)})$.

If $q < 1$, i.e., $\log_b(a) < l$, then $\frac{q^{k-1}-1}{q-1}$ converges to $\frac{1}{1-q}$ for $k \longrightarrow \infty$. So $\frac{q^{k-1}-1}{q-1} = O(1)$ and $a^{\lfloor\log_b(\lfloor n\rfloor)\rfloor} + cn^l \leq n^{\log_b(a)} + cn^l = O(n^l)$.

If $\log_b(a) = l$, then $da^{\lfloor\log_b(\lfloor n\rfloor)\rfloor} + cn^l\lfloor\log_b(\lfloor n\rfloor)\rfloor = O(n^l + n^l\log_b(n)) = O(n^l\log_b(n))$. The assertion of the lemma is thus shown. □

The solution method – expanding the right-hand side – immediately implies the uniqueness of the solution.

Corollary 1.27. *The (closed) solution* (S1) *of the recurrence* (R1) *is determined by the parameters a, b, c, d and l of the recurrence, and hence it is unique.*

Remark. Let $n = b^k$. We set $x_k = T_{(\overline{b})}(b^k)$. Then

$$x_1 = ad + cb^l \text{ and } x_k = ax_{k-1} + c\left(b^l\right)^k \text{ for } k > 1.$$

Using the substitution $n = b^k$, we transform the recurrence (R1) into a linear difference equation. We present the solution of this difference equation as an exercise (Exercise 12). Another method to solve the recurrence (R1) is obtained by applying the inverse transformation $k = \log_b(n)$ (Lemma B.23).

We formulate the prerequisites for the application of the master theorem. We split the input of size $n \in \mathbb{N}$ for a recursive algorithm A into a instances of size $\lfloor\frac{n}{b}\rfloor$ or of size $\lceil\frac{n}{b}\rceil$. Then the solutions for the a subinstances are computed recursively. The running time to split an instance and to combine the results of the recursive calls of these subinstances is cn^l.

The function $T_{\lfloor\overline{b}\rfloor}$ is defined recursively by

(R2) $T_{\lfloor\overline{b}\rfloor}(n) = d$ for $n < b$ and $T_{\lfloor\overline{b}\rfloor}(n) = aT_{\lfloor\overline{b}\rfloor}\left(\left\lfloor\frac{n}{b}\right\rfloor\right) + cn^l$ for $n \geq b$,

---

22 Recursion breaks down after $k - 1 = \lfloor\log_b(n)\rfloor$ steps. We say $\lfloor\log_b(n)\rfloor$ is the *recursion depth* of the equation (R1).

23 $a^{\log_b(n)} = (b^{\log_b(a)})^{\log_b(n)} = (b^{\log_b(n)})^{\log_b(a)} = n^{\log_b(a)}$.

where $a \geq 1$, $b > 1$ and c, d, l are constants from $\mathbb{N}_0$. The function $T_{\lceil \frac{}{b} \rceil}$ is defined analogously by replacing in $T_{\lfloor \frac{}{b} \rfloor}$ the function $\lfloor \frac{}{b} \rfloor$ with the function $\lceil \frac{}{b} \rceil$.

(R3) $T_{\lceil \frac{}{b} \rceil}(n) = d$ for $n < b$ and $T_{\lceil \frac{}{b} \rceil}(n) = a T_{\lceil \frac{}{b} \rceil}\left(\left\lceil \frac{n}{b} \right\rceil\right) + cn^l$ for $n \geq b$.

Let $n = \sum_{i=0}^{k-1} n_i b^i = n_{k-1} \ldots n_1 n_0$, $n_{k-1} \neq 0$, in the base-b numeral system and let $q = a/b^l$.

The function $S(n, \lambda)$, which is only used with $\lambda = b/(b-1)$ and $\lambda = (b-1)/b$, is defined by

$$S(n, \lambda) = \begin{cases} d' a^{\lfloor \log_b(n) \rfloor} + c(\lambda n)^l \, \dfrac{q^{\lfloor \log_b(n) \rfloor} - 1}{q-1} & \text{if } q \neq 1, \\[2mm] d' a^{\lfloor \log_b(n) \rfloor} + c(\lambda n)^l \lfloor \log_b(n) \rfloor & \text{if } q = 1. \end{cases}$$

Depending on λ and n, d' is defined by

$$d' = \begin{cases} d & \text{if } \lambda = (b-1)/b \text{ or } \lambda = b/(b-1) \text{ and } n \leq (b-1)b^{k-1}, \\ ad + cb^l & \text{if } \lambda = b/(b-1) \text{ and } n > (b-1)b^{k-1}. \end{cases}$$

Proposition 1.28 (*master theorem*). *Let $T_{(\frac{}{b})}$ be the function of Lemma 1.26.*

1. *Then $T_{\lfloor \frac{}{b} \rfloor}(n) \leq T_{(\frac{}{b})}(n) \leq T_{\lceil \frac{}{b} \rceil}(n)$ for $n \in \mathbb{N}$.*
2. *For $n = n_{k-1} b^{k-1}$, the inequality from above becomes an equation, i.e., for $T_{\lfloor \frac{}{b} \rfloor}(n)$ and $T_{\lceil \frac{}{b} \rceil}(n)$ the formulas for $T_{(\frac{}{b})}(n)$ of Lemma 1.26 apply.*
3. *Further, if $n \neq n_{k-1} b^{k-1}$ then $S\left(n, (b-1)/b\right)$ is a lower bound of $T_{\lfloor \frac{}{b} \rfloor}(n)$ and $S(n, b/(b-1))$ is an upper bound for $T_{\lceil \frac{}{b} \rceil}$.*
4. *The asymptotic statements for $T_{(\frac{}{b})}(n)$ from Lemma 1.26 apply to $T_{\lfloor \frac{}{b} \rfloor}(n)$ and $T_{\lceil \frac{}{b} \rceil}(n)$.*

Proof. Lemma 1.25 implies the inequality in point 1.

For $n = n_{k-1} b^{k-1}$, we have $\lfloor \frac{n}{b^i} \rfloor = \lceil \frac{n}{b^i} \rceil = \frac{n}{b^i}$, $i = 0, \ldots, k-1$. Thus, the inequality becomes an equation.

We now show the statement for the lower bound of $T_{\lfloor \frac{}{b} \rfloor}(n)$. For this purpose we set

$$U(n) = \frac{n - (b-1)}{b}.$$

Then $U(n) \leq \lfloor \frac{n}{b} \rfloor$. Let

$$T_U(n) = d \text{ for } n < b, \, T_U(n) = a T_U(U(n)) + cn^l \text{ for } n \geq b.$$

We set

$$m_0 = n \text{ and } m_i = \frac{m_{i-1} + 1 - b}{b} \text{ for } i \geq 1.$$

This is a linear difference equation with constant coefficients. Hence, by Corollary 1.16[24]

$$m_i = \frac{n}{b^i} + \frac{1}{b^i} - 1 \text{ and from there } \left(\frac{b-1}{b}\right)\frac{n}{b^i} \le m_i \text{ for } i = 0, \ldots, k-2.$$

We have $U^i(n) = m_i$. With Lemma 1.25 and $\lambda = (b-1)/b$, we get

$$T_U(n) = a^{k-1}d + c\sum_{i=0}^{k-2} a^i m_i^l \ge a^{k-1}d + c(\lambda n)^l \sum_{i=0}^{k-2} \left(\frac{a}{b^l}\right)^i$$

$$= \begin{cases} da^{k-1} + c(\lambda n)^l \frac{q^{k-1}-1}{q-1} & \text{if } b^l \neq a, \\ \\ da^{k-1} + c(\lambda n)^l (k-1) & \text{if } b^l = a \end{cases}$$

(Appendix B (F.5)). We replace k by $\lfloor \log_b(n) \rfloor + 1$ and get $S(n, (b-1)/b) \le T_U(n) \le T_{\lfloor \frac{n}{b} \rfloor}(n)$. For the last inequality, Lemma 1.25 is used.

To show the upper bound for $T_{\lceil \frac{n}{b} \rceil}(n)$, we use the following notation:

$$\left\lceil \frac{n}{b} \right\rceil_0 := n \text{ and } \left\lceil \frac{n}{b} \right\rceil_i := \left\lceil \frac{\left\lceil \frac{n}{b} \right\rceil_{i-1}}{b} \right\rceil \text{ for } i \ge 1.$$

We show first that

$$\left\lceil \frac{n}{b} \right\rceil_i = \left\lceil \frac{n}{b^i} \right\rceil \le \frac{b}{b-1}\frac{n}{b^i} \text{ for } i = 0, \ldots, k-2.$$

Let $n = \sum_{i=0}^{k-1} n_i b^i = n_{k-1} \ldots n_1 n_0$, $n_{k-1} \neq 0$, in the base-b numeral system. For $i = 0, \ldots, k-2$ we show

$$\left\lceil \frac{n}{b^i} \right\rceil \le \frac{b}{b-1}\frac{n}{b^i} \text{ or equivalently } (b-1)\left\lceil \frac{n}{b^i} \right\rceil \le \frac{n}{b^{i-1}}.$$

If $i = 0$ or $n_{i-1} \ldots n_0 = 0$, there is nothing to show. Let $i \ge 1$ and $n_{i-1} \ldots n_0 \neq 0$. Then for the left-hand side l and for the right-hand side r we have

$$l = n_{k-1}b^{k-i} + n_{k-2}b^{k-i-1} + \ldots + n_i b + b -$$
$$(n_{k-1}b^{k-i-1} + n_{k-2}b^{k-i-2} + \ldots + n_i + 1)$$
$$\le n_{k-1}b^{k-i} + n_{k-2}b^{k-i-1} + \ldots + n_i b + (b-1) - b^{k-i-1}$$
$$= n_{k-1}b^{k-i} + (n_{k-2}-1)b^{k-i-1} + n_{k-3}b^{k-i-2} + \ldots + n_i b + (b-1)$$
$$\le n_{k-1}b^{k-i} + n_{k-2}b^{k-i-1} + \ldots n_i b + n_{i-1}$$
$$\le r$$

---

[24] Please note the index shift, because here the start condition is given for m_0 and not for m_1.

By Lemma 1.25 we get

$$T_{\lceil \frac{n}{b} \rceil}(n) = d'a^{k-1} + c\sum_{i=0}^{k-2} a^i \left(\left\lceil \frac{n}{b} \right\rceil_i \right)^l \leq d'a^{k-1} + c(n\lambda)^l \sum_{i=0}^{k-2} \left(\frac{a}{b^l} \right)^i$$

$$= \begin{cases} d'a^{k-1} + c(\lambda n)^l \left(\frac{q^{k-1}-1}{q-1} \right) & \text{if } b^l \neq a, \\ \\ d'a^{k-1} + c(\lambda n)^l (k-1) & \text{if } b^l = a. \end{cases}$$

Again, we replace k by $\lfloor \log_b(n) \rfloor + 1$ and get the upper bound for $T_{\lceil \frac{n}{b} \rceil}$. Statement 4 is a consequence of statements 1 and 3 (with Lemma 1.26). $\quad\square$

Remark. We summarize the results of our investigations. The running time $T(n)$ of a divide and conquer algorithm that splits instances of size n into instances of size $\lfloor \frac{n}{b} \rfloor$ or $\lceil \frac{n}{b} \rceil$ can be exactly determined for $n = n_{k-1}b^{k-1}$. In the case $n \neq n_{k-1}b^{k-1}$, we specify functions that bound $T_{\lfloor \frac{n}{b} \rfloor}(n)$ narrowly downwards and $T_{\lceil \frac{n}{b} \rceil}(n)$ narrowly upwards. The recursion depth of each of the equations (R1), (R2) and (R3) is $\lfloor \log_b(n) \rfloor$ for $n \in \mathbb{N}$. The statements about the order of the running time follow immediately from the derived formulas for $S\left(n, (b-1)/b \right)$ and $S\left(n, b/(b-1) \right)$.

We will present a first application of the master theorem in the following section.

The Algorithm of Strassen for the Multiplication of Matrices. We consider the product of two 2×2 square matrices with coefficients from a (not necessarily commutative) ring[25]:

$$\begin{pmatrix} a_{11} & a_{12} \\ a_{21} & a_{22} \end{pmatrix} \cdot \begin{pmatrix} b_{11} & b_{12} \\ b_{21} & b_{22} \end{pmatrix} = \begin{pmatrix} c_{11} & c_{12} \\ c_{21} & c_{22} \end{pmatrix}.$$

The standard method calculates the scalar product of each row of the first matrix with each column of the second matrix, and requires eight multiplications and four additions of the coefficients.

The following equations, which Strassen[26] published in [Strassen69], reduce the number of multiplications to 7.

$$\begin{aligned} m_1 &= f_1 \cdot j_1 := (a_{11} + a_{22}) \cdot (b_{11} + b_{22}), \\ m_2 &= f_2 \cdot j_2 := (a_{21} + a_{22}) \cdot b_{11}, \\ m_3 &= f_3 \cdot j_3 := a_{11} \cdot (b_{12} - b_{22}), \\ \text{(S.1)} \qquad m_4 &= f_4 \cdot j_4 := a_{22} \cdot (b_{21} - b_{11}), \\ m_5 &= f_5 \cdot j_5 := (a_{11} + a_{12}) \cdot b_{22}, \\ m_6 &= f_6 \cdot j_6 := (a_{21} - a_{11}) \cdot (b_{11} + b_{12}), \\ m_7 &= f_7 \cdot j_7 := (a_{12} - a_{22}) \cdot (b_{21} + b_{22}). \end{aligned}$$

---

[25] In the application it is a matter of matrix rings. The result of multiplying two matrices depends on the order of the factors. Matrix rings are generally not commutative.

[26] Volker Strassen (1936 –) is a German mathematician.

The product $(c_{ij})_{\substack{i=1,2 \\ j=1,2}}$ is computed from $m_1, \ldots, m_7$:

(S.2)
$$c_{11} = m_1 + m_4 - m_5 + m_7,$$
$$c_{12} = m_3 + m_5,$$
$$c_{21} = m_2 + m_4,$$
$$c_{22} = m_1 - m_2 + m_3 + m_6.$$

The calculation of $(c_{ij})_{\substack{i=1,2 \\ j=1,2}}$ is done by seven multiplications and 18 additions. The equations can easily be verified by recalculation.

The following algorithm calculates the product of two $n \times n$ square matrices A, B with coefficients from a ring R for $n = 2^k$. We apply the reduction of the number of multiplications from eight to seven recursively. For this, the inputs A and B are each divided into four $n/2 \times n/2$ matrices. Now A, B and C are 2×2 matrices with $n/2 \times n/2$ matrices as coefficients:

$$\begin{pmatrix} A_{11} & A_{12} \\ A_{21} & A_{22} \end{pmatrix} \cdot \begin{pmatrix} B_{11} & B_{12} \\ B_{21} & B_{22} \end{pmatrix} = \begin{pmatrix} C_{11} & C_{12} \\ C_{21} & C_{22} \end{pmatrix}.$$

So we are looking at 2×2 matrices over the matrix ring of the $n/2 \times n/2$ matrices, where the equations (S.1) and (S.2) to calculate the product of two 2×2 matrices also apply. The algorithm is designed according to the divide and conquer design method (Section 1.5.2).

Algorithm 1.29.
　　matrix StrassenMult(matrix $A[1..n, 1..n]$, $B[1..n, 1..n]$)
　1　if $n = 1$
　2　　then return $A[1, 1] \cdot B[1, 1]$
　3　for $k \leftarrow 1$ to 7 do
　4　　　$(F_k, J_k) \leftarrow$ Divide(k, A, B)
　5　　　$M_k \leftarrow$ StrassenMult(F_k, J_k)
　6　$C \leftarrow$ Combine$(M_1, \ldots, M_7)$
　7　return C

For $n = 1$ the product is computed immediately, and for $n = 2$ the algorithm performs the operations of the equations (S.1) and (S.2) with elements from the ring R.

The calculation of the inputs $(F_1, J_1), \ldots, (F_7, J_7)$ for the recursive calls is done by Divide (line 4) according to the equations (S.1). It requires 10 additions of square matrices of dimension $n/2$. After termination of the recursive calls of StrassenMult, the results are combined to give the return value C (by the equations (S.2)). For this, eight more additions of square matrices of dimension $n/2$ are necessary.

Hence, the number of arithmetic operations (additions, subtractions and multiplications) fulfills the following recurrence

$$T(n) = 7 \cdot T\left(\frac{n}{2}\right) + 18 \left(\frac{n}{2}\right)^2 \text{ for } n \geq 2 \text{ and } T(1) = 1.$$

We now apply Proposition 1.28 and get

$$T(n) = 7^{\log_2(n)} + 6n^2 \left(\left(\frac{7}{4} \right)^{\log_2(n)} - 1 \right)$$

$$= n^{\log_2(7)} + 6n^2 \left(n^{\log_2(\frac{7}{4})} - 1 \right)$$

$$= 7n^{\log_2(7)} - 6n^2 = 7^{k+1} - 3 \cdot 2^{2k+1}.$$

The number of arithmetic operations is of order $O(n^{\log_2(7)}) = O(n^{2.807})$.

For any n we set $k = \lceil \log_2(n) \rceil$. We complete A and B to $2^k \times 2^k$ matrices, by setting the missing coefficients to 0. Then we apply Algorithm 1.29. For the number $T(n)$ of arithmetic operations, we get

$$T(n) = 7^{\lceil \log_2(n) \rceil} + 6n^2 \left(\left(\frac{7}{4} \right)^{\lceil \log_2(n) \rceil} - 1 \right)$$

$$\leq 7 \cdot 7^{\log_2(n)} + 6n^2 \left(\frac{7}{4} \left(\frac{7}{4} \right)^{\log_2(n)} - 1 \right)$$

$$= 7n^{\log_2(7)} + 6n^2 \left(\frac{7}{4} n^{\log_2(\frac{7}{4})} - 1 \right)$$

$$= \frac{35}{2} n^{\log_2(7)} - 6n^2.$$

For any n we have an estimate for the number of arithmetic operations. Since the running time is proportional to the number of arithmetic operations, StrassenMult's running time is $O(n^{\log_2(7)}) = O(n^{2.807})$ for all $n \in \mathbb{N}$.[27]

In [CopWin90] an algorithm is developed that solves the problem of multiplying square matrices of dimension n in a running time of order $O(n^{2.375477})$. Since then optimizations have been published which decrease the exponent from the third digit after the decimal point.

However, the assumption is that the problem of multiplying square matrices is solvable in time $O(n^2)$.

1.5 Design Techniques for Algorithms

The design of an algorithm is done individually depending on the problem. However, there are design principles that have proven themselves and provide good algorithms. The first method is recursion. It is often easy to reduce a problem to a problem of the same type but of a smaller scope. In this situation recursion can be applied. Other methods are divide and conquer – often in conjunction with recursion – greedy algorithms, dynamic programming and branch and bound algorithms. In this section, we introduce these design techniques using prominent examples.

---

[27] The running time of the standard algorithm is in $O(n^3)$.

1.5.1 Recursion

Recursion is a powerful tool in the development of algorithms, and it is often easy to prove the correctness of a recursive algorithm and to calculate its running time. We explain this using the example of the towers of Hanoi. This is a puzzle which is attributed to Lucas[28]. The towers of Hanoi appeared in 1883 as a toy under the pseudonym "N. Claus de Siam", an anagram of "Lucas d'Amiens". The game, shown in Figure 1.3, consists of three upright rods A, B and C and a tower. The tower consists of n perforated discs of different diameters, arranged according to size, with the largest disc at the bottom and the smallest disc at the top, lined up on rod A.

The aim of the game is to move the complete tower from A to B.

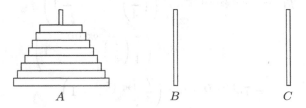

$$A \qquad\qquad B \qquad\qquad C$$

Fig. 1.3: Towers of Hanoi.

1. One step allows you to move a disc from one rod to another.
2. Never place a disc on a smaller one.
3. Rod C serves as a clipboard.

It is not immediately clear that the problem has a solution at all. However, with recursion the problem can quite simply be solved as follows:

Algorithm 1.30.
TowersOfHanoi(int n; rod A, B, C)
   1   if $n > 0$
   2   then TowersOfHanoi($n - 1, A, C, B$)
   3   move disc n from A to B
   4   TowersOfHanoi($n - 1, C, B, A$)

The function TowersOfHanoi outputs a sequence of working steps that lead to the goal. We shall prove our assertion by induction on n. If there is only one disc, the target is reached by line 3: move the disc from A to B. Constraint 2 above is observed.

We now assume that TowersOfHanoi for $n - 1$ discs indicates a sequence of steps that lead to the goal and respect the constraint. The call

---

[28] François Édouard Anatole Lucas (1842 – 1891) was a French mathematician and is known for his work in number theory.

TowersOfHanoi($n - 1, A, C, B$) moves the first $n - 1$ discs from A to C. B serves as clipboard. Then the largest disc is moved from A to B. Next the call TowersOfHanoi($n - 1, C, B, A$) moves the $n - 1$ discs from C to B. Now A serves as clipboard. The second condition is maintained with all movements.

Since every recursive call lowers n by 1, $n = 0$ occurs and the algorithm terminates. These considerations show that our algorithm works correctly.

Even now that we know that the problem of the Towers of Hanoi has a solution, it does not seem obvious what a solution without recursion should look like. This shows that recursion provides a powerful method for designing algorithms. The steps we get using recursion can also be achieved iteratively (Exercise 15).

We now analyze TowersOfHanoi. The number of steps is easy to describe. Let x_n be the number of steps to move a tower of n discs from one rod to another. Then

$$x_1 = 1, \ x_n = 2x_{n-1} + 1, \ n \geq 2.$$

This is a linear difference equation of the first order. According to Corollary 1.16 it has the solution $x_n = 2^{n-1} + 2^{n-1} - 1 = 2^n - 1$.

However, recursion does not always provide an efficient solution. This is shown by the function that calculates the Fibonacci numbers recursively, analogously to the defining equation (Algorithm 1.23).

Recursion is used to define trees, to traverse trees and more generally to traverse graphs (Chapter 4 and Algorithm 5.12). The algorithm quicksort (Algorithm 2.1), the algorithm for the search for the kth-smallest element (Algorithm 2.30) and the algorithm for binary search (Algorithm 2.28)) use recursion together with the divide and conquer method. The Algorithm of Karger, Klein and Tarjan – a randomized algorithm for computing a minimum spanning tree in a graph – uses divide and conquer with recursion virtuously (Algorithm 6.50).

1.5.2 Divide and Conquer

With the divide and conquer strategy, the problem is first divided into smaller independent subproblems. The subproblems should be easier to control than the overall problem. The subproblems are solved recursively. Then the solutions of the subproblems are combined to form a solution to the overall problem. The application of this principle leads to a simpler algorithm, as in the following example of integer multiplication. This also results in a significant improvement of the running time.

The product of positive integers

$$c = \sum_{i=0}^{n-1} c_i b^i \text{ and } d = \sum_{i=0}^{n-1} d_i b^i$$

– represented in the numeral system with base b – is computed according to
the school method as follows:

$$e = cd = \sum_{i=0}^{2n-1} \overline{e}_i b^i.$$

The coefficients $\overline{e}_i$ are calculated from

$$e_i = \sum_{j+k=i} c_j d_k.$$

Additionally, carry-overs have to be considered, i.e., calculations are modulo
b and the carry-over from the previous position has to be added.

With this method, every digit of c is multiplied by every digit of d. Therefore, n^2 multiplications of digits are necessary. When calculating with paper
and pencil, we use the decimal system. We have n^2 digits to multiply according to multiplication tables. If c and d are large numbers, we use a computer
and display the numbers with the base $b = 2^{32}$, for example, if it is a 32-bit
computer. Then the multiplication of digits is performed by the processor.

However, there are procedures for multiplying numbers that are faster if
the numbers are large. The algorithm of Karatsuba[29] uses the divide and
conquer design method (see [KarOfm62]).

Let c and d be $2n$-digit numbers. To apply Karatsuba's method, we write

$$c = c_1 b^n + c_0, \; d = d_1 b^n + d_0,$$

where c_0, c_1, d_0 and d_1 are at most n-digit numbers. When calculating the
product
$$cd = c_1 d_1 b^{2n} + (c_1 d_0 + c_0 d_1) b^n + c_0 d_0,$$

a trick is used to reduce the four multiplications of n-digit numbers to three
multiplications. Calculate $f := (c_1 + c_0)(d_1 + d_0)$. Then

$$c_1 d_0 + c_0 d_1 = f - c_1 d_1 - c_0 d_0.$$

Thereby $c_1 + c_0$ and $d_1 + d_0$ can have at most $n+1$ digits. The calculation of f
is a bit more complex than with n-digit numbers. We neglect this additional
effort in the following considerations.

Figure 1.4 illustrates the advantage with a geometric figure. Only the
areas of the white squares have to be calculated.

---

[29] Anatoly Alexeyevich Karatsuba (1937 – 2008) was a Russian mathematician
working in computer science, number theory and analysis.

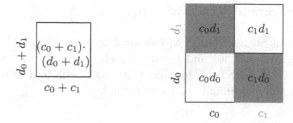

Fig. 1.4: Reduction from four to three multiplications.

The advantage of this reduction from four to three multiplications pays off especially if we use it recursively. This is done in the following Algorithm 1.31.

Algorithm 1.31.
int Karatsuba(int p, q)
1   if $p < m$ and $q < m$
2   then return $p \cdot q$
3   $l_p \leftarrow \text{len}(p)$, $l_q \leftarrow \text{len}(q)$
4   $l \leftarrow \lceil \max(l_p, l_q)/2 \rceil$
5   $low_p \leftarrow p \bmod b^l$, $low_q \leftarrow q \bmod b^l$
6   $hi_p \leftarrow \text{rshift}_l(p)$, $hi_q \leftarrow \text{rshift}_l(q)$
7   $z_0 \leftarrow \text{Karatsuba}(low_p, low_q)$
8   $z_1 \leftarrow \text{Karatsuba}(hi_p, hi_q)$
9   $z_2 \leftarrow \text{Karatsuba}(low_p + hi_p, low_q + hi_q)$
10 return $z_1 b^{2l} + (z_2 - z_1 - z_0)b^l + z_0$

The recursion is aborted if both factors are smaller than a given limit m. In this case, the multiplication is executed immediately (by the processor of the computer). The summands of the additions are large numbers. The function $\text{len}(x)$ returns the number of digits of x and rshift_l shifts by l digits to the right.

Let $M(n)$ be the number of multiplications necessary to multiply two n-digit numbers. Then

$$M(n) = d \text{ for } n < m \text{ and } M(n) = 3M\left(\left\lceil \frac{n}{2} \right\rceil\right).$$

The multiplications with powers of b are shift operations and are not counted with the multiplications. With Proposition 1.28 we conclude

$$M(n) = O(n^{\log_2(3)}) = O(n^{1.585}).$$

We get a procedure that manages with much less than n^2 multiplications.

There is a procedure that is even faster for very large numbers. It uses the discrete Fourier transform method from analysis and was published by

Schönhage[30] and Strassen[31] in [SchStr71].

The algorithms StrassenMult (Algorithm 1.29), quicksort (Algorithm 2.1), quickselect (Algorithm 2.30) and binary search (Algorithm 2.28) as well as the algorithm KKT − MST (Algorithm 6.50) to calculate a minimum spanning tree apply the divide and conquer principle.

1.5.3 Greedy Algorithms

We consider a *unit-time task scheduling problem*. Given are tasks

$$a_i = (t_i, p_i), \ i = 1, \ldots, n,$$

t_i is the deadline in time units for a_i and p_i is the premium paid when a_i is completed before the deadline t_i. The tasks must be processed sequentially. Each task needs one time unit to be processed. We are now looking for a processing schedule that maximizes the total profit.

Example. Let $a = (1, 7)$, $b = (1, 9)$, $c = (2, 5)$, $d = (2, 2)$ and $e = (3, 7)$ be tasks. For the execution in the first step, all tasks are possible. In the second step, the tasks that have a deadline 1, no longer need to be considered and in the third step, the tasks that have deadlines 1 and 2 earn no profit.

A possible approach to the solution is to select in each step a task that appears to be optimal. A task is selected that maximizes the profit at the moment. A locally optimal solution should result in an optimal solution. In the previous example, this procedure produces the schedule b, c, e.

This strategy is called a *greedy strategy* and an algorithm that implements such a strategy is called a *greedy algorithm*. The situation in which the greedy strategy leads to success can be formalized.

Definition 1.32. Let S be a finite set and $\tau \subset \mathcal{P}(S)$ a set of subsets of S. (S, τ) is called a *matroid* if $\tau \neq \emptyset$ and

1. τ is closed regarding subsets, i.e., for $A \subset B$ and $B \in \tau$ we also have $A \in \tau$. This is sometimes called the *hereditary property*.
2. For $A, B \in \tau$, $|A| < |B|$, there is an $x \in B \setminus A$ with $A \cup \{x\} \in \tau$. This condition is called the *exchange property*.

The elements of τ are called *independent* sets.

This definition is already contained in a work by H. Whitney[32] from 1935 ([Whitney35]). There have been extensive investigations about matroids and

---

[30] Arnold Schönhage (1934 –) is a German mathematician and computer scientist.
[31] Volker Strassen (1936 –) is a German mathematician.
[32] Hassler Whitney (1907 – 1989) was an American mathematician. He is famous for his contributions to algebraic and differential topology and to differential geometry.

greedy algorithms, see for example Schrijver's monograph "Combinatorial Optimization" [Schrijver03].

We consider a matroid $M = (S, \tau)$ with a weight function

$$w : S \longrightarrow \mathbb{R}_{>0}.$$

Let $A \in \tau$. $w(A) := \sum_{a \in A} w(a)$ is called the *weight* of A.

The *optimization problem* for (S, τ) now consists of finding an $\tilde{A} \in \tau$ with

$$w(\tilde{A}) = \max\{w(A) \mid A \in \tau\}.$$

$\tilde{A}$ is called an *optimal solution* of the optimization problem.

We now want to apply this notation to the task scheduling problem. Let $S = \{a_1, \ldots a_n\}$ be the set of tasks.

τ must be defined so that the elements of τ represent a solution to the task scheduling problem (a solution with maximum profit is wanted). A subset of S is said to be *admissible* for the task scheduling problem if there is an order for the elements of A (a schedule for A) so that all tasks from A can be completed before their deadline date. We refer to such an order as an admissible order. Let τ be the set of admissible subsets of S. We assign to the task scheduling problem the pair (S, τ). We will first show that (S, τ) is a matroid. Then, the task scheduling problem is an optimization problem for a matroid.

Proposition 1.33. (S, τ) *is a matroid.*

Proof. 1. We have $\emptyset \in \tau$, so $\tau \neq \emptyset$. Obviously, τ has the hereditary property. A schedule for a subset results from a schedule of the superset by deleting tasks.

2. It remains to show that the exchange property holds. Let $A, B \in \tau$ and $|A| < |B| =: l$. We write the elements of B in an admissible order:

$$b_1 = (t_1, p_1), b_2 = (t_2, p_2), \ldots, b_l = (t_l, p_l).$$

Since each task needs a time unit to be processed, $t_j \geq j$, $j = 1, \ldots, l$.

Let k be maximum with $b_k \notin A$, i.e., $b_k \notin A$ and $b_{k+1}, \ldots, b_l \in A$. $|A \setminus \{b_{k+1}, \ldots, b_l\}| = |A| - (l - k) = |A| - |B| + k < k$.

We show that $A \cup b_k \in \tau$ by specifying a schedule for $A \cup b_k$. We first execute the tasks of $A \setminus \{b_{k+1}, \ldots, b_l\}$ in the (admissible) order of $A \setminus \{b_{k+1}, \ldots, b_l\}$ and then the tasks $b_k, b_{k+1}, \ldots, b_l$ (in that order). The task b_j is executed at a time $\leq j$, $j = k, \ldots, l$. Because $t_j \geq j$, $j = 1, \ldots, l$, we get a valid order for $A \cup \{b_k\}$, i.e., $A \cup \{b_k\} \in \tau$. This shows the exchange property for τ. $\square$

Example. Figure 1.5 shows the power set for the set of tasks $S = \{a, b, c, d, e\}$ from the previous example. Between the admissible subsets of our task scheduling problem above, the subset relationship is given. They form a matroid.

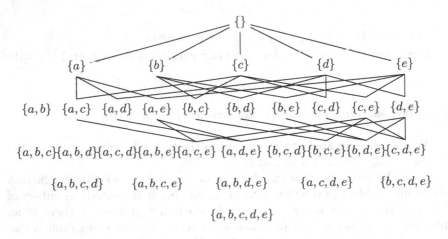

Fig. 1.5: The matroid for the task scheduling example.

Let (S, τ) be a matroid with weight function $w : S \longrightarrow \mathbb{R}_{>0}$. The following algorithm, a generic solution to the matroid optimization problem, calls an algorithm Sort to sort S by weights in descending order, i.e.,

$$w(s_1) \geq w(s_2) \geq \ldots \geq w(s_n).$$

Algorithm 1.34.
   set Optimum(Matroid (S, τ))
  1   $\{s_1, \ldots, s_n\} \leftarrow \text{Sort}(S); O \leftarrow \emptyset$
  2   for $i \leftarrow 1$ to n do
  3   if $O \cup \{s_i\} \in \tau$
  4   then $O \leftarrow O \cup \{s_i\}$
  5   return O

Example. Let the tasks $a = (1, 7)$, $b = (1, 9)$, $c = (2, 5)$, $d = (2, 2)$ and $e = (3, 7)$ be given. Our algorithm first chooses b. The test with a is negative. Then we select e and finally c. $\{b, e, c\}$ is admissible and maximum. The schedule for $\{b, e, c\}$ is (b, c, e).

In general, the matroid is not explicitly but only conceptually given. The test "$O \cup \{s_i\} \in \tau$" corresponds for the task scheduling problem to check: Is $O \cup \{s_i\}$ admissible for the task scheduling problem, i.e., a schedule of

$O \cup \{s_i\}$ must be specified so that all tasks can be completed before their deadline date.

Proposition 1.35. *Let $M = (S, \tau)$ be a matroid and $w : \tau \longrightarrow \mathbb{R}_{>0}$ a weight function on M, then the algorithm* Optimum *returns an optimal solution to the optimization problem for (M, w).*

Proof. The algorithm returns an element O from τ. Let $S = \{s_1, \ldots, s_n\}$ and $O = \{s_{i_1}, \ldots, s_{i_k}\}$ be sorted by weight in descending order, and let $\tilde{O}$ be an optimal solution. First we show that $|O| = |\tilde{O}|$.

From $|O| > |\tilde{O}|$ it follows from the exchange property that there is an $s \in O \setminus \tilde{O}$ with $\tilde{O} \cup \{s\} \in \tau$. This is a contradiction because $\tilde{O}$ is optimal.

From $|O| < |\tilde{O}|$ it again follows from the exchange property that there is an $s \in \tilde{O} \setminus O$, so $O \cup \{s\} \in \tau$. Due to the subset property, each subset of $O \cup \{s\}$ is an element of τ. But then s would have been selected in line 4 of the algorithm when processing the list L, a contradiction.

Let $\tilde{O} = \{s_{j_1}, \ldots, s_{j_k}\}$ and $w(s_{j_1}) \geq w(s_{j_2}) \geq \ldots \geq w(s_{j_k})$. Suppose $w(\tilde{O}) > w(O)$. Then there would be an $\tilde{l}$ with $w(s_{j_{\tilde{l}}}) > w(s_{i_{\tilde{l}}})$. Let l be the smallest index with this property. Since S is sorted descending by weight, $j_l < i_l$ holds. Let $A = \{s_{i_1}, \ldots, s_{i_{l-1}}\}$ and $\tilde{A} = \{s_{j_1}, \ldots, s_{j_l}\}$. Following the exchange property, there is an $s \in \tilde{A} \setminus A$ with $A \cup \{s\} \in \tau$. Since $w(s_{j_1}) \geq w(s_{j_2}) \geq \ldots \geq w(s_{j_l})$, we get $w(s) \geq w(s_{j_l}) > w(s_{i_l})$, a contradiction to the choice of s_{i_l} in line 4 of the algorithm. So $w(\tilde{O}) = w(O)$. Hence, O is an optimal solution. $\qquad\square$

Remark. Let τ only satisfy the hereditary property (first condition of Definition 1.32). Then the greedy algorithm Optimum calculates an optimal solution if and only if τ is a matroid ([Schrijver03, Theorem 40.1]).

Greedy algorithms include Algorithm 1.43 for solving the fractal knapsack problem, Huffman's algorithm (4.43) for data compression, Dijkstra's algorithm (Section 6.2) for computing the shortest paths in weighted graphs, and the algorithms of Prim (Section 6.2), Kruskal (Section 6.3) and Borůvka (Section 6.4) for computing minimum spanning trees in weighted graphs. The LZ77 algorithm uses a greedy strategy to parse strings (Section 4.6.4).

1.5.4 Dynamic Programming

Using the method of dynamic programming we calculate an optimal solution of a problem in a simple way from the optimal solutions of partial problems. This method has been known for a long time. A systematic treatment was performed by Bellman[33] (see [Bellman57]). The key in developing a solution by the method of dynamic programming is to find a recursive formula for an optimal solution. This formula is called *Bellman's optimality equation.*

---

[33] Richard Bellman (1920 – 1984) was an American mathematician.

Dynamic programming refers to a solution method using tables and not to a programming technique. A simple algorithm that implements this method is to calculate the first n Fibonacci numbers iteratively. The table is an array $Fib[0..n]$ initialized with $Fib[0] = 0$ and $Fib[1] = 1$. The further entries are calculated with $Fib[i] = Fib[i-1] + Fib[i-2]$ for $i = 2, \ldots, n$.

$$Fib = 0, 1, 1, 2, 3, 5, \ldots$$

This algorithm is at the same time a typical example for the application of the dynamic programming method. The recursive method fails here, because common partial problems are recomputed again and again (Algorithm 1.23). The dynamic programming method solves each subproblem exactly once and stores the result in a table. If you only want to calculate the nth Fibonacci number, this can be done much more efficiently with Algorithm 1.20.

The RMQ Problem. We apply the design method of dynamic programming to calculate a solution to the *range-minimum-query (RMQ)* problem. The solution shown here follows [BeFa00].

The RMQ problem deals, as the name implies, with the calculation of the minimum in a subarray of an array of numbers. More precisely, an index is to be determined within the subarray that specifies a position at which the minimum of the subarray is located.

Example. In Figure 1.6 the minimum of the subarray a[5..12] is located at position 10.

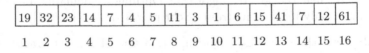

19	32	23	14	7	4	5	11	3	1	6	15	41	7	12	61
1	2	3	4	5	6	7	8	9	10	11	12	13	14	15	16

Fig. 1.6: The RMQ problem.

First we specify the problem and introduce notations. Let $a[1..n]$ be an array of numbers. An algorithm $\mathrm{rmq}_a(i,j)$ for the RMQ problem returns for indices i and j with $1 \le i \le j \le n$ an index k with $i \le k \le j$ and

$$a[k] = \min\{a[l] \mid i \le l \le j\}.$$

The solution developed here calculates a lookup table $t_a[1..n, 1..n]$, which stores the index of an element with minimal value for $i \le j$:

$$t_a[i,j] = \mathrm{rmq}_a(i,j).$$

After the table t_a has been created, a query can be answered with one table access. Because

$$\min a[i..i] = a[i] \text{ and}$$

$$\min a[i..j] = \min\{\min a[i..j-1], \min a[i+1..j]\},$$

we get a recursive formula for the calculation of $t_a[i, j]$:

$$t_a[i, i] = i,$$

$$t_a[i, j] = \begin{cases} t_a[i, j-1] & \text{if } a[t_a[i, j-1]] \leq a[t_a[i+1, j]] \text{ and} \\ t_a[i+1, j] & \text{otherwise.} \end{cases}$$

The idea of dynamic programming is to calculate the values $t_a[i, j]$ one after the other and store them in a table.

$$t_a[1, 1] \; t_a[1, 2] \; t_a[1, 3] \quad \ldots$$
$$t_a[2, 2] \; t_a[2, 3]$$
$$t_a[3, 3] \quad \vdots$$
$$t_a[4, 4]$$
$$\ddots \quad \vdots$$
$$t_a[n, n]$$

We set the diagonal elements $t_a[i, i] = i$. Starting from the diagonal we calculate the columns in the order from left to right and from bottom to top. For the calculation of $t_a[i, j]$, the values $t_a[i, j-1]$ and $t_a[i+1, j]$ are required. These values have already been calculated. They are in the table and can be easily read.

Algorithm 1.36.
compTab(item $a[1..n]$)
1   index i, j
2   for $j \leftarrow 1$ to n do
3       $t_a[j, j] \leftarrow j$
4   for $i \leftarrow j - 1$ to 1 do
5   if $a[t_a[i, j-1]] < a[t_a[i+1, j]]$
6   then $t_a[i, j] \leftarrow t_a[i, j-1]$
7   else $t_a[i, j] \leftarrow t_a[i+1, j]$

The running time of compTab is of the order $O(n^2)$.

Example. For $a = \{7, 4, 5, 11, 3, 1\}$ we receive for the table t_a

	1	2	3	4	5	6
1	1	2	2	2	5	6
2		2	2	2	5	6
3			3	3	5	6
4				4	5	6
5					5	6
6						6

We optimize the procedure by calculating a lookup table only for indices $i < j$ whose distance $j - i$ is $2^k - 1$. We calculate a lookup table t_a^+ for the index pairs

$$(i, i + 2^k - 1), i = 1, \ldots, n \text{ and for all } k \geq 0 \text{ with } i + 2^k - 1 \leq n.$$

We have $\text{rmq}_a(i, i + 2^k - 1) = t_a^+[i, k]$ and $\text{rmq}_a(i - 2^k + 1, i) = t_a^+[i - 2^k + 1, k]$. The following consideration shows that this is sufficient.

For the index pair $i < j$ and $k = \lfloor \log_2(j - i + 1) \rfloor$, we get

$$j - i + 1 = 2^{\log_2(j-i+1)} < 2^{\lfloor \log_2(j-i+1) \rfloor + 1} = 2 \cdot 2^k$$

and thus also

$$j - 2^k + 1 \leq i + 2^k - 1.$$

Hence, we have

$$[i, j] = [i, i + 2^k - 1] \cup [j - 2^k + 1, j].$$

So with $i' := \text{rmq}_a(i, i + 2^k - 1) = t_a^+[i, k]$ and $j' := \text{rmq}_a(j - 2^k + 1, j)$ we get

$$\text{rmq}_a(i, j) = \begin{cases} i' & \text{if } a[i'] \leq a[j'] \text{ and} \\ j' & \text{otherwise.} \end{cases}$$

The value $\text{rmq}_a(i, j)$ can be computed by the queries

$$\text{rmq}_a(i, i + 2^k - 1) \text{ and } \text{rmq}_a(j - 2^k + 1, j).$$

For both queries, the distance between the indices is a power of 2 minus 1.

We now set up a recursive formula for t_a^+. Because

$$\min a[i..i] = a[i] \text{ and } \min a[i..i + 2^k - 1] =$$
$$\min\{\min a[i..i + 2^{k-1} - 1], \min a[i + 2^{k-1}..i + 2^k - 1]\}, k \geq 1,$$

we get the following recursive formula for t_a^+:

$$t_a^+[i, 0] = i,$$

$$t_a^+[i, k] = \begin{cases} t_a^+[i, k - 1] \text{ if } a[t_a^+[i, k - 1]] \leq a[t_a^+[i + 2^{k-1}, k - 1]] \text{ and} \\ t_a^+[i + 2^{k-1}, k - 1] \text{ otherwise.} \end{cases}$$

The idea now, as above, is to calculate and save the columns of the table

$$
\begin{array}{llll}
t_a^+[1, 0] & t_a^+[1, 1] & \cdots & \\
t_a^+[2, 0] & t_a^+[2, 1] & & \\
\vdots & \vdots & \vdots & \ddots \\
t_a^+[n - 4, 0] & t_a^+[n - 4, 1] & t_a^+[n - 4, 2] & \\
t_a^+[n - 3, 0] & t_a^+[n - 3, 1] & t_a^+[n - 3, 2] & \\
t_a^+[n - 2, 0] & t_a^+[n - 2, 1] & & \\
t_a^+[n - 1, 0] & t_a^+[n - 1, 1] & & \\
t_a^+[n, 0] & & & \\
\end{array}
$$

one after the other.

The first column is $t_a^+[i, 0] = i$, $i = 1, \ldots, n$. For the following columns, we use the recursive formula. For the calculation of the kth column $t_a^+[i, k]$, we need the values $t_a^+[i, k-1]$ and $t_a^+[i + 2^{k-1}, k-1]$ from the $(k-1)$th column. Since we calculate the columns one after the other from left to right, these values are already in the table t_a^+ and we can simply read them out.

Example. Let $a = [7, 4, 5, 11, 3, 1, 14, 17, 2, 6]$. Then

	1	2	3	4	5	6	7	8	9	10
0	1	2	3	4	5	6	7	8	9	10
1	2	2	3	5	6	6	7	9	9	
2	2	5	6	6	6	6	9			
3	6	6	6							

is the matrix transposed to t_a^+.

For the ith row of the table t_a^+, the inequality $i + 2^l - 1 \le n$ or equivalently $l \le \log_2(n - i + 1)$ is valid for the largest column index l. The table thus has

$$\sum_{i=1}^{n}(l_i + 1) = \sum_{i=1}^{n}(\lfloor \log_2(n - i + 1) \rfloor + 1)$$

$$= n + \sum_{i=1}^{n} \lfloor \log_2(i) \rfloor$$

$$= (n + 1)(\lfloor \log_2(n) \rfloor + 1) - 2^{\lfloor \log_2(n) \rfloor + 1} + 1$$

entries (Lemma B.15).

An algorithm that implements the calculation iteratively can be implemented analogously to Algorithm 1.36. It is of the order $O(n \log_2(n))$.

Proposition 1.37. *Every RMQ request for an array a of length n can be answered in constant time, after preprocessing with running time $O(n \log_2(n))$.*

Remarks:

1. In Section 6.1.3, we specify an algorithm with linear running time for the RMQ problem. First for an array in which two consecutive entries differ only by $+1$ or -1 and then for any array.
2. The RMQ problem is equivalent to the LCA problem. This consists of determining in a rooted tree the common ancestor of two nodes which has the greatest distance to the root (Section 6.1.3). The LCA problem and thus also the RMQ problem is a basic algorithmic problem that has been studied intensively. An overview is given in the article "Lowest common ancestors in trees" by Farach-Colton in [Kao16].
3. Range minimum queries have applications in many situations, for example, document retrieval, compressed suffix trees, Lempel-Ziv compression and text indexing (Fischer: Compressed range minimum queries in [Kao16]).

The Edit Distance. A further application of the design method of dynamic programming is the calculation of the edit distance of two strings. The edit distance quantifies how similar two strings are.

Definition 1.38. The *edit distance* of two strings is the minimum number of operations to convert one string into the other string. The operations allowed are insert (i), delete (d) and substitute (s). Keeping a character (k) should not be counted as an operation.

The definition of the edit distance is attributed to Levenshtein[34] ([Leven65]). No algorithm for the calculation is given in that article. In our presentation we refer to the paper [WagFis74], which follows a more general approach.

Example. The edit distance between "remedy" and "ready" is two. The operations keep r, keep e, substitute m with a, delete e, keep d and finally keep y convert "remedy" to "ready".

Proposition 1.39. *Let* $a_1 \ldots a_n$ *and* $b_1 \ldots b_m$ *be strings. The edit distance* $d(a_1 \ldots a_n, b_1 \ldots b_m)$, *or* $d(n,m)$ *for short, is calculated recursively.*

$$d(0,0) = 0, d(i,0) = i, d(0,j) = j,$$
$$d(i,j) = \min\{d(i,j-1)+1, d(i-1,j)+1, d(i-1,j-1)+[a_i \neq b_j]\},$$

where $[a_i \neq b_j] = 1$ *if* $a_i \neq b_j$ *and 0 otherwise.*

Proof. When converting $a_1 \ldots a_i$ to $b_1 \ldots b_j$, we distinguish between the following cases

(1) delete a_i (at the end) and convert $a_1 \ldots a_{i-1}$ to $b_1 \ldots b_j$,
(2) convert $a_1 \ldots a_i$ to $b_1 \ldots b_{j-1}$ and add b_j,
(3) convert $a_1 \ldots a_{i-1}$ to $b_1 \ldots b_{j-1}$ and substitute a_i with b_j or
(4) convert $a_1 \ldots a_{i-1}$ to $b_1 \ldots b_{j-1}$ and keep the last character.

Since $d(i,j)$ is produced by one of the four cases, $d(i,j) \geq \min\{d(i,j-1)+1, d(i-1,j)+1, d(i-1,j-1)+[a_i \neq b_j]\}$.
Since the conversion of $a_1 \ldots a_i$ into $b_1 \ldots b_j$ must be done by one of the four cases considered, and since $d(i,j)$ is the minimum distance, $d(i,j) \leq \min\{d(i,j-1)+1, d(i-1,j)+1, d(i-1,j-1)+[a_i \neq b_j]\}$. This shows the assertion. □

We can without effort convert the formula from Proposition 1.39 into a recursive function. Although there are only $(n+1)(m+1)$ partial problems, the running time of this function is exponential. That is because the recursive function calculates the same distances over and over again. The following procedure provides a more efficient algorithm.

---

[34] Vladimir Levenshtein (1935 – 2017) was a Russian mathematician.

We calculate the values

$$d(0,0)\ d(0,1)\ d(0,2) \dots d(0,m)$$
$$d(1,0)\ d(1,1)\ d(1,2) \dots$$
$$d(2,0)\ d(2,1)\quad \dots$$
$$\vdots$$

one after the other and save them in a table. We start with the calculation of the first row and the first column. We calculate the following columns from top to bottom and from left to right. When calculating $d(i,j)$, we need the values $d(i,j-1)$, $d(i-1,j)$ and $d(i-1,j-1)$. These values are already calculated. They are in the table, and we can simply read them out. The table consists of n rows and m columns. Our calculation takes place in time $O(nm)$. We summarize the result in the following proposition.

Proposition 1.40. *Let $a = a_1 \dots a_n$ and $b = b_1 \dots b_m$ be strings of length n and m. With the method of dynamic programming, we can calculate the edit distance from a to b in time $O(nm)$.*

We specify the algorithm in pseudo-code.

Algorithm 1.41.
```
Dist(char a[1..n], b[1..m])
 1    int i, j, d[0..n, 0..m]
 2    for i ← 0 to n do
 3        d[i, 0] ← i
 4    for j ← 1 to m do
 5        d[0, j] ← j
 6    for i ← 1 to n do
 7        for j ← 1 to m do
 8            if a_i = b_j
 9                then k ← 0
10                else  k ← 1
11            d[i, j] ← Min(d[i, j − 1] + 1,
12                          d[i − 1, j] + 1, d[i − 1, j − 1] + k)
```

After the termination of Dist, $d[n,m]$ contains the edit distance of $a[1..n]$ and $b[1..m]$.

We now modify the algorithm Dist so that it also calculates the sequence of operations that determines the edit distance. To do this, we store how the value of $d[i,j]$ comes about. We use a second matrix $op[0..n, 0..m]$, in which we set the empty set as the initial value for each cell. Then we extend Dist with

$$op[i,0] = \{d\}, 0 \le i \le n,$$

$$op[0,j] = \{i\}, 0 \le j \le m,$$

$$op[i,j] = \begin{cases} op[i,j] \cup \{d\} & \text{(delete) if } d[i,j] = d[i-1,j]+1, \\ op[i,j] \cup \{i\} & \text{(insert) if } d[i,j] = d[i,j-1]+1, \\ op[i,j] \cup \{s\} & \text{(substitute) if } d[i,j] = d[i-1,j-1]+1, \\ op[i,j] \cup \{k\} & \text{(keep) if } d[i,j] = d[i-1,j-1]. \end{cases}$$

After terminating Dist, it is possible to obtain a sequence of operations corresponding to the edit distance by passing op from $op[n,m]$ to $op[0,0]$. The resulting path contains the operations. We start in $op[n,m]$. The next node in the path is determined by the choice of entry from $op[i,j]$. The next possible node is

$$\begin{array}{ll} op[i-1,j] & \text{if } d \in op[i,j], \\ op[i,j-1] & \text{if } i \in op[i,j] \text{ or} \\ op[i-1,j-1] & \text{if } s \text{ or } k \in op[i,j]. \end{array}$$

The path – and thus also the sequence of the operations – is not uniquely determined.

Example. We calculate the edit distance between "ready" and "remedy" and a minimal sequence of operations that converts "ready" into "remedy".

We get the distance matrix d

d		r	e	m	e	d	y
	0	1	2	3	4	5	6
r	1	0	1	2	3	4	5
e	2	1	0	1	2	3	4
a	3	2	1	1	2	3	4
d	4	3	2	2	2	2	3
y	5	4	3	3	3	3	2

and the operation matrix op

o		r	e	m	e	d	y
		i	i	i	i	i	i
r	d	k	i	i	i	i	i
e	d	d	k	i	i	i	i
a	d	k	d	s	i,s	i,s	i,s
d	d	d	d	d,s	s	k	i
y	d	d	d	d,s	d,s	d	k

The sequence of operations is k, k, s, i, k, k.

Remarks:

1. The calculated sequence of operations for a word pair (v, u) results from the sequence of operations for (u, v) by swapping operations i (insert) and d (delete).

   "remedy" can be converted into "ready" by means of the operations sequence k, k, s, d, k, k.

2. The matrix d calculated for the word pair $(a_1 \ldots a_n, b_1 \ldots b_m)$ also contains the edit distances of all prefix pairs $(a_1 \ldots a_i, b_1 \ldots b_j), 1 \leq i \leq n, 1 \leq j \leq m$. Accordingly, the *op* matrix contains the entries for reconstructing an operation sequence for each prefix pair.

   The edit distance $d(read, re) = d[4, 2] = 2$. Starting with $op[4, 2]$ you get the unique operation sequence k, k, d, d.

3. The edit distance and its calculation is used in algorithmic biology. Here the similarity of DNA sequences is measured with the edit distance. The individual operations are weighted differently. The method is also used in the field of pattern recognition. There one usually speaks of the *Levenshtein distance*.

The algorithm of Warshall-Floyd is constructed according to the design method of dynamic programming (Section 6.7).

1.5.5 Branch and Bound with Backtracking

Branch and bound is a basic design principle for algorithms and can be applied in many situations. The idea of branch and bound was already developed in the 1960s to solve integer optimization problems.

Branch and bound requires that the solution space $\mathcal{L}$ of the computational problem consists of n-tuples $(x_1, \ldots, x_n) \in S_1 \times \ldots \times S_n$, where S_i, $i = 1, \ldots, n$, is a finite set. These n-tuples $(x_1, \ldots, x_n) \in \mathcal{L}$ are defined by certain conditions. The solution space is often provided with the structure of a tree (Definition 4.1).

For example, permutations of the sets $\{1, \ldots, i\}$, $1 \leq i \leq n$, can be assigned to a tree. We define π_2 as the successor of π_1 if π_2 continues the permutation π_1 and is defined on one more element. Permutations of $\{1, \ldots, n\}$ are located in the leaves of the tree.

When branch and bound is used, the solution space is searched for a solution. A bounding function limits the search space by truncating subtrees that cannot contain a desired solution. Breadth-first, depth-first and priority-first search define different visit sequences when searching the solution tree.

Backtracking uses depth-first search (Algorithm 4.5). If the bounding function is used to determine that a subtree with root w contains no solution, the search is continued in the parent node of w: a backward step is performed (backtracking). We explain branch and bound with backtracking in more detail using the eight queens problem and the knapsack problem.

The Eight Queens Problem. The eight queens problem was published by Bezzel[35] in 1848. It consists in positioning eight queens on a chess board in such a way that no two queens threaten each other. More precisely, the problem is to indicate the number of possible solutions of the problem. Even the famous mathematician Gauss[36] dealt with the problem.

---

[35] Max Friedrich Wilhelm Bezzel (1824 – 1871) was a German chess player.

[36] Carl Friedrich Gauss (1777 – 1855) was a German mathematician. He is recognized as one of the most outstanding mathematicians of his time.

Figure 1.7 shows one of the 92 solutions to the eight queens problem.

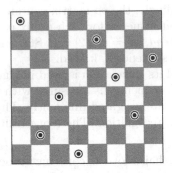

Fig. 1.7: A solution to the eight queens problem.

If a queen stands on a square F, the second queen cannot be positioned on a square contained in the row, column, or one of the two diagonals that pass through the square F.

Therefore, the queens must be positioned in different rows. Hence, a solution to the problem is defined by specifying the column for each row, i.e., a solution is an 8-tuple $(q_1, \ldots, q_8) \in \{1, \ldots, 8\}^8$, where q_j is the column for the jth row. In addition, $(q_1, \ldots, q_8)$ must fulfill the condition of mutual "non-threat".

Since two queens have to be positioned in different columns, a solution $(q_1, \ldots, q_8)$ must accomplish particularly $q_i \neq q_j$ for $i \neq j$. $(q_1, \ldots, q_8)$ is thus a permutation $(\pi(1), \ldots, \pi(8))$. The set of all permutations of $(1, \ldots, 8)$ can be represented by a tree with nine levels. Each node in level i has $8 - i$ successors. So the tree has $1 + 8 + 8 \cdot 7 + 8 \cdot 7 \cdot 6 + \ldots + 8! = 69,281$ nodes, as shown in Figure 1.8.

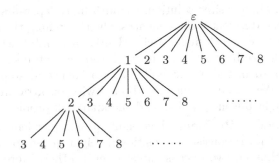

Fig. 1.8: The solution tree for the eight queens problem.

A permutation q is given in the tree by a path P from the root to a leaf. If a node k in the ith level belongs to P, k specifies the ith component of q.

The solutions can now be found by traversing the tree using depth-first search. In each node it is checked whether the permutation $(q_1, \ldots, q_i)$ is still part of a solution. If this is the case, the subsequent nodes in the next level are examined. If $(q_1, \ldots, q_i)$ is not part of a solution, the search is continued at the previous level. Thus, a backtracking step takes place. The search is aborted and continued from the higher-level node.

The following algorithm Queens implements this solution without explicitly displaying the tree. The representation is implicitly given by the descending paths of the recursion.

Queens gives a solution to the n queens problem, which generalizes the problem for n queens and a chessboard with $n \times n$ squares.

Algorithm 1.42.
Queens(int $Q[1..n], i$)
1   if $i = n + 1$
2   then print(Q)
3   for $j \leftarrow 1$ to n do
4   if testPosition$(Q[1..n], i, j)$
5   then $Q[i] \leftarrow j$
6   Queens$(Q[1..n], i + 1)$

boolean testPosition(int $Q[1..n], i, j$)
1   for $k \leftarrow 1$ to $i - 1$ do
2   if $Q[k] = j$ or $Q[k] = j + i - k$ or $Q[k] = j - i + k$
3   then return false
4   return true

The call Queens$(Q[1..n], 1)$ calculates all solutions of the n queens problem and outputs them with print(Q). The function testPosition checks for the ith row whether a queen can be positioned in the jth column. To do this, it must be checked whether the jth column or one of the straight lines $y = x + (j - i)$ or $y = -x + (j + i)$ (through (i, j)) already contains a queen. This is done in line 2 of testPosition for the line k, $k = 1, \ldots, i - 1$.

The 92 solutions for the eight queens problem can be computed with a PC in less than one second. Recently, a working group at TU Dresden succeeded in computing all solutions of the 27 queens problem. There are 234,907,967,154,122,528 solutions. Field Programmable Gate Arrays (FPGA), which allow massive parallel computing, were used for the calculation. These computed for one year with all their idle time to achieve the result ([Queens@TUD-Team16]).

The Knapsack Problem. In the knapsack problem, there is a fixed-size knapsack and pieces of luggage. The aim is to pack the knapsack as full as possible with a suitable selection of the pieces. More abstractly and more generally, the problem is formulated as follows:

Given are $m \in \mathbb{N}$, $w = (w_1, \ldots, w_n)$ and $p = (p_1, \ldots, p_n) \in \mathbb{N}^n$. Searched for is $x = (x_1, \ldots, x_n) \in \{0, 1\}^n$ with

$$\sum_i^n x_i w_i \leq m \text{ and } \sum_i^n x_i p_i \text{ is maximal.}$$

The number m is called the *capacity*, the vector w the *weight vector* and the vector p the *profit vector*. The problem is to calculate a solution that maximizes the profit ($\sum_i^n x_i p_i$) while observing the capacity limit ($\sum_i^n x_i w_i \leq m$). A solution that satisfies this is called an *optimal solution*.

More precisely, this problem is the *0,1 knapsack problem*. The 0,1 knapsack problem is one of the so-called *NP-complete* problems. Under the assumption that P $\neq$ NP[37] is true there is no polynomial running time algorithm to solve the problem. Computational problems from complexity class P can be solved by a deterministic Turing machine in polynomial time, those computational problems from complexity class NP by a non-deterministic Turing machine. A deterministic Turing machine can verify solutions from NP in polynomial time. The NP-complete problems prove to be the most difficult problems from NP. If a single NP-complete problem has a solution which we can compute in polynomial time, it is possible to solve all problems in NP in polynomial time. The complexity classes P, NP and others are studied in theoretical computer science. We refer interested readers to textbooks on computability and complexity theory, such as [GarJoh79] and [HopMotUll07].

The knapsack problem has a long history. The main methods to solve the problem are the dynamic programming and the branch and bound method. Many theoretical and application-oriented papers have been published about the problem. A comprehensive overview can be found in [MartToth90] or [KelPisPfe04].

First we weaken the requirements of the solutions and also allow vectors $x = (x_1, \ldots, x_n) \in [0, 1]^n$ with fractions as components of the solutions. In this case, we call the problem the *fractal knapsack problem*. First we solve the fractal knapsack problem by the following algorithm greedyKnapsack. It goes back to a paper by Dantzig[38] from the year 1957.

The algorithm pursues the following obvious greedy strategy to maximize the profit: Pack the items in descending order of their *profit density* $\frac{p_i}{w_i}$, $i = 1, \ldots, n$, more precisely; start with the item with the highest profit density,

---

[37] The decision of the problem P $\neq$ NP is included in the list of Millennium Problems drawn up in 2000 by the Clay Mathematics Institute. The list contains seven problems; among the six unsolved problems is the P $\neq$ NP problem.

[38] George Bernard Dantzig (1914 – 2005) was an American mathematician. He developed the simplex method, the standard method for solving linear optimization problems.

continue packing the items in descending order of their profit density until the barrier m is reached and fill the remaining capacity with a portion of the next item. To do this, we sort $w = (w_1, \ldots, w_n)$ and $p = (p_1, \ldots, p_n)$ so that $\frac{p_1}{w_1} \geq \frac{p_2}{w_2} \geq \ldots \geq \frac{p_n}{w_n}$. The function greedyKnapsack has for $i = 1$ the call parameters weight vector $w[1..n]$, profit vector $p[1..n]$ and the vector $x[1..n]$, which is initialized with 0, and the capacity m of the knapsack. The vector $x[1..n]$ contains the solution after termination. We assume without loss of generality that $\sum_{i=1}^{n} w_i > m$. The function greedyKnapsack returns the largest index j with $x[j] \neq 0$ and the achieved profit P.

Algorithm 1.43.
(int, real) greedyKnapsack(int $p[i..n]$, $w[i..n]$, $x[i..n]$, m)
```
1    index j; int c ← 0; P ← 0
2    for j ← i to n do
3        c ← c + w[j]
4        if c < m
5        then x[j] ← 1
6             P ← P + p[j]
7        else x[j] ← (w[j]−(c−m))/w[j]
8             P ← P + p[j] · x[j]
9             break
10   return (j, P)
```

Proposition 1.44. *If we call Algorithm 1.43 with the parameter $i = 1$, it calculates an optimal solution for the instance $(p[1..n], w[1..n], m)$ of the fractal knapsack problem.*

Proof. For the result $x = (x_1, \ldots, x_n)$ of Algorithm 1.43, we have $\sum_{i=1}^{n} x_i w_i = m$. If $x_i = 1$ for $i = 1, \ldots, n$, then x is an optimal solution. Otherwise, there is a j with $1 \leq j \leq n$, $x_1 = \ldots = x_{j-1} = 1$ and $0 < x_j \leq 1$, $x_{j+1} = \ldots = x_n = 0$.

We now assume that $x = (x_1, \ldots, x_n)$ is not optimal. Let k be maximum, so that for all optimal solutions $(\tilde{y}_1, \ldots, \tilde{y}_n)$ we have $\tilde{y}_1 = x_1, \ldots, \tilde{y}_{k-1} = x_{k-1}$ and $\tilde{y}_k \neq x_k$. For this k we obtain $k \leq j$, because if $k > j$ we get $x_k = 0$, and we conclude that $\tilde{y}_k > 0$ and $\sum_{i=1}^{n} w_i \tilde{y}_i > \sum_{i=1}^{n} w_i x_i = m$, a contradiction.

Let $(y_1, \ldots, y_n)$ be an optimal solution with $y_1 = x_1, \ldots, y_{k-1} = x_{k-1}$ and $y_k \neq x_k$. Now, we show that $y_k < x_k$. For $k < j$ we get $x_k = 1$, hence $y_k < x_k$. It remains to discuss the case $k = j$. Suppose $y_j > x_j$. Then $\sum_{i=1}^{n} w_i y_i > \sum_{i=1}^{n} w_i x_i = m$, a contradiction. Therefore, $k \leq j$ and $y_k < x_k$ is shown.

From $y_1 = \ldots = y_{k-1} = 1$ we get

$$w_k(x_k - y_k) = \sum_{i=k+1}^{n} w_i \alpha_i \text{ with } \alpha_i \leq y_i.$$

We now change the solution $(y_1, \ldots, y_n)$ at the positions $k, \ldots, n$. More precisely, we define $(z_1, \ldots, z_n)$ as follows: Choose $z_i = y_i$, $i = 1, \ldots, k-1$, $z_k = x_k$ and $z_i = y_i - \alpha_i$, for $i = k+1, \ldots, n$. Then

$$\sum_{i=1}^{n} p_i z_i = \sum_{i=1}^{n} p_i y_i + p_k(z_k - y_k) - \sum_{i=k+1}^{n} p_i \alpha_i$$

$$\geq \sum_{i=1}^{n} p_i y_i + \left(w_k(z_k - y_k) - \sum_{i=k+1}^{n} w_i \alpha_i \right) \frac{p_k}{w_k} - \sum_{i=1}^{n} p_i y_i.$$

Since $(y_1, \ldots, y_n)$ is optimal, $\sum_{i=1}^{n} p_i z_i = \sum_{i=1}^{n} p_i y_i$ follows. Therefore, $(z_1, \ldots, z_n)$ is optimal, a contradiction to the choice of k. So $(x_1, \ldots, x_n)$ is optimal. □

Now we solve the 0,1 knapsack problem and may assume that $w_i \leq m$ for $i = 1, \ldots, n$ and $\sum_{i=1}^{n} w_i > m$. We will use Algorithm 1.43 and assume therefore that the order of $p[1..n]$ and $w[1..n]$ yields a decreasing sequence $\frac{p[1]}{w[1]} \geq \frac{p[2]}{w[2]} \geq \cdots \geq \frac{p[n]}{w[n]}$.

We consider the following binary tree B (Definition 4.3). Nodes are the binary vectors $(x_1, \ldots, x_i)$, $i = 0, \ldots, n$. The node $(x'_1, \ldots, x'_{i+1})$ is a successor of $(x_1, \ldots, x_i)$ if $x'_j = x_j$ for $j = 1, \ldots i$ (see Figure 1.9). The tree has $2^{n+1} - 1$ nodes spread over $n + 1$ levels (numbered from 0 to n).

The solutions to the knapsack problem are located in the 2^n leaves. These are all in the nth level. But not all leaves are solutions of the knapsack problem. Some may violate the capacity limit, others may not reach the maximum possible profit. Completely traversing the tree and then checking the capacity limit and optimality condition in each leaf gives a correct result. However, since the number of nodes of B increases exponentially in the number of items, this procedure leads to an algorithm of exponential running time. The idea is to recognize in time that a subtree cannot contain an optimal solution.

If the capacity condition is violated in a node v, it is violated for all nodes in the subtree that has v as root. If in the node v the sum of the profit that has already been achieved and the profit that is still to be expected does not exceed the maximum profit achieved so far, we do not examine the subtree with root v any further. With this strategy, the following algorithm solves the 0,1 knapsack problem. It consists of the function knapSack, which starts the execution, and the function traverse, which traverses B by depth-first search (Algorithm 4.5). As with the solution of the eight queens problem, we do not explicitly present the solution tree B as a data structure.

Algorithm 1.45.
int: $p[1..n]$, $w[1..n]$, $x[1..n]$, $\tilde{x}[1..n]$

knapSack(int $p[1..n]$, $w[1..n]$, m)
1    $(i, p'') \leftarrow$ greedyKnapsack($p[1..n]$, $w[1..n]$, $\tilde{x}[1..n]$, m)
2   if $\tilde{x}[i] < 1$
3   then $\tilde{x}[i] \leftarrow 0$
4   traverse($x[1..1]$, m, 0)
5   return $\tilde{x}$

traverse(int $x[1..j]$, m', p')
1   int : $\tilde{p}$
2    $\tilde{p} \leftarrow \sum_{k=1}^{n} p[k]\tilde{x}[k]$
3   if $j \leq n$
4   then $(i, p'') \leftarrow$ greedyKnapsack($p[j..n]$, $w[j..n]$, $x[j..n]$, m')
5   if $p' + p'' > \tilde{p}$
6   then if $w[j] \leq m'$
7   then $x[j] \leftarrow 1$
8   traverse($x[1..j + 1]$, $m' - w[j]$, $p' + p[j]$)
9           $x[j] \leftarrow 0$, traverse($x[1..j + 1]$, m', p')
10   else if $p' > \tilde{p}$ then $\tilde{x} \leftarrow x$

Remarks:

1. The function knapSack calls greedyKnapsack (line 1). This calculates a solution $\tilde{x}$ to the fractal knapsack problem. If $\tilde{x}$ is an integer solution, then an optimal solution has been found, consisting of integers. Otherwise, we set the last component of the solution $\tilde{x}$ which is different from 0 to 0 and get a solution in $\{0, 1\}^n$. After the termination of traverse($x[1..1]$, m, 0) called in line 4 of knapSack, $\tilde{x}$ contains the first optimal solution found.
2. The parameters of traverse are the current node $(x_1, \ldots, x_j)$, the capacity m' remaining in the node $(x_1, \ldots, x_j)$, and the profit p' earned up to node $(x_1, \ldots, x_{j-1})$. The algorithm greedyKnapsack calculates an optimal solution of the fractal subproblem restricted to $[j..n]$ (Proposition 1.44). The profit of the 0,1 solution is always less than or equal to the profit of the optimal fractal solution.
3. We initialize the solution $(\tilde{x}_1, \ldots, \tilde{x}_n)$ with greedyKnapsack, and then update it whenever we discover a solution with a higher profit (line 10).
4. The condition in line 5 checks whether the subtree with root $(x_1, \ldots, x_j)$ can contain an optimal solution. This is the case if the profit p' obtained up to the node $(x_1, \ldots, x_{j-1})$ plus the profit p'' of an optimal solution for the fractal problem restricted to $[j..n]$ is greater than the profit $\tilde{p} = \sum_{i=1}^{n} p_i \tilde{x}_i$ of the solution $(\tilde{x}_1, \ldots, \tilde{x}_n)$, the current optimal solution. If this is the case, we continue the search in the next level with $x_j = 0$ and with $x_j = 1$ if the remaining capacity allows it (line 6: $w[j] \leq m'$). The

variable j specifies the level of the tree where the node $(x_1,\ldots,x_j)$ is located. In particular, a leaf is reached for $j = n$.

5. If the condition in line 5 does not occur, we cut off the subtree under the node $(x_1,\ldots,x_{j-1})$, i.e., we search neither the subtree with root $(x_1,\ldots,x_{j-1},0)$ nor the subtree with root $(x_1,\ldots,x_{j-1},1)$ for an optimal solution.

6. The notation $x[1..j]$ also passes the parameter j when the function is called. If we call traverse with $j = n + 1$, we update $\tilde{x}$ if the profit $p' = \sum_{k-1}^{n} p_k x_k$, which is given by the node $(x_1,\ldots,x_n)$, is greater than the profit of the solution stored in $\tilde{x}$, i.e., if $p' > \sum_{k=1}^{n} p_k \tilde{x}_k$ (line 10).

Example. Figure 1.9 shows a solution tree for the knapsack problem with five pieces of luggage, $p = (10, 18, 14, 12, 3)$, $w = (2, 6, 5, 8, 3)$ and $m = 12$.

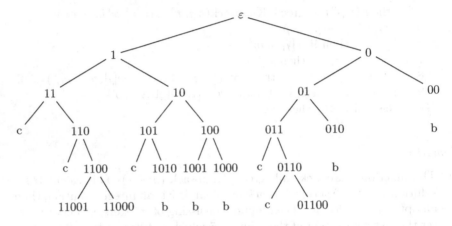

Fig. 1.9: Solution tree for five items.

The greedy solution is 11000 and makes profit $p' = 28$. This is first updated with 11001. The assigned profit is $p' = 31$. c stands for a violated capacity condition (row 6: $w[j] > m'$) and b for a violated bounding condition (row 5: $p' + p'' \leq \tilde{p}$). The optimal solution is 01100 and yields profit 32.

1.6 Randomized Algorithms

Originally, randomized algorithms were mainly used in computational number theory and cryptography. Important examples are the primality tests of Solovay-Strassen and of Miller-Rabin (see for example [DelfsKnebl15]). In cryptography, probabilistic methods are the key technology for secure cryptographic methods (ibid.). In the meantime, there is a wide field of applications for probabilistic methods. They belong to the basic techniques for the construction of simple and efficient algorithms. In this section, we follow the description in "Randomized Algorithms" by Motwani and Raghavan, which provides a good insight into the field of randomized algorithms ([MotRag95]).

The control flow in randomized algorithms depends on random decisions, such as the result of a coin toss. If we apply a randomized algorithm twice for a computation with the same input, then different results of the coin tosses can lead to different results of the computation. For theoretical purposes, randomized algorithms are modeled analogously to (deterministic) algorithms with randomized Turing machines, see e.g., [HopMotUll07].

Random Walk on a Line. The following algorithm is completely random. The result depends only on the result of a series of coin tosses, where the probability is p for heads and $1 - p$ for tails. This is a random walk on the number line $\mathbb{Z}$. At the start we position a figure F at the zero point of $\mathbb{Z}$. In each step, depending on a coin toss we move F one unit to the right $(+1)$ or one unit to the left (-1).

Algorithm 1.46.

```
int randomWalk(int n)
1   int x ← 0
2   for i = 1 to n do
3       choose at random z ∈ {−1,1}
4       x := x + z
5   return x
```

The random variable X describes the return value x (the endpoint of the random walk). It can take the values $-n, \dots, n$.

The variable X has the value x if k times 1 and $n - k$ times -1 happened and if $x = k - (n - k) = 2k - n$, i.e., $k = (n + x)/2$. We get as generating function of X

$$G_X(z) = \sum_{x=-n}^{n} \binom{n}{\frac{n+x}{2}} p^{(x+n)/2}(1-p)^{(n-x)/2} z^x$$

$$= \sum_{x=0}^{2n} \binom{n}{\frac{x}{2}} p^{x/2}(1-p)^{n-x/2} z^{x-n}$$

$$= \frac{1}{z^n} \sum_{x=0}^{n} \binom{n}{x} p^x (1-p)^{n-x} \left(z^2\right)^x$$

$$= \frac{(pz^2 + (1-p))^n}{z^n}$$

(see Definition A.15, Definition A.11 and Appendix B (F.3)). We get

$$G_X'(1) = n(2p-1),\, G_X''(1) = 4n\left(n\,(p-1/2)^2 - p\,(p-1/2) + 1/4\right).$$

For the expected value we get $\mathrm{E}(X) = n(2p-1)$ and for the variance $\mathrm{Var}(X) = 4np(1-p)$ (Proposition A.12). The recalculation of the formulas is a routine task.

For $p = \frac{1}{2}$ the expected value of X is 0. We expect the random walk to end again at the origin after n steps. The variance $\text{Var}(X) = n$. We would therefore be surprised if the random walk ends in many cases more than $\sigma(X) = \sqrt{n}$ positions remote from the origin.

Example. The histogram in Figure 1.10 shows the relative frequencies of the endpoints of 10,000 simulated random walks, each consisting of 50 steps.

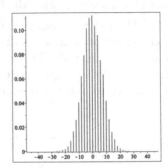

Fig. 1.10: Distribution of the endpoints of 10,000 random walks.

Since the endpoints are even for an even number of steps, only the even coordinates are given. The coin is a fair coin, heads and tails have equal probability, $\frac{1}{2}$. The random walk ends in 68% of the performed experiments, as expected, in the interval [-7,7]. The experimentally determined distribution hardly deviates from the computed distribution.

1.6.1 Comparing Polynomials

We consider the problem of deciding whether two finite sequences of integers

$$\alpha_1, \ldots, \alpha_n \text{ and } \beta_1, \ldots, \beta_n$$

contain the same elements. If we sort the two sequences and then compare the sequences element by element, we obtain a solution that has a running time of order $O(n \log_2(n))$ (see Chapter 2).

We get a more efficient solution using the polynomials

$$f(X) = \prod_{i=1}^{n}(X - \alpha_i) \text{ and } g(X) = \prod_{i=1}^{n}(X - \beta_i)$$

assigned to $\alpha_1, \ldots, \alpha_n$ and $\beta_1, \ldots, \beta_n$. Let $f(X)$ and $g(X) \in \mathbb{Z}[X]$ be polynomials with integers as coefficients. The task now is to determine whether $f(X) = g(X)$.

If the coefficients of $f(X)$ and $g(X)$ are known, this can simply be done by comparing the individual coefficients. However, there are also situations in which the coefficients are not known. This is the case, for example, if we only know the zeros of $f(X)$ and $g(X)$. As we know, two normalized polynomials are equal if $f(X)$ and $g(X)$ have the same zeros $\alpha_1, \ldots, \alpha_n$ and $\beta_1, \ldots, \beta_n$.

Multiplying out the products and then comparing the polynomials does not provide a faster algorithm than the solution just given. We obtain a faster algorithm if we apply the idea of fingerprints. The fingerprint of $f(X)$ is $f(x)$. x is an argument that we can use in f. For our procedure we choose the argument x from a finite set $A \subset \mathbb{Z}$ randomly and compare

$$f(x) = g(x).$$

We calculate $f(x) = \prod_{i=1}^{n}(x - \alpha_i)$ with n multiplications without calculating the coefficients. We get the following algorithm.

Algorithm 1.47.
    boolean OnePassPolyIdent(polynomial f, g)
    1   choose at random $x \in A$
    2   if $f(x) \neq g(x)$
    3   then return false
    4   return true

The element x is called a *witness* for $f(X) \neq g(X)$ if $f(x) \neq g(x)$.

If $f(X) = g(X)$, then $f(x) = g(x)$ is also true, and the result is correct. If $f(X) \neq g(X)$, it may well be that $f(x) = g(x)$. In this case, OnePassPolyIdent is wrong. Now we investigate the probability with which OnePassPolyIdent is incorrect. For simplicity, we assume that $\deg(f - g) = n - 1$ and select A from $\mathbb{Z}$ with $|A| = 2(n - 1)$ in advance. If $f(X) \neq g(X)$, then $f(X) - g(X) \neq 0$ is a polynomial of degree $n - 1$ and thus has – allowing for multiplicity – at most $n - 1$ zeros. OnePassPolyIdent is wrong if a zero of $f - g$ is selected in line 1. The probability of this is $\leq (n - 1)/2(n - 1) = 1/2$. Let p be the probability that OnePassPolyIdent computes correctly. So $p = 1$ if $f(X) = g(X)$ and $p \geq 1/2$ if $f(X) \neq g(X)$. At a first glance, an algorithm that errs in many cases with a probability up to $1/2$ seems to be of little use. However, the error probability can be made arbitrarily small by independent repetitions – a standard procedure with randomized algorithms.

Algorithm 1.48.
    boolean PolyIdent(polynomial f, g; int k)
    1   for $i = 1$ to k do
    2   choose at random $x \in A$
    3   if $f(x) \neq g(x)$
    4   then return false
    5   return true

The probability that PolyIdent is wrong k times – for k independent repetitions of the choice of x – is less than or equal to $1/2^k$. Then the probability of success is greater than or equal to $1 - 1/2^k$. By appropriate choice of k, we achieve that it is arbitrarily close to 1.

A randomized algorithm is called a Monte Carlo algorithm if it produces a correct result with high probability and a Las Vegas algorithm if it always returns a correct result. This is formulated more precisely as follows.

Definition 1.49. Let $\mathcal{P}$ be a computational problem. A randomized algorithm A for $\mathcal{P}$ is called a

1. *Monte Carlo algorithm* if
   a. The result $A(x)$ is very likely correct.
   b. The running time is polynomial.
2. *Las Vegas algorithm* if
   a. The result $A(x)$ is always correct.
   b. The expected value of the running time is polynomial.

We give an example of a Las Vegas algorithm. The algorithm PolyDif proves that two polynomials of degree n are different. It is based on the same facts as the algorithm PolyIdent.

Algorithm 1.50.
    boolean PolyDif(polynomial f, g)
      1   while true do
      2   choose at random $x \in A$
      3   if $f(x) \neq g(x)$
      4   then return true

If $f(X) = g(X)$, the algorithm does not terminate. We calculate the expected value of the number I of iterations of the while loop in PolyDif for the case $f(X) \neq g(X)$. We consider the event $\mathcal{E}$ that the random choice of $x \in A$ does not return a zero of $f(X) - g(X)$. If p is the relative frequency of non-zeros, then $\mathrm{p}(\mathcal{E}) = p$. The random variable I is geometrically distributed with parameter p. The expected value $\mathrm{E}(I) = 1/p$ (Proposition A.20).

If the algorithm will be used for practical purposes, the loop must be terminated at some point. In this case, the algorithm outputs "no result obtained". Probably the two polynomials are the same. For $p = 1/2$ after k iterations the error probability is at most $1/2^k$.

When calculating $f(x) = \prod_{i=1}^{n}(x - \alpha_i)$ in the algorithm PolyIdent, very large numbers may occur. Then a multiplication is not an elementary operation. The effort depends on the length of the numbers. This problem can also be solved using fingerprints.

1.6.2 Verifying the Identity of Large Numbers

We demonstrate the advantage of the probabilistic method with the problem of checking whether objects are equal. We consider objects x_1 and x_2 that are elements of a large set X. The task is to determine whether $x_1 = x_2$ holds. For example, x_1, x_2 can be large numbers or sequences of numbers.

The idea is to use a *hash function*

$$h : X \longrightarrow Y$$

and compare $h(x_1) = h(x_2)$. Hash functions are introduced in Section 3.2. Usually hash functions map elements of very large sets X – X can even have infinitely many elements – to elements of sets of moderate size. We call the hash value $h(x)$ the *fingerprint* of x. The comparison of elements in Y is less complicated. Of course, this only brings an advantage if the calculation of $h(x_1)$ and $h(x_2)$ and comparing $h(x_1) = h(x_2)$ costs less than comparing $x_1 = x_2$. We will get to know situations where this is the case. Another problem is that $h(x_1) = h(x_2)$ can be valid without $x_1 = x_2$. In this case, we say (x_1, x_2) is a *collision* of h (see Definition 3.1). The method of tracing the comparison of objects $x_1 = x_2$ back to the comparison of fingerprints $h(x_1) = h(x_2)$ can only be used if for $x_1 \neq x_2$ the collision probability $p(h_p(x) = h_p(y))$ is small (Definition 3.5).

Let x and y be natural numbers with $x, y < 2^l$. We now apply the idea of fingerprints to determine whether $x = y$ holds.

For the following application, we need hash functions which are multiplicative. Since the universal families from Section 3.2.2 do not have this property, we specify a suitable family of hash functions.

We randomly select a prime p from a suitable set of primes P and consider the family $(h_p)_{p \in P}$,

$$h_p : \{0,1\}^l \longrightarrow \{0,\dots,p-1\}, \ x \longmapsto x \bmod p.$$

Since the proof of the prime number property is complex, one chooses a random number of appropriate size for applications that require a large prime number, and tests the prime number property with a probabilistic prime number test such as the Miller-Rabin test ([DelfsKnebl15, Algorithm A.93]). For composite numbers, this test returns the correct result "composite". However, the result "prime number" is only correct with high probability. By repeating the test independently, we can ensure that the error probability is arbitrarily small. Probabilistic primality tests are also very efficient when testing large numbers.

We first specify the set P of prime numbers from which we randomly select a prime. Let z be a number and

$$\pi(z) = |\{p \text{ Prime} \mid p \leq z\}|.$$

According the Prime Number Theorem[39], for large z

---

[39] For a simple proof of the Prime Number Theorem, see [Newman80].

$$\pi(z) \approx \frac{z}{\ln(z)}$$

is valid. Since $\pi(z)$ is unbounded, we can select z so large that $\pi(z) \approx tl$ for each constant t. We consider for this z the set $P = \{p \text{ prime} \mid p \leq z\}$.

Proposition 1.51. *Let $x \neq y$. Then the collision probability for randomly selected $p \in P$ is*

$$\mathrm{p}(h_p(x) = h_p(y)) \leq \frac{1}{t}.$$

Proof. Let $x \neq y$ and $z := x - y$. We have $h_p(x) = h_p(y)$ if and only if $h_p(z) = 0$. But this is equivalent to p being a divisor of z. Since $|z| < 2^l$, z has at most l prime divisors. We get

$$\mathrm{p}(h_p(x) = h_p(y)) \leq \frac{l}{|P|} \approx \frac{l}{tl} = \frac{1}{t}.$$

This shows the assertion. $\square$

We get the following algorithm that tests numbers for equality.

Algorithm 1.52.
    boolean IsEqual(int x, y)
    1   choose at random $p \in P$
    2   if $x \not\equiv y \bmod p$
    3   then return false
    4   return true

If $x = y$, then $x \equiv y \bmod p$ is also true, and the result is correct. If $x \neq y$, it may well be that $x \equiv y \bmod p$. In this case, IsEqual is wrong. Its error probability is $\approx \frac{1}{t}$. By k independent repetitions of the test, we can lower the error probability to $\approx \frac{1}{t^k}$. For $t = 2$ the error probability is $\approx \frac{1}{2}$ or $\approx \frac{1}{2^k}$, respectively.

We now use this probabilistic method in the algorithm PolyIdent to test $f(x) = g(x)$. The calculation of

$$h_p(f(x)) = \left(\prod_{i=1}^{n}(x - \alpha_i)\right) \bmod p = \left(\prod_{i=1}^{n}(x - \alpha_i) \bmod p\right) \bmod p$$

can be done modulo p. Exactly the same rule applies to the calculation of $h_p(g(x))$. For this reason the number of digits in the n multiplications is limited by $\log_2(p)$.

Algorithm 1.53.
   boolean OnePassPolyIdent(polynomial f, g; int k)
    1   choose at random $x \in A$
    2   for $i \leftarrow 1$ to k do
    3   choose at random $p \in P$
    4   if $f(x) \not\equiv g(x) \bmod p$
    5   then return false
    6   return true

If $f(X) = g(X)$, OnePassPolyIdent returns a correct result as before. The comparison $f(x) = g(x)$, done in the lines 2 – 4 with the probabilistic method of Algorithm 1.52, is only correct with high probability ($\geq 1 - 1/2^k$). The probability of success of OnePassPolyIdent decreases slightly in the case $f(X) \neq g(X)$ ($\geq 1/2 - 1/2^k$). Through independent repetitions the probability of success – as with PolyIdent – can be brought close to 1 again.

1.6.3 Comparing Multivariate Polynomials

We now discuss the fundamentals necessary to extend the algorithm for comparing univariate polynomials to multivariate polynomials.

Proposition 1.54. *Let $\mathbb{F}$ be a finite field with q elements*[40]*, and let $f(X_1, \ldots, X_n) \in \mathbb{F}[X_1, \ldots, X_n]$ be a polynomial of degree d, $d > 0$. Let $N(f) = \{(x_1, \ldots, x_n) \mid f(x_1, \ldots, x_n) = 0\}$ denote the set of zeros of f. Then*

$$|N(f)| \leq d \cdot q^{n-1}.$$

Proof. We show the assertion by induction on the number n of variables. For $n = 1$ the assertion is correct, because a polynomial in a variable of degree d over a field has at most d zeros. We show that $n - 1$ implies n. Let

$$f(X_1, \ldots, X_n) = \sum_{i=0}^{k} f_i(X_1, \ldots, X_{n-1})X_n^i, f_k(X_1, \ldots, X_{n-1}) \neq 0.$$

We assume without loss of generality that $k \geq 1$; otherwise, we develop $f(X_1, \ldots, X_n)$ according to another variable. The polynomial $f_k(X_1, \ldots, X_{n-1})$ has degree $\leq d - k$. By the induction hypothesis applied to

$$N(f_k) = \{(x_1, \ldots, x_{n-1}) \mid f_k(x_1, \ldots, x_{n-1}) = 0\},$$

we get $|N(f_k)| \leq (d - k)q^{n-2}$. For every $(x_1, \ldots, x_{n-1}) \in N(f_k)$, there are at most q zeros of $f(x_1, \ldots, x_{n-1}, X_n)$. For every $(x_1, \ldots, x_{n-1}) \notin N(f_k)$, the polynomial $f(x_1, \ldots, x_{n-1}, X_n)$ has degree k. Consequently, for each $(x_1, \ldots, x_{n-1}) \notin N(f_k)$ there are at most k zeros of $f(x_1, \ldots, x_{n-1}, X_n)$. Then with $l = |N(f_k)|$

---

[40] The number of elements is a prime power, $q = p^n$. For $q = p$ see Appendix B, Corollary B.11.

$$|N(f)| \le l \cdot q + (q^{n-1} - l)k \le (d-k) \cdot q^{n-1} + k \cdot q^{n-1} = d \cdot q^{n-1}.$$

Thus, the assertion is shown. □

Corollary 1.55. *Let* $\mathbb{F}$ *be a finite field and* $f(X_1, \ldots, X_n) \in \mathbb{F}[X_1, \ldots, X_n]$ *be a polynomial of degree* d, $d > 0$. *Then the probability that an element* $(x_1, \ldots, x_n)$ *randomly chosen in* $\mathbb{F}^n$ *is a zero of* f *is less than or equal to* d/q.

Remarks:

1. The preceding corollary allows us to implement a randomized algorithm for $d \le q/2$ for multivariate polynomials, analogous to Algorithm 1.48.
2. Corollary 1.55 was published independently by Schwartz[41] and Zippel[42]. In the literature it is called the Schwartz-Zippel Lemma.
3. The preceding corollary has an interesting application in graph algorithms. The problem of whether a given bipartite graph has a perfect matching is reduced to the question of whether a given polynomial is the zero polynomial (Proposition 5.8). The randomized algorithm mentioned in point 1, which tests multivariate polynomials for equality, can be used to decide this question.

1.6.4 Random Numbers

The algorithms in this section use the statement "choose at random". An implementation of this statement requires random numbers. True random numbers require physical processes such as dice, radioactive decay or quantum effects. A uniformly distributed n-bit random number can be obtained by tossing a fair coin n times. However, this method is not suitable for implementation with a computer. We use *pseudo-random numbers*. Pseudo-random numbers are generated by a *pseudo-random number generator*. A *generator* is a deterministic algorithm that generates a long sequence of digits (bits) from a short randomly chosen starting value, called the *seed*.

There is special hardware for the generation of random numbers. The Trusted Platform Module (TPM), for example, is a chip that offers basic security functions as well as the generation of random numbers. Good sources of randomness that are available without additional hardware are time differences between events within a computer that originate from mechanically generated information, such as timing between network packets, rotation latency of hard disks and timing of mouse and keyboard inputs. A good starting value can be calculated from a combination of these events.

There are different procedures with regard to the quality of the pseudo-random numbers and the running time of the generating algorithms. Cryptographic algorithms, for example, require high-quality pseudo-random numbers. The security of cryptographic methods is closely linked to the generation

---

[41] Jacob Theodore Schwartz (1930 - 2009) was an American mathematician and computer scientist.
[42] Richard Zippel is an American computer scientist.

of unpredictable random numbers. The theoretical aspects of the generation of pseudo-random numbers in cryptography are described comprehensively in [DelfsKnebl15, Chapter 8].

For our purposes, it is sufficient that the sequence of pseudo-random numbers has no obvious regularity and passes certain statistical tests, such as the χ^2- test. These aspects are discussed in detail in [Knuth98].

Example. We consider three 0-1 sequences of length 50. Which of the three sequences in Figure 1.11 is a random sequence?

```
0001011101 1100101010 1111001010 1100111100 0101010100
0000000000 0000000000 0000001010 1100111100 0101010100
0000000000 0000000000 0000000000 0000000000 0000000001
```

Fig. 1.11: 0-1-sequences.

Although each of the three sequences has the probability $1/2^{50}$ if we randomly select it in $\{0, 1\}^{50}$, intuitively the first sequence appears typical for a random sequence, the second less typical and the third atypical.

This can be justified as follows. If we create a sequence by tossing a fair coin, the random variable X that counts the number of ones in the sequence is binomially distributed with the parameters $(50, 1/2)$ (Definition A.15). The expected value $E(X) = 25$ and the standard deviation $\sigma(X) = \sqrt{50}/2 = 3.54$ (Proposition A.16). A sequence of length 50, where the number of ones (and thus also the number of zeros) deviates strongly from 25, does not seem typical for a random sequence. Therefore, the first sequence with 26 ones seems typical and the third sequence with one untypical.

Another method to decide the above question is by information theory. For a uniformly distributed random sequence of length 50, the information content is 50 bits. The information content is closely related to the length of the shortest coding of the sequence. The information content of a bit sequence $\approx$ the length of a shortest possible coding of the bit sequence (Proposition 4.39). The third sequence has a short encoding 0(49),1 (49 times the zero followed by the one).[43] Consequently, the information content is small and so is the randomness involved in generating the sequence. A sequence of 50 bits which was generated like the first sequence with coin tosses cannot be encoded with fewer than 50 bits if the original sequence is to be decoded again from the encoded sequence.

The most commonly used pseudo-random generator (for non-cryptographic applications) is the *linear congruence generator*. It is determined by the following parameters: $m, a, c, x_0 \in \mathbb{Z}$ with $0 < m$, $0 \leq a < m$, $0 \leq c < m$ and $0 \leq x_0 < m$. m is called the *modulus* and x_0 is called the *start value* of the linear congruence generator. Starting from x_0 we calculate according to the rule

---

[43] The method of encoding used here is called *run-length encoding*.

$$x_{n+1} = (ax_n + c) \bmod m, \; n \geq 1,$$

the pseudo-random sequence. The effects of the choice of the parameters a, c and m on the safety of the pseudo-random sequence and on the length of the period are studied in detail in [Knuth98, Chapter 3].

This section serves as an introduction to probabilistic methods, which we will discuss in the following text. Quicksort, quickselect, search trees and hash functions are efficient on average. The consequence is that if the inputs are chosen randomly, appropriate running times can be expected. The idea is to replace random input by randomness in the algorithm (by using random numbers). Following this idea, we get probabilistic methods for sorting and searching in sorted arrays (Algorithm 2.10 and Algorithm 2.30), universal families of hash functions (Section 3.2.2) and randomized binary search trees (Section 4.4). We solve the graph problems of computing a minimal cut and a minimum spanning tree using randomized algorithms (Sections 5.7 and 6.6).

All algorithms, except the algorithm for computing a minimal cut, are Las Vegas algorithms. Thus, they always deliver correct results. The algorithm for computing a minimal cut is a Monte Carlo algorithm. For all problems there are also solutions by deterministic algorithms. However, these are less efficient.

1.7 Pseudo-code for Algorithms

We formulate our algorithms with pseudo-code. Pseudo-code is much more precise and compact than a colloquial formulation. Pseudo-code allows us to formulate the algorithms with sufficient precision without having to go into the details of an implementation in a concrete programming language – such as C or Java. On the basis of pseudo-code, conclusions can be drawn about the correctness and the running time can be calculated.

We agree on the following notation:

1. In our pseudo-code there are variables and elementary data types like in Java or C.
2. The assignment operator is "←", the equality operator is "=".
3. We use control structures, as in the programming languages Java or C. In detail, it is about for and while loops, conditional statements (if-then-else) and the call of functions. Unlike in Java or C, for loops always terminate. After leaving the loop, the run variable has the value that caused the termination.
4. We make the block structure visible by indenting it. Since the coding of the algorithms in question always fits on one page, we do not mark the beginning and end of the block conventionally. In the following algorithm,

Euclid's[44] algorithm, which calculates the largest common divisor of a and b, the body of the while loop includes the indented lines 2, 3 and 4.

Algorithm 1.56.
int gcd(int a, b)
1   while $b \neq 0$ do
2       $r \leftarrow a \bmod b$
3       $a \leftarrow b$
4       $b \leftarrow r$
5   return $|a|$

5. Elementary data types are *value types*, i.e., a variable contains the elementary data object.
6. Structure data types aggregate one or more variables, possibly of different type. They are *reference types*. A variable contains a reference (pointer) to the data object. The structure member operator "." is used to access a component. Besides the declaration of the reference type, the new operator has to be used to allocate memory for the data object.

We show the definition of structure data types using the definition of a list element:

    type listElem = struct
        char c
        listElem   *next*

A data object of type listElem consists of the components c and *next*. The variable c can store a character and *next* can store a reference to a listElem type data object. The definition allows self referencing.

We now use data objects of type ListElem to store the characters A, B and C in a linked list, as shown in Figure 1.12.

A variable *start* of type listElem stores a reference to the first data object. With *start.c* you can access the character and with *start.next* the reference.

The variable *next* stores a reference to a data object of type listElem or null. The null reference indicates that the end of the list is reached. We use the null reference when a reference variable does not reference an object.

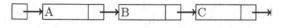

Fig. 1.12: Linked list.

7. Arrays are reference types (see the point before). Individual elements are accessed by the [ ] – operator. When defining an array, we specify the

---

[44] Euclid of Alexandria was a Greek mathematician, who probably lived in Alexandria in the third century B.C. Euclid described the algorithm in his famous work "The Elements" in an equivalent form.

range of the indices. The expression int $a[1..n]$ defines an array of integers of dimension n, indexed from 1 to n. Later it is possible to access partial arrays with $a[i..j]$, $1 \leq i \leq j \leq n$. For $i = j$ we access the ith element, and for short we write $a[i]$. If an array $a[1..n]$ is defined as a parameter of a function, it is agreed that we can access the variable n, the length of the array, inside the called function.

8. Our pseudo-code contains functions similar to those in the programming languages Java or C. We pass parameters to functions always "by value", i.e., the called function receives a copy of the parameter in its own variable. A change of the variable only affects the called function. It is not visible in the calling function. If x is a reference variable and parameter of a function, an assignment $x \leftarrow y$ only affects the called function; an assignment $x.prop \leftarrow a$ is also visible in the calling function.

Variables that we define within a function are only visible in the function. Variables defined outside of functions are globally visible.

1.8 Textbooks on Algorithms and Data Structures

I used the following textbooks for the preparation of the lectures from which this book originates. They were a valuable source in the selection and presentation of the algorithms covered. In the text one can surely find traces of the referenced textbooks.

First I would like to mention "The Art of Computer Programming" (Volumes 1–3) by Knuth ([Knuth97], [Knuth98]), [Knuth98a]). This standard work presents the treated topics comprehensively. The methodology developed is very precise. It would be an omission not to use this work in the preparation of a lecture course on Algorithms and Data Structures.

"Concrete Mathematics" by Graham, Knuth and Patashnik develops mathematical methods for the analysis of algorithms using numerous examples ([GraKnuPat94]). This book is an exorbitant treasure trove not only for computer scientists, but also for friends of "concrete mathematics".

During my first lectures at the beginning of the 1990s I also used Wirth's "Algorithmen und Datenstrukturen" ([Wirth83]). Further, there is the classic "The Design and Analysis of Computer Algorithms" ([AhoHopUll74]), which also contains many interesting subjects from today's point of view, and "Data Structures and Algorithms" ([AhoHopUll83]), both by Aho, Hopcroft and Ullman, as well as "Algorithms" by Sedgewick ([Sedgewick88]), which was published in its fourth edition ([SedWay11]) with Wayne as an additional author.

Among the newer textbooks is "Introduction to Algorithms" by Cormen, Leiserson and Rivest ([CorLeiRiv89]), which is available in its third edition, with Stein as an additional author ([CorLeiRivSte09]) and "Algorithms and Data Structures" by Mehlhorn and Sanders ([MehSan08]).

Motwani and Raghavan cover randomized algorithms comprehensively in "Randomized Algorithms" ([MotRag95]).

The biographical data of persons given in the text are taken from the respective Wikipedia entries.

Exercises.

1. Show that $n = \frac{2^k - 1}{3}$, where $k \in \mathbb{N}$ is even, is a natural number, and that Algorithm 1.2 terminates with input n.

2. We consider sorting by insertion – InsertionSort.

   Algorithm 1.57.
   ```
   InsertionSort(item a[1..n])
   1   index i, j; item x
   2   for i ← 2 to n do
   3       x ← a[i], a[0] ← x, j ← i − 1
   4       while x < a[j] do
   5           a[j + 1] ← a[j], j ← j − 1
   6       a[j + 1] ← x
   ```

   a. Illustrate the operation of the algorithm using appropriate input arrays.

   b. Show that InsertionSort is correct.

3. Let A_1, A_2 and A_3 be algorithms with the following running times

   $$T_1(n) = c_1 n, \ T_2(n) = c_2 n^3 \text{ and } T_3(n) = c_3 2^n,$$

   where the c_i, $i = 1, 2, 3$, are constants. For each algorithm let m_i, $i = 1, 2, 3$, be the maximum size of the input which can be processed within a fixed time t on a computer. How do the numbers m_i, $i = 1, 2, 3$, change if the computer is replaced by a k times faster computer?

4. Arrange the following functions in ascending order with respect to asymptotic growth. To do this, estimate the asymptotic growth of each function. Then compare two consecutive terms of the sequence by calculation. For all calculations use only the rules for fractions, powers and logarithms.

   $$f_1(n) = n,$$
   $$f_2(n) = \sqrt{n},$$
   $$f_3(n) = \log_2(n),$$
   $$f_4(n) = \log_2(\sqrt{n}),$$
   $$f_5(n) = \log_2(\log_2(n)),$$
   $$f_6(n) = \log_2(n)^2,$$

   $$f_7(n) = \frac{n}{\log_2(n)},$$
   $$f_8(n) = \sqrt{n}\log_2(n)^2,$$
   $$f_9(n) = (1/3)^n,$$
   $$f_{10}(n) = (3/2)^n,$$
   $$f_{11}(n) = \sqrt{\log_2(\log_2(n))\log_2(n)},$$
   $$f_{12}(n) = 2^{f_{11}(n)}.$$

5. For which (i,j) does $f_i = O(f_j)$ hold?

$$f_1(n) = n^2. \qquad\qquad f_2(n) = n^2 + 1000n.$$

$$f_3(n) = \begin{cases} n & \text{if } n \text{ is odd,} \\ n^3 & \text{if } n \text{ is even.} \end{cases} \qquad f_4(n) = \begin{cases} n & \text{if } n \le 100, \\ n^3 & \text{if } n > 100. \end{cases}$$

6. Let $f_1(n) = n(\sqrt[n]{n} - 1)$ and $f_2(n) = \binom{n}{k} k!$.
   Determine the orders of $f_1(n)$ and $f_2(n)$.

7. A capital sum k is subject to an annual interest rate of $p\ \%$. After each year, the capital increases by the interest and by a constant amount, c. Specify a formula for the capital k after n years.

8. Solve the following difference equations:

   a. $x_1 = 1$, $\qquad\qquad$ b. $x_1 = 0$,

   $\quad x_n = x_{n-1} + n,\ n \ge 2.$ $\qquad x_n = \frac{n+1}{n} x_{n-1} + \frac{2(n-1)}{n},\ n \ge 2.$

9. How often is the string "hello!" output by the following algorithm (depending on n)?

   Algorithm 1.58.
   ```
   DoRec(int n)
   1   if n > 0
   2     then for i ← 1 to 2n do
   3             DoRec(n − 1)
   4           k ← 1
   5           for i ← 2 to n + 1 do
   6               k ← k · i
   7           for i ← 1 to k do
   8               print(hello!)
   ```

10. Use difference equations to determine how often the string "hello!" is output by the following algorithm (depending on n).

    Algorithm 1.59.
    ```
    DoRec(int n)
    1   if n > 0
    2     then for i ← 1 to n − 1 do
    3             DoRec(i)
    4           print(hello!), print(hello!)
    ```

11. Let $n \in \mathbb{R}_{\ge 0}$, $T(n) = T(\sqrt{n}) + r(n)$ for $n > 2$ and $T(n) = 0$ for $n \le 2$. Calculate for $r(n) = 1$ and $r(n) = \log_2(n)$ a closed solution for $T(n)$. Use Lemma B.23.

12. Let $a \geq 1$, $b > 1$, d, $l \geq 0$ and

$$x_1 = ad + cb^l, \; x_k = ax_{k-1} + c(b^l)^k \text{ for } k > 1.$$

Specify a closed solution to the equation. Use the inverse transformation $k = \log_b(n)$ to calculate a solution to the recurrence (R1).

13. Let $T(n) = aT\left(\lfloor \frac{n}{2} \rfloor\right) + n^l$, $T(1) = 1$. Specify estimates for $a = 1, 2$ and $l = 0, 1$.

14. The function $\text{Fib}(n)$ for calculating the nth Fibonacci number is implemented recursively (analogously to the defining formula). How big is the required stack in terms of n?

15. Implement TowersOfHanoi iteratively. To do this, examine the tree that is defined by the recursive calls from TowersOfHanoi.

16. Implement the algorithm Optimum for the task scheduling problem.

17. An amount of n (Euro-)Cents is to be paid out. The coins[45] should be chosen in such a way that the number of coins is minimized. Develop a greedy algorithm and show that the greedy strategy leads to success.

18. Proposition 1.39 contains a recursive formula for calculating the edit distance. Convert the formula into a recursive function and specify a lower limit for the running time.

19. Let $a_1 \ldots a_n$ be a string of characters. A substring of $a_1 \ldots a_n$ is created by deleting characters in the string $a_1 \ldots a_n$. Develop an algorithm according to the dynamic programming method that calculates the length of the largest common substring for two strings $a_1 \ldots a_n$ and $b_1 \ldots b_m$.

20. Let $a_1 \ldots a_n$ be a sequence of integers. $f(i,j) = \sum_{k=i}^{j} a_k$. We are looking for

$$m := \max_{i,j} f(i,j).$$

Specify an algorithm using the dynamic programming method that calculates m.

21. Let $a = a_1 \ldots a_n$ and $b = b_1 \ldots b_m$, $m \leq n$, be strings of characters. The problem is to decide whether b is a substring of a, and if so, to specify the smallest i with $a_i \ldots a_{i+m-1} = b_1 \ldots b_m$. The problem is called "pattern matching" in strings. Develop a randomized algorithm to solve the problem using the fingerprint technique.

---

[45] The euro coin series comprises eight different denominations: 1, 2, 5, 10, 20 and 50 cent, 1 € (= 100 cent) and 2 €.

2. Sorting and Searching

Let $a_1, \ldots, a_n$ be a finite sequence. The elements of the sequence should be elements of an ordered set. The order relation is $\leq$. We are looking for a permutation π of the indices $\{1, \ldots, n\}$, so that the sequence $a_{\pi(1)} \leq a_{\pi(2)} \leq \ldots \leq a_{\pi(n)}$ is arranged in ascending order. More precisely, we are interested in an algorithm that will bring about this arrangement. We call such an algorithm a sorting procedure.

Sorting procedures can be divided into sorting procedures for data stored in main memory and those for data stored in secondary storage. In this section, we will only consider sorting procedures for data in main memory. The elements to be sorted are stored in an array a. The sorting should be done in the array a (except for variables, if possible without additional memory) by exchanging elements on the basis of comparisons. A measure of the efficiency of the algorithms is the number of comparisons and exchanges depending on n. n denotes the length of the array.

When sorting data in main memory, we differentiate between simple sorting methods such as *selection sort*, *insertion sort* and *bubble sort* and the more efficient methods *heapsort* and *quicksort*. The simple methods have a running time of order $O(n^2)$. Quicksort and heapsort run in time $O(n \log_2(n))$, quicksort on average and heapsort in the worst case. We discuss them in detail in this chapter.

An important application of sorting algorithms is to simplify the subsequent search. Unsorted arrays require sequential search. In sorted arrays we can perform a binary search. The order of the running time improves considerably, from $O(n)$ to $O(\log(n))$. Besides sequential and binary search, we also deal with the problem of finding the kth-smallest element of a finite sequence. We can solve this problem by sorting the sequence first and then accessing the kth element. Quickselect, however, provides a much more efficient solution.

2.1 Quicksort

Quicksort implements the divide and conquer strategy (Section 1.5.2). We divide the problem of sorting a sequence of length n into smaller subproblems. A subproblem is to sort a subsequence. The subproblems are of the same type

© Springer Nature Switzerland AG 2020
H. Knebl, *Algorithms and Data Structures*, https://doi.org/10.1007/978-3-030-59758-0_2

as the overall problem. It is a good idea to solve the subproblems recursively. The solutions to the subproblems are then combined to form a solution to the overall problem.

Let F be the sequence to sort. For quicksort, the decomposition of the problem consists of choosing a *pivot element* x from F and dividing F into two sequences F_1 and F_2. F_1 contains only elements that are $\leq x$ and F_2 only elements that are $\geq x$. We then recursively apply quicksort to F_1 and F_2. In the case of quicksort, assembling the partial solutions "F_1 and F_2 sorted" into the total solution "F sorted" simply consists of outputting the elements of F_1 one after the other in sorted order, then x and finally F_2 again in sorted order.

We store the sequence F to be sorted in an array a. Quicksort sorts on the basis of comparisons and exchanges in the input array a.

The algorithm quicksort was published by Hoare ([Hoare62]).

Algorithm 2.1.
```
    QuickSort(item a[i..j])
    1   item x; index l, r; boolean loop ← true
    2   if i < j
    3       then x ← a[j], l ← i, r ← j − 1
    4           while loop do
    5               while a[l] < x do l ← l + 1
    6               while a[r] > x do r ← r − 1
    7               if l < r
    8                   then exchange a[l] and a[r]
    9                       l = l + 1, r = r − 1
    10                  else  loop ← false
    11              exchange a[l] and a[j]
    12              QuickSort(a[i..l − 1])
    13              QuickSort(a[l + 1..j])
```

The call QuickSort($a[1..n]$) sorts an array $a[1..n]$. Before the first call of QuickSort we set $a[0]$ as sentinel.[1] The sentinel is chosen such that $a[0] \leq a[i]$, $1 \leq i \leq n$.

Example. We consider the application of QuickSort to the sequence 67, 56, 10, 41, 95, 18, 6, 42. Figure 2.1 shows the hierarchy of the QuickSort calls. The nodes of the tree are formed by partial arrays, which we pass as call parameters. Each node that is not a leaf has exactly two successors. We see that recursive calls with one element or even with no element can take place. This should be avoided when implementing the algorithm. We get the sequence of the call times by the pre-order output and the sequence of the termination times by the post-order output of the nodes of the tree (see Definition 4.4).

---
[1] The sentinel element makes sure that we do not access array a with a negative index.

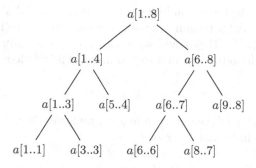

Fig. 2.1: Call hierarchy for QuickSort.

The call QuickSort($a[1..1]$) terminates as the first call. The smallest element is then at the first position.

Below are the pivot elements and their corresponding decompositions.

sequence:		67	56	10	41	95	18	6	42
pivot element:						42			
partition:		6	18	10	41		56	67	95
pivot elements:					41				95
partition:		6	18	10			56	67	
pivot elements:			10					67	
partition:		6		18			56		
sorted sequence:		6	10	18	41	42	56	67	95

After termination of the call QuickSort($a[i..j]$), the subarray with the indices $i..j$ is sorted.

Proposition 2.2. *QuickSort sorts the array a in ascending order.*

Proof. We first show that QuickSort terminates.

1. The while loop in line 5 terminates at the first run at the latest for $l = j$, because the pivot element is at the very right.
2. The while loop in line 6 terminates at the first run at the latest for $r = i-1$ (if the pivot element is the smallest element). The pivot element of the previous decomposition or the sentinel $a[0]$ (if $i = 1$) is located at position $i - 1$. Therefore, $a[i - 1] \leq a[r]$ for $i \leq r \leq j$.
3. If $l < r$, we swap $a[l]$ and $a[r]$. After incrementing l and decrementing r, the elements left of $a[l]$ are $\leq x$ and the elements right of $a[r]$ are $\geq x$. Hence, all subsequent passes of the two inner while loops terminate. After each iteration of the while loop in line 4, the distance $r - l$ decreases. Therefore, $l \geq r$ occurs, i.e., the while loop terminates.

Correctness now immediately follows by induction on n, the number of elements of a. The assertion is obviously true when $n = 1$. The partial arrays for which we call QuickSort recursively have at most $n - 1$ elements. Therefore, we may assume by the induction hypothesis that the partial arrays are sorted in ascending order. After termination of the outer while loop (line 4), we have $i \leq l \leq j$, $a[i], \ldots, a[l-1] \leq x$ and $a[l+1], \ldots, a[j] \geq x$. Thus, we can store the element x at the position l in a sorted order. The whole array a is sorted accordingly.   □

Remarks:

1. After termination of the outer while loop, we have $l \geq r$. Since $a[l-1] < x$ holds, we conclude that $l = r$ or $l = r + 1$.

2. Let $n = j - (i - 1)$ be the number of elements. There are n or $n + 1$ comparisons (lines 5 and 6). By a small modification, you can achieve that $n - 1$ comparisons with elements of a are sufficient (Exercise 7). The comparisons with elements from a are called essential comparisons. Comparisons between indices require less effort, because indices are usually implemented with register variables and elements in an array have a complex structure compared to indices. Comparisons between indices, therefore, are insignificant. We count only essential comparisons. Since each swap involves two elements, the number of swaps in line 8 is limited by $\lfloor \frac{n-1}{2} \rfloor$.

3. In the algorithm above, recursive calls for an array with one or without elements occur. This should be avoided when implementing the algorithm. Even recursive calls for small arrays should be avoided, because quicksort is only superior to a simple sorting method such as insertion sort if the number of elements in the array to be sorted is sufficiently large. Therefore, it is recommended to use insertion sort if the number of elements is small, i.e., if it is below a given bound. In [Knuth98a] this is analyzed exactly and a bound for n is calculated. This bound is 10 for the computer considered there.

2.1.1 Running Time Analysis

We assume that the array $a[1..n]$ to be sorted contains different elements. The effort for lines 2 - 11 is cn, where c is constant. We split $a[1..n]$ into arrays of length $r - 1$ and $n - r$. For the running time $T(n)$, we get recursively:

$$T(n) = T(r-1) + T(n-r) + cn, c \text{ constant.}$$

The Best and the Worst Case. The pivot element determines the two parts during disassembly. Equally large parts or parts of strongly different sizes can be produced. In extreme cases, one part is empty. This is the case if the pivot element is the largest or the smallest element. Figure 2.2 shows the trees that represent the recursive call hierarchy of QuickSort in these two cases. In the nodes we note the number of elements of the array that we pass as a parameter. Nodes for which no comparisons take place are omitted. The first tree represents the case of equal-sized parts. The second tree represents the case in which in each step one part is empty.

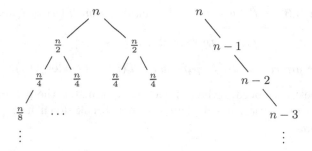

Fig. 2.2: The best and the worst case.

In the first case, the height of the tree is $\lfloor \log_2(n) \rfloor$. On each level of the tree there are approximately n elements. The sum of all comparisons on the same recursion level, i.e., in one level of the tree, is approximately n. In total, the number of comparisons is of order $O(n \log_2(n))$.

In the second case, the height of the tree is n. On the ith level $n - (i + 1)$ comparisons take place. The total number of comparisons is $\sum_{i=0}^{n-1} n-(i+1) = \sum_{i=1}^{n-1} i = \frac{n(n-1)}{2} = O(n^2)$.

Proposition 2.26 states that $O(n \log_2(n))$ is a lower limit of the number of comparisons in the worst case required by a comparison sort algorithm, i.e. an algorithm that sorts based on the comparison of two elements. The QuickSort algorithm gives an upper limit on the number of comparisons, which leads to the following consideration.

Let $C(n)$ be the number of comparisons[2] which QuickSort needs to sort n elements. Then

$$C(n) \leq \max_{1 \leq r \leq \lfloor \frac{n}{2} \rfloor} C(r - 1) + C(n - r) + (n - 1).$$

We show by induction on n that $C(n) \leq \frac{n(n-1)}{2}$. For $n = 1$ no comparison is necessary, the assertion is true. By applying the induction hypothesis, we conclude that

$$C(n) \leq \max_{1 \leq r \leq \lfloor \frac{n}{2} \rfloor} \frac{(r - 1)(r - 2)}{2} + \frac{(n - r)(n - r - 1)}{2} + (n - 1).$$

The function on the right, over which we form the maximum, is decreasing for $r \in [1, \lfloor \frac{n}{2} \rfloor]$. The induction assertion follows immediately. This shows that the number of comparisons of QuickSort is limited downwards by $O(n \log_2(n))$ and upwards by $\frac{n(n-1)}{2}$. Since the running time is proportional to the number of comparisons, there are analogous limits for the running time.

We investigate the running time of QuickSort in the best and worst case.

---

[2] We consider an optimized version of quicksort that manages with $n - 1$ comparisons (see the remarks after the proof of Proposition 2.2).

Proposition 2.3. *In the best case, the running time $T(n)$ of QuickSort satisfies*

$$T(n) \leq b2^{\lfloor \log_2(n) \rfloor} + cn\lfloor \log_2(n) \rfloor,$$

where b and c are constants. In particular, $T(n) = O(n \log_2(n))$.

Proof. The best case occurs when in each recursion step the process delivers roughly equal quantities. $n-1$ elements then break down into $\lceil \frac{n-1}{2} \rceil$ and $\lfloor \frac{n-1}{2} \rfloor$ elements.

$$T(n) = T\left(\left\lfloor \frac{n-1}{2} \right\rfloor\right) + T\left(\left\lceil \frac{n-1}{2} \right\rceil\right) + cn,$$

$$T(1) = b.$$

We have $\lfloor \frac{n-1}{2} \rfloor \leq \lfloor \frac{n}{2} \rfloor$ and $\lceil \frac{n-1}{2} \rceil = \lfloor \frac{n}{2} \rfloor$. Since T is increasing, we get

$$T(n) \leq 2T\left(\left\lfloor \frac{n}{2} \right\rfloor\right) + cn.$$

We replace "$\leq$" with "$=$" and get by Proposition 1.28 the formula of the assertion.   □

QuickSort is in the best case much more efficient than the simple sorting methods selection sort, insertion sort and bubble sort. The running times of these methods are of order $O(n^2)$. In the worst case QuickSort also runs in time $O(n^2)$.

Proposition 2.4. *Let $T(n)$ be the running time of QuickSort in the worst case, then*

$$T(n) = \frac{c}{2}n^2 + \left(\frac{c}{2} + b\right)n - c,$$

where b and c are constants. In particular, $T(n) = O(n^2)$.

Proof. The worst case occurs when in each recursion step the decomposition process returns an empty array and an $(n-1)$-element array.

$$T(n) = T(n-1) + T(0) + cn, n \geq 2, T(0) = T(1) = b,$$

has according to Proposition 1.15 the solution

$$T(n) = b + \sum_{i=2}^{n}(ci + b) = bn + c\left(\frac{n(n+1)}{2} - 1\right)$$

$$= \frac{c}{2}n^2 + \left(\frac{c}{2} + b\right)n - c.$$

This shows the assertion.   □

Remark. In Algorithm 2.1 the worst case occurs for a sorted array.

The Average Case. The analysis for the average running time is carried out under the assumption that all elements are pairwise distinct. We designate the elements to be sorted in ascending order with $a_1 < a_2 < \ldots < a_n$. The probability that a_i is at the last position n is $\frac{1}{n}$, because there are $(n-1)!$ permutations π with $\pi(i) = n$ and $n!$ permutations in total and $\frac{(n-1)!}{n!} = \frac{1}{n}$.

If a_i is at the last position, $\{a_1, a_2, \ldots, a_n\}$ breaks down into $\{a_1, \ldots, a_{i-1}\}$, $\{a_{i+1}, \ldots, a_n\}$ and $\{a_i\}$. First we show that after partitioning there is a uniform distribution on $\{a_1, \ldots, a_{i-1}\}$ and on $\{a_{i+1}, \ldots, a_n\}$.

After the decomposition with the pivot element a_i, we get – before executing line 11 – the sequence

$$(2.1) \qquad a_{\pi(1)}, a_{\pi(2)}, \ldots, a_{\pi(i-1)}, a_{\tilde{\pi}(i+1)}, a_{\tilde{\pi}(i+2)}, \ldots, a_{\tilde{\pi}(n)}, a_i.$$

π is a permutation on $\{1, \ldots, i-1\}$ and $\tilde{\pi}$ is a permutation on $\{i+1, \ldots, n\}$.

We now determine the number of arrangements of $\{a_1, \ldots, a_n\}$ that result after decomposition in the sequence (2.1). For each choice of j positions in $(1, \ldots, i-1)$ and of j positions in $(i+1, \ldots, n)$, $j \geq 0$, exactly one sequence is determined which requires j swaps during partitioning and results after partitioning in the sequence (2.1). Therefore, there are

$$(2.2) \qquad \binom{i-1}{j}\binom{n-i}{j}$$

output sequences that after partitioning using j swaps result in (2.1).

Let $m = \min\{i-1, n-i\}$. The number l of all sequences that result in the sequence (2.1) after partitioning is

$$l = \sum_{j=0}^{m} \binom{i-1}{j}\binom{n-i}{j} = \binom{n-1}{i-1}$$

(Lemma B.17). The number l is independent of the order of the sequence (2.1). For all permutations π on $\{1, \ldots, i-1\}$ and for all permutations $\tilde{\pi}$ on $\{i+1, \ldots, n\}$, we get the same number l. Therefore, all orders on $\{a_1, \ldots, a_{i-1}\}$ and on $\{a_{i+1}, \ldots, a_{n-1}\}$ have equal probability. The uniform distribution on $\{a_1, a_2, \ldots, a_n\}$ therefore leads to the uniform distribution on $\{a_1, \ldots, a_{i-1}\}$ and on $\{a_{i+1}, \ldots, a_n\}$.

The discussions of the average running time, the average number of comparisons and the average number of exchanges are based on [Knuth98a].

Average Number of Comparisons. Our quicksort algorithm makes n or $n+1$ comparisons. However, for n elements, $n-1$ comparisons suffice. We only have to compare the pivot element once with each of the other $n-1$ elements. This requires controlling the indices of a in the algorithm. When determining the average number of comparisons, we assume an optimized algorithm that manages with $n-1$ comparisons (see the remarks after the proof of Proposition 2.2). The calculation of the average number of comparisons for Algorithm 2.1 is an exercise (Exercise 4). Let $C(n)$ denote the average number of comparisons and $\tilde{C}(n,i)$ the average number of comparisons if the ith element is the pivot element. We get

$$\tilde{C}(n,i) = C(i-1) + C(n-i) + n - 1.$$

$C(n)$ is the average of the $\tilde{C}(n,i)$, $i = 1, \ldots, n$:

$$C(n) = \frac{1}{n} \sum_{i=1}^{n} \tilde{C}(n,i)$$

$$= \frac{1}{n} \sum_{i=1}^{n} (C(i-1) + C(n-i) + n - 1)$$

$$= \frac{2}{n} \sum_{i=0}^{n-1} C(i) + n - 1, n \geq 2.$$

The aim is to transform the recursion $C(n) = \frac{2}{n} \sum_{i=0}^{n-1} C(i) + n - 1$ by a suitable substitution into a difference equation. For recursions where the nth member depends on the sum of all predecessors, this is done with the substitution

$$x_n = \sum_{i=0}^{n} C(i).$$

Then

$$x_n - x_{n-1} = \frac{2}{n} x_{n-1} + n - 1.$$

We get the difference equation

$$x_1 = C(0) + C(1) = 0,$$
$$x_n = \frac{n+2}{n} x_{n-1} + n - 1, n \geq 2.$$

This equation has the solution

$$x_n = (n+1)(n+2)\left(H_{n+1} + \frac{3}{n+2} - \frac{5}{2}\right)$$

(see page 16, equation (d)). We get

$$C(n) = x_n - x_{n-1} = \frac{2}{n} x_{n-1} + n - 1 = 2(n+1)H_n - 4n.$$

We summarize the result in the following Proposition.

Proposition 2.5. *Let $C(n)$ be the average number of comparisons in quicksort, $n \geq 1$. Then*

$$C(n) = 2(n+1)H_n - 4n.$$

The average is over all arrangements of the array to be sorted.

The Average Number of Exchanges. $E(n)$ denotes the average number of exchanges and $\tilde{E}(n,i)$ the average number of exchanges in line 8 of Algorithm 2.1 if the ith element is the pivot element. We first calculate $\tilde{E}(n,i)$ for $n \geq 2$. Let $L = \{1,\ldots,i-1\}$ and $R = \{i+1,\ldots,n\}$. To calculate the probability $p(\tilde{E}(n,i) = j)$ for j exchanges, we consider the following experiment. We draw $i-1$ numbers $z_1,\ldots,z_{i-1}$ from $L \cup R$ and set $a[k] = z_k$, $k = 1,\ldots,i-1$. The result of our experiment requires j exchanges if j of the numbers were drawn from R and $i-1-j$ of the numbers were drawn from L. This is independent of the order in which we draw the numbers. For this reason

$$p(\tilde{E}(n,i) = j) = \frac{\binom{n-i}{j}\binom{i-1}{i-1-j}}{\binom{n-1}{i-1}}.$$

The random variable $\tilde{E}(n,i)$ is hyper-geometrically distributed. By Proposition A.24 the expected value $E(\tilde{E}(n,i))$ satisfies

$$E(\tilde{E}(n,i)) = (i-1)\frac{n-i}{n-1}.$$

With the last exchange, which brings a_i to the ith position (line 11 in Algorithm 2.1), the result is $\frac{(i-1)(n-i)}{n-1} + 1$.

Lemma 2.6. *The average number of exchanges (without recursion) averaged over all pivot elements is for $n \geq 2$*

$$\frac{1}{n}\sum_{i=1}^{n} E(\tilde{E}(n,i) + 1) = \frac{n+4}{6}.$$

Proof. The average number of exchanges (without recursion) averaged over all pivot elements

$$\frac{1}{n}\sum_{i=1}^{n} E(\tilde{E}(n,i) + 1)$$

$$= \frac{1}{n}\sum_{i=1}^{n}\left(\frac{(i-1)(n-i)}{n-1} + 1\right)$$

$$= \frac{1}{(n-1)n}\sum_{i=1}^{n}((n+1)i - n - i^2) + 1$$

$$= \frac{1}{(n-1)n}\left(\frac{n(n+1)^2}{2} - n^2 - \frac{n(n+1)(2n+1)}{6}\right) + 1$$

$$= \frac{1}{6(n-1)}(n-1)(n-2) + 1 = \frac{n+4}{6}.$$

This shows the assertion.   □

For the average number of exchanges $\tilde{E}(n, i)$ with pivot element a_i, we get

$$\tilde{E}(n, i) = E(i-1) + E(n-i) + \frac{(i-1)(n-i)}{n-1} + 1.$$

Hence, the average number of exchanges $E(n)$ results in

$$E(n) = \frac{1}{n} \sum_{i=1}^{n} \tilde{E}(n, i)$$

$$= \frac{1}{n} \sum_{i=1}^{n} \left(E(i-1) + E(n-i) + \frac{(n-i)(i-1)}{n-1} + 1 \right)$$

$$= \frac{2}{n} \sum_{i=0}^{n-1} E(i) + \frac{n+4}{6}, n \geq 2.$$

Analogously to above, the substitution $x_n = \sum_{i=0}^{n} E(i)$ yields

$$x_n - x_{n-1} = \frac{2}{n} x_{n-1} + \frac{n+4}{6}$$

and

$$x_1 = E(0) + E(1) = 0,$$
$$x_n = \frac{n+2}{n} x_{n-1} + \frac{n+4}{6}, n \geq 2.$$

This equation has the solution

$$x_n = \frac{(n+1)(n+2)}{6} \left(H_{n+1} - \frac{2}{n+2} - \frac{5}{6} \right)$$

(page 16, equation (d)). We obtain

$$E(n) = x_n - x_{n-1} = \frac{2}{n} x_{n-1} + \frac{n+4}{6} = \frac{1}{3}(n+1)H_n - \frac{1}{9}n - \frac{5}{18}.$$

We summarize the result in the following Proposition.

Proposition 2.7. *The average number of exchanges $E(n)$ satisfies*

$$E(n) = \frac{1}{3}(n+1)H_n - \frac{1}{9}n - \frac{5}{18},$$

$n \geq 2$. *The average number is composed of all arrangements of the array to be sorted.*

Remark. We call exchange in Algorithm 2.1 in line 11 also for $l = j$. The calculation of the formula $E(n)$ for the modified algorithm which avoids this unnecessary call is an exercise (Exercise 5).

Analogous to the formulas in Proposition 2.5 and Proposition 2.7, we obtain a formula for the average running time $T(n)$ of QuickSort:

$$T(n) = 2c(n+1)H_n + \frac{1}{3}(2b - 10c)n + \frac{1}{3}(2b - c),$$

where b and c are constants. The average is calculated over all arrangements of the array to be sorted. In particular, $T(n) = O(n \ln(n))$ holds. We set the recalculation as an exercise (Exercise 6).

2.1.2 Memory Space Analysis

The implementation of function calls uses a *stack frame* on a memory area, the *stack*, that the operating system provides. The call of the function occupies the stack frame and when the function is terminated it is released again. The stack frame is used to store the call parameters, the local variables and the return address. A function call is active at a moment t if the call took place before t and has not terminated at time t. For each active call, its stack frame occupies memory on the stack. The *recursion depth* indicates the maximum number of active calls of a function. When executing a recursive function, the memory consumption increases linearly with the recursion depth.

$S(n)$ is the recursion depth of QuickSort, depending on the number n of elements to sort.

Proposition 2.8. *Let $S(n)$ be the recursion depth of QuickSort. Then*

$$S(n) \begin{cases} \leq \lfloor \log_2(n) \rfloor + 1 & \text{in the best case,} \\ = n & \text{in the worst case.} \end{cases}$$

Proof.

1. The best case occurs when the $n-1$ elements are split into $\lceil \frac{n-1}{2} \rceil$ and $\lfloor \frac{n-1}{2} \rfloor$ elements. We have $\lfloor \frac{n-1}{2} \rfloor \leq \lfloor \frac{n}{2} \rfloor$ and $\lceil \frac{n-1}{2} \rceil = \lfloor \frac{n}{2} \rfloor$. Since S is increasing,

$$S(n) \leq S\left(\left\lfloor \frac{n}{2} \right\rfloor\right) + 1.$$

We replace "$\leq$" with "$=$" and get the recurrence

$$S(n) = S\left(\left\lfloor \frac{n}{2} \right\rfloor\right) + 1,$$

whose solution by Proposition 1.28 is $S(n) = \lfloor \log_2(n) \rfloor + 1$.
2. In the worst case, a single-element subset is split off in each recursion step. Thus,

$$S(n) = S(n-1) + 1 = \ldots = S(1) + n - 1 = n.$$

This shows the assertion of the proposition. $\square$

Remark. The memory consumption varies considerably. We can implement QuickSort in such a way that the best case always occurs. First the recursive call for the smaller part of the decomposition takes place. The second recursive call is the last statement in the function. It is a *tail recursion*. Tail recursions are generally eliminated by jump statements, with reuse of the memory for the variables on the stack (Exercise 8). We eliminate the final recursion. For the implementation that we thereby obtain, the number of active calls is limited by $\lfloor \log_2(n) \rfloor + 1$.

2.1.3 Quicksort Without Stack

We can convert any recursive function into an iteration by explicitly setting up a stack, thereby replacing the stack which is supplied by the operating system and implicitly used by the function calls. Quicksort, however, we can program iteratively without using an additional stack, i.e., we do not need any additional memory besides local variables. The problem that needs to be solved is that we can only process one part immediately after the decomposition. Information about the other part has to be buffered for later processing. If we process the right part first, we have to cache the initial index of the left part. The idea now is to store this information in the array itself. The quicksort variant without an additional stack is published in [Ďurian86].

We now explain the idea of Ďurian's algorithm.

1. We are looking at a decomposition that differs slightly from the decomposition in Algorithm 2.1 (see the quicksort variant, Exercise 11). The decomposition for the subarray $a[i..j]$ uses a pivot element x. We rearrange the elements of a so that $a[k] < x$ for $i \leq k \leq l-1$, $a[l] = x$ and $a[k] \geq x$ for $l+1 \leq k \leq j$. See Figure 2.3.
2. Let $a[i..j]$ be the right part of the decomposition of $a[g..j]$ and $x = a[i]$ be the pivot element for this decomposition. The elements to the left of position i are smaller than x, especially $a[i-1] < x$, and the elements to the right of position i are $\geq x$ i.e., $x \leq a[k], i \leq k \leq j$.
3. We now split $a[i..j]$ with the pivot element y into the parts $a[i..l-1]$ and $a[l..j]$. We store the pivot element y in position l and swap $a[i]$ with $a[l-1]$. From l we determine i by searching. At position $i-1$ is the first element (to the left of the position l) which is smaller than x (x is at position $l-1$). We determine this element by a sequential search.

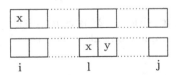

Fig. 2.3: Decomposition with additional information.

4. First we call QuickSort for the right part $a[l..j]$. After QuickSort terminates for this part, we determine the initial index for the left part as described in point 3 and process the left part further.
5. QuickSort has now only one recursive call at the very end – a tail recursion. As described above, this is easy to eliminate.

2.1.4 Randomized Quicksort

We have shown that the average running time of QuickSort is of order $O(n \log_2(n))$. We average over all arrangements of the sequence to be sorted. This implies that if we randomly select the input, we expect a running time of order $O(n \log_2(n))$. This prerequisite is unrealistic in applications. The order of the input is predefined. The idea now is to provide the assumption about the randomness of the arrangement by "randomness in the algorithm". This kind of randomness can always be guaranteed.

The obvious idea is first to apply a random permutation to the input, which requires the calculation of a random permutation. To do this, we have to compute a random number at least $n - 1$ times. It may be necessary to exchange elements n times. Less effort would be required to choose the pivot element at random. Here we only have to determine a random number once. In the randomized version RandQuickSort (Algorithm 2.10) of quicksort the function $\text{Random}(i, j)$, which returns a uniformly chosen number from $\{i, \ldots, j\}$, determines the pivot element.

For each deterministic method of determining the pivot element, there is a sequence of elements for which the "worst case" – i.e., the running time is of order $O(n^2)$ – occurs. In the randomized version of quicksort there are no such bad inputs anymore. The probability that we choose the "worst" pivot element in every recursive call is $1/n!$, where n is the number of elements in the sequence to be sorted. Because of this small probability, we expect that RandQuickSort will always have good running time behavior.

We assume that all elements in the array $a[1..n]$ which is input into RandQuickSort are different. We describe the function Random with the random variable R, which can take values from $\{i, \ldots, j\}$. R is uniformly distributed, i.e., $\text{p}(R = r) = \frac{1}{n}$ for $i = 1$ and $j = n$. The expected value of the running time T_n of RandQuickSort is calculated with Lemma A.9:

$$E(T_n) = \sum_{r=1}^{n} E(T_n \mid R = r) \text{p}(R = r).$$

$(T_n \mid R = r) = T_{r-1} + T_{n-r} + cn$ and the linearity of the expected value imply

$$E(T_n \mid R = r) = E(T_{r-1}) + E(T_{n-r}) + cn$$

and hence

$$E(T_n) = \sum_{r=1}^{n} E(T_n \mid R = r) p(R = r)$$

$$= \frac{1}{n} \sum_{r=1}^{n} (E(T_{r-1}) + E(T_{n-r}) + cn)$$

$$= cn + \frac{2}{n} \sum_{r=0}^{n-1} E(T_r), n \geq 2.$$

Analogously to the average running time of quicksort, we have the following.

Proposition 2.9. *Let T_n be the expected running time of RandQuickSort. Then*

$$E(T_n) = 2c(n+1)H_n + \frac{1}{3}(2b - 10c)n + \frac{1}{3}(2b - c),$$

where b and c are constants. In particular, $E(T_n) = O(n \ln(n))$ holds.

Algorithm 2.10.
RandQuickSort(item $a[i..j]$)
1   item x; index l, r
2   if $i < j$
3   then exchange $a[j]$ and $a[\text{Random}(i, j)]$
4            $x \leftarrow a[j], l \leftarrow i, r \leftarrow j - 1$
5   while true do
6   while $a[l] < x$ do $l \leftarrow l + 1$
7   while $a[r] > x$ do $r \leftarrow r - 1$
8   if $l < r$
9   then exchange $a[l]$ and $a[r]$
10                        $l \leftarrow l + 1, r \leftarrow r - 1$
11   else break
12   exchange $a[l]$ and $a[j]$
13   RandQuickSort($a[i..l - 1]$)
14   RandQuickSort($a[l + 1..j]$)

Remark. The random variable C_n, which counts the number of comparisons, has the expectation

$$E(C_n) = 2(n+1)H_n - 4n.$$

For the variance $\text{Var}(C_n)$, the following formula holds:

$$\text{Var}(C_n) = 7n^2 - 4(n+1)^2 H_n^{(2)} - 2(n+1)H_n + 13n,$$

where $H_n^{(2)} = \sum_{i=1}^{n} \frac{1}{i^2}$[3]. The full derivation of the formula uses generating functions (see [IliPen10]).

When calculating the expected value of the number of exchanges, we take the exchange in line 3 into account. We have

$$E(E_n) = \frac{1}{3}(n+1)H_n + \frac{7}{18}n - \frac{41}{18}, n \geq 2.$$

---

[3] In contrast to the harmonic series, the series $\sum_{i=1}^{\infty} \frac{1}{i^2}$ converges. The limit is $\frac{\pi^2}{6}$.

2.2 Heapsort

Heapsort belongs to the sorting methods "sorting by selection". When sorting by selection, we look for a smallest element x in the sequence F to be sorted. We remove x from F and recursively apply the sorting method to F without x. In selection sort, we use the naive method for determining the minimum – inspect the n elements of the sequence one by one. The running time of this method is of order $O(n)$. Heapsort uses the data structure of a *binary heap*. This essentially improves the running time for determining the minimum (from order $O(n)$ to order $O(\log_2(n))$). The algorithm heapsort was published by Williams[4] in [Williams64], after preliminary work by Floyd[5].

We first look at the data structure of a binary heap.

2.2.1 Binary Heaps

Definition 2.11. Elements of a totally ordered set are stored in an array $h[1..n]$.

1. h is said to be a *(binary) heap* if

$$h[i] \leq h[2i], 1 \leq i \leq \left\lfloor \frac{n}{2} \right\rfloor, \text{ and } h[i] \leq h[2i+1], 1 \leq i \leq \left\lfloor \frac{n-1}{2} \right\rfloor.$$

2. The heap $h[1..n]$ conforms to the structure of a binary tree (Definition 4.3) if we declare $h[1]$ as root. For $i \geq 1$ and $2i \leq n$, the element $h[2i]$ is left and for $2i+1 \leq n$, the element $h[2i+1]$ is right successor of $h[i]$. With this tree structure, the heap condition is: If n_1 and n_2 are successors of k, then $n_i \geq k, i = 1, 2$.

Remarks:

1. Alternatively, the binary tree structure is described as follows: The first element $h[1]$ is the root. Then we insert the following elements into the levels of the tree one after the other from left to right and from top to bottom. We get a balanced binary tree, i.e., the height is minimum and the leaves are on at most two levels. The resulting path length from the root to a leaf is no greater than $\lfloor \log_2(n) \rfloor - 1$ (Lemma 2.16).
2. If a is an arbitrary array, the leaves – the nodes that do not have any successors ($i > \lfloor \frac{n}{2} \rfloor$) – fulfill the heap condition.
3. A heap $h[1..n]$ is sorted along each of its paths. In particular, $h[1] \leq h[j]$ holds, $1 \leq j \leq n$, i.e., $h[1]$ is the minimum.

---

[4] John William Joseph Williams (1929 – 2012) was a British-Canadian computer scientist.

[5] Robert W. Floyd (1936 – 2001) was an American computer scientist and Turing Award winner.

Example. In Figure 2.4 we give the array 6, 41, 10, 56, 95, 18, 42, 67 the structure of a binary tree.

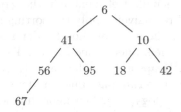

Fig. 2.4: Heap with tree structure.

The algorithm DownHeap (Algorithm 2.12) is central and essential for heapsort. DownHeap is based on the following observation: If the heap condition is only violated in the root of h, then we can establish the heap condition for the entire array by "percolating down" – a simple efficient procedure. Percolating down means: Start at the root and swap with the smaller successor until the heap condition is established.

Algorithm 2.12.
DownHeap(item $a[l..r]$)
1   index i, j; item x
2    $i \leftarrow l, j \leftarrow 2 \cdot i, x \leftarrow a[i]$
3   while $j \leq r$ do
4   if $j < r$
5   then if $a[j] > a[j+1]$
6   then $j \leftarrow j+1$
7   if $x \leq a[j]$
8   then break
9        $a[i] \leftarrow a[j], i \leftarrow j, j \leftarrow 2 \cdot i$
10   $a[i] \leftarrow x$

Remarks:

1. In DownHeap we follow a path that starts at $a[l]$. We index the current node with j and the parent node with i.
2. In lines 5 and 6, the smaller successor becomes the current node.
3. If x is less than or equal to the current node, x can be placed at position i. The insertion position i on the descent path is determined. In line 10 we assign x to a at the position i where a gap exists. The heap condition is restored at a.
4. If x is larger than the current node, in line 9 we copy the current node $a[j]$ one position up in the traversed path. This creates a gap in the path that has been traversed. Then we make the current node the predecessor and the successor the current node.

Example. In the left-hand tree in Figure 2.5, the heap condition is only violated by the root. By percolating down the element 60, we establish the heap condition. We move the 60 downwards on the path 60-37-45-58 until the heap condition is established. Here, this is only the case after 60 has been localized in a leaf.

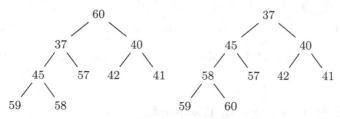

Fig. 2.5: Percolating down of the root.

Heapsort works in two phases to sort an array. In the first phase, we rearrange the elements of a so that a fulfills the heap condition (BuildHeap). In the second phase, the actual sorting process takes place. After the first phase, the minimum is at the first position of a (at the root of the tree). DownHeap is used by the algorithm BuildHeap to build the heap.

Algorithm 2.13.
  BuildHeap(item $a[1..n]$)
  1   index l
  2   for $l \leftarrow n$ div 2 downto 1 do
  3   DownHeap($a[l..n]$)

Example. Figure 2.6 shows heap construction for 50, 40, 7, 8, 9, 18, 27, 10, 30, 17, 33.

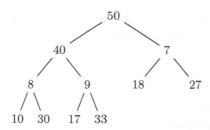

Fig. 2.6: The heap condition is violated at nodes 40 and 50.

The heap is built with DownHeap from bottom to top and from right to left. In this order, node 40 is the first node in which the heap condition is violated. We establish the heap condition in the subtree with root 40 by percolating down. The result is the first tree of the following figure. Now the heap condition is only violated at the root. The second tree in Figure 2.7 shows the result after the heap condition is established in the entire tree.

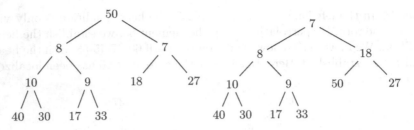

Fig. 2.7: Establishing the heap condition.

2.2.2 The Sorting Phase of Heapsort

Once a heap has been created, the actual sorting process takes place in the second phase. After the first phase, the minimum is at the first position of a. We now swap the first element with the last element and continue with the first $n-1$ elements of a. The heap condition is now only violated at the root. We restore the heap condition by percolating down the root (DownHeap). We continue the procedure recursively and get the elements sorted in reverse order.

Example. Sorting phase of heapsort:

$$
\begin{array}{llllllll}
6 & 41 & 10 & 56 & 95 & 18 & 42 & 67 \\
\hline
67 & 41 & 10 & 56 & 95 & 18 & 42 & |6 \\
10 & 41 & 18 & 56 & 95 & 67 & 42 & |6 \\
\hline
42 & 41 & 18 & 56 & 95 & 67 & |10 & 6 \\
18 & 41 & 42 & 56 & 95 & 67 & |10 & 6
\end{array}
$$
$$\vdots$$

The example starts with a heap and shows the first two sorting steps with the root subsequently percolating down.

Algorithm 2.14.
  HeapSort(item $a[1..n]$)
  1   index l, r
  2   for $l \leftarrow n$ div 2 downto 1 do
  3   DownHeap($a[l..n]$)
  4   for $r \leftarrow n$ downto 2 do
  5   exchange $a[1]$ and $a[r]$
  6   DownHeap($a[1..r-1]$)

The following proposition immediately follows by induction.

Proposition 2.15. *Heapsort sorts the array $a[1..n]$ into descending order.*

Remark. We sort a into ascending order if we write ">" instead of "<" in line 5 of Algorithm 2.12 and "≤" instead of "≥" in line 7.

2.2.3 Running Time Analysis

HeapSort (Algorithm 2.14) consists of two for loops. In each of the two for loops, the function DownHeap (Algorithm 2.12) is called. The analysis of HeapSort therefore requires the analysis of DownHeap. The running time of HeapSort depends essentially on the number of iterations of the while loop in DownHeap. We capture these with the counters I_1 and I_2. $I_1(n)$ indicates how often the while loop in Downheap is iterated for all calls in line 3 of HeapSort. I_2 counts the same event for all calls in line 6. $I_1(n)$ is also the number of iterations of the while loop in Downheap, accumulated over all calls by BuildHeap (Algorithm 2.13, line 3). We give bounds for $I_1(n)$ and $I_2(n)$.

To analyze the running time of BuildHeap we need the following lemma.

Lemma 2.16. *Let $a[1..r]$ be the input for DownHeap (Algorithm 2.12), $1 \leq l \leq r$, and let k be the number of iterations of the while loop in DownHeap. Then*

$$k \leq \left\lfloor \log_2 \left(\frac{r}{l} \right) \right\rfloor.$$

Proof. We get the longest path with the sequence $l, 2l, 2^2l, \ldots, 2^{\tilde{k}}l$, where $\tilde{k}$ is maximal with $2^{\tilde{k}}l \leq r$. Thus,

$$\tilde{k} = \left\lfloor \log_2 \left(\frac{r}{l} \right) \right\rfloor.$$

Since the number of iterations of the while loop in DownHeap is limited by the length of the path starting at the node $a[l]$, the bound also applies to the number of iterations. From $k \leq \tilde{k}$ the assertion follows. $\square$

Proposition 2.17.

1. *Let $I_1(n)$ be the number of iterations of the while loop in DownHeap, accumulated over all calls to Downheap in BuildHeap. Then*

$$I_1(n) \leq 3 \left\lfloor \frac{n}{2} \right\rfloor - \log_2 \left(\left\lfloor \frac{n}{2} \right\rfloor \right) - 2.$$

2. *Let $T(n)$ be the running time of BuildHeap in the worst case, then*

$$T(n) \leq c I_1(n),$$

where c is a constant. In particular, $T(n) = O(n)$.

Proof. Lemma B.15 implies

$$I_1(n) \leq \sum_{l=1}^{\lfloor n/2 \rfloor} \left\lfloor \log_2 \left(\frac{n}{l} \right) \right\rfloor \leq \sum_{l=1}^{\lfloor n/2 \rfloor} \log_2 \left(\frac{n}{l} \right)$$

$$= \left\lfloor \frac{n}{2} \right\rfloor \log_2(n) - \sum_{l=1}^{\lfloor n/2 \rfloor} \log_2(l)$$

$$\leq \left\lfloor \frac{n}{2} \right\rfloor \log_2(n) - \sum_{l=1}^{\lfloor n/2 \rfloor} \lfloor \log_2(l) \rfloor$$

$$= \left\lfloor \frac{n}{2} \right\rfloor \log_2(n) - \left(\left(\left\lfloor \frac{n}{2} \right\rfloor + 1 \right) \log_2 \left(\left\lfloor \frac{n}{2} \right\rfloor \right) - 2 \left(2^{\lfloor \log_2(\lfloor \frac{n}{2} \rfloor) \rfloor} - 1 \right) \right)$$

$$\leq \left\lfloor \frac{n}{2} \right\rfloor \log_2 \left(\frac{n}{\lfloor \frac{n}{2} \rfloor} \right) - \log_2 \left(\left\lfloor \frac{n}{2} \right\rfloor \right) + 2 \left\lfloor \frac{n}{2} \right\rfloor - 2$$

$$\approx 3 \left\lfloor \frac{n}{2} \right\rfloor - \log_2 \left(\left\lfloor \frac{n}{2} \right\rfloor \right) - 2.$$

This shows the first statement.[6] Statement 2 follows immediately from statement 1. □

Lemma 2.18. *Let $n \geq 2$ and $I_2(n)$ be the number of iterations of the while loop in* DownHeap, *accumulated over all calls in line 6 of* HeapSort. *Then*

$$I_2(n) \leq n \lfloor \log_2(n - 1) \rfloor - n + 2.$$

Proof. By Lemma B.15 and $n \leq 2 \cdot 2^{\lfloor \log_2(n-1) \rfloor}$ follows

$$I_2(n) \leq \sum_{r=1}^{n-1} \lfloor \log_2(r) \rfloor = n \lfloor \log_2(n - 1) \rfloor - 2 \left(2^{\lfloor \log_2(n-1) \rfloor} - 1 \right)$$

$$\leq n \lfloor \log_2(n - 1) \rfloor - n + 2.$$

Thus, the assertion of the Lemma is shown. □

We summarize the result of the running time analysis for HeapSort in the following proposition.

Proposition 2.19.

1. *Let $T(n)$ be the running time (in the worst case) of* HeapSort. *Then*

$$T(n) = c_1(I_1(n) + I_2(n)) + c_2(n - 1)$$
$$\leq c_1 \left(3 \left\lfloor \frac{n}{2} \right\rfloor - n + n \lfloor \log_2(n - 1) \rfloor - \log_2 \left(\left\lfloor \frac{n}{2} \right\rfloor \right) + 2 \right) + c_2(n - 1),$$

where c_1 and c_2 are constants. In particular, $T(n) = O(n \log_2(n))$.

2. *Let $C(n)$ be the number of the essential comparisons in* HeapSort. *Then*

$$C(n) = 2(I_1(n) + I_2(n))$$
$$\leq 2 \left(3 \left\lfloor \frac{n}{2} \right\rfloor - n + n \lfloor \log_2(n - 1) \rfloor - \log_2 \left(\left\lfloor \frac{n}{2} \right\rfloor \right) + 2 \right).$$

---

[6] For even n, equality holds in the last line. For odd n, the term can be estimated by $3 \left\lfloor \frac{n}{2} \right\rfloor - \log_2 \left(\left\lfloor \frac{n}{2} \right\rfloor \right) - 1$.

2.2.4 Heapsort Optimizations

The path that is produced by percolating down an element x, i.e., by selecting the smaller successor as the next node, is called the *path of the smaller successor*. On this path, which leads from the root of the tree to a leaf, lies the insertion position for x. In one execution of the inner loop, the algorithm DownHeap determines the next node and checks whether the insertion position has already been reached. There are two comparisons in each step (lines 5 and 7 in Algorithm 2.12).

The idea to speed up the algorithm is first to calculate the path of the smaller successor – from the root to a leaf – (see [Carlson87]). This requires only one comparison in each execution of the inner loop.

Algorithm 2.20.
    index DownHeapO(item $a[l..r]$)
  1   index i, j; item x
  2   $i \leftarrow l, j \leftarrow 2 \cdot i, x \leftarrow a[i]$
  3   while $j \leq r$ do
  4   if $j < r$
  5   then if $a[j] > a[j+1]$
  6   then $j \leftarrow j+1$
  7       $i \leftarrow j, j \leftarrow 2 \cdot i$
  8   return i

Remarks:

1. We indicate the current node with j and the parent node with i.
2. In the while loop, we follow the path of the smaller successor until the leaf, which is indexed by i after the loop terminates.

Example. In Figure 2.8 the path of the smaller successor is given by the indices 1, 3, 6, 13, 27 and 55. The smaller number indicates the index of the respective element.

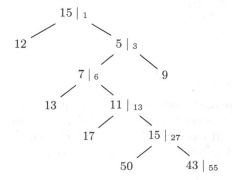

Fig. 2.8: The path of the smaller successor.

We denote the indices of the path from the root to a leaf by $v_1, \ldots, v_\ell$. Then

$$v_{k-1} = \left\lfloor \frac{v_k}{2} \right\rfloor, \; 2 \leq k \leq \ell, \; v_1 = 1.$$

We get the binary representation for v_{k-1} if we delete the last digit in the binary representation for v_k. The index k of v_k also indicates the number of binary digits of v_k. The kth node v_k in the path is given by the k highest-valued bits of v_ℓ. Therefore, we can immediately access any node on the path if the index of the last node is known.

We discuss two ways to determine the insertion position.

Sequential Search. If the insertion position lies in the last part of the path, i.e., in a lower level of the tree, we find the insertion position by sequentially searching from the end of the path after a few steps.

This modification has a positive effect in the second phase of heapsort. In the second phase, in each step we copy a large element into the root. This element then percolates down into the tree. The insertion position lies in the last part of the path. This variant of DownHeap follows an idea of Wegener[7] ([Wegener93]).

Algorithm 2.21.
    index SequentialSearch(item $a[1..n]$, index v)
    1   $x \leftarrow a[1]$
    2   while $x < a[v]$ do $v \leftarrow v$ div 2
    3   return v

SequentialSearch determines the insertion place for x from the end node of the path of the smaller successor by sequential search.

The following function Insert inserts x into the path at position v. The index v is given by its binary representation $v = w_1 \ldots w_\ell$.

Algorithm 2.22.
    Insert(item $a[1..n]$, index $v = w_1 \ldots w_\ell$)
    1   int k; item $x \leftarrow a[1]$
    2   for $k \leftarrow 2$ to ℓ do
    3       $a[w_1 \ldots w_{k-1}] \leftarrow a[w_1 \ldots w_k]$
    4   $a[v] \leftarrow x$

Remarks:

1. In the for loop we move the elements on the path of the smaller successor, which we call P, one position up. To do this, we go through P again from top to bottom and calculate the nodes of P from the index of the end node v_ℓ. The index of the jth node of P is given by the j most significant bits of v_ℓ.

---

[7] Ingo Wegener (1950 – 2008) was a German computer scientist.

2. In DownHeap, there are two comparisons in each node. In DownHeapO, there's only one comparison. Let t be the number of nodes in the path P and $\tilde{t}$ be the number of nodes up to the insertion position. Then DownHeap makes $2\tilde{t}$ comparisons and DownHeapO with SequentialSearch together $t + t - \tilde{t} = 2t - \tilde{t}$ comparisons. If the insertion position is in the last third of P, the number of comparisons in DownHeapO and SequentialSearch is smaller, because $2t - \tilde{t} < 2\tilde{t}$ if $\tilde{t} > \frac{2}{3}t$.

3. Heapsort requires on average $2n \log_2(n) - O(n)$ comparisons. With DownHeapO and SequentialSearch, there are only $n \log_2(n) + O(n)$ comparisons. However, it is complicated to analyze (see [Wegener93]).

Binary Search. We denote the indices of the path from the root to a leaf by $v_1, \ldots, v_\ell$. The sequence $a[v_2], \ldots, a[v_\ell]$ is sorted in ascending order. In this sequence we determine the insertion position by binary search. Starting from v_ℓ, we calculate $v_{\ell-\lfloor \ell/2 \rfloor}$

$$v_{\ell-\lfloor \ell/2 \rfloor} = \left\lfloor \frac{v_\ell}{2^{\lfloor \ell/2 \rfloor}} \right\rfloor = w_1 \ldots w_{\ell-\lfloor \ell/2 \rfloor},$$

where v_ℓ has the binary representation $v_\ell = w_1 \ldots w_\ell$.

The following algorithm determines the index of the insertion position on the path leading from the root to the node v using the method of binary search (Algorithm 2.36). The node v is represented by its binary representation $v = w_1 \ldots w_k$.

Algorithm 2.23.
```
    index BinarySearch(item a[1..n], index v = w₁...wₖ)
    1   index l, r; item x
    2   l ← 2, r ← k, x ← a[w₁]
    3   while l <= r do
    4       m ← (l + r) div 2
    5       if a[w₁...wₘ] < x
    6           then l ← m + 1
    7           else r ← m − 1
    8   return w₁...wₗ₋₁
```

Proposition 2.24. *Algorithm 2.23 calculates the insertion position for $x = a[1]$.*

Proof. Let $w_1 \ldots w_i$ be the insertion position for x. The invariant of the while loop is

$$l - 1 \leq i < r.$$

We show the invariant by induction on the number of iterations of while. The statement is valid for $l = 2$ and $r = k$, so for 0 iterations. For $j \geq 1$ we consider the jth iteration of while. By l_{j-1} and r_{j-1} or l_j and r_j we denote the values of l and r after the $(j-1)$th or jth iteration. By (∗) we denote the condition $l = r$.

First we consider the case that l_{j-1} and r_{j-1} fulfill the condition $(*)$. According to the induction hypothesis, we have $l_{j-1} - 1 \leq i < r_{j-1}$. From $a[w_1..w_m] < x$ follows $m \leq i$ and $l_j = m + 1$. Thus, $l_j - 1 \leq i$. Further, $l_j = r_{j-1} + 1 = r_j + 1$ holds. From $a[w_1..w_m] \geq x$ follows $i < m$. Because $l_j = l_{j-1}$, we have $l_j \leq i$. We set $r_j = m - 1$ (in line 7), so $l_j = l_{j-1} = m = r_j + 1$. The invariant also applies to the jth iteration of while (for $a[w_1..w_m] < x$ and $a[w_1..w_m] \geq x$). Further, $l_j > r_j$, and while terminates in the next step with $r_j = l_j - 1$. Hence, after termination of while $i = l - 1$.

If $l_{j-1} < r_{j-1}$ holds, $2l_{j-1} < l_{j-1} + r_{j-1} < 2r_{j-1}$, and if $r_{j-1} + l_{j-1}$ is odd, it follows that $2l_{j-1} \leq r_{j-1} + l_{j-1} - 1 < 2r_{j-1}$. In total, we get $l_{j-1} \leq m < r_{j-1}$. Either $l_j = r_j$ follows and in the next loop iteration $(*)$ occurs, or $l_j < r_j$ and $r_j - l_j < r_{j-1} - l_{j-1}$. If $l \neq r$ the distance $r - l$ decreases with each iteration, thus the case $(*)$ must occur.

From $(*)$ and the invariant of the while loop, it follows that $w_1 \ldots w_{l-1}$ is the insertion position for x. $\square$

Example. In Figure 2.9 we determine the insertion position for $a[1] = 15$ with Algorithm 2.23. The algorithm terminates with $l = 5$ and $w_1 w_2 w_3 w_4 = 1101 = 13$.

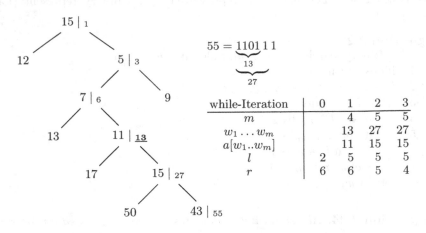

while-Iteration	0	1	2	3
m		4	5	5
$w_1 \ldots w_m$		13	27	27
$a[w_1..w_m]$		11	15	15
l	2	5	5	5
r	6	6	5	4

Fig. 2.9: Binary search for the insertion position.

We now estimate the number of significant comparisons using DownHeapO and binary search for the insertion position. Let $C_2(n)$ be the number of essential comparisons in the sorting phase of heapsort. Then

$$C_2(n) \leq \sum_{r=2}^{n-1} \lfloor \log_2(r) \rfloor + \sum_{r=2}^{n-1} (\lfloor \log_2(\lfloor \log_2(r) \rfloor) \rfloor + 1)$$

$$\leq n(\lfloor \log_2(n-1) \rfloor - 1) + 3 + (n-2)(\lfloor \log_2(\log_2(n-1)) \rfloor + 1)$$
$$= n\lfloor \log_2(n-1) \rfloor + (n-2)(\lfloor \log_2(\log_2(n-1)) \rfloor) + 1.$$

The number of elements in a path is $\leq \lfloor \log_2(r) \rfloor$. Therefore, we need only $\lfloor \log_2(\lfloor \log_2(r) \rfloor) \rfloor + 1$ essential comparisons for binary search (Algorithm 2.36). We have already estimated the first sum. The second inequality follows immediately. Since the number of comparisons in the heap build-up phase is linear, we do not estimate them more precisely. The number $C(n)$ of the essential comparisons is bounded above by

$$C(n) \leq 2\left(3\left\lfloor \frac{n}{2} \right\rfloor - \log_2\left(\left\lfloor \frac{n}{2} \right\rfloor\right) - 2\right) +$$
$$n\lfloor \log_2(n-1) \rfloor + (n-2)(\lfloor \log_2(\log_2(n-1)) \rfloor) + 1.$$

2.2.5 Comparison of Quicksort and Heapsort

We have estimated the number of essential comparisons for two heapsort variants in the worst case. For quicksort, the average number of comparisons is $2(n+1)H_n - 4n$ (Proposition 2.5). The function graphs in Figure 2.10 represent the limits for the number of essential comparisons for heapsort and the average number of comparisons for quicksort.

The curves show that heapsort with binary search is clearly superior to ordinary heapsort. The curve for quicksort displays the lowest number of comparisons. However, we emphasize again that the graph for heapsort is an estimate of the worst case, and that for quicksort is the exact solution for the average number of comparisons.

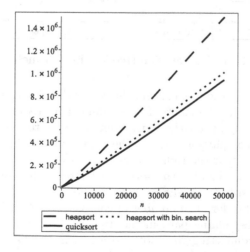

Fig. 2.10: Comparison of sorting methods.

2.3 A Lower Bound for Sorting by Comparison

Quicksort and heapsort assume an ordered set, i.e., the $\leq$-operator can be applied to the elements to be sorted. Both algorithms exchange elements based on a comparison with the $\leq$-operator. *Comparison-based sorting algorithms* only use the $\leq$-operator and no structural properties of the elements to be sorted. In Exercise 1, we cover situations that allow sorting with the running time $O(n)$. The algorithms use structural properties of the elements to be sorted.

Sorting pairwise distinct elements $a[1], \ldots, a[n]$ with a comparison-based algorithm is equivalent to determining a permutation on $\{1, \ldots, n\}$. This permutation π returns the sorted order:

$$a[\pi(1)] < a[\pi(2)] < \ldots < a[\pi(n)].$$

We will determine π using a binary decision tree. In each node a comparison using the $<$-operator is applied. A leaf indicates the sorted order of the elements. A binary decision tree for n pairwise distinct elements has $n!$ leaves.

Example. Figure 2.11 shows a binary decision tree for a, b and c. It shows the necessary comparisons to determine the order for a, b, c.

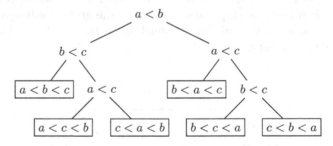

Fig. 2.11: The decision tree for three elements.

The inner nodes of the tree contain the comparisons; the leaves of the tree contain all possible arrangements. Each arrangement requires the execution of the comparisons lying on the path from the root to the respective leaf. If the result of a comparison is true, the next node of the path is the left successor, otherwise it is the right successor.

An algorithm that creates the sorted order based on comparisons must perform the comparisons on the path from the root to the leaf node that specifies the sorted order. The number of comparisons therefore matches the length of the corresponding path in the decision tree. A lower limit for the length of a path connecting the root and a leaf in the binary decision tree is a lower limit for the number of comparisons that a sorting method which requires only an ordered set must perform.

Lemma 2.25. *Let B be a binary tree with n leaves. Then the maximum length of a path from the root to a leaf is greater than or equal to $\log_2(n)$.*

Proof. Let t_B be the maximum length of a path from the root to a leaf in B. Then $n \leq 2^{t_B}$. This implies $t_B \geq \log_2(n)$.   □

Proposition 2.26. *If a comparison-based sorting algorithm sorts n elements, then it requires in the worst case at least $n \log_2(n) - O(n)$ comparisons.*

Proof. The number of comparisons is equal to the length of a path in the decision tree with $n!$ leaves. With Stirling's[8] approximation formula

$$n! \approx \sqrt{2\pi n}\left(\frac{n}{e}\right)^n > \left(\frac{n}{e}\right)^n.$$

Let $C(n)$ be the number of comparisons in the worst case. Then

$$C(n) \geq \log_2(n!) > n\log_2(n) - n\log_2(e) = n\log_2(n) - O(n).$$

This shows the assertion.   □

2.4 Searching in Arrays

In this section, we discuss the problem of finding a specific element in an array a. If a is unsorted, we have to search *sequentially*, i.e., we inspect the elements of a one by one until the desired element is found. The running time is of order $O(n)$. A sorted array allows *binary search*. The running time of this method is $O(\log_2(n))$. Another method with logarithmic running time is the Fibonacci search (see Chapter 4, Exercise 11). If the array is searched sufficiently often, then the computational effort of sorting pays off. In addition to sequential and binary searches, we also cover the search for the kth-smallest element. Here we do not specify the element explicitly. We specify the element by a property.

2.4.1 Sequential Search

The algorithm of the sequential search – SequSearch – searches for an element x among the first n elements of an array $a[0..n]$. We inspect the elements from $a[0..n-1]$ one after the other until x is found or the end of a is reached. The algorithm needs the variable $a[n]$ as sentinel element.

Algorithm 2.27.
```
    index SequSearch(item a[0..n], x)
    1   index i
    2   a[n] ← x, i ← 0
    3   while a[i] ≠ x do
    4       i ← i + 1
    5   return i
```

---

[8] James Stirling (1692–1770) was a Scottish mathematician.

Remarks:

1. At position n in the array we set the searched element x as sentinel ($n \geq 1$). The sentinel prevents us from accessing a with indices $> n$ if x is not stored in a.
2. The function SequSearch searches for x in a and finds the smallest index l with $x = a[l]$. SequSearch returns n if x is not stored.
3. Let $I(n)$ be the number of iterations of the while loop in the worst case. Then $I(n) = n$.
4. If all stored elements in a are searched for and the elements in a are pairwise distinct, the average number of iterations of the while loop is $1/2(n-1)$.

2.4.2 Binary Search

The following binary search algorithm, BinSearch, searches for an element x in a sorted array a with n elements. It follows the divide and conquer strategy (Section 1.5.2). We compare the element x to be searched for with the element $a[i]$ in the middle. If the comparison $a[i] = x$ is true, the wanted element is found. If x is less than $a[i]$, x, if present, is to the left of $a[i]$ and if x is greater than $a[i]$, it is to the right of $a[i]$. The subarray in which we continue to search is about half the size of the original array. The solution to the problem is reduced to the solution to the subproblem. Therefore, we do not need to assemble the solutions to the subproblems.

Algorithm 2.28.
    index BinSearch(item $a[0..n-1], x$)
    1   index l, r, i
    2   $l \leftarrow 0$, $r \leftarrow n-1$
    3   repeat
    4       $i \leftarrow (l+r)$ div 2
    5   if $a[i] < x$
    6   then $l \leftarrow i+1$
    7   else $r \leftarrow i-1$
    8   until $a[i] = x$ or $l > r$
    9   if $a[i] = x$
    10   then return i
    11   else return -1

Remarks:

1. $a[l..r]$ contains $r - (l-1) = r - l + 1$ elements. The index $i = (l+r)$ div 2 references the "middle element" in $a[l..r]$. BinSearch returns the index for x or -1 if x is not in a.
2. If there are equal elements in the array, BinSearch returns the index of any of the equal elements. Then we can simply determine the first or last of the same elements.

3. Each iteration of the repeat-until loop contains two comparisons with array elements. Another version of the binary search (Algorithm 2.36) optimizes the number of comparisons. There is only one comparison per iteration. In total, the number of comparisons is halved. It is limited by $\lfloor \log_2(n) \rfloor + 1$.

Example. Figure 2.12 specifies all access paths that are created when searching all elements in $a[1..11]$. A binary search tree (Definition 4.6) is used for the navigation when searching in $a[1..11]$.

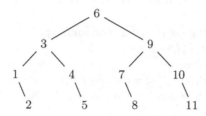

Fig. 2.12: All access paths.

Proposition 2.29. *Let $I(n)$ be the number of iterations of the repeat-until loop in the worst case. Then*

$$I(n) \le \lfloor \log_2(n) \rfloor + 1.$$

The number of comparisons is $2I(n)$ and is therefore $\le 2(\lfloor \log_2(n) \rfloor + 1)$.

Proof. In each iteration we divide $n-1$ elements into $\lceil \frac{n-1}{2} \rceil$ and $\lfloor \frac{n-1}{2} \rfloor$ elements. We have $\lfloor \frac{n-1}{2} \rfloor \le \lfloor \frac{n}{2} \rfloor$ and $\lceil \frac{n-1}{2} \rceil = \lfloor \frac{n}{2} \rfloor$. Since I is increasing, $I\left(\lfloor \frac{n-1}{2} \rfloor\right) \le I\left(\lfloor \frac{n}{2} \rfloor\right)$.
In the worst case, the repeat-until loop terminates with $l > r$. $I(n)$ performs the recursion

$$I(n) \le I\left(\left\lfloor \frac{n}{2} \right\rfloor\right) + 1, I(1) = 1.$$

This implies the assertion with Proposition 1.28. □

2.4.3 Searching for the kth-Smallest Element

Let $a_1, a_2, \ldots, a_n$ be a finite sequence. An element a of this sequence is called the *kth-smallest element* or *element of rank k* if a could be at position k in a sorted order of the sequence. If there are several identical elements a in the sequence, the rank of a is not uniquely determined.

The problem of finding the kth-smallest element in a sequence can of course be solved by first sorting the elements and then accessing the kth element. The computational effort to sort the sequence is of order $O(n \ln(n))$, e.g., if we use the QuickSort algorithm. We introduce a randomized algorithm that finds the kth element without sorting. The expected value of its running time is of order $O(n)$.

We call this algorithm QuickSelect. It is created by modifying QuickSort. After the call QuickSelect($a[1..n], k$) the algorithm returns the element of rank k. The precondition for QuickSelect is that we can apply the $<$-operator to the elements of a and that $1 \leq k \leq n$ holds.

Algorithm 2.30.

```
QuickSelect(item a[i..j], int k)
 1    item x, index l, r, boolean loop ← true
 2    if i < j
 3      then exchange a[j] and a[Random(i, j)]
 4           x ← a[j], l ← i, r ← j − 1
 5           while loop do
 6               while a[l] < x do l ← l + 1
 7               while a[r] > x do r ← r − 1
 8               if l < r
 9                 then exchange a[l] and a[r]
10                      l ← l + 1, r ← r − 1
11                 else  loop ← false
12               exchange a[l] and a[j]
13               if k < l
14                 then return QuickSelect(a[i..l − 1], k)
15                 else  if k > l
16                         then return QuickSelect(a[l + 1..j], k − l)
17               return a[l]
18    return a[i]
```

The running time in the worst case is – as with quicksort – of order $O(n^2)$. In QuickSelect we select the pivot element randomly. The choice of the pivot element is determined by the random variable R with value range $\{1, \ldots, n\}$. R is uniformly distributed, i.e., $p(R = r) = \frac{1}{n}$.

Proposition 2.31. *The algorithm* QuickSelect *returns the kth element of a. The expected value of the running time is linear.*

Proof. The statement follows by induction on n. This is certainly true when $n = 1$, because QuickSelect returns $a[1]$. Let $n \geq 2$. After termination of the outer while loop (line 5), we have $a[1], \ldots, a[l-1] \leq x$ and $a[l+1], \ldots, a[n] \geq x$. If $k < l$, then the kth element is to the left of position l, and if $k > l$, then the kth element is to the right of position l. By the induction hypothesis, the call QuickSelect($a[1..l − 1], k$) returns the kth element and the call QuickSelect($a[l + 1..n], k − l$) the $(k − l)$th element. In both cases, the kth element of a is returned. If $l = k$, $a[l]$ is the kth element.

The expected value of the running time $T(n)$ of QuickSelect is calculated according to Lemma A.9.

$$E(T(n)) = \sum_{r=1}^{n} E(T(n) \mid R = r) p(R = r) + cn$$

$$= \sum_{r \in I} E(T(n) \mid R = r) \frac{1}{n} + \sum_{r \notin I} E(T(n) \mid R = r) \frac{1}{n} + cn$$

$$\leq \sum_{r \in I} E\left(T\left(\left\lfloor \frac{3n}{4} \right\rfloor\right)\right) \frac{1}{n} + \sum_{r \notin I} E(T(n)) \frac{1}{n} + cn$$

$$= \frac{1}{2} E\left(T\left(\left\lfloor \frac{3n}{4} \right\rfloor\right)\right) + \frac{1}{2} E(T(n)) + cn.$$

where $I = [n/4, 3n/4]$ and c is a constant. Thus,

$$E(T(n)) \leq E\left(T\left(\frac{3n}{4}\right)\right) + 2cn.$$

Set $b = \frac{4}{3}$, $n = b^k$ and $x_k = E(T(b^k))$. Then $x_1 = 2c$ and $x_k = x_{k-1} + 2cb^k = 2c + 2c \sum_{i=2}^{k} b^i = 8cb^k - \frac{26}{3}c$ (Proposition 1.15).
For $k = \log_b(n)$ and by Lemma B.23 follows $E(T(n)) \leq 8cn - \frac{26}{3}c = O(n)$.

$\square$

Exercises.

1. a. An array contains only records with a component that contains only 1 or 2. Specify an algorithm that sorts the array by this component *in situ* with running time $O(n)$. Is there an algorithm that sorts the array *in situ* with running time $O(n)$ if elements 1, 2 and 3 occur?
    b. An array contains records with the keys $1, 2, \ldots, n$. Specify an algorithm that will sort the array *in situ* with running time $O(n)$.

2. In this exercise the following statement about the mean value of inversions can be used. Let $a[1..n]$ be an array. $(a[i], a[j])$ is an *inversion* if $i < j$ and $a[j] < a[i]$ holds. In both algorithms, the number of inversions is equal to the number of exchanges.
   For example, (3,1,4,2) has the inversions (3,1), (3,2) and (4,2).
   Thus, three exchange operations are necessary.
   Averaged over all arrangements, there are $\frac{1}{2}\binom{n}{2} = \frac{n(n-1)}{4}$ inversions, because $(a[i], a[j])$ is either an inversion in a or an inversion in the reverse array.
   Show that

Algorithm 2.32.

BubbleSort(item $a[1..n]$)

```
1   index i, j; item x
2   for i ← 1 to n − 1 do
3       for j ← n downto i + 1 do
4           if a[j] < a[j − 1]
5               then exchange a[j] and a[j − 1]
```

is correct and analyze the running time and then also the running time of sorting by insertion (Algorithm 1.57).

3. A sorting algorithm is referred to as *stable* if the order of identical elements is not changed. Which of the algorithms insertion sort, selection sort, bubble sort, quicksort and heapsort are stable?

4. Let $C(n)$ be the average number of comparisons in Algorithm 2.1. Show that
$$C(n) = 2(n + 1)H_n - \frac{8n + 2}{3}.$$

5. In Algorithm 2.1 in line 11, avoid the unnecessary call of exchange for $l = j$ and show that for the modified algorithm the average number of exchanges is
$$E(n) = \frac{1}{3}(n + 1)H_n - \frac{5n + 8}{18}.$$

6. Let $T(n)$ be the average running time of QuickSort. Then
$$T(n) = 2c(n + 1)H_n + \frac{1}{3}(2b - 10c)n + \frac{1}{3}(2b - c),$$

where b and c are constants. The average is calculated over all arrangements of the array to be sorted. In particular, $T(n) = O(n \ln(n))$ holds.

7. Modify Algorithm 2.1 so that it can do with $n - 1$ comparisons in the decomposition process. Analyze the number of comparisons in the best case.

8. Specify and analyze an implementation of the iterative version of quicksort.

9. Let $a[1..n]$ be an array of numbers. Specify an algorithm that identifies in time $O(n)$ the first k elements in $a[1..n]$ for small k $\left(k \le {}^n/\log_2(n)\right)$ without additional memory.

10. The algorithm below is a quicksort variant that is attributed to N. Lomuto (see [CorLeiRivSte09]).

Algorithm 2.33.

QuickSortVariant(item $a[i..j]$)

```
1    item x, index l
2    if i < j
3      then x ← a[j], l ← i
4           for k ← i to j − 1 do
5                if a[k] ≤ x
6                    then exchange a[k] and a[l]
7                         l ← l + 1
8           exchange a[l] and a[j]
9           QuickSort(a[i..l − 1])
10          QuickSort(a[l + 1..j])
```

a. Compare QuickSortVariant with Algorithm 2.1. Discuss their pros and cons.

b. Specify the invariant of the for loop and show that the algorithm is correct.

11. Show that the following variant of quicksort is correct and determine its running time.

Algorithm 2.34.

QuickSort(item $a[i..j]$)

```
1    index l, r, p, item x
2    if p ← Pivot(a[i..j]) ≠ 0
3      then x ← a[p], l ← i, r ← j
4           repeat
5                exchange a[l] and a[r]
6                while a[l] < x do l ← l + 1
7                while a[r] ≥ x do r ← r − 1
8           until l = r + 1
9           QuickSort(a[i..l − 1])
10          QuickSort(a[l..j])
```

index Pivot(item $a[i..j]$)

```
1    index l, item x
2    x ← a[i]
3    for l ← i + 1 to j do
4        if a[l] > x
5            then return l
6            else if a[l] < x
7                     then return i
8    return 0
```

12. Modify the QuickSort algorithm to ensure a logarithmically limited recursion depth. Hint: Eliminate the tail recursion in Algorithm 2.34 from the previous exercise.

13. Develop a formula for the maximum number of assignments when Heap-Sort is executed, and when running HeapSort with binary search.

14. Give an example that shows that the upper bound $\sum_{l=1}^{\lfloor \frac{n}{2} \rfloor} \lfloor \log_2 \left(\frac{n}{l} \right) \rfloor$ in estimating the number of iterations of the while loop in DownHeap for all calls in BuildHeap is attained (see proof of Proposition 2.17).

15. **Mergesort.** Mergesort splits the array $a[i..j]$ into two almost equal parts and sorts the two parts recursively. The two parts are then joined to form a sorted sequence.

    Algorithm 2.35.
    MergeSort(item $a[i..j]$; index i, j)
    ```
    1   index l
    2   if i < j
    3     then l ← (i + j) div 2
    4          MergeSort(a[i..l])
    5          MergeSort(a[l + 1..j])
    6          Merge(a[i..j], l + 1)
    ```

    Merge merges the sorted partial arrays $a[i..l]$ and $a[l + 1..j]$.
    a. Specify an implementation of *Merge*. Pay attention to the memory consumption.
    b. Analyze the running time.

16. Let $a[1..n]$ be an array of numbers. Specify an algorithm with running time $O(n)$ that returns the k smallest elements in $a[1..n]$ without using additional memory.

17. Compare the following version of the binary search with Algorithm 2.28 and show that the number of significant comparisons is limited by $\lfloor \log_2(n) \rfloor + 1$.

    Algorithm 2.36.
    index BinSearch(item $a[0..n - 1], x$)
    ```
    1   index l, r, i, l ← 0, r ← n − 1
    2   while l < r do
    3       i ← (l + r − 1) div 2
    4       if a[i] < x
    5           then l ← i + 1
    6           else r ← i
    7   return l
    ```

3. Hashing

The number of accesses to search for a stored object is of order $O(\log_2(n))$ when using sorted arrays or binary search trees. With hashing, we ideally find a stored object with one single access. We achieve this by calculating the address of the object.

In a hash application, we store objects in a hash table. Here we call an object a data record. A data record contains a *key*, which is assigned uniquely to the data record, i.e., the map of the set of data records into the set of keys is injective.[1] When storing these records in a hash table, only the key is relevant for the organization. We therefore identify the data record with its key and speak only of keys that we store, search or delete.

We assume that the set of keys is a set of numbers. This is not a restriction, because we can code the key set over a number system, for example, the binary numbers.

The efficiency mentioned above can only be achieved by not completely filling the hash table. A careful analysis shows which running time we achieve depending on the fill factor of the hash table. Conversely, we can use the results of this analysis to size the hash table so that we can achieve a desired running time – for example, a key should be found with a maximum of two accesses.

3.1 Basic Terms

Definition 3.1. Let X be the set of possible keys. A *hash procedure* consists of a *hash table* H with m cells and a *hash function* $h : X \longrightarrow \{1, \ldots, m\}$. For $k \in X$, $h(k)$ is the table index that we use to store k.

If two keys $k_1, k_2 \in X$, $k_1 \neq k_2$, are stored and the result is the same table index, i.e., $h(k_1) = h(k_2)$, we speak of a *collision*.

Since hash functions are not injective – hash functions allow collisions – in addition to the hash table and the hash function, a *procedure for handling collisions* is necessary for a hash procedure, as shown in Figure 3.1.

---

[1] A map $f : X \longrightarrow Y$ is said to be injective if whenever $x, y \in X$ and $x \neq y$, then $f(x) \neq f(y)$.

© Springer Nature Switzerland AG 2020
H. Knebl, *Algorithms and Data Structures*, https://doi.org/10.1007/978-3-030-59758-0_3

Remark. The set of actual keys K is often not known in advance. One only knows that K is a subset of a very large set X, the set of possible keys. A function that injectively maps X is not practical, or is even impossible, if X requires a hash table whose size exceeds the available memory. Therefore, we accept collisions. We introduce procedures for handling collisions in Section 3.3. The size of the hash table is approximately the size of K and typically much less than $|X|$.

In [Knuth98a], extensive material is provided on hash procedures, and in [MotRag95], on probabilistic hash procedures that covers the aspects discussed here.

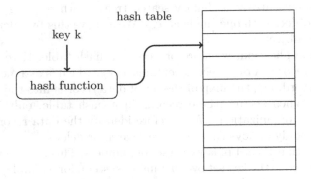

Fig. 3.1: Hash procedures.

3.2 Hash Functions

In a hash procedure, the hash function maps each key to a table location. This assumes that the hash function can be calculated by an efficient algorithm. All examples of hash functions that we discuss can be calculated with a few simple arithmetic operations.

A second requirement for hash functions is that they should minimize collisions. With *universal families of hash functions*, quantitative statements are possible. The underlying assumptions are realizable in applications.

The following example shows that collisions are possible even with a few keys and a large table.

Example. Let X be a set of people. The function

$$h : X \longrightarrow \{1, \ldots, 365\}$$

assigns the day on which a person in X has his or her birthday (without taking leap years into account). We assume that h is a random function, i.e., the birthdays appear random to us. If there are more than 23 people, the probability of a collision is $\geq 1/2$. It is astonishing that we have to expect a collision with so few people if we choose the birthday at random.

Under this assumption – random choice (with replacement) of the birthday from the set of days of a year $\{1, \ldots, 365\}$ – we can calculate the following: If we choose n elements from an m–element set, the probability p that no collision will occur

$$p = p(m, n) = \frac{1}{m^n} \prod_{i=0}^{n-1} (m - i) = \prod_{i=1}^{n-1} \left(1 - \frac{i}{m}\right).$$

For all real numbers x, we have $1 - x \leq e^{-x}$ (Corollary B.19). Thus,

$$p \leq \prod_{i=1}^{n-1} e^{-i/m} = e^{-(1/m)\sum_{i=1}^{n-1} i} = e^{-n(n-1)/2m}.$$

The collision probability is $1-p$ and $1-p \geq \frac{1}{2}$ if $n \geq \frac{1}{2}\left(\sqrt{1 + 8\ln 2 \cdot m} + 1\right)$ $\approx 1.18 \sqrt{m}$. For $m = 365$ this results in $1.18 \sqrt{365} \approx 22.5$.

3.2.1 Division and Multiplication

The arithmetic operations multiplication and division with remainder (Proposition B.1) provide suitable hash functions. Most processors perform the multiplication of two numbers much faster than their division.

Definition 3.2 *(division with remainder).* Let $m \in \mathbb{N}$.

$$h : K \longrightarrow \{0, \ldots, m - 1\}, \ k \longmapsto k \bmod m.$$

Example. Let $K = \{2, 4, \ldots, 200\}$. For $m = 100$ we have $h(k) = h(k + 100)$. There are 50 collisions. If we choose $m = 101$, then 0 collisions take place. The example suggests that prime numbers are better suited as divisors.

Definition 3.3 *(multiplication).* Let $c \in \mathbb{R}, 0 < c < 1$.

$$h : K \longrightarrow \{0, \ldots, m - 1\}, \ k \longmapsto \lfloor m\{kc\} \rfloor,$$

where for $x \in \mathbb{R}$ the expression $\{x\}$ denotes the fractional part of x, i.e., $\{x\} := x - \lfloor x \rfloor$.

Remark. Let $g = \frac{1}{2}(1 + \sqrt{5})$ be the ratio of the golden mean (Definition 1.22). The best results are obtained with a choice of $c = \frac{1}{g}$ (see [Knuth98a, Chapter 6.4]).

Although there are real numbers in the definition of h, which are usually approximated on a computer by floating-point numbers, this function can easily be implemented with integer arithmetic if $m = 2^p$ with $p \leq w$, where

w denotes the word size of the computer. Only a multiplication of two integers and a shift operation is necessary.

$$h(k) = \lfloor 2^p \{k \cdot c \cdot 2^w \cdot 2^{-w}\} \rfloor = \lfloor 2^p \{k(\lfloor c \cdot 2^w \rfloor + \{c \cdot 2^w\})2^{-w}\} \rfloor$$
$$= \lfloor 2^p \{k \lfloor c \cdot 2^w \rfloor 2^{-w} + k\{c \cdot 2^w\}2^{-w}\} \rfloor.$$

Write

$$k \lfloor c \cdot 2^w \rfloor = q2^w + r$$

and set $k\{c \cdot 2^w\}2^{-w} = 0$. Then

$$h(k) = \lfloor 2^p \{q + r \cdot 2^{-w}\} \rfloor = \lfloor 2^p \{r \cdot 2^{-w}\} \rfloor.$$

If k and c are stored in registers of the processor, $h(k)$ results from the p most significant bits of r, the least significant part of kc. We get these p bits of r by a right shift operation by $w - p$ bits.

Example. Let $w = 8$ be the word size of our computer, $m = 2^p = 2^6 = 64$ the size of our hash table, $c = 0.618 = 0.10011110$ the used multiplicative constant and $k = 4 = 100$ the key that should be stored.
Then $h(k)$ is calculated by

$$10011110 \cdot 100 = 10|01111000.$$

So $h(k) = 011110 = 30$.

3.2.2 Universal Families

Hash functions are designed to minimize collisions. Random functions have this property. However, they cannot be implemented. Universal families of hash functions introduced in [CarWeg79] minimize collisions and are easy to implement. We first look at random functions.

Let X be the set of possible keys, $n := |X|$ and $m \in \mathbb{N}$. We define a random function

$$h : X \longrightarrow \{0, \dots, m - 1\}$$

by the following construction. For each argument x, we randomly choose a value $y \in \{0, \dots, m - 1\}$. We store the pairs (x, y) in a table. The random function h is described by this table – an entry (x, y) defines the assignment $x \longmapsto y$. If the function value $y = h(x)$ is to be calculated for $x \in X$, check the table to see whether x is listed as an argument.

(1) If yes, use the table entry (x, y) and set $h(x) = y$,
(2) else choose $y \in \{0, \dots, m - 1\}$ randomly, put $h(x) = y$ and enter (x, y) into the table.

In the application of a hash function h, the *collision probability*

$$p(h(x_1) = h(x_2)), x_1, x_2 \in X, x_1 \neq x_2,$$

should be small. For a random function h this is true: $p(h(x_1) = h(x_2)) = \frac{1}{m}$.

Example. A random function distributes points evenly in the plane, as shown in Figure 3.2.

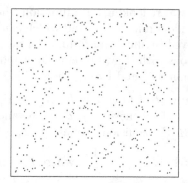

Fig. 3.2: Coordinates generated by a random function.

The above procedure for constructing a random function generates a specific function with the probability $\frac{1}{m^n}$. Thus, we get the uniform distribution on the set $\mathcal{F}(X, Y)$ of all maps from X to Y.

Another method to get a random function is to randomly choose a function from $\mathcal{F}(X, Y)$. Both methods yield the uniform distribution on $\mathcal{F}(X, Y)$. We define random functions as follows.

Definition 3.4. A *random function* is a function randomly chosen from $\mathcal{F}(X, Y)$.

Remark. The collision probability now refers to the random choice of h.

$$\mathrm{p}(h(x_1) = h(x_2)) = \frac{|\{f \in \mathcal{F}(X, Y) \mid f(x_1) = f(x_2)\}|}{|\mathcal{F}(X, Y)|}$$

$$= \frac{m^{n-1}}{m^n} = \frac{1}{m}.$$

We can generalize this definition of the collision probability to any family of functions.

Definition 3.5. Let $\mathcal{H}$ be a family of functions $h : X \longrightarrow Y$ and $x_1, x_2 \in X, x_1 \neq x_2$. For randomly selected $h \in \mathcal{H}$, the collision probability is

$$\mathrm{p}(h(x_1) = h(x_2)) := \frac{|\{h \in \mathcal{H} \mid h(x_1) = h(x_2)\}|}{|\mathcal{H}|}.$$

Example. Let $X = \{0, 1\}^l$ and $Y = \{0, 1\}^r$. We can create a random function using a table with 2^l lines each with r bits. The collision probability is $\frac{1}{2^r}$. For example, if $l = 64$ and $r = 16$, the collision probability is only $\frac{1}{2^{16}}$. To save a single random function, however, you need $16 \cdot 2^{64}$ bits $= 2^{65}$ bytes.

The example shows that random functions are huge objects. Therefore, they are not implementable.

For a hash function, we are looking for a function whose collision probability is small – as with random functions – and which can also be implemented efficiently. This is achieved by universal families of hash functions. They behave like random functions with regard to collisions and can be implemented efficiently (see Proposition 3.20 and Proposition 3.7).

Definition 3.6. A family $\mathcal{H}$ of functions $h : X \longrightarrow Y$ is called *a universal family of hash functions* if whenever $x_1, x_2 \in X$ and $x_1 \neq x_2$, then for randomly selected $h \in \mathcal{H}$, the collision probability is

$$p(h(x_1) = h(x_2)) \leq \frac{1}{m}, \text{ where } m = |Y|.$$

A hash function $h : X \longrightarrow Y$ should distribute the actual keys $K \subset X$ equally, i.e., it should hold that

$$n_{h,y} := |h^{-1}(y) \cap K| = \frac{|K|}{m} \text{ for all } y \in Y.$$

The effort required to handle a collision with a value y depends on the number of keys mapped to that value. It is proportional to $n_{h,y}$ (Section 3.3). Ideally, there will be no collisions. This is equivalent to $n_{h,y} \leq 1$ for all $y \in Y$. If we randomly select the keys or use a random function h, we expect that $n_{h,y} = \frac{|K|}{m}$ (Exercise 10 and Proposition 3.16). However, random functions cannot be implemented, and we cannot influence the distribution of keys. The application in which we use the hash procedure determines the distribution on the keys. A solution to this problem is to use a universal family of hash functions.

Universal families of hash functions and their variants also play an important role in information theory and cryptography (see [DelfsKnebl15, Chapters 10.1 and 10.3]). There are universal families of hash functions that use efficient binary arithmetic. Since we do not introduce the finite extension of $\mathbb{F}_2$, we now give two examples of universal families based on the less efficient modular arithmetic. For a natural number m,

$$\mathbb{Z}_m = \{[0], \ldots, [m-1]\}$$

denotes the set of residue classes modulo m. We identify $\mathbb{Z}_m$ with $\{0, \ldots, m-1\}$, the set of remainders modulo m (see Definition B.8). For a prime $m = p$, $\mathbb{Z}_p$ is a field and $\mathbb{Z}_p^r$, $r \in \mathbb{N}$, a vector space over the field $\mathbb{Z}_p$ (see Corollary B.11).

Proposition 3.7. *Let p be a prime, let $a, b \in \mathbb{Z}_p$, $m \in \mathbb{N}$, $2 \leq m \leq p$ and*

$$h_{a,b} : \{0, \ldots, p-1\} \longrightarrow \{0, \ldots, m-1\}, \ x \longmapsto ((ax+b) \bmod p) \bmod m.$$

The family $\mathcal{H} = \{h_{a,b} \mid a, b \in \mathbb{Z}_p, a \neq 0\}$ is universal.

Proof. First, we show that $|\mathcal{H}| = |\{(a, b) \mid a, b \in \mathbb{Z}_p, a \neq 0\}| = p(p-1)$. We distinguish between:

1. Let $a, a', b, b' \in \mathbb{Z}_p$, $a \neq a'$. We show that $h_{a,b} \neq h_{a',b'}$ holds.
   If $a \neq 0$, then the map

$$f_{a,b} : \mathbb{Z}_p \longrightarrow \mathbb{Z}_p, \ x \longmapsto (ax + b) \bmod p$$

   is bijective.
   Consequently, whenever $a \neq a'$, then $f_{a,b} - f_{a',b'} = f_{a-a',b-b'}$ is a bijective map. For $x \in \mathbb{Z}_p$ with $(f_{a,b} - f_{a',b'})(x) = [1]$, we get $h_{a,b}(x) \neq h_{a',b'}(x)$.
2. Now let $a = a'$ and $b > b'$ (without loss of generality). If m does not divide $b - b'$, then $h_{a,b}(0) \neq h_{a,b'}(0)$. If m divides $b - b'$, then we have with $y = p - b$

$$h_{a,b}(a^{-1}y) = ((p - b + b) \bmod p) \bmod m = 0 \text{ and}$$
$$\begin{aligned} h_{a',b'}(a^{-1}y) &= ((p - b + b') \bmod p) \bmod m \\ &= ((p - (b - b')) \bmod p) \bmod m \\ &= (p - (b - b')) \bmod m \\ &= p \bmod m \neq 0. \end{aligned}$$

We have shown that whenever $(a, b) \neq (a', b')$, then $h_{a,b} \neq h_{a',b'}$. Therefore,

$$|\mathcal{H}| = |\{(a, b) \in \mathbb{Z}_p^2 \mid a \neq 0\}| = p(p-1).$$

Let $x, y \in \mathbb{Z}_p$, $x \neq y$. We now show that

$$|\{(a, b) \mid a, b \in \mathbb{Z}_p, a \neq 0, h_{a,b}(x) = h_{a,b}(y)\}| \leq \frac{p(p-1)}{m}.$$

Let

$$\varphi : \mathbb{Z}_p^2 \longrightarrow \mathbb{Z}_p^2, \ (a, b) \longmapsto A \begin{pmatrix} a \\ b \end{pmatrix}, \text{ where } A = \begin{pmatrix} x & 1 \\ y & 1 \end{pmatrix}$$

Since $x \neq y$, φ is bijective (see [Fischer14, Chapter 2]).

$$\varphi(\{(a, b) \in \mathbb{Z}_p^2 \mid a \neq 0\}) = \{(r, s) \in \mathbb{Z}_p^2 \mid r \neq s\}$$

and

$$\varphi(\{(a, b) \in \mathbb{Z}_p^2 \mid a \neq 0, h_{a,b}(x) = h_{a,b}(y)\})$$
$$= \{(r, s) \in \mathbb{Z}_p^2 \mid r \neq s, r \equiv s \bmod m\}.$$

Hence,

$$|\{(a, b) \in \mathbb{Z}_p^2 \mid a \neq 0, h_{a,b}(x) = h_{a,b}(y)\}|$$
$$= |\{(r, s) \in \mathbb{Z}_p^2 \mid r \neq s, r \equiv s \bmod m\}|.$$

Since each (fixed) r has a maximum of $\lfloor \frac{p}{m} \rfloor$ s with $s \neq r$ and $s \equiv r \bmod m$ (these are the elements $r+m, \ldots, r+\lfloor \frac{p}{m} \rfloor m$) and since there are p possibilities for r,

$$\{(r,s) \in \mathbb{Z}_p^2 \mid r \neq s, r \equiv s \bmod m\} \leq \left\lfloor \frac{p}{m} \right\rfloor \cdot p.$$

From $\lfloor \frac{p}{m} \rfloor \leq \frac{p-1}{m}$, it follows that $\lfloor \frac{p}{m} \rfloor \cdot p \leq \frac{p(p-1)}{m}$. Since $|\mathcal{H}| = (p-1)p$, the assertion is shown. $\qquad\square$

Remark. Let m be the desired number of table indices and $n = |X|$. For a universal family $\mathcal{H} = \{h_{a,b} \mid a, b \in \mathbb{Z}_p, a \neq 0\}$, a prime number $p \geq n$ is necessary. So we need a prime p with about $\lceil \log_2(n) \rceil$ bits. Further, we need two random numbers, a and b, each with about $\lceil \log_2(n) \rceil$ bits. The calculation of the hash value is done by simple arithmetic operations.

Example. Let $X = \{0, 1, \ldots, 100\,000\}$, $p = 100\,003$ and $m = 10\,000$. p is a prime number. Randomly choose $a, b \in \mathbb{Z}_p$, $a \neq 0$, and use $h_{a,b}(x) = ((ax + b) \bmod 100\,003) \bmod 10\,000$ as the hash function. You need only 8 bytes to store the hash function from above.

Proposition 3.8. *Let p be a prime, $a = (a_1, \ldots, a_r) \in \mathbb{Z}_p^r$ and*

$$h_a : \mathbb{Z}_p^r \longrightarrow \mathbb{Z}_p, \quad (x_1, \ldots, x_r) \longmapsto \sum_{i=1}^r a_i x_i \bmod p.$$

The family $\mathcal{H} = \{h_a \mid a \in \mathbb{Z}_p^r\}$ is universal.

Proof. First, we will show that $|\mathcal{H}| = p^r$. From $h_a(x) = 0$ for all $x \in \mathbb{Z}_p^r$, we conclude $a_i = h_a(e_i) = 0$ for $i = 1, \ldots, r$, i.e., $a = 0$.[2] Let $h_a(x) = h_{a'}(x)$ for all $x \in \mathbb{Z}_p^r$. Then $h_a(x) - h_{a'}(x) = h_{a-a'}(x) = 0$ and $a = a'$ follows. So $|\mathcal{H}| = |\mathbb{Z}_p^r| = p^r$ is shown.
Let $x, y \in \mathbb{Z}_p^r$ be given, $x \neq y$. We show

$$\frac{1}{|\mathcal{H}|} \left| \{a \in \mathbb{Z}_p^r \mid h_a(x) = h_a(y)\} \right| \leq \frac{1}{p}.$$

From $h_a(x) = h_a(y)$ it follows that $h_a(x - y) = 0$ (and vice versa) i.e.,

$$(a_1, \ldots, a_r) \begin{pmatrix} x_1 - y_1 \\ \vdots \\ x_r - y_r \end{pmatrix} = 0.$$

Since $x - y \neq 0$, the linear map defined by $x - y$ has rank 1 and a kernel of dimension $r - 1$[3] (see [Fischer14, Chapter 2]). Thus,

$$\left| \{a \in \mathbb{Z}_p^r \mid h_a(x - y) = 0\} \right| = p^{r-1},$$

thereby proving our assertion. $\qquad\square$

---

[2] $e_i = (0, \ldots, 0, 1, 0, \ldots, 0)$, where 1 is at the ith position, is the ith unit vector.
[3] The vectors perpendicular to a vector $\neq 0$ in $\mathbb{Z}_p^r$ form a subspace of the dimension $r - 1$.

Remark. Let m be the desired number of table indices. For a universal family $\mathcal{H} = \{h_a \mid a \in \mathbb{Z}_p^r\}$, a prime number $p \geq m$ is necessary. So we need a prime p with approximately $\lceil \log_2(m) \rceil$ bits. Further, we need r random numbers $a_1, \ldots, a_r$ with approximately $\lceil \log_2(m) \rceil$ bits.

To be able to apply h_a to $x \in X$, we develop x in the base-p numeral system (Proposition B.2). r must be selected to be so large that $x \leq p^r - 1$ is valid for all $x \in X$ (see Lemma B.3). The hash value is calculated by simple arithmetical operations in $\mathbb{Z}_p$.

Procedure Using Universal Families. If we use a universal family $\mathcal{H}$ of hash functions, we turn the hash procedure into a probabilistic procedure. This is done by randomly selecting the hash function. The random choice of the hash function h makes the number $n_{h,y}$ of elements from K which h maps to y into a random variable. Its expected value is similar to that of a random function $\frac{|K|}{m}$ (see Proposition 3.16 and Proposition 3.20).

We implement the procedure by passing the hash function as a parameter.

1. When initializing the procedure, we randomly select $h \in \mathcal{H}$.
2. We then use this function h for the entire run time of the procedure, i.e., we perform all insert and search operations with this hash function h.

3.3 Collision Resolution

Designing a hash function that maps possible keys one-to-one to table indices would be impractical, or even impossible, if there are many more possible keys than actually stored keys. Hash functions are not injective. Different keys may be mapped to the same hash value. We call this situation a collision (see Definition 3.1). Fortunately, there are efficient procedures to resolve the problems caused by collisions. We discuss the methods chaining and open addressing.

3.3.1 Collision Resolution by Chaining

The methods for collision resolution by chaining organize the keys which are mapped to the same hash value in a linearly linked list. When searching for a key, we search the linked list. Depending on the organization of the chained lists, we distinguish between chaining with overflow area and separate chaining.

Chaining With Overflow. We split the hash table into a *primary area* and an *overflow area*. The hash function calculates indices of cells in the primary table. The cells in the overflow area store keys that do not fit in the primary area due to collisions.

To manage the colliding keys, we add a field to the entries in the hash table for an index, which points into the overflow area, as shown in Figure 3.3. We organize all keys with the same hash value in a linked list.

Memory management must be implemented for the cells in the overflow area. This can be done using a linked list of free cells.

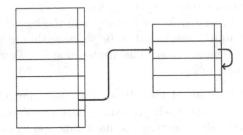

Fig. 3.3: Primary and overflow areas.

Separate Chaining. We store all keys in the nodes of a linked list. The hash table contains anchors to the linked lists, as shown in Figure 3.4. The hash function maps keys to indices of the hash table. The node elements for the linked lists are allocated and released as required.

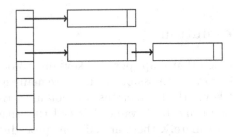

Fig. 3.4: Separate chaining.

Usually the programming language used for implementation supports this. High-level programming languages often offer dynamic memory management in the so-called *heap memory*. The operating system provides a contiguous memory area, the heap memory, for a running program. A program can allocate and release memory blocks from the heap memory at runtime. The advantage over chaining with overflow area is therefore that no memory management has to be implemented. Since memory management on heap memory manages blocks of variable length, it is less efficient than the memory management adapted to the situation above.

When initializing the hash procedure, it should be known how many data records can be expected. Then the question arises as to how to define the dimension of the hash table and possibly the overflow area. The procedure of separate chaining is only limited by the amount of heap memory available. However, if we define too small a hash table, long linked lists result. This results in poor running time behavior. The problem of dimensioning is dealt with in Section 3.4.1.

3.3.2 Open Addressing

For open addressing we use a hash table T with m cells. In contrast to chaining, the entries are without additional information. In case of a collision, we look for a replacement place within the table T. The replacement place also depends on the current load of the table. The address is therefore not fixed from the outset. Therefore, we call this procedure *open addressing*.

Definition 3.9.

1. By a *probing sequence*, we refer to a sequence of indices $i_1, i_2, i_3, \ldots$ of the hash table.
2. By a *probing sequence for $k \in X$*, we mean a probing sequence uniquely assigned to k, i.e., a map $i : X \longrightarrow \{1, \ldots, m\}^{\mathbb{N}}$ defines $i(k)$, the probing sequence for $k \in X$.

Remarks:

1. Those cells of the hash table that can contain $k \in X$ are defined by the probing sequence for k. Within this sequence, the address is open.
2. Since the table is finite, only finite probing sequences are used.

Before discussing various methods of calculating probing sequences, let us indicate how we will use these probing sequences. We describe how the algorithms for inserting, searching and deleting work in principle.

Algorithms For Inserting, Searching and Deleting.

1. Insertion: Inspect the cells with the indices $i_1, i_2, i_3 \ldots$, which are given by the probing sequence for k, and use the first "empty cell" to store k. If the index of this cell is i_l, then $i_1, i_2, \ldots, i_l$ is the probing sequence used for k.
2. Searching: Let $k \in X$, and $i_1, i_2, \ldots$ be the probing sequence for k. We inspect the cells with the indices $i_1, i_2, \ldots$ until we find k or decide that $k \notin T$.
3. Deleting: Search for k. If k is stored, mark the cell containing k as "deleted".

Remarks:

1. We can reoccupy deleted cells. However, the indices of deleted cells may occur in probing sequences of other elements. This cannot happen with cells that have never been occupied, which we call untouched cells. Therefore, we have to distinguish between deleted and untouched cells among the free cells. Deleted cells may not shorten the probing sequences for other entries.

2. We can turn deleted cells into untouched cells if the index of the cell does not occur in any of the used probing sequences for the table entries.

We treat different types of probing sequences. All probing sequences should meet the following requirements:

1. An efficient algorithm is available for the calculation of each probing sequence, just as with hash functions.
2. Each probing sequence should contain all free cells of the table.

Definition 3.10. Let $h : X \longrightarrow \{0, \ldots, m-1\}$ be a hash function. *Linear probing* uses the probing sequence

$$i(k)_j = (h(k) + j) \bmod m, j = 0, \ldots, m-1.$$

The probing sequence consists of the indices $h(k), (h(k) + 1) \bmod m,$ $\ldots, (h(k) + m - 1) \bmod m$, where m equals the length of the hash table. The probing sequence meets the requirements from above. When deleting, we set a cell to untouched if the following cell is free. However, the problem of cluster formation occurs, which we explain with an example.

Example. Figure 3.5 shows cluster formation during linear probing. The occupied cells have a gray background.

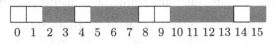

$$0 \;\; 1 \;\; 2 \;\; 3 \;\; 4 \;\; 5 \;\; 6 \;\; 7 \;\; 8 \;\; 9 \;\; 10 \;\; 11 \;\; 12 \;\; 13 \;\; 14 \;\; 15$$

Fig. 3.5: Clustering.

Let p_i be the probability that cell i is allocated. We observe:

1. $p_{14} = 5p_9$ holds if all values are equally probable.
2. If cell 4 is occupied, two clusters unite.

Another method for calculating probing sequences is quadratic probing.

Definition 3.11. Let $h : X \longrightarrow \{0, \ldots, m-1\}$ be a hash function. *Quadratic probing* uses the probing sequence

$$i(k)_j = (h(k) \pm j^2) \bmod m, j = 0, \ldots, m-1,$$

i.e., the sequence $h(k), (h(k) + 1) \bmod m, (h(k) - 1) \bmod m, \ldots$.

In quadratic probing, we only consider indices whose distance from the hash value is a square modulo m.

Proposition 3.12. *Let $m = p$ be a prime and $p \equiv 3 \bmod 4$. In quadratic probing modulo p, all indices of the hash table appear in each probing sequence.*

Proof. We know from Corollary B.14 that $\mathbb{Z}_p = \{\pm[i^2] \mid i = 0, \ldots, (p-1)/2\}$. The translation used in the calculation of a probing sequence by $c = h(k)$ defines a bijective map on $\mathbb{Z}_p$. Thus, all table indices occur in a probing sequence with quadratic probing.   □

The problem of primary clustering in linear probing no longer occurs in quadratic probing. Clustering is not completely suppressed, however, because the probing sequence deterministically depends on the hash value. The following method of double hashing is based on the model in which not only a hash value, but also the step size of the probing sequence is randomly selected.

Definition 3.13. Let $h : X \longrightarrow \{0, \ldots, m-1\}$ and $h^* : X \longrightarrow \{1, \ldots, m-1\}$ be hash functions. *Double hashing* uses the probing sequence

$$i(k)_j = (h(k) + jh^*(k)) \bmod m, j = 0, \ldots, m-1,$$

i.e., the sequence $h(k), (h(k) + h^*(k)) \bmod m, (h(k) + 2h^*(k)) \bmod m, \ldots$.

Remarks:

1. The formula is similar to that of linear probing. In double hashing, we start probing from the hash value $h(k)$ with the increment $h^*(k)$. The step size is not constant. The hash function h^* determines the step size for each key k.
2. It is recommended to select the hash functions h and h^* independently (see the remark after Proposition 3.23). For universal families of hash functions, this means that we select the hash functions h and h^* randomly and independently of each other. Consequently, whenever $x_1, x_2 \in X$ and $x_1 \neq x_2$, then

$$\mathrm{p}(h(x_1) = h(x_2) \text{ and } h^*(x_1) = h^*(x_2)) \leq \frac{1}{m^2},$$

   i.e., the probability that the hash values and the step sizes are equal is less than or equal to $1/m^2$.
3. The above probing sequence is a linear congruence sequence $x_{n+1} = (ax_n + c) \bmod m$, $a = 1$, $c = h^*(k)$ and $x_0 = h(k)$. We use linear congruence sequences to generate pseudo-random numbers (see Section 1.6.4).

Proposition 3.14. *If $h^*(k)$ and m are relatively prime, then*

$$|\{(h(k) + jh^*(k)) \bmod m \mid j = 0, \ldots, m-1\}| = m.$$

In this situation all table indices occur in a probing sequence.

Proof. Let $i, j \in \{0, \ldots, m-1\}$, $i > j$. Suppose $(h(k) + ih^*(k)) \bmod m = (h(k) + jh^*(k)) \bmod m$. We conclude that m divides $(i - j)h^*(k)$. Since m and $h^*(k)$ are relatively prime, m divides the number $i - j$. This is a contradiction because $i - j < m$. Thus, the numbers $(h(k) + jh^*(k)) \bmod m, j = 0, \ldots, m-1$, are pairwise distinct.   □

Remarks:

1. The prerequisite of the proposition is fulfilled for a prime number m or for $m = 2^k$ and an h^* with odd values. Then all table indices occur in a probing sequence.
2. Bertrand's[4] Postulate says that between n and $2n$, $n \in \mathbb{N}$, there is a prime number (see [RemUll08]). Thus, there is always a prime number of suitable size.

Remark. To choose the dimension of the hash procedures, assumptions about the number of keys to be stored are necessary. If the estimated number is significantly less than the number actually required, performance problems arise. The desired property of the hash procedures to provide the operations insert, search and delete with a constant time requirement is then no longer fulfilled. In the case of chaining with an overflow area or open addressing, the procedures fail if the number of keys exceeds the planned capacity. In practice, this problem is solved by saving the contents of the existing hash table (including the elements in the separate chains) to a new larger hash table and deleting the previous table when a certain fill level is reached. This procedure is often referred to as *rehashing*.

3.4 Analysis of Hashing

We are interested in the questions of how many comparisons on average are necessary to find a stored object, and how many comparisons are necessary to decide that an object is not stored. The two methods of collision resolution require separate considerations.

3.4.1 Chaining

In the case of chaining, we are not only interested in the number of comparisons if the search is successful or unsuccessful, but also in the number of collisions to be expected. This number must be known in order to adequately choose the dimension of the overflow area.

Let us first consider the case where the hash function is a random function. The random experiment consists of inserting n keys with a random function into an empty hash table. Let X be the set of possible keys. The hash function

$$h : X \longrightarrow \{0, \dots, m-1\}$$

is a random function, i.e., we choose the values for each argument in $\{0, \dots, m-1\}$ at random and uniformly distributed (see Section 3.2.2).

---

[4] Joseph Louis François Bertrand (1822 – 1900) was a French mathematician.

Random functions are not implementable. Universal families of hash functions are a good approximation of random functions. They behave with respect to collisions like random functions (see Section 3.2.2).

By $K = \{k_1, \ldots, k_n\} \subset X$, we denote the set of keys actually present.

Proposition 3.15. Let $h : X \longrightarrow \{0, \ldots, m-1\}$ be a random function and let

$$n_j = |\{k \in K \mid h(k) = j\}|, \; j = 0, \ldots, m - 1.$$

The random variable n_j can take the values $0, \ldots, n$. The probability p_i, which indicates that i keys are mapped to the value j, is

$$p_i := p_{ij} = p(n_j = i) = \binom{n}{i} \left(\frac{1}{m}\right)^i \left(1 - \frac{1}{m}\right)^{n-i}.$$

The random variable n_j is binomially distributed, with parameters $(n, p = \frac{1}{m})$ (Definition A.15).

Proof. Assuming that h is a random function, the insertion of n keys is the independent repetition of the experiment "insertion of one key". This is a Bernoulli experiment, and the probability that the index j will occur exactly i times is given by the binomial distribution.   □

Proposition 3.16. The expected value of the random variable n_j is

$$\mathrm{E}(n_j) = \frac{n}{m}.$$

Proof. The assertion follows from Proposition A.16.   □

Remark. For the number w_i of values with i pre-images, it holds that

$$w_i = |\{j \mid n_j = i\}| = \sum_{j=0}^{m-1} \delta_{n_j i}, i = 0, \ldots, n,$$

where $\delta_{n_j i} = 1$[5] if and only if $n_j = i$, otherwise $\delta_{n_j i} = 0$. If i keys are mapped to one value, $i - 1$ of the keys lead to collisions. For the number *col* of collisions, the following holds

$$col = \sum_{i=2}^{n} w_i(i - 1)$$

with the random variables w_i and *col*.

Proposition 3.17. Let H be a hash table with m cells in the primary area and n stored elements. The expected number of values with i pre-images is mp_i. The expected number of collisions is $n - m(1 - p_0)$.

---

[5] δ_{ij} denotes the Kronecker delta. Leopold Kronecker (1823 – 1891) was a German mathematician.

Proof.

$$E(w_i) = E\left(\sum_{j=0}^{m-1} \delta_{nji}\right) = \sum_{j=0}^{m-1} E(\delta_{nji}) = \sum_{j=0}^{m-1} p(\delta_{nji} = 1)$$

$$= \sum_{j=0}^{m-1} p(n_j = i) = \sum_{j=0}^{m-1} p_i = m p_i.$$

$$E(col) = E\left(\sum_{i=2}^{n} w_i(i-1)\right) = \sum_{i=2}^{n} (i-1)E(w_i)$$

$$= \sum_{i=2}^{n} (i-1)m p_i = m \sum_{i=2}^{n} (i-1)p_i = m\left(\sum_{i=2}^{n} ip_i - \sum_{i=2}^{n} p_i\right)$$

$$= m\left(\frac{n}{m} - p_1 - (1 - (p_0 + p_1))\right) = n - m(1 - p_0).$$

We used $\sum_{i=1}^{n} ip_i = \frac{n}{m}$. This follows from Proposition 3.16. □

Definition 3.18. Let H be a hash table with m cells in the primary area, and let n be the number of stored elements. We call $B := \frac{n}{m}$ the *load factor* of H.

We approximate the binomial distribution by the Poisson distribution (see page 315) $p_i \approx r_i = \frac{B^i}{i!}e^{-B}$ and calculate the percentage $E(w_i)/m \cdot 100 = p_i \cdot 100$ of the values occupied by i keys for $i = 0, 1, 2$ and the percentage $\frac{E(col)}{n} \cdot 100$ of the keys that cause collisions for $B = 0.1, 0.5, 1, 1.5$ and 3.

	$B = 0.1$	$B = 0.5$	$B = 1$	$B = 1.5$	$B = 3$
$p_0 \cdot 100$	90.5	60.7	36.8	22.3	5.0
$p_1 \cdot 100$	9.0	30.3	36.8	33.5	14.9
$p_2 \cdot 100$	0.5	7.6	18.4	25.1	22.4
$\frac{E(col)}{n} \cdot 100$	4.8	21.3	36.8	48.2	68.3

We can use this table to define the dimensions of the primary and overflow areas. So we expect with a load factor of 1, i.e., the number of keys is the same as the number of cells in the primary area, that 36.8 % of the cells in the primary area remain free and that 36.8 % of the keys lead to collisions. The dimension of the overflow area must be chosen accordingly. The load factor influences the performance of the procedure and vice versa. Exact information can be obtained from the following.

Proposition 3.19. *Let $h : X \longrightarrow \{0, \ldots, m-1\}$ be a random function, $K = \{k_1, \ldots, k_n\}$ the set of stored keys and $B = \frac{n}{m}$ the load factor.*

1. *The expected number of comparisons for a successful search is $1 + \frac{1}{2}B$.*
2. *The expected number of comparisons for an unsuccessful search is $B + e^{-B}$.*

Proof. 1. If we search for all keys of a chain of length i, the number of comparisons is $i(i+1)/2$. Since there are w_i chains of length i, the number of comparisons, if we search for all keys, is equal to $\sum_{i=1}^{n} \frac{i(i+1)}{2} w_i$. We get for the number of comparisons per key

$$V = \frac{1}{n} \sum_{i=1}^{n} \frac{i(i+1)}{2} w_i.$$

For the expected value $\mathrm{E}(V)$, we get

$$\mathrm{E}(V) = \frac{1}{n} \sum_{i=1}^{n} \frac{i(i+1)}{2} \mathrm{E}(w_i) = \frac{1}{n} \sum_{i=1}^{n} \frac{i(i+1)}{2} m p_i = \frac{1}{2} \frac{m}{n} \left(\frac{(n-1)n}{m^2} + 2\frac{n}{m} \right)$$

$$= \frac{1}{2} \left(\frac{n-1}{m} + 2 \right) = 1 + \frac{n-1}{2m} \approx 1 + \frac{1}{2}B.$$

Here we have used

$$\sum_{i=1}^{n} i(i+1)p_i = \sum_{i=1}^{n} i^2 p_i + \sum_{i=1}^{n} i p_i = \frac{n(n-1)}{m^2} + 2\frac{n}{m}.$$

The last "=" follows by Proposition A.16:

$$\sum_{i=1}^{n} i p_i = \frac{n}{m} \text{ and } \sum_{i=1}^{n} i^2 p_i = \frac{n(n-1)}{m^2} + \frac{n}{m}.$$

2. If the search is unsuccessful, we must search the entire linked list. The linked list has length n_j. So n_j comparisons are necessary if $n_j > 0$. For $n_j = 0$, one access is necessary. For the number V of comparisons, $V = \delta_{n_j 0} + n_j$ holds. Thus,

$$\mathrm{E}(V) = \mathrm{E}(\delta_{n_j 0}) + \mathrm{E}(n_j) = p_0 + \frac{n}{m} = e^{-B} + B.$$

The assertion of the proposition is shown. □

Instead of a random function h, we will now consider a randomly chosen $h \in \mathcal{H}$, where $\mathcal{H}$ is a universal family of hash functions. We get statements for universal families of hash functions (Corollary 3.21) analogous to Proposition 3.19. Let

$$\delta_h(x, y) = \begin{cases} 1 & \text{if } h(x) = h(y) \text{ and } x \neq y, \\ 0 & \text{otherwise.} \end{cases}$$

δ_h is the indicator function for collisions. The number of elements of $\{k \in K \setminus \{x\} \mid h(k) = h(x)\}$ is calculated as follows

$$\delta_h(x, K) = \sum_{k \in K \setminus \{x\}} \delta_h(x, k).$$

Remark. Let $n_{h(x)} = |\{k \in K \mid h(k) = h(x)\}|$ be the number of keys $k \in K$ with $h(k) = h(x)$. Then

$$
\delta_h(x, K) = \begin{cases} n_{h(x)} & \text{if } x \notin K, \\ \\ n_{h(x)} - 1 & \text{if } x \in K. \end{cases}
$$

We consider $\delta_h(x, K)$ as a random variable depending on h.

Proposition 3.20. *Let $\mathcal{H} = \{h : X \longrightarrow \{0, \dots, m-1\}\}$ be a universal family of hash functions, $K = \{k_1, \dots, k_n\}$ the set of stored keys and $x \in X$. Then the expected value (regarding the uniformly distributed random choice of $h \in \mathcal{H}$) is*

$$
\mathrm{E}(\delta_h(x, K)) \leq \begin{cases} \frac{n}{m} & \text{if } x \notin K, \\ \\ \frac{n-1}{m} & \text{if } x \in K. \end{cases}
$$

In all cases $\mathrm{E}(\delta_h(x, K)) \leq \frac{n}{m}$ is valid.

Proof.

$$
\mathrm{E}(\delta_h(x, K)) = \sum_{h \in \mathcal{H}} \frac{1}{|\mathcal{H}|} \delta_h(x, K) = \sum_{h \in \mathcal{H}} \frac{1}{|\mathcal{H}|} \sum_{k \in K \setminus \{x\}} \delta_h(x, k)
$$

$$
= \frac{1}{|\mathcal{H}|} \sum_{k \in K \setminus \{x\}} \sum_{h \in \mathcal{H}} \delta_h(x, k)
$$

$$
= \sum_{k \in K \setminus \{x\}} \frac{|\{h \in \mathcal{H} \mid h(k) = h(x)\}|}{|\mathcal{H}|}
$$

$$
\leq \frac{|K \setminus \{x\}|}{m} = \begin{cases} \frac{n}{m} & \text{if } x \notin K, \\ \\ \frac{n-1}{m} & \text{if } x \in K. \end{cases}
$$

The last inequality uses the fact that the collision probability of the family $\mathcal{H}$ is less than or equal to $1/m$. □

Remarks:

1. Let $x \in K$. For the expected value of $n_{h(x)}$, the following inequality holds:

$$
\mathrm{E}(n_{h(x)}) \leq (n-1)/m + 1
$$
$$
\approx n/m + 1.
$$

We expect a randomly selected $h \in \mathcal{H}$ to distribute the keys evenly among the table indices. This is independent of the distribution on X according to which we select the keys.

2. The effort required for an insert operation (or search operation) for an element with a hash value $h(x)$ is proportional to $n_{h(x)}$. The bounds $E(n_{h(x)}) \leq \frac{n}{m}$ for insert and $E(n_{h(x)}) \leq \frac{n-1}{m} + 1$ for a successful search do not depend on $h(x)$.
3. The probability that $\delta_h(x, K)$ takes values greater than the expected value is estimated by the inequality of Markov (Proposition A.10). For each real number $r > 0$,

$$p(\delta_h(x, K) \geq rE(\delta_h(x, K))) \leq \frac{1}{r}.$$

This means $|\{h \in \mathcal{H} \mid \delta_h(x, K) \geq rE(\delta_h(x, K))\}| \leq \frac{|\mathcal{H}|}{r}$.
Let $\tilde{H} = \{h \in \mathcal{H} \mid \delta_h(x, K) \geq rn/m\}$. Then $|\tilde{H}| \leq \frac{|\mathcal{H}|}{r}$.

Corollary 3.21. *Let $\mathcal{H} = \{h : X \longrightarrow \{0, \ldots, m-1\}\}$ be a universal family of hash functions, $K = \{k_1, \ldots, k_n\}$ the set of stored keys and $B = \frac{n}{m}$ the load factor. Then*

1. *The expected value of the number of comparisons for a successful search is $< 1 + \frac{1}{2}B$.*
2. *The expected value of the number of comparisons for an unsuccessful search is $\leq 1 + B$.*

The expected value refers to the random choice of h.

Proof. 1. Let $h \in \mathcal{H}$ be chosen, $x \in K$ and $j = h(x)$. The number of comparisons, if we search all keys with hash value j, is equal to $(n_j(n_j + 1))/2$. The expected number of comparisons per key is $V = (n_j + 1)/2$. From the linearity of the expected value and Proposition 3.20, it follows that

$$E(V) = E\left(\frac{1}{2}(n_j + 1)\right) \leq \frac{1}{2}\left(2 + \frac{n-1}{m}\right) < 1 + \frac{1}{2}B.$$

2. Let $x \notin K$, and let V be the number of comparisons in an unsuccessful search for x. Then one comparison is necessary if there is no key with hash value j in K and n_j otherwise. Therefore, $V = \delta_{n_j 0} + n_j$. With Proposition 3.20, it follows that

$$E(V) = E(\delta_{n_j 0}) + E(n_j) = p(n_j = 0) + E(n_j) \leq 1 + B.$$

This shows the assertion. □

3.4.2 Open Addressing

Model. A hash table has m cells and n cells are occupied, where $n < m$ holds. The choice of a probing sequence $i_1, \ldots, i_k$ of length k corresponds to the choice of $k - 1$ occupied places and the choice of one free place. We assume that all probing sequences of the length k are equally probable. This is the assumption of *uniform probing* or *uniform hashing*.

We denote by sl_n the length of a probing sequence to insert the $(n+1)$th key. The random variable sl_n counts how often we have to do the experiment "select a place" until we reach the first empty place. The sample is taken without replacing the drawn element.

Proposition 3.22. *The probability p_j which specifies that sl_n has length j satisfies*

$$p_j = \mathrm{p}(sl_n = j) = \frac{\binom{n}{j-1}}{\binom{m}{j-1}} \frac{m-n}{m-(j-1)}, \quad j = 1, \ldots, n+1.$$

Proof. The random variable sl_n is negatively hyper-geometrically distributed with the parameters $N = m$, $M = m - n$ and the bound $r = 1$ (see Definition A.25 and the explanation afterwards). M is the number of free cells. sl_n counts the repetitions until we probe a free cell for the first time. □

Proposition 3.23 *(uniform probing).* *In a hash table with m cells, n cells are used ($n < m$ holds). The load factor is $B = \frac{n}{m}$.*

1. *To insert the $(n+1)$th element, the mean length of a probing sequence is $\frac{1}{1-B}$.*
2. *When searching for an element, the mean length of a probing sequence is $\frac{1}{B} \ln\left(\frac{1}{1-B}\right)$.*

Proof. 1. The expected value of the negative hyper-geometric distribution is calculated with the notations of Proposition A.26 $N = m$ and $M = m - n$.

$$\mathrm{E}(sl_n) = \frac{N+1}{M+1} = \frac{m+1}{m-n+1} = \frac{\frac{m+1}{m}}{\frac{m+1}{m} - \frac{n}{m}} \approx \frac{1}{1-B}.$$

2. There are n elements in the table. $sl_0, \ldots, sl_{n-1}$ are the lengths of the probing sequences for the n elements. The mean length sl of a probing sequence when searching is $sl = \frac{1}{n} \sum_{j=0}^{n-1} sl_j$.

$$
\begin{aligned}
\mathrm{E}(sl) &= \frac{1}{n} \sum_{j=0}^{n-1} \mathrm{E}(sl_j) = \frac{1}{n} \sum_{j=0}^{n-1} \frac{m+1}{m-j+1} \\
&= \frac{m+1}{n} (H_{m+1} - H_{m-n+1}) \\
&\approx \frac{m+1}{n} (\ln(m+1) - \ln(m-n+1)) \\
&= \frac{m+1}{n} \ln\left(\frac{m+1}{m+1-n}\right) \\
&\approx \frac{1}{B} \ln\left(\frac{1}{1-B}\right).
\end{aligned}
$$

We approximated $H_n = \sum_{k=1}^{n} \frac{1}{k}$ by $\ln(n)$ (see B.5). $\qquad\qquad\qquad$ □

Remark. If in double hashing the hash functions h and h^* are independently selected from a family of universal hash functions, the mean lengths of the probing sequences are similar to uniform hashing. However, the analysis is much more complicated. In [SieSch95] it is shown that the mean length of a probing sequence when inserting an element is $\frac{1}{1-B} + O(\frac{1}{m})$.

Proposition 3.24 *(Linear probing). In a hash table with m cells, n cells are occupied. B is the load factor.*

1. *The mean length of a probing sequence is $\frac{1}{2}\left(1 + \frac{1}{1-B}\right)$ if the search is successful.*

2. *The mean length of a probing sequence is $\frac{1}{2}\left(1 + \left(\frac{1}{1-B}\right)^2\right)$ if the search is not successful.*

Proof. See [Knuth98a]. $\qquad\qquad\qquad$ □

We now compare the procedures uniform hashing (UH), double hashing with a universal family (DU), chaining with a universal family (CU) and chaining with a random function (CR).
The number of comparisons for a successful search depending on $B = \frac{n}{m}$, as shown in Figure 3.6.

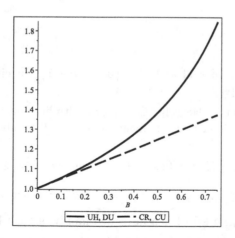

Fig. 3.6: Comparison – successful search.

The number of comparisons for an unsuccessful search depending on $B = \frac{n}{m}$, as shown in Figure 3.7.

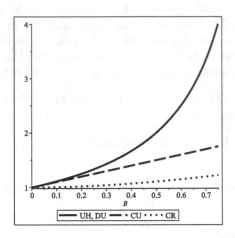

Fig. 3.7: Comparison – unsuccessful search.

Remark. At a first glance, the procedures with chaining appear to be superior. However, these methods require memory to store the links. If the memory required for the links is large compared to the memory required for the data sets, there may be an advantage to open addressing methods.

Exercises.

1. Let $M = \{0, \ldots, m-1\}$ and $N = \{0, \ldots, n-1\}$. Specify the percentage of injective maps $f : M \longrightarrow N$.

2. A hash table has 2,048 cells. Consider multiplication by $c = 0.618$ as a hash function. Determine the hash values for all numbers 2^k, $0 \leq k \leq 10$.

3. Let p be a prime, $\mathbb{Z}_p$ the field with p elements and $a \in \mathbb{Z}_p$.

$$h_a : \mathbb{Z}_p \times \mathbb{Z}_p \longrightarrow \mathbb{Z}_p, \ (x, y) \longmapsto ax + y.$$

Show: $\mathcal{H} = \{h_a \mid a \in \mathbb{Z}_p\}$ is a universal family of hash functions.

4. Let p be a prime and $\mathbb{Z}_p$ be the field with p elements. Show that the set of linear maps $A : \mathbb{Z}_p^k \longrightarrow \mathbb{Z}_p^l$ is a universal family of hash functions.

5. Let $i(s)_j := (s + j \cdot c) \bmod m$, $j = 0, 1, 2, \ldots$, be a probing sequence.
   a. Use this probing sequence to enter the following keys in an initially empty hash table: 261, 321, 453, 781, 653, 1333, 109, 235, 800. Set $c = 7$ and $m = 21$.

b. In the probing sequence under point a, not all locations in the hash table are probed. For which c are all places in the hash table probed using $i(s)_j := (s+j \cdot c) \bmod m$, $j = 0, 1, 2, \ldots$? Justify your statement.

6. 10,000 data records are managed in main memory. A hash procedure with primary and overflow areas is used. On average, a data record should be found with two accesses.

a. Determine the load factor.

b. What should be the dimensions of the primary and overflow areas?

7. A hash procedure in main memory is used to manage 1,000 records. Collision resolution is achieved by double hashing. We use the family of functions

$$h_{a,b} : \{0, \ldots, p-1\} \longrightarrow \{0, \ldots, m-1\},\ x \longmapsto ((ax+b) \bmod p) \bmod m,$$

where $p = 2{,}003$ and $2 \leq m \leq p$. We assume that double hashing behaves like uniform hashing if h and h^* are independently selected. On average, a record should be found with two accesses. How should the dimension of the hash table be defined to achieve this goal? How should m be chosen? Specify the smallest suitable m.

8. With LZ77 data compression (Section 4.6.4), finding a matching segment can be accelerated by the use of hash procedures. Work out the details of this idea.

9. a. The uniqueness problem is to decide whether n given objects are pairwise distinct. Specify an algorithm to solve this problem.

b. Given are numbers $z_1, \ldots, z_n \in \mathbb{Z}$ and $s \in \mathbb{Z}$. Specify an algorithm that decides whether there are two numbers z_i and z_j with $s = z_i + z_j$.

10. Let $h : S \longrightarrow \{0, \ldots, m-1\}$ be a hash function, and S the set of possible keys. Assume that h distributes the possible keys evenly:

$$|h^{-1}(j)| = \frac{|S|}{m},\ j = 0, \ldots, m-1.$$

We assume that n keys $k_1, \ldots, k_n$ are randomly selected and stored in a hash table H with m cells. Let $n_j = |\{s_i \mid h(s_i) = j\}|, j = 0, \ldots, m-1$. Calculate the expected value $E(n_j)$.

11. **Hash procedures on hard disks.** Hash methods can also be used for data on secondary storage. Records are stored here in blocks. A block can contain several records. The value set of the hash function is equal to the set of block addresses. A block contains a maximum of b records. Let n be the number of records and m the number of blocks. Then we understand by the load factor $\beta = \frac{n}{m}$ the number of records per address. The load factor for the memory is $B = \frac{n}{bm}$. Perform the analysis of the hash procedures for the above situation and solve the following task.

5,000 records are to be stored in a file. A hash method with primary and overflow areas is to be used. 10,000 records can be stored in the primary area. Answer the following questions for block sizes 1 and 5:
   a. How many blocks remain free in the primary area?
   b. How many blocks must be provided in the overflow area?
   c. How many records lead to collisions during insertion?

12. **Stack symbol tables and hash procedures.** Symbol tables are used to manage the names of a source program in the translation process. The accesses to symbol tables to be implemented are Insert, Delete and Search.
An entry in the symbol table consists of
(a) the name of the variables (labels, procedure, . . .) and
(b) additional information.
The organization of a symbol table as a stack supports the rules for visibility in languages with a block structure.
The following rules apply to the visibility of names:
   a. A name is visible in the block in which it is declared (and also in subordinate blocks).
   b. A name is unique in a block (without nesting).
   c. If a name is declared twice in two nested blocks, the inner block refers to the inner declaration (most closely nested rule).
The translation process is sequential. A block is called active if the compiler has passed the beginning of the block (begin block) but not the end of the block (end block). This results in the following requirements of the compiler regarding the organization of the symbol tables:
   a. Access must only be given to names in active blocks.
   b. Names should be arranged according to the nesting structure (from inside to outside —most closely nested first).
Since the effort required to access symbol tables is significant, efficient access methods are necessary. A hash procedure is superimposed on the organization of the symbol tables as a stack. Find out which operations are necessary at the beginning and end of a block, for inserting, searching and deleting. Work out the details of the procedure.

4. Trees

In sorted arrays, you can find a stored element with $O(\log_2(n))$ comparisons, where n is the number of stored elements. Another way to sort elements is to provide *binary search trees*. Binary search trees are designed to be used when elements are inserted or deleted dynamically. It is desirable that the insertion and deletion operations keep the tree as balanced as possible, i.e., the number of levels should be small.

Binary search trees are balanced on average (averaged over all possible arrangements of the elements to be stored). In the worst case, binary search trees degenerate into linear lists. Then the number of necessary comparisons when searching for an element is of order $O(n)$, compared to $O(\log_2(n))$ in the balanced case.

Ideally the number of levels is $\lfloor \log_2(n) \rfloor + 1$, and the leaves are on one or two levels, where n denotes the number of stored elements. The effort to achieve this ideal case is not justifiable. Therefore, we do not strive to achieve this ideal case.

AVL trees are almost balanced (only about 45% worse than ideal). We achieve this with little additional computational effort. The effort required to search for an element is comparable to the effort required to search in a sorted array. Another method to prevent binary search trees from degenerating is to use randomized binary search trees. The average path length for binary search trees will become the expected length of paths in randomized binary search trees. The path length increases by a maximum of 39% compared to the ideal case.

Binary search trees and their variants are used to organize data in main memory. For the organization of data in secondary storage, we discuss B-trees. These are balanced search trees that are designed to minimize disk I/O operations. B-tree nodes may have many children, hence the number of levels is small; it is always of order $O(log_2(n))$.

Code trees for the graphical representation of codes for data compression will complete the chapter. We show that the problem of unique decodability is decidable and discuss Huffman codes including adaptive Huffman codes, arithmetic coding and the ubiquitous Lempel-Ziv codes.

© Springer Nature Switzerland AG 2020

H. Knebl, *Algorithms and Data Structures*, https://doi.org/10.1007/978-3-030-59758-0_4

4.1 Rooted Trees

Trees are special graphs (see Chapter 5). A graph is a *tree* if there is exactly one path between two nodes that connects them. If we designate a node as the root of the tree and give the edges a direction, we get a rooted tree. Trees occur frequently in computer science, and we have already encountered them in the previous Chapters 1 and 2; see, for example, the branch and bound method (Section 1.5.5), binary heaps (Section 2.2.1) or decision trees (Section 2.3). We now specify the term rooted tree.

Definition 4.1.

1. A *rooted tree* $B = (V, E, r)$ consists of a finite set of *nodes* V, a finite set of *directed edges* $E \subset V \times V$ and a *root* $r \in V$. We define recursively:
   a. A node r is a rooted tree $(B = (\{r\}, \emptyset, r))$.
   b. Let $B_1 = (V_1, E_1, r_1), \ldots, B_k = (V_k, E_k, r_k)$ be trees with the roots $r_1, \ldots, r_k$. We extend the node set V by a new root r and the edge set E by the edges (r, r_i), $i = 1, \ldots, k$. Then

$$(V_1 \cup \ldots \cup V_k \cup \{r\}, \{(r, r_i) \mid i = 1, \ldots, k\} \cup E_1 \cup \ldots \cup E_k, r)$$

   is a tree with root r.
   The *empty tree* is explained as deviating from this structure. It has no nodes and no edges.
2. Let $e = (v, w) \in E$, then v is called the *predecessor* or *parent* of w and w is called the *successor* or *child* of v. The edges in B are directed. A node that has no successors is called a *leaf*.
3. A *path P in B* is a sequence of nodes $v_0, \ldots, v_n$ with: $(v_i, v_{i+1}) \in E, i = 0, \ldots, n - 1$. n is called the *length* of P.
4. Let $v, w \in V$. The node w is called *accessible* from the node v if there is a path P from v to w, i.e., there is a path $P = v_0, \ldots, v_n$ with $v_0 = v$ and $v_n = w$. If w is accessible from v, v is said to be an *ancestor* of w and w is said to be a *descendant* of v.
   Each node v of B can be regarded as the root of the subtree of the nodes accessible from v. If v has the successors $v_1, \ldots, v_k$, the subtrees $B_1, \ldots, B_k$ with the roots $v_1, \ldots, v_k$ are called the *subtrees of v*.

Remark. In a tree, each node v has exactly one path leading from the root to v; each node except the root has exactly one predecessor.

Definition 4.2.

1. The *height of a node* v is the maximum of the lengths of all paths starting at v.
2. The *depth of a node* v is the length of the path from the root to v. The nodes of depth i form the *ith level* of the tree.
3. The *height and depth of the tree* is the height of the root. The empty tree has height -1 and depth -1.

Remark. Let B be a tree of height h, and let n be the number of nodes of B. If each node of B has at most d successors, then

$$n \le \sum_{i=0}^{h} d^i = \frac{d^{h+1} - 1}{d - 1}.$$

Definition 4.3. Let B be a rooted tree. If each node v in B has at most two successors, B is called a *binary tree*. The two successors are distinguished as the *left successor* and *right successor* and the two subtrees of v as the *left subtree* and *right subtree*.

Remark. Let n be the number of nodes in a binary tree of height h. Then the number n of nodes satisfies $n \le 2^{h+1} - 1$ or equivalent; the height h is at least $\log_2(n + 1) - 1$, i.e., $\lceil \log_2(n + 1) \rceil - 1 \le h$. The bound is reached for a binary tree in which all levels are completely filled.

The following algorithms use linked lists of node elements to implement binary trees. A node element is defined by

> type node = struct
>> item   *element*
>> node   *left, right*
>> node   *parent*

The reference *parent* to the predecessor is optional. We only need it if we access the predecessor node in an algorithm. A tree is of type tree and is defined by its root node or a reference to the root node. The access to a component of *node* is done with the .-operator (see Section 1.7).

Definition 4.4. We perform depth-first search (DFS) on a binary tree (see Section 5.4.2 and Algorithm 4.5). Its nodes are output in different sequences. We define the following alternatives:

1. For *pre-order output*, first write out the node, then the nodes of the left subtree, and then the nodes of the right subtree.
2. For *in-order output*, first write out the nodes of the left subtree, then the node, and then the nodes of the right subtree.
3. For *post-order output*, first write out the nodes of the left subtree, then the nodes of the right subtree, and finally the node.

Each procedure has to be applied recursively starting from the root.

The recursive definition of a tree allows DFS to be easily implemented by a recursive algorithm.

Algorithm 4.5.
> TreeDFS(node a)
>> 1   if $a.left \ne$ null then TreeDFS($a.left$)
>> 2   if $a.right \ne$ null then TreeDFS($a.right$)
>> 3   mark node a as visited

Example. Figure 4.1 shows depth-first search in a binary tree.

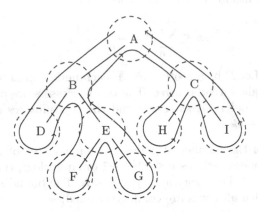

Fig. 4.1: Depth-first traversal.

The path that starts and ends in node A represents the visit order of the nodes by Algorithm 4.5. The first entry of the path into the environment U_v of a node v, which is represented by the dotted circle around v, corresponds to the call of TreeDFS in v, and the last exit of the environment U_v corresponds to the termination of this call.

4.2 Binary Search Trees

We use a binary search tree to store an ordered set S if S is in a large "universe" U, $|S|$ is small compared to $|U|$ and the ability to add or delete elements is required.

Definition 4.6. A *binary search tree* for an ordered set S is a binary tree $B = (V, E)$ with a bijective map $l : V \longrightarrow S$ (each node is marked with an $s \in S$), so that each node v satisfies:

1. Each node w in the left subtree of v satisfies $l(w) < l(v)$.
2. Each node w in the right subtree of v satisfies $l(w) > l(v)$.

Proposition 4.7. *DFS with in-order output yields the elements stored in the nodes of B in sorted order.*

Proof. For one node the statement is correct. Since the elements stored in the left subtree of the root are output before the element stored in the root and the elements stored in the right subtree of the root are output after the element stored in the root, the statement follows by induction on the number of nodes of B. □

Example. The in-order output of the binary tree in Figure 4.2 yield a sorted sequence. The super indices indicate the output order for an in-order traversal.

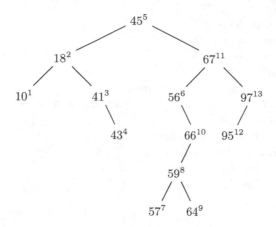

Fig. 4.2: Depth-first search and in-order output.

4.2.1 Searching and Inserting

Searching for an element in a binary search tree is analogous to binary search (Algorithm 2.28). First we check whether the element e to be searched for is stored in the root. If this is not the case and e is smaller than the element stored in the root, we continue the search (recursively) in the left subtree of the root. If e is greater than the element stored in the root, we (recursively) continue the search in the right subtree of the root. When implementing the search using the Search function, we avoid recursion. We replace the recursion with an iteration. When Search is called, the tree and the element to be searched for must be passed.

Algorithm 4.8.
```
node Search(tree t, item e)
1   node a ← t
2   while a ≠ null and  a.element ≠ e do
3       if e < a.element
4           then a ← a.left
5           else  a ← a.right
6   return a
```

The Insert function is used to insert an element. When Insert is called, a tree and the element e to be inserted must be passed. Insert first performs a search for e. If e is already in the tree, there is nothing to do. Otherwise, the search ends in a leaf b. We add a new node for e at b and store e in it.

Algorithm 4.9.
   Insert(tree t, item e)
    1   node $a \leftarrow t, b \leftarrow$ null
    2   while $a \neq$ null and $a.element \neq e$ do
    3      $b \leftarrow a$
    4   if $e < a.element$
    5   then $a \leftarrow a.left$
    6   else $a \leftarrow a.right$
    7 if $a =$ null
    8   then $a \leftarrow$ new(node), $a.element \leftarrow e$
    9         $a.left \leftarrow$ null, $a.right \leftarrow$ null, $a.parent \leftarrow b$
  10   if $b =$ null
  11   then $t \leftarrow a$, return
  12   if $e < b.element$
  13   then $b.left \leftarrow a$
  14   else $b.right \leftarrow a$

4.2.2 Deletion

When deleting an element e, we consider the following cases:

1. There is no node with element e: There is nothing to do.
2. If the node with the element e is a leaf, we can simply remove the node from the tree. We change the reference in the predecessor to null.
3. We can also remove the node v of e from the chained list if v has only one successor. The predecessor of v must reference the successor of v. The binary search tree property is not affected.
4. If the node v of e has two successors, the node v cannot be removed from the concatenated list. We look in the left subtree of v for the largest element $\tilde{e}$. This element is stored in the node which is furthest to the right in the left subtree of v. The node $\tilde{v}$ of $\tilde{e}$ has at most one (left) successor. We swap e with $\tilde{e}$. Then we remove the node $\tilde{v}$ together with e according to point 3 from the tree. Since $\tilde{e}$ was the largest element in the left subtree of v, the elements in the left subtree of v are now smaller than $\tilde{e}$. The elements in the right subtree of v are larger than e and thus also larger than $\tilde{e}$. The binary search tree property is thus fulfilled in v. The node $\tilde{v}$ of $\tilde{e}$ is called the *symmetric predecessor* of v.

Example. We will delete the node marked 45 in the first tree of Figure 4.3.

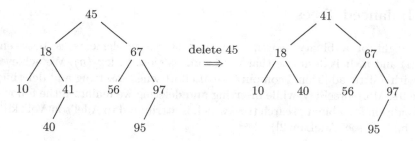

Fig. 4.3: Deleting an element in a binary search tree.

We implement deleting of an element by the following algorithm.

Algorithm 4.10.
Delete(tree t, item e)
1   node $b, a \leftarrow t$
2   $a \leftarrow$ Search(t, e)
3   if a = null then return
4   if $a.right \neq$ null and $a.left \neq$ null
5   then DelSymPred(a), return
6   if $a.left =$ null
7   then $b \leftarrow a.right$
8   else $b \leftarrow a.left$
9   if $t = a$
10   then $t \leftarrow b$, return
11   if $a.parent.left = a$
12   then $a.parent.left \leftarrow b$
13   else $a.parent.right \leftarrow b$
14   $b.parent \leftarrow a.parent$
15   return

DelSymPred(node a)
1   node $b \leftarrow a$
2   if $a.left.right =$ null
3   then $c \leftarrow a.left$, $a.left \leftarrow c.left$
4   else $b \leftarrow a.left$
5   while $b.right.right \neq$ null do
6                $b \leftarrow b.right$
7           $c \leftarrow b.right$, $b.right \leftarrow c.left$
8   $a.element \leftarrow c.element$
9   $c.left.parent \leftarrow b$

4.3 Balanced Trees

The height of a binary search tree that stores n elements is between $\log_2(n)$ and n. It is desirable that the height is close to $\log_2(n)$. We achieve this with a little additional computational effort when inserting and deleting elements. More precisely, while inserting and deleting we maintain the following condition for a binary search tree, which is attributed to Adel'son-Vel'skiĭ[1] and Landis[2] (see [AdeLan62]).

Definition 4.11 *(AVL condition)*. A binary tree is said to be *balanced* if for each node v the heights of the left and right subtree of v differ at most by 1. Balanced binary search trees are also called *AVL trees*.

The Fibonacci trees, which we introduce in the following definition, are balanced trees. Binary trees are used as navigation structures for binary search in sorted arrays (see Section 2.4.2). Analogously to binary search trees, Fibonacci trees serve as navigation structures for the Fibonacci search in sorted arrays. During Fibonacci search, the array in which the search will be performed is divided using two consecutive Fibonacci numbers, and the array is not just halved as with binary search. The details are the subject of Exercise 11.

Definition 4.12. The sequence of *Fibonacci trees* $(\mathrm{FB}_k)_{k \geq 0}$ is analogous to the sequence of the Fibonacci numbers $(f_k)_{k \geq 0}$ (see Definition 1.19). It is recursively defined by

1. FB_0 and FB_1 consist of the node 0.
2. Let $k \geq 2$. Choose the kth Fibonacci number f_k as root, take FB_{k-1} as left and FB_{k-2} as right subtree.
3. Increase each node in the right subtree by f_k.

The height of FB_k is $k - 1$ for $k \geq 1$. Therefore, the Fibonacci trees are balanced.

Figure 4.4 shows $\mathrm{FB}_2 - \mathrm{FB}_5$.

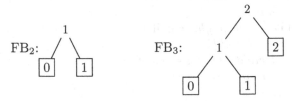

---

[1] Georgy Maximovich Adel'son-Vel'skiĭ (1922 – 2014) was a Russian and Israeli mathematician and computer scientist.
[2] Evgenii Mikhailovich Landis (1921 – 1997) was a Russian mathematician.

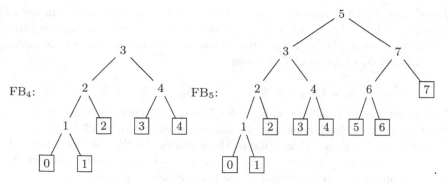

Fig. 4.4: The Fibonacci trees $FB_2 - FB_5$

The tree B_k is the tree of the inner nodes of FB_k, i.e., the nodes which are not leaf nodes. The sequence $(B_k)_{k \geq 0}$ is analogous to the sequence of the Fibonacci trees. The start of induction is given by $B_0 = B_1 = \emptyset$. The tree B_k, $k \geq 2$, has f_k as root, B_{k-1} as left and B_{k-2} as the right subtree of the root. The nodes of B_{k-2} are increased by f_k, as shown in Figure 4.5.

Inductively we obtain

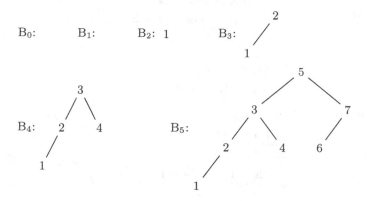

Fig. 4.5: The inner nodes $B_0 - B_5$ of the corresponding Fibonacci trees.

B_k is a balanced tree of height $k - 2$ with a minimum number of nodes. The following proposition provides information about the number of nodes of B_k.

Proposition 4.13. *Let b_h be the number of nodes of a balanced tree of height h with a minimum number of nodes. Then*

$$b_h = f_{h+3} - 1,$$

where f_{h+3} is the $(h+3)$th Fibonacci number.

Proof. Let T_h be a balanced tree of height h with a minimum number of nodes. The left subtree of the root has height $h-1$. Then the right subtree of the root has height $h-2$, because we assume a minimum number of nodes. The number b_h of nodes of T_h satisfies

$$b_0 = 1, \; b_1 = 2, \; b_h = b_{h-1} + b_{h-2} + 1, \; h \geq 2.$$

This is an inhomogeneous second-order linear difference equation with constant coefficients. Such equations are discussed in Section 1.3.2.

We calculate a special solution of the equation by the solution approach $\varphi_h = c$, c constant, and get $c = 2c + 1$ or $c = -1$. The general solution b_h results from the general solution of the homogeneous equation

$$b_h = \lambda_1 g^h + \lambda_2 \hat{g}^h, \lambda_1, \lambda_2 \in \mathbb{R},$$

solved in the proof of Proposition 1.21, and the special solution φ_h:

$$b_h = \lambda_1 g^h + \lambda_2 \hat{g}^h - 1, \lambda_1, \lambda_2 \in \mathbb{R},$$

where $g = \frac{1}{2}(1 + \sqrt{5})$ and $\hat{g} = \frac{1}{2}(1 - \sqrt{5})$ are the solutions of $x^2 = x + 1$ (Section 1.3.2, Proposition 1.21).

From the initial conditions $b_0 = 1$, $b_1 = 2$, results

$$\lambda_1 g^0 + \lambda_2 \hat{g}^0 - 1 = 1,$$
$$\lambda_1 g^1 + \lambda_2 \hat{g}^1 - 1 = 2.$$

We get

$$\lambda_2 = 2 - \lambda_1,$$
$$\lambda_1 g + (2 - \lambda_1)(1 - g) = 3.$$

This implies:

$$\lambda_1 = \frac{2g + 1}{2g - 1} = \frac{g^3}{\sqrt{5}},$$

$$\lambda_2 = 2 - \frac{2g + 1}{\sqrt{5}} = -\frac{2g + 1 - 2\sqrt{5}}{\sqrt{5}}$$

$$= -\frac{2(g - \sqrt{5}) + 1}{\sqrt{5}} = -\frac{2\hat{g} + 1}{\sqrt{5}} = -\frac{\hat{g}^3}{\sqrt{5}}.$$

In our calculation, we used that g and $\hat{g}$ solve the equation $2x + 1 = x + x + 1 = x + x^2 = x(x + 1) = xx^2 = x^3$. This results in the following solution

$$b_h = \frac{1}{\sqrt{5}} \left(g^{h+3} - \hat{g}^{h+3} \right) - 1 = f_{h+3} - 1.$$

$\square$

Proposition 4.14 *(Adel'son-Vel'skiĭ and Landis). Let h be the height of a balanced tree with n nodes. Then*

$$h < 1.45 \log_2(n + 2) - 1.33.$$

Proof. The number n of nodes satisfies

$$n \geq b_h = f_{h+3} - 1 = round\left(\frac{g^{h+3}}{\sqrt{5}}\right) - 1 > \frac{g^{h+3}}{\sqrt{5}} - 2.$$

This implies $\sqrt{5}(n+2) > g^{h+3}$. The result is

$$h < \log_g(\sqrt{5}(n+2)) - 3 \approx 1.45 \log_2(n+2) - 1.33,$$

thereby proving our assertion. □

4.3.1 Insert

Since an AVL tree is a binary search tree, we use the search function of a binary search tree (Algorithm 4.8). When inserting, we first proceed as with a binary search tree (Algorithm 4.9). The search for the element e to be inserted ends in a leaf, if e is not stored in the tree. At this leaf, we anchor a new node and fill it with the element to be inserted. This may violate the AVL condition. Then we reorganize the tree and restore the AVL condition. We check for each node n on the search path, starting from the leaf, whether the tree is balanced at n, i.e., whether the heights of the two subtrees of n differ at most by 1. If this is not the case, we achieve this by a balancing operation. The algorithm does not need the heights of the two subtrees of a node, but only the difference between the two heights, the balance factor of the node. The binary search tree property must be invariant under the balancing procedure. We achieve this with *rotations*, which are sketched in Figure 4.6.

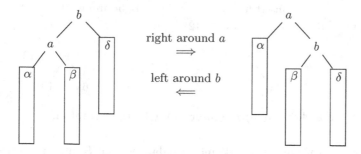

Fig. 4.6: Right, left rotation.

The right rotation around a brings b one level down and a one level up. The left rotation around b brings a one level down and b one level up. Since the elements in β are larger than a and smaller than b, the binary search tree property is preserved by right and left rotations.

Definition 4.15. Let a be a node in a binary tree. The *balance factor* bf(a) of a is height of the right minus the height of the left subtree of a. For balance factors we write $-$ for -1, $+$ for $+1$, $--$ for -2 and $++$ for $+2$.

Example. In Figure 4.7, the balance factors are the superscripts at each node. The tree is not AVL-balanced.

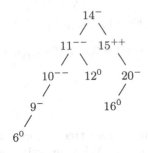

Fig. 4.7: Balance factors.

Remarks:

1. In a balanced tree, there are only nodes with the balance factors $-$, 0 and $+$.
2. A negative (positive) balance factor of a node indicates that the left (right) subtree has greater height.

Example. We insert 6 into the left-hand tree in Figure 4.8.

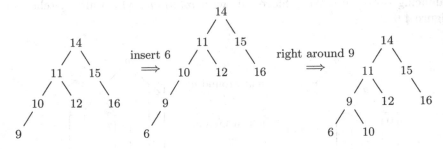

Fig. 4.8: Example – insertion with right rotation.

Assume that we insert a node into a balanced tree B, and after insertion we have $\mathrm{bf}(a) = --$ or $\mathrm{bf}(a) = ++$ for some node a; then the balanced tree condition is violated at a.

We now discuss the case $\mathrm{bf}(a) = --$. The symmetrical case $\mathrm{bf}(a) = ++$ is to be treated analogously. Let a be a node with $\mathrm{bf}(a) = --$ and b be the root of the left subtree of a.

In general, the following holds for $\mathrm{bf}(b)$ before inserting and after inserting a node in the subtree rooted at b:

before	0	$-$	$+$	$-,+$
after	$-,+$	$--$	$++$	0

Because of bf$(a) = --$ the height of b increased by one after inserting. Since in both cases of the last column the height of b remains unchanged, these cases can not occur.

In the cases bf$(b) = --$ or bf$(b) = ++$, we continue with the subtree with root b. Thus, the cases bf$(a) = --$, bf$(b) = -$ and bf$(a) = --$, bf$(b) = +$ remain.

We now specify the balancing operation for bf$(a) = --$ and bf$(b) = -$. The height adjustment is done by a right rotation around b. We sketch this in Figure 4.9.

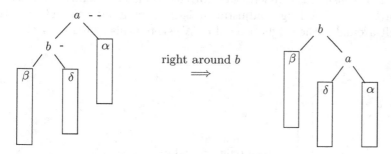

Fig. 4.9: Insert with right rotation.

Let h be the height of α. Then the height of δ is equal to h and the height of β after inserting the node is equal to $h + 1$.
After the rotation, we have bf$(a) = 0$ and bf$(b) = 0$. Therefore, the right tree fulfills the AVL condition in the nodes a and b. The height of the considered subtree is $h + 2$ before insertion and after rotation. Therefore, no further balancing operations are necessary.

Example. Figure 4.10 shows a situation where it is not possible to restore the AVL condition with one rotation.

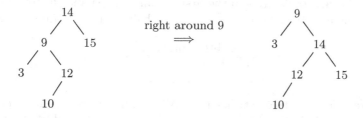

Fig. 4.10: A simple rotation does not balance.

Example. In this example we establish the AVL condition by a double rotation – first a left rotation, then a right rotation, as shown in Figure 4.11.

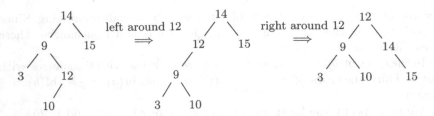

Fig. 4.11: Example – insert with double rotation.

We now consider the general case for the balancing operation for $\mathrm{bf}(a) = --$, $\mathrm{bf}(b) = +$. The height adjustment is done by a left and right rotation, first left around c, then right around c. We sketch this in Figure 4.12.

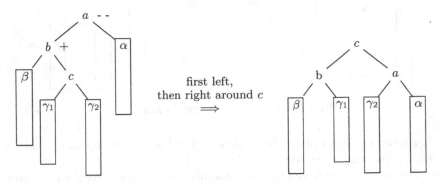

Fig. 4.12: Insert with double rotation.

Let h be the height of α. Then the height of β is equal to h and the heights of γ_1 and γ_2 before insertion are equal to $h-1$. Because the height of b increases by one after insertion, either the height of γ_1 or γ_2 after inserting is equal to h. The figure shows the second case.

The following table gives in the first column the balance factor of c after the insertion and in the further columns the balance factors after reorganization.

$\mathrm{bf}(c)$	$\mathrm{bf}(a)$	$\mathrm{bf}(b)$	$\mathrm{bf}(c)$
+	0	−	0
−	+	0	0

Therefore, the right tree satisfies the AVL condition at the nodes a, b and c. The height of the considered subtree before insertion and of the subtree after the rotations is $h+2$. Therefore, no further balancing operations are necessary on the insertion path.

The following algorithms implement insertion into an AVL tree. The first parameter of AVLInsert is the tree, the second parameter the root of the tree and the third parameter the element e to insert.

We add to the node object the balance factor component.
type balFac $= 0, -, --, +, ++$ and
    type node $=$ struct
          item   *element*
          node   *left, right*
          node   *parent*
          balFac *bf*

Algorithm 4.16.

```
boolean AVLInsert(tree t, node a, item e)
1   if e < a.element
2     then b ← a.left
3           if b = null then insertNode(b, e), return true
4           if AVLInsert(t, b, e)
5             then if a.bf = + then a.bf ← 0, return false
6                   if a.bf = 0 then a.bf ← −, return true
7                   if b.bf = −
8                     then R-Rot(t, b), return false
9                     else  c ← b.right
10                         LR-Rot(t, c), return false
11    else  if e > a.element
12            then b ← a.right
13                  if b = null then insertNode(b, e), return true
14                  if AVLInsert(t, b, e)
15                    then if a.bf = − then a.bf ← 0, return false
16                          if a.bf = 0 then a.bf ← +, return true
17                          if b.bf = +
18                            then L-Rot(t, b), return false
19                            else  c ← b.left
20                                 RL-Rot(t, c), return false
21    return false
```

We specify the algorithms for right and left-right rotation. The left and right-left rotation are to be implemented analogously.

Algorithm 4.17.

```
R-Rot(tree t, node b)
1   a ← b.parent, c ← a.parent
2   a.bf ← 0, b.bf ← 0
3   a.parent ← b, b.parent ← c, a.left ← b.right, b.right ← a
4   if c = null
5     then t ← b
6     else  if c.right = a
7             then
8                   c.right ← b
9             else  c.left ← b
```

Algorithm 4.18.
    LR-Rot(tree t, node c)
    1   $b \leftarrow c.parent,\ a \leftarrow b.parent,\ d \leftarrow a.parent$
    2   if $c.bf = +$
    3   then $b.bf \leftarrow -,\ a.bf \leftarrow 0$
    4   else $b.bf \leftarrow 0,\ a.bf \leftarrow +$
    5   $c.bf \leftarrow 0$;
    6   $a.parent \leftarrow c,\ b.parent \leftarrow c,\ c.parent \leftarrow d$
    7   $a.left \leftarrow c.right,\ b.right \leftarrow c.left,\ c.left \leftarrow b,\ c.right \leftarrow a$
    8   if $d = \text{null}$
    9   then $t \leftarrow c$
    10   else if $d.right = a$
    11   then
    12                      $d.right \leftarrow c$
    13   else $d.left \leftarrow c$

Remarks:

1. AVLInsert determines the insertion path and the target leaf by recursive descent analogously to depth-first search (Algorithm 4.5). Then the function insertNode adds a new node to the target leaf and stores e in it. On the way back to the root, the rotations are performed and the balance factors are corrected.

2. When AVLInsert is executed, the descent path is implicitly stored on the call stack. The node component *parent*, which is used by R-Rot and LR-Rot, is not accessed in AVLInsert.

3. AVLInsert returns true in line 6 or line 16 if the height of the subtree with root b has increased. It may be necessary to update the balance factor $a.bf$. If the balance factor in a is neither 0 nor +, then $a.bf = -$. So after termination of the call in line 4, $a.bf = --$. Then a right rotation (R-Rot) or a left-right rotation (LR-Rot) is necessary in this subtree. If AVLInsert returns false, no further updates are necessary on the descent path.

4. The lines 15 – 20 following the call of AVLInsert in line 14 are symmetrical to the lines 5 – 10 for the descent on the right.

5. If e is in the tree. Then e is the element at a node a; neither of the comparisons in lines 1 and 11 is true. AVLInsert returns false at line 21.

6. With an alternative iterative implementation of AVLInsert, we insert an element with the algorithm Insert (Algorithm 4.9). To create the AVL condition, we then pass through the path given by the *parent* component of the node. Thereby we carry out the necessary rotations and updates of the balance factors (compare with Algorithm 4.19).

4.3.2 Delete

The AVL condition and the binary search tree property must be invariant under deleting. We delete first as in a binary search tree (Algorithm 4.10) and then possibly establish the AVL condition by balancing activities.

Example. In Figure 4.13 we delete 16:

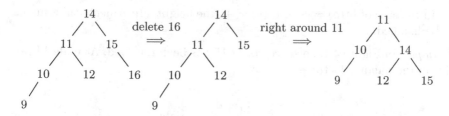

Fig. 4.13: Example – delete with right rotation.

To perform the balancing action, we consider the path P which leads from the root to the predecessor of the node that we remove from the tree. We denote by a the node furthest from the root at which the tree is no longer balanced. We consider the case $\mathrm{bf}(a) = --$. The symmetrical case $\mathrm{bf}(a) = ++$ can be treated analogously.

Let b be the root of the left subtree of a and α the right subtree of a. Let h be the height of α before deleting the node. Because of $\mathrm{bf}(a) = --$ the height of the subtree α decreases by one after deleting the node. The subtree with root b and thus the balance factor $\mathrm{bf}(b)$ remains unchanged.

We now consider the case $\mathrm{bf}(a) = --$, $\mathrm{bf}(b) = -$ or 0. The height adjustment is done by a right rotation around b. We sketch this in Figure 4.14.

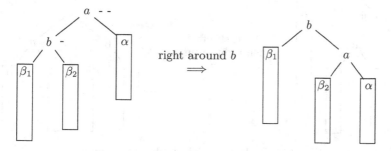

Fig. 4.14: Deletion with right rotation.

Then the height of β_1 is equal to h and the height of β_2 is equal to $h-1$ or h (remember $\mathrm{bf}(b) = -$ or 0). The figure shows the first case. The height of the subtree with root a was $h+2$ before deleting the node.

In the right-hand tree, we have $\mathrm{bf}(a) = -$ and $\mathrm{bf}(b) = +$ if before deleting $\mathrm{bf}(b) = 0$, and we have $\mathrm{bf}(a) = \mathrm{bf}(b) = 0$ if before deleting $\mathrm{bf}(b) = -$.

Therefore, the AVL condition is fulfilled in the right-hand tree at nodes a and b. In the case $bf(b) = -$, the height of the reorganized tree decreases. It only has height $h + 1$. This may require balancing actions for higher nodes in the path P.

In the case of $bf(a) = --$, $bf(b) = +$, the height adjustment still remains to be handled.

Example. In Figure 4.15, a successor of 15 has been removed. At node 14, we obtain the balance factor $--$.

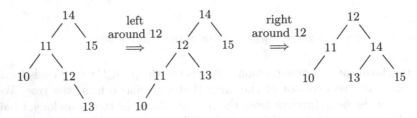

Fig. 4.15: Example – delete with double rotation.

We will now consider the general case. The height balance is done by a left-right rotation, first left around c then right around c. We sketch this in Figure 4.16.

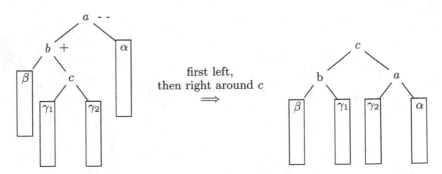

Fig. 4.16: Deletion with double rotation.

After deleting the node, the subtree α has height $h-1$. Because $bf(b) = +$, the height of the right subtree of b is h, and the height of β is $h - 1$. Either one of the subtrees γ_1 or γ_2 has height $h - 1$ and the other height $h - 2$, or both have height $h - 1$. The original tree had height $h + 2$ before the node was deleted.

The following table shows the balance factor of c before reorganization in the first column. The other columns show the balance factors after reorganization.

bf(c)	bf(a)	bf(b)	bf(c)
0	0	0	0
+	0	−	0
−	+	0	0

Therefore, the right tree fulfills the AVL condition at nodes a, b and c and has height $h + 1$. This may require balancing activities for higher nodes in the path P.

Example. When deleting a node, rotations may occur along the path up to the root. This occurs for trees consisting of the inner nodes of the Fibonacci trees (Definition 4.12) when we delete the element furthest to the right. In Figure 4.17 we delete the element 12 in the tree B_8.

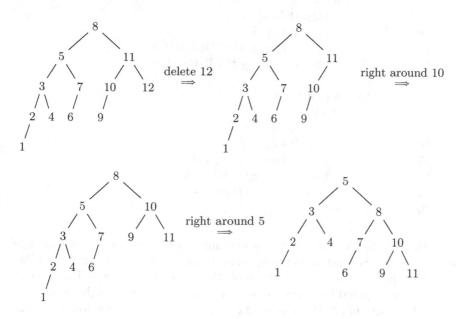

Fig. 4.17: Example – delete with multiple rotations.

Balancing requires first a right rotation around 10 and then a right rotation around 5. The last tree shows the result.

To delete an element we use Delete (Algorithm 4.10). Delete must be modified so that the predecessor a of the removed node b is returned. Furthermore, the return value contains the information whether b was the left ($bal = +$) or right ($bal = -$) successor of a. After calling AVLRepair with these parameters, we go through the path P from a to the root. Thereby we perform the rotations to establish the AVL condition and update the balance factors. The rotations we use when inserting a node (Algorithms 4.17 and 4.18) have to be adjusted regarding the correction of the balance factors.

The variable h controls whether balancing operations are necessary at higher nodes.

Algorithm 4.19.
AVLRepair(tree t, node a, int bal)
1   node b, c; int $h \leftarrow bal$
2   while $a \neq$ null and $h \neq 0$ do
3        $a.bf \leftarrow a.bf + h$, $next \leftarrow a.parent$
4   if $a = next.left$ then $h \leftarrow +$ else $h \leftarrow -$
5   if $a.bf = --$
6   then $b \leftarrow a.left$
7   if $b.bf = -$
8   then R-Rot(t, b)
9   else if $b.bf = 0$
10   then $h \leftarrow 0$, R-Rot(t, b)
11   else $c \leftarrow b.right$, LR-Rot(t, c)
12   if $a.bf = ++$
13   then $b \leftarrow a.right$
14   if $b.bf = +$
15   then L-Rot(t, b)
16   else if $b.bf = 0$
17   then $h \leftarrow 0$, L-Rot(t, b)
18   else $c \leftarrow b.left$, RL-Rot(t, c)
19   if $a.bf = -$ or $a.bf = +$ then $h \leftarrow 0$
20        $a \leftarrow next$

Remark. Inserting a node requires a maximum of two rotations. Performing a rotation requires constant running time. Together with the effort for finding the insert position, the running time of AVLInsert is $O(\log(n))$. The number of rotations required to delete an element is limited by the height of the tree. Since the height of an AVL tree is of order $O(\log(n))$ (Proposition 4.14), the running time $T(n)$ for deleting an element is $O(\log(n))$.

4.4 Randomized Binary Search Trees

We assume that n elements are stored in a binary search tree. The maximum number of nodes in a search path is between $\log_2(n)$ and n, depending on the tree. We calculate the average number of nodes in a search path.

Proposition 4.20. *If we insert n elements into an empty binary search tree, then the average number of nodes in a search path $P(n)$ is*

$$P(n) = 2\,\frac{n+1}{n}\mathrm{H}_n - 3.^3$$

We calculate the average of all search paths and all possible arrangements of the n elements.

Proof. The probability that the ith element (in the sorted order) v_i is the first element to insert is $\frac{1}{n}$.

Let $\tilde{P}(n,i)$ be the average number of nodes in a search path if v_i is the root. In this case, we get the tree in Figure 4.18.

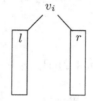

Fig. 4.18: A binary search tree.

In the left subtree l of the root, there are $i-1$ and in the right subtree r, there are $n-i$ nodes. Therefore, the following recursive formula holds for the average number of nodes in a search path with fixed root v_i.

$$\tilde{P}(n,i) = \frac{1}{n}((P(i-1)+1)(i-1) + (P(n-i)+1)(n-i)+1)$$
$$= \frac{1}{n}(P(i-1)(i-1) + P(n-i)(n-i)) + 1.$$

$$P(n) = \frac{1}{n}\sum_{i=1}^{n}\tilde{P}(n,i)$$
$$= \frac{1}{n}\sum_{i=1}^{n}\left(\frac{1}{n}(P(i-1)(i-1) + P(n-i)(n-i)) + 1\right)$$
$$= 1 + \frac{2}{n^2}\sum_{i=1}^{n-1}iP(i).$$

The aim is to transform this recurrence into a difference equation by a suitable substitution. This recurrence is similar to the recurrence we have seen in the

---

[3] H_n is the nth harmonic number (Definition B.4).

running time calculation of QuickSort (Section 2.1.1). As in that case, the nth element depends on all the predecessors. A similar substitution leads to success.

We set $x_n := \sum_{i=1}^{n} iP(i)$ and get the difference equation

$$x_n = nP(n) + \sum_{i=1}^{n-1} iP(i)$$

$$= \frac{2}{n} \sum_{i=1}^{n-1} iP(i) + \sum_{i=1}^{n-1} iP(i) + n$$

$$= \frac{2}{n} x_{n-1} + x_{n-1} + n$$

$$= \frac{n+2}{n} x_{n-1} + n, n \geq 2, x_1 = P(1) = 1 .$$

This equation has the solution

$$x_n = (n+1)(n+2)(H_{n+2} + \frac{1}{n+2} - 2).$$

(page 16, equation (d)). For $P(n)$ we get

$$P(n) = 1 + \frac{2}{n^2} \sum_{i=1}^{n-1} iP(i) = 1 + \frac{2}{n^2} x_{n-1}$$

$$= 1 + \frac{2}{n^2} n(n+1) \left(H_{n+1} + \frac{1}{n+1} - 2 \right)$$

$$= 2 \frac{n+1}{n} H_n - 3 .$$

This shows the assertion.   □

Remarks:

1. For large n, $P(n) \approx 2\ln(n)$. The average number of nodes in a search path in the optimal case is $\approx \log_2(n)$. Since $\frac{2\ln(n)}{\log_2(n)} \approx 1.39$, the average number of nodes in a search path is a maximum of 39% greater than in the optimal case.
2. If we save the elements in a random order, we get the average value as the expected value for the number of nodes of a search path. The aim is to construct the search tree as if the elements to be saved were randomly selected. We achieve this by the following construction.

4.4.1 The Treap Data Structure

The data structure Treap (= Tr(ee) + (H)eap) overlays a binary search tree with the heap structure (Definition 2.11). Treaps are used in [AragSeid89] to implement randomized search trees. The elements $e = (k, p)$ to be stored in the treap consist of the key component k and the priority component p. In a binary search tree, the priority is defined by the order in which we insert the elements into the search tree. In a binary search tree, the element which we first insert becomes the root. Now the element with the lowest priority should become the root. We assign the priorities randomly and thus achieve that a search tree is built just as with randomly selected elements. In particular, each element has probability $1/n$ of being the root.

Definition 4.21. A binary search tree is called a *treap* if for each node, beside the search tree property, the heap condition is also satisfied:

1. The keys of the elements stored in the right subtree of a node v are greater than the key of the element of v. This key in turn is larger than the keys of the elements stored in the left subtree of v.
2. The priority of an element e, stored in node v, is less than the priority of the two elements stored in the successor nodes of v.

Example. Figure 4.19 shows an example of a treap.

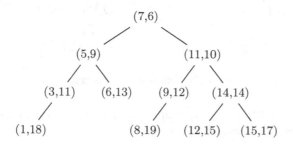

Fig. 4.19: A treap.

Proposition 4.22. *Let S be a set of elements (k, p) with pairwise distinct priorities p. Then there is exactly one treap T that stores S.*

Proof. We shall prove our assertion by induction on $n := |S|$. For $n = 0$ and $n = 1$, there is nothing to prove. Let $n \geq 1$, and let $(k, p) \in S$ be the element of minimum priority. This is the root of the treap. The left subtree of the root is $S_1 := \{(\tilde{k}, \tilde{p}) \in S \mid \tilde{k} < k\}$ and the right subtree of the root is $S_2 := \{(\tilde{k}, \tilde{p}) \in S \mid \tilde{k} > k\}$. Then $|S_1| < n$ and $|S_2| < n$. By the induction assumption, there is exactly one treap T_1 for S_1 and exactly one Treap T_2 for S_2. With T_1 and T_2, also T is uniquely determined. □

Corollary 4.23. *Let S be a set of elements (k, p). Then the treap T that stores S does not depend on the order in which we insert the elements. If we consider the priorities for all the elements to be fixed in advance, the result will be a unique treap independent of the insertion sequence.*

4.4.2 Search, Insert and Delete in Treaps

When searching for elements, we use the search function of a binary search tree (Algorithm 4.8). When inserting, we first proceed as in a binary search tree (Algorithm 4.9). In the target node of the search, a leaf, we anchor a new node and fill it with the element to be inserted. Then we reorganize the tree in order to establish the heap condition. We move a node up by a left or right rotation until the heap condition is established.

Example. We insert $(13, 7)$ into the treap in Figure 4.19: First we insert as in a binary search tree, as shown in Figure 4.20.

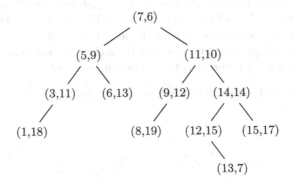

Fig. 4.20: Example for insert.

Then the node$(13, 7)$ is rotated upwards until the heap condition is established. The result is shown in Figure 4.21

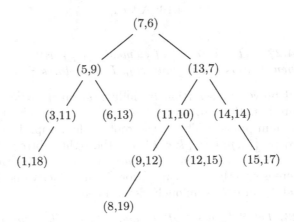

Fig. 4.21: Example – the heap property is established.

When removing a node, the procedure is the reverse of that for inserting a node. First we move the node down by left or right rotations. We always rotate with the successor with the lower priority. At the lowest level, we simply delete the node.

4.4.3 Treaps with Random Priorities

We examine treaps whose elements have priorities that are random and pairwise distinct. Using randomly chosen priorities, we expect a binary tree, like a tree which emerges from a random choice of keys. The question arises as to the additional computational effort that needs to be made, i.e., the number of rotations that are necessary when inserting or deleting an element.

We first consider the deletion of a node in a binary tree in which all levels are fully occupied. Half of the nodes are at the lowest level. We can delete one of these nodes without any rotation. A quarter of the nodes are at the second-lowest level. Deleting one of these nodes requires only one rotation. We continue counting the rotations and get $\frac{1}{2} \cdot 0 + \frac{1}{4} \cdot 1 + \frac{1}{8} \cdot 2 + \ldots < 1$ as the mean value.

In the case of a treap with random priorities, the following proposition also gives information about the expected value of the number of necessary rotations.

Proposition 4.24. *If we insert n elements into an empty treap and randomly choose the priority of the elements with respect to the uniform distribution, then the following assertions hold.*

1. *The expected value $P(n)$ of the number of nodes in a search path is*

$$P(n) = 2\, \frac{n+1}{n} H_n - 3.$$

2. *The expected value of the number of rotations for inserting or removing an element is less than 2.*

Proof. 1. The probability is $\frac{1}{n}$ that the ith element (in the sorted order) has the lowest priority, i.e., that it is the root of the treap. The proof is analogous to the proof of Proposition 4.20.

We consider the number of rotations which are necessary to delete a node. For reasons of symmetry, the number of rotations for inserting a node is equal to the number of rotations for deleting it. Let the element a to be deleted be the $(k+1)$th element in the sorted sequence.

Let R be the path that starts from the left successor of a and always pursues the right successor of a node and L be the path that starts from the right successor of a and always pursues the left successor of a node. Let $R : b, d, \ldots, u$, $L : c, e, \ldots, v$, $R' : d, \ldots, u$, $L' : e, \ldots, v$, and let LT_b be the left subtree of b and RT_c the right subtree of c. We consider a right rotation around b, as shown in Figure 4.22.

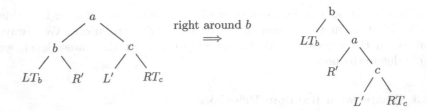

Fig. 4.22: Right rotation.

We bring the node a one level lower by executing a right rotation around b. The number of nodes in R decreases by one; the number of nodes in L does not change. The situation with left rotations is analogous. Before a reaches the leaf level, a must rotate around all nodes of $L \cup R$. Since we reduce the number of nodes in $L \cup R$ by one for each rotation and $L \cup R = \emptyset$ is valid for a leaf node, the number of rotations is equal to the sum of the nodes in the two paths L and R.

We show for the expected value l of the number of nodes of L and for the expected value r of the number of nodes of R:

$$ l = 1 - \frac{1}{k+1}, \; r = 1 - \frac{1}{n-k}. $$

From these two equations, it follows that $l + r \leq 2$ and thus statement 2 of the proposition is true. By symmetry, it is sufficient to show one formula. We show the formula for l.

Let $x_1 < x_2 < \ldots x_k < x_{k+1} < \ldots < x_n$. Let us now look at the binary search tree that is created when we randomly permute $(x_1, x_2, \ldots, x_n)$ and insert the elements in the new order. We realize the random permutation by randomly drawing the elements with respect to the uniform distribution one after the other from $\{x_1, x_2, \ldots, x_n\}$ (without replacement). This tree is equal to the tree which we get if we select all priorities in advance and insert the elements in ascending order (by priority). No rotations are necessary for this order. The elements are inserted as leaves, taking into account the binary search tree condition. However, the treap does not depend on this insertion order.

Let P be the path starting from the root of the left subtree of the node that stores x_{k+1} and always pursues the right successor of a node. Let l_k be the expected value of the number of nodes in P. Then $l = l_k$. We want to determine l_k. The problem depends only on the order of the elements $x_1, x_2, \ldots, x_k, x_{k+1}$. The elements $x_{k+2}, \ldots, x_n$ are not on P. They are irrelevant for this question.

We choose the first element $x \in \{x_1, x_2, \ldots, x_k, x_{k+1}\}$ randomly with respect to the uniform distribution. We distinguish between two cases:

1. $x = x_{k+1}$.
2. $x = x_i, 1 \leq i \leq k$.

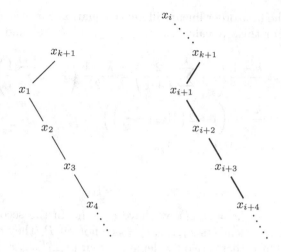

Fig. 4.23: Left subtree – right leg.

In Figure 4.23, the listing of possible keys in P has been started. Not all of these elements must necessarily occur.

An element x is on P if and only if

(1) $x < x_{k+1}$, i.e., $x \in \{x_1, x_2, \ldots x_k\}$ and
(2) x is greater than any element selected before x from $\{x_1, x_2, \ldots x_k\}$.

Let us consider the first case ($x = x_{k+1}$). Let $\tilde{l}_k$ be the random variable indicating how often condition (2) occurs. Once we have chosen the next element x_i, condition (2) can no longer be fulfilled for $x_1, \ldots, x_{i-1}$. Condition (2) can at most be fulfilled for the $k - i$ elements $x_{i+1}, \ldots, x_k$. Recursively, we get the results: Condition (2) is fulfilled $1 + \tilde{l}_{k-i}$ times. Averaged over all i we conclude

$$\tilde{l}_k = \frac{1}{k} \sum_{i=1}^{k} (1 + \tilde{l}_{k-i}) = 1 + \frac{1}{k} \sum_{i=0}^{k-1} \tilde{l}_i, k \geq 1,$$

$$\tilde{l}_0 = \tilde{l}_{k-k} = 0 \text{ (the first element is } x_k\text{)}.$$

To solve this equation we set $x_k = \sum_{i=0}^{k} \tilde{l}_i$. We get

$$x_k = \tilde{l}_k + \sum_{i=0}^{k-1} \tilde{l}_i = \frac{1}{k} x_{k-1} + x_{k-1} + 1.$$

Hence

$$x_1 = \tilde{l}_1 = 1,$$
$$x_k = \frac{k+1}{k} x_{k-1} + 1, k \geq 2.$$

Now we solve the first-order linear difference equation with the methods from Section 1.3.1. For this, we calculate $\pi_k = \prod_{i=2}^{k} \frac{i+1}{i} = \frac{k+1}{2}$ and

$$
\begin{aligned}
x_k &= \frac{k+1}{2} \left(1 + \sum_{i=2}^{k} \frac{2}{i+1} \right) = \frac{k+1}{2} \left(1 + 2 \sum_{i=3}^{k+1} \frac{1}{i} \right) \\
&= \frac{k+1}{2} \left(1 + 2 \left(\mathrm{H}_{k+1} - \frac{3}{2} \right) \right) \\
&= (k+1)(\mathrm{H}_{k+1} - 1).
\end{aligned}
$$

We get

$$
\tilde{l}_k = x_k - x_{k-1} = \mathrm{H}_k.
$$

In the first case $(x = x_{k+1})$, we have $l_k = \tilde{l}_k$. In the second case $(x = x_i, 1 \le i \le k)$, the elements $x_1, \dots, x_{i-1}$ are not on P (they are in the left subtree of x_i). On P there are only elements from $\{x_{i+1}, \dots, x_k\}$. Recursively, it follows that the number of elements in P is l_{k-i}. Averaged over all i results:

$$
l_k = \frac{1}{k+1} \tilde{l}_k + \sum_{i=1}^{k} \frac{1}{k+1} l_{k-i} = \frac{1}{k+1} \tilde{l}_k + \frac{1}{k+1} \sum_{i=0}^{k-1} l_i, k \ge 1,
$$
$$
l_0 = 0.
$$

Now we solve this equation and set $x_k = \sum_{i=0}^{k} l_i$. We get:

$$
x_k = l_k + \sum_{i=0}^{k-1} l_i = \frac{1}{k+1} x_{k-1} + x_{k-1} + \frac{1}{k+1} \tilde{l}_k.
$$

Thus

$$
\begin{aligned}
x_1 &= l_1 = \frac{1}{2} \tilde{l}_1 = \frac{1}{2}, \\
x_k &= \frac{k+2}{k+1} x_{k-1} + \frac{1}{k+1} \tilde{l}_k, k \ge 2.
\end{aligned}
$$

We reduced the problem to the solution of an inhomogeneous difference equation of first order. We solve this equation with the methods from Section 1.3.1.

We compute $\pi_i = \prod_{j=2}^{i} \frac{j+2}{j+1} = \frac{i+2}{3}$ and

$$
\begin{aligned}
x_k &= \frac{k+2}{3} \left(\frac{1}{2} + 3 \sum_{i=2}^{k} \tilde{l}_i \frac{1}{i+1} \frac{1}{i+2} \right) \\
&= \frac{k+2}{3} \left(\frac{1}{2} + 3 \sum_{i=2}^{k} \tilde{l}_i \left(\frac{1}{i+1} - \frac{1}{i+2} \right) \right)
\end{aligned}
$$

$$= \frac{k+2}{3}\left(\frac{1}{2} + 3\left(\sum_{i=3}^{k+1} \tilde{l}_{i-1}\frac{1}{i} - \sum_{i=4}^{k+2} \tilde{l}_{i-2}\frac{1}{i}\right)\right)$$

$$= \frac{k+2}{3}\left(\frac{1}{2} + 3\left(\frac{1}{3}\tilde{l}_2 + \sum_{i=4}^{k+1}\left(\tilde{l}_{i-1} - \tilde{l}_{i-2}\right)\frac{1}{i} - \frac{\tilde{l}_k}{k+2}\right)\right)$$

$$= \frac{k+2}{3}\left(\frac{1}{2} + 3\left(\frac{1}{2} + \sum_{i=4}^{k+1} \frac{1}{i-1}\frac{1}{i} - \frac{\mathrm{H}_k}{k+2}\right)\right)$$

$$= \frac{k+2}{3}\left(\frac{1}{2} + 3\left(\frac{1}{2} + \sum_{i=4}^{k+1} \frac{1}{i-1} - \frac{1}{i} - \frac{\mathrm{H}_k}{k+2}\right)\right)$$

$$= \frac{k+2}{3}\left(\frac{1}{2} + 3\left(\frac{1}{2} + \sum_{i=3}^{k} \frac{1}{i} - \sum_{i=4}^{k+1}\frac{1}{i} - \frac{\mathrm{H}_k}{k+2}\right)\right)$$

$$= \frac{k+2}{3}\left(\frac{1}{2} + 3\left(\frac{1}{2} + \frac{1}{3} - \frac{1}{k+1} - \frac{\mathrm{H}_k}{k+2}\right)\right)$$

$$= \frac{k+2}{3}\left(3 - \frac{3}{k+1} - 3\frac{\mathrm{H}_k}{k+2}\right)$$

$$= k + 1 - \mathrm{H}_{k+1}.$$

We get

$$l_k = x_k - x_{k-1} = 1 - \frac{1}{k+1}.$$

Since the expected value of l_k and r_k for each node is less than one, we expect on average less than two rotations. □

Remark. AVL trees and randomized binary search trees have similar performance characteristics. Randomized binary search trees provide expected values; AVL trees always meet the specified limits.

If further operations are required, such as the combination of two trees T_1 and T_2, where the keys in T_1 are smaller than the keys in T_2, this can be easily implemented with randomized binary search trees. Select a new root with appropriate key and priority component, make T_1 the left and T_2 the right successor of the root and then delete the root.

4.5 B-Trees

B-trees were developed by Bayer[4] and McCreight[5] to store data on external storage media (see [BayMcC72]). The external storage media are typically hard disk drives. These allow "quasi-random" access to the data. With quasi-random access, we address data blocks – not individual bytes as with random

---

[4] Rudolf Bayer (1939 –) is a German computer scientist.
[5] Edward Meyers McCreight is an American computer scientist.

access – and transfer them between main memory and external storage. Essentially, the number of accesses to the external memory affects the computing time of applications for storing data on external storage media. The access time for two bytes in a single data block is approximately half as long as the access time for bytes in different data blocks. B-trees minimize the number of accesses to the external storage medium.

We manage large amounts of data with databases. The data must be persistently stored and are typically of large volume. Therefore, the use of secondary storage is necessary. Database systems organize the stored data using B-trees.

Definition 4.25. A rooted tree is called a *B-tree of order d* if the following holds:

1. Each node has a maximum of d successors.
2. Each node other than the root and leaves has at least $\lceil \frac{d}{2} \rceil$ successors.
3. The root contains at least two successors if it is not a leaf.
4. All leaves are on the same level.

Remark. Let B be a B-tree of order d and height h. For the minimum number of nodes of B, we get

$$1 + 2 + 2\left\lceil\frac{d}{2}\right\rceil + \ldots + 2\left\lceil\frac{d}{2}\right\rceil^{h-1} = 1 + 2\sum_{i=0}^{h-1}\left\lceil\frac{d}{2}\right\rceil^{i} = 1 + 2\frac{\left\lceil\frac{d}{2}\right\rceil^{h} - 1}{\left\lceil\frac{d}{2}\right\rceil - 1}.$$

The maximum number of nodes is

$$1 + d + d^2 + \ldots + d^h = \sum_{i=0}^{h} d^i = \frac{d^{h+1} - 1}{d - 1}.$$

In total, the number n of nodes is limited by

$$1 + 2\frac{\left\lceil\frac{d}{2}\right\rceil^{h} - 1}{\left\lceil\frac{d}{2}\right\rceil - 1} \le n \le \frac{d^{h+1} - 1}{d - 1}.$$

We call the nodes of a B-tree *pages*. The transfer of data from main memory to the hard disk takes place in blocks of fixed size. The block size depends on the external storage medium used. We select the size of a page so that the transfer from main memory to the secondary storage is possible with one access.

Small-order B-trees are less suitable for organizing data on external storage media due to their small page size. They are another way to efficiently manage data in main memory. B-trees of order four, for example, are an equivalent structure to red-black trees (Exercise 17). Red-black trees are another variant of balanced binary search trees (Exercise 10).

To store an ordered set X we use the B-tree structure as follows:

1. A page contains elements of X in sorted order and addresses of successor nodes. Addresses are not used in leaf pages.
2. Let d be the order of the B-tree. For each page, it holds that:

$$\text{number of addresses} = \text{number of elements} + 1.$$

This results in the following conditions for the number of elements on a page.

  a. The root contains at least one element.
  b. Each node other than the root contains at least $\lfloor \frac{d-1}{2} \rfloor$ $(= \lceil \frac{d}{2} \rceil - 1)$ elements.
  c. Each node contains a maximum of $d - 1$ elements.
3. The logical data structure of a page is given by :

$$\boxed{a_0 \,|\, x_1 \,|\, a_1 \,|\, x_2 \,|\, a_2 \,|\, \ldots \,|\, a_{l-1} \,|\, x_l \,|\, a_l \,|\, \ldots \ldots}$$

where a_i, $i = 0, \ldots, l$, denotes the address of a subsequent page and x_i, $i = 1, \ldots, l$, an element stored on the page. We have $x_1 < x_2 < \ldots < x_l < \ldots$. For an element x, l_x denotes the address to the left of x, and r_x the address to the right of x. For an address a, $S(a)$ is the page that is addressed by a. Elements $u \in S(l_x)$ and $z \in S(r_x)$ satisfy

$$u < x < z.$$

Remark. Due to the arrangement defined above, the elements are stored in sorted order in the B-tree. If we traverse and output the B-tree "in-order", i.e., (1) start with the first element x of the root page, first output (recursively) the elements in $S(l_x)$, then x and then (recursively) the elements on the page $S(r_x)$, (2) continue the procedure with the second element of the root page, and so on, then the output is sorted in ascending order.

Example. Figure 4.24 shows a B-tree for the set {A,B,E,H,L,M,N,O,P,Q,R,T, V,W}.

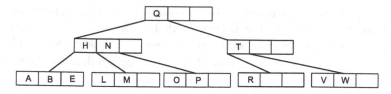

Fig. 4.24: A B-tree example.

4.5.1 Path Lengths

Since all leaves of a B-tree lie on the same level, all paths from the root to a leaf have the same length. The length of a path is limited by the height of the B-tree and determines the number of page accesses required for searching, inserting and deleting an element.

Proposition 4.26. *Let S be a set stored in a B-tree of order d, $|S| = n$. Then the height h of the tree meets*

$$\log_d(n+1) - 1 \le h \le \log_{q+1}\left(\frac{n+1}{2}\right), \; q = \left\lfloor \frac{d-1}{2} \right\rfloor.$$

In particular, the height h of the tree is logarithmic in the number of elements stored in the tree: $h = O(\log_2(n))$.

Proof. Let min be the minimum and max the maximum number of elements in a B-tree of height h. Then

$$min = 1 + 2q + 2(q+1)q + \ldots + 2(q+1)^{h-1}q$$

$$= 1 + 2q\sum_{i=0}^{h-1}(q+1)^i = 1 + 2q\frac{(q+1)^h - 1}{q} = 2(q+1)^h - 1 \le n.$$

Thus, $h \le \log_{q+1}\left(\frac{n+1}{2}\right)$.

$$max = (d-1) + d(d-1) + \ldots + d^h(d-1)$$

$$= (d-1)\sum_{i=0}^{h}d^i = (d-1)\frac{d^{h+1}-1}{d-1} \ge n.$$

This implies $\log_d(n+1) - 1 \le h$. $\qquad\qquad\square$

Example. Let $d = 127, n = 2^{21} + 1 (\approx 2Mio)$. Then $q = 63$ and $h \le \log_{64}(2^{20} + 1) \approx 3.3$. We store the elements in a B-tree with four levels.

In the next two sections, we study algorithms for searching, inserting and deleting elements. The efficiency of these algorithms is determined by the number of necessary accesses to the secondary storage. These, in turn, depend on the height h of the B-tree. With Proposition 4.26, we conclude that the number of accesses to secondary storage is of order $O(\log_{q+1}\left(\frac{n+1}{2}\right))$, where $q = \left\lfloor \frac{d-1}{2} \right\rfloor$, d denotes the order of the B-tree and n denotes the number of stored elements.

4.5.2 Search and Insert

The pages of a B-tree reside on secondary storage. The root of a B-tree is always in main memory. More pages are in main memory only as far as possible and necessary. We address the pages of a B-tree in main memory with the data type *page*.

The secondary storage addresses are of type *address*. Here $1, 2, 3, \ldots$ denote valid page addresses; the page address 0 plays the role of null in linked lists.

The Find, Insert and Delete algorithms use access functions provided by the abstract data type B-Tree. These are the following functions:

1. ReadPage(*address a*) reads the page with address a from secondary storage and returns a reference to the page in main memory.
2. WritePage(*address a, page p*) transfers a page p from main memory to secondary storage at address a. If $a = 0$, WritePage allocates a new page in secondary storage and returns its address. Otherwise, WritePage returns a.
3. PageSearch(*page p, item e*) searches for e in the page that references p and returns a pair (i, adr). If $i > 0$ holds, e is the ith element in p. If $i = 0$, e is not on the page p. If in this case p is a leaf, PageSearch returns the address $adr = 0$. If p is not a leaf, PageSearch returns the address of the page which is the root of the subtree which could contain e.

The first two functions hide the details about the transfer of pages to and from secondary storage.

First we specify the function to search for elements. e is the element to search for and p is the root of the B-tree.

Algorithm 4.27.

```
(page, index) BTreeSearch(page p, item e)
1   while true do
2       (i, adr) ← PageSearch(p, e)
3       if i > 0
4           then return (p, i)
5           else if adr ≠ 0
6               then p ← ReadPage(adr)
7               else return(p, 0)
```

BTreeSearch returns in *page* the page where e is located. With the returned index i, we can access e on the page.

If e is not in the B-tree, the search ends in a leaf. BTreeSearch returns 0 in *index* (valid indices start at 1). *page* is the page in which e would be inserted.

When inserting an element e, we first use BTreeSearch to search for the node which has to store e. Suppose the search with BTreeSearch ends unsuccessfully in a leaf of the B-tree. If the leaf is not yet full, we insert e into this leaf. If the leaf is full, we allocate a new page. We copy about half of the elements from the old page into the new page and insert an element together with the address of the new page into the predecessor page. The insertion of an element is not limited to the leaves; it may be continued on lower levels.

First, we demonstrate the insertion of an element with the following example.

Example. We insert D into the B-tree of Figure 4.25.

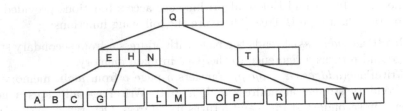

Fig. 4.25: Inserting an element.

Since the page that should store D is already full, we allocate a new page. The elements A, B, D are distributed on two pages, the middle element C goes to the predecessor page. Since the predecessor page is full, we allocate another new page. We distribute the elements C, E, N on two pages; the middle element H goes to the predecessor page. We get the B-tree which is shown in Figure 4.26.

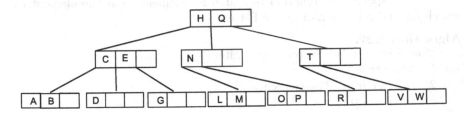

Fig. 4.26: Inserting an element.

We now consider the general case of a full page

$$\boxed{a_0\,|\,x_1\,|\,a_1\,|\,x_2\,|\,a_2\,|\,\ldots\ldots\,|\,a_{l-1}\,|\,x_l\,|\,a_l}$$

with $l = d - 1$, where d denotes the order of the B-tree. Insert e, b ($b = 0$, if the target is a leaf page):

$$\boxed{a_0\,|\,x_1\,|\,a_1\,|\,\ldots\,|\,a_{i-1}\,|\,e\,|\,b\,|\,x_i\,|\,a_i\,|\,\ldots\ldots\,|\,a_{l-1}\,|\,x_l\,|\,a_l} = \boxed{\tilde{a}_0\,|\,\tilde{x}_1\,|\,\ldots\ldots\,|\,\tilde{a}_l\,|\,\tilde{x}_{l+1}\,|\,\tilde{a}_{l+1}}$$

Find the element $\tilde{x}_k$ in the middle and split into

$$\boxed{\tilde{a}_0\,|\,\tilde{x}_1\,|\,\ldots\ldots\,|\,\tilde{x}_{k-1}\,|\,\tilde{a}_{k-1}} \text{ and } \boxed{\tilde{a}_k\,|\,\tilde{x}_{k+1}\,|\,\ldots\ldots\,|\,\tilde{a}_l\,|\,\tilde{x}_{l+1}\,|\,\tilde{a}_{l+1}}$$

We allocate a new page for the right part $\boxed{\tilde{a}_k\,|\,\tilde{x}_{k+1}\,|\,\ldots\ldots\,|\,\tilde{a}_l\,|\,\tilde{x}_{l+1}\,|\,\tilde{a}_{l+1}}$. Let $\tilde{b}$ be the address of the new page. Insert $\tilde{x}_k, \tilde{b}$ (in sorted order) into the predecessor page.

Because the address to the left of $\tilde{x}_k$ references the old page, which is now $\boxed{\tilde{a}_0 \mid \tilde{x}_1 \mid \cdots \cdots \mid \tilde{x}_{k-1} \mid \tilde{a}_{k-1}}$, the algorithm preserves the B-tree properties. The elements stored in it are smaller than $\tilde{x}_k$. The B-tree remains sorted after the division of a node. After splitting a full node, each node has at least $\lfloor \frac{d-1}{2} \rfloor$ elements and at least $\lfloor \frac{d-1}{2} \rfloor + 1$ $(= \lceil \frac{d}{2} \rceil)$ successors. Splitting preserves the lower limit of the number of elements a page must contain.

We extend the abstract data type B-tree by the function

$(boolean\ insert, item\ f,\ adr\ b)$ PageInsert$(page\ p,\ item\ e,\ address\ a)$.

PageInsert inserts the element e with address a on to the page p, which is in main memory, and writes the page to secondary storage. If the page p is full, PageInsert allocates a new page, splits the elements and writes both pages to secondary storage. If the return value $insert$ is true, the case of a full page has occurred. In this case, an element has to be inserted on to the predecessor page. This element is $(item\ f,\ adr\ b)$.

Algorithm 4.28.
BTreeInsert(page t, item e)
  1 $(p, i) \leftarrow$ BTreeSearch(t, e)
  2 if $i \neq 0$ then $return$
  3 $b \leftarrow 0$
  4 repeat
  5      $(insert, e, b) \leftarrow$ PageInsert(p, e, b)
  6   if $insert$
  7   then if $p.predecessor \neq 0$
  8   then $p \leftarrow$ ReadPage$(p.predecessor)$
  9   else $p \leftarrow$ new page
  10 until $insert =$ false

Remarks:

1. First, BTreeSearch determines the leaf into which e is to be inserted. PageInsert then inserts e into the leaf. If $insert$ is true, then we read the predecessor page from secondary storage. The middle element (e, b) will be added to the predecessor page as long as the page splits, i.e., $insert =$ true.
   The algorithm from above reads pages from secondary storage again on the path from the leaf to the root. However, it is possible to avoid this by a more careful implementation.
2. If an element is to be inserted into a full root node, PageInsert allocates a new page and distributes the elements of the old root between the old root and the new page. In line 9, BTreeSearch allocates a page for a new root. Then we insert the middle element into the new root (line 5). The height of the tree increases by one.
3. The balance is not lost because the tree grows from the bottom to the top.

4.5.3 Deleting Elements

Deleting an element must be done in accordance with the B-tree structure. The following points must be observed:

1. Since the condition "number of addresses = number of elements + 1" is fulfilled for inner pages, it is initially only possible to remove an element from a leaf page. If the element x to be deleted is not in a leaf, swap x with its successor (or predecessor) in the sorted order. It is stored in a leaf. Now, we remove x from the leaf page. After removing x, the sorted order is restored.

2. If we remove an element and underflow arises, we have to reorganize the B-tree. *Underflow* exists if a node different from the root contains fewer than $\lfloor (d-1)/2 \rfloor$ elements. We first try to balance between directly adjacent pages. We designate two nodes in the B-tree as *directly adjacent* if they are adjacent on the same level and have the same predecessor. If it is not possible to balance between directly adjacent pages, we combine two directly adjacent pages into one and then release one of the two pages. We get an element from the predecessor page, i.e., we continue deleting recursively. Because

$$\left\lfloor \frac{d-1}{2} \right\rfloor - 1 + \left\lfloor \frac{d-1}{2} \right\rfloor + 1 \le d - 1$$

   the elements from the page with underflow, the neighboring page and the element from the predecessor fit on to one page.

   If underflow enters the root, i.e., the root contains no elements, we free the root page.

3. Balancing between directly adjacent pages S_1 (left node) and S_2 (right node) is done via the predecessor node S of both pages. For an element $x \in S$, we denote by l_x the address to the left of x and r_x the address to the right of x. l_x references S_1 and r_x references S_2. The elements in S_1 are smaller than x and the elements in S_2 are larger than x. We discuss the case where the balance occurs from S_1 to S_2. The reverse case should be treated analogously. The largest element v in S_1 (it stands at the far right) goes to S to the place of x and x goes to S_2 and occupies there the place which lies at the far left. Now, we have to adjust the tree. We replace the missing address l_x in S_2 with r_v: $l_x = r_v$. We delete the address r_v in S_1. The elements in S_1 are smaller than v, the elements in S_2 are larger than v. The elements in $S(l_x)$ are larger than v, but smaller than x. The B-tree remains sorted after adjustment.

Example. We will now look at examples of the various cases that can occur during deletion. We delete the element U in the B-tree of order 4 in Figure 4.27.

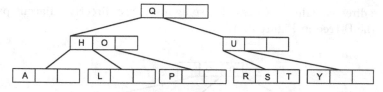

Fig. 4.27: Deleting U.

For this, we exchange U with T. Now U is in a leaf, and we can delete U. We get the B-tree in Figure 4.28.

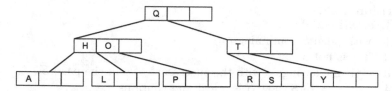

Fig. 4.28: Deleting an element in a leaf page.

Next, we delete Y. Now underflow occurs; there is a balance with the direct neighbor. We get the B-tree in Figure 4.29.

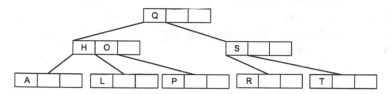

Fig. 4.29: Deleting an element with adjustment.

Finally, we delete T. Underflow occurs again, we merge directly adjacent pages. After another underflow in the predecessor node, a balance is made with the direct neighbor. We get the B-tree in Figure 4.30.

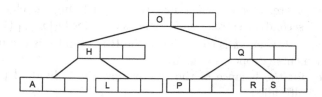

Fig. 4.30: Deleting an element with internal adjustment.

Finally, we delete A. Because of underflow, we merge directly adjacent pages. Underflow occurs again in the predecessor node. Since no adjustment

with the direct neighbor is possible, we again merge directly adjacent pages.
We get the B-tree in Figure 4.31.

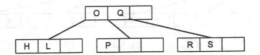

Fig. 4.31: Deleting an element with height reduction.

After deleting the root, the height of the B-tree decreases by one.

Algorithm 4.29.
    BTreeDel(item e)
    1   with page S containing e
    2   if S is not a leaf
    3   then exchange e with the successor* of e in the page $\tilde{S}$
    4         $S \leftarrow \tilde{S}$ (now S is a leaf and contains e)
    5   delete e from the page S
    6   while underflow in S do
    7   if S = root
    8   then free S , return
    9   attempt to balance between immediate neighbors
   10   if balance successful
   11   then return
   12   combine directly adjacent pages
   13    $S \leftarrow$ predecessor of S

---

* The successor in the sorted sequence is located in a leaf.

Remarks:

1. By definition, B-trees are completely balanced. The maintenance of the
   B-tree structure during insertion and deletion is ensured by simple algorithms. In the worst case, all nodes of the search path from a leaf
   to the root are affected when inserting or deleting an element. The
   number of secondary storage operations is of order $O(\log_{q+1}\left((n+1)/2\right))$,
   $q = \lfloor (d-1)/2 \rfloor$, where d is the order of the B-tree and n is the number of
   stored elements (Proposition 4.26).
   The price for the balance of the tree is that the individual pages may
   only be "half" filled.
2. The addresses appearing on the leaf pages all have the value 0 and therefore we do not need to store them. However, we note that it is a leaf.
3. When inserting, just like while deleting, it is possible to balance between
   directly adjacent pages. Instead of immediately creating a new page if

a page is full, we first check whether there is still room on a directly adjacent page. We need a new page if two pages are full. This increases the utilization of memory; every page except the root is filled to at least $2/3$ full. This B-tree variant is called a B*-tree. In addition to more efficient memory usage, B*-trees have a lower height than B-trees for a given number of stored elements (see Proposition 4.26).

4. Database applications store data records. These records are identified by keys. The length of the key is often small compared to the length of the whole data set. We implement an index to speed up access to the data records. The index consists of search keys, and we organize it as a B-tree. Due to the lower memory requirements for a search key, it is possible to store many search keys on a page. This increases the degree of a node and causes the tree to have lower height. The leaf pages of the B-tree contain the references to the data pages. This structure, consisting of index and data pages, is called a B+-tree.

The set of search keys can consist of keys of the data records. In fact, a search key s in a leaf must separate the keys of the following data pages, i.e., it must be valid that the keys in the left successor are $< s$ and the keys in the right successor are $> s$. Therefore, deleting a record may not require changing the search keys.

If we organize the data pages in a double linked list, then it is possible to access the predecessor or successor of a data page in constant time. As a consequence, we can perform range queries of data very efficiently, i.e., output data whose keys lie within an interval.

This type of access is called the *indexed sequential access method* (ISAM). It enables both sequential (in a sorted order) and index-based access to the data records of a database.

Example. Figure 4.32 shows a B+-tree.

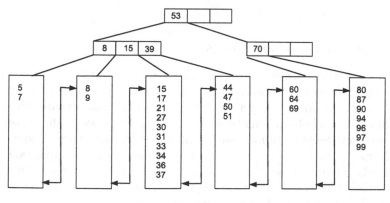

Fig. 4.32: B+-tree.

4.6 Code Trees

In this section, we use code trees to graphically represent codes for data compression. Therefore, we first introduce basic terms from coding theory. In the sections on adaptive Huffman coding, arithmetic codes and Lempel-Ziv codes, we are guided by [HanHarJoh98], an excellent introduction to information theory and data compression.

Definition 4.30.

1. An *alphabet* is a non-empty finite set X. The elements $x \in X$ are called *symbols*.
2. A finite sequence of symbols $x = x_1 \ldots x_n$, $x_i \in X$, $i = 1, \ldots, n$, is called a *word* or *message over* X. $|x| := n$ is called the *length of* x. ε is the word without symbols, the *empty word*. The length of ε is 0, $|\varepsilon| = 0$.
3. $X^* := \{x \mid x \text{ is a word over } X\}$ is called the *set of messages over* X.
4. $X^n := \{x \in X^* \mid |x| = n\}$ denotes the *set of messages of length n over* X, $n \in \mathbb{N}_0$.

Example. An important example is binary messages. The set of binary messages is $\{0, 1\}^*$ and the set of binary messages of length n is $\{0, 1\}^n$.

Definition 4.31. Let $X = \{x_1, \ldots, x_m\}$ and $Y = \{y_1, \ldots, y_n\}$ be alphabets. An *encoding of X over Y* is an injective map

$$C : X \longrightarrow Y^* \backslash \{\varepsilon\},$$

i.e., different messages receive different codes. By C we also denote the image of C. It consists of the *codewords* $C(x_1), \ldots, C(x_m)$ and is called a *code of order m over Y*.

Example. Let $X = \{a, b, c, d\}$. An encoding of X over $\{0, 1\}$ is given by:
$a \longmapsto 0, b \longmapsto 111, c \longmapsto 110, d \longmapsto 101$ or
$a \longmapsto 00, b \longmapsto 01, c \longmapsto 10, d \longmapsto 11$.

4.6.1 Uniquely Decodable Codes

When compressing a message from X^*, the *encoder* generates the coded message, a string from Y^*. In order to encode the symbols from X, a code over Y is used. To encode a string from X^*, the encoder concatenates the code words for the symbols that make up the string. The task of the *decoder* is to reconstruct the original messages from the coded messages. Uniquely decodable means that a string from Y^* has at most one decomposition into code words. Thus, the use of a uniquely decodable code enables the decoder to determine the sequence of the coded messages. This is why we also call uniquely decodable codes *lossless codes*.

Definition 4.32. Let $X = \{x_1, \ldots, x_m\}$ and $Y = \{y_1, \ldots, y_n\}$ be alphabets and $C : X \longrightarrow Y^* \backslash \{\varepsilon\}$ an encoding of X over Y.

1. The extension of C to X^* is defined by

$$C^* : X^* \longrightarrow Y^*,\ \varepsilon \longmapsto \varepsilon, x_{i_1} \ldots x_{i_k} \longmapsto C(x_{i_1}) \ldots C(x_{i_k}).$$

2. The encoding C or the code $\{C(x_1), \ldots, C(x_n)\}$ is called *uniquely decodable* if the extension $C^* : X^* \longrightarrow Y^*$ is injective.

We can prove unique decodability, for example, by specifying an algorithm for unique decoding. A coded string must be unambiguously broken down into a sequence of code words. By specifying two decompositions of a string, we show that a code cannot be uniquely decoded.

Example.

1. The code $C = \{0, 01\}$ is uniquely decodable. We decode $c = c_{i_1} \ldots c_{i_k}$ by

$$c_{i_1} = \begin{cases} 0 & \text{if } c = 0 \text{ or } c = 00 \ldots, \\ 01 & \text{if } c = 01 \ldots, \end{cases}$$

and continue recursively with $c_{i_2} \ldots c_{i_k}$.

2. $C = \{a, c, ad, abb, bad, deb, bbcde\}$ is not uniquely decodable, because $abb|c|deb|ad = a|bbcde|bad$ are two decompositions into code words.

Criterion for Unique Decodability. Let $C = \{c_1, \ldots, c_m\} \subset Y^* \setminus \{\varepsilon\}$. C is not uniquely decodable if there is a counterexample to unique decodability, i.e., for a $c \in Y^*$ there are two decompositions into code words. More precisely, if there are $(i_1, \ldots, i_k)$ and $(j_1, \ldots, j_l)$ with

$$c_{i_1} \ldots c_{i_k} = c_{j_1} \ldots c_{j_l} \text{ and } (i_1, \ldots, i_k) \neq (j_1, \ldots, j_l).$$

Searching for a counterexample, we start with all codewords that have a codeword as prefix. For each of these code words, we check whether the associated postfix either splits another code word as prefix or is prefix of a code word. We define for a code C the sequence

$$
\begin{aligned}
C_0 &:= C, \\
C_1 &:= \{w \in Y^* \setminus \{\varepsilon\} \mid \text{ there is a } w' \in C_0 \text{ with } w'w \in C_0\}, \\
C_2 &:= \{w \in Y^* \setminus \{\varepsilon\} \mid \text{ there is a } w' \in C_0 \text{ with } w'w \in C_1\} \\
&\quad \cup \{w \in Y^* \setminus \{\varepsilon\} \mid \text{ there is a } w' \in C_1 \text{ with } w'w \in C_0\}, \\
&\ \vdots
\end{aligned}
$$

$$
\begin{aligned}
C_n &:= \{w \in Y^* \setminus \{\varepsilon\} \mid \text{ there is a } w' \in C_0 \text{ with } w'w \in C_{n-1}\} \\
&\quad \cup \{w \in Y^* \setminus \{\varepsilon\} \mid \text{ there is a } w' \in C_{n-1} \text{ with } w'w \in C_0\}.
\end{aligned}
$$

We denote by C_n^1 and C_n^2 the sets which define C_n.

The elements $w \in C_1$ are postfixes of code words (the corresponding prefix is also a code word). We have to look at them further. There are two cases:
(1) Either $w \in C_1$ splits off another code word as prefix (the rest of w is in C_2) or
(2) $w \in C_1$ is a prefix of a code word $c \in C$ and the rest of c is in C_2.
We process the elements of C_2 recursively, i.e., we form the sets $C_3, C_4, \ldots$.
We find a counterexample to the unique decodability if

$$C_n \cap C_0 \neq \emptyset \text{ for an } n \in \mathbb{N}.$$

Example. Again, we consider the code $C = \{a, c, ad, abb, bad, deb, bbcde\}$ from above.

C_0	C_1	C_2	C_3	C_4	C_5
a					
c					
ad	d	eb			
abb	bb	cde	de	b	$\boldsymbol{ad}, bcde$
bad					
deb					
$bbcde$					

Since $ad \in C_5 \cap C_0$, we get a counterexample to unique decoding: $abbcdebad$ has the decompositions $a|bbcde|bad$ and $abb|c|deb|ad$.

If C can be uniquely decoded, then $C_n \cap C = \emptyset$ for all $n \in \mathbb{N}$. The following proposition, published in [SarPat53], asserts the equivalence of the two statements.

Proposition 4.33. *For a code $C = \{c_1, \ldots, c_m\}$ the following statements are equivalent:*

1. *C is uniquely decodable.*
2. *$C_n \cap C = \emptyset$ for all $n \in \mathbb{N}$.*

Proof. Let $\mathcal{M} = \{w \in Y^* \mid$ there exists $c_{i_1}, \ldots, c_{i_k}, c_{j_1}, \ldots, c_{j_l} \in C$ with: $c_{i_1} \ldots c_{i_k} w = c_{j_1} \ldots c_{j_l}$ and w is a proper postfix of $c_{j_l}.\}$. We show that

$$\mathcal{M} = \bigcup_{n \geq 1} C_n.$$

The relationship $C_n \subseteq \mathcal{M}$ is shown by induction on n. For $n = 1$ the statement follows directly from the definition of C_1. Now assume $n > 1$, and let the statement already be shown for $n-1$, i.e., $C_{n-1} \subseteq \mathcal{M}$. Let $w \in C_n^1$. Then there is a $w' \in C_0$ with $w'w \in C_{n-1}$. By the induction hypothesis, there is a representation $c_{i_1} \ldots c_{i_k} w'w = c_{j_1} \ldots c_{j_l}$, so that $w'w$ and thus also w is a proper postfix of c_{j_l}. Therefore, $w \in \mathcal{M}$. If $w \in C_n^2$, there is a $w' \in C_{n-1}$ with $w'w \in C_0$. According to the induction hypothesis, there is a representation $c_{i_1} \ldots c_{i_k} w' = c_{j_1} \ldots c_{j_l}$ with w' is a proper postfix of c_{j_l}. We add w on both sides at the end and get the representation $c_{i_1} \ldots c_{i_k} w' w = c_{j_1} \ldots c_{j_l} w$, which proves $w \in \mathcal{M}$.

It remains to be shown that $\mathcal{M} \subseteq \bigcup_{n \geq 1} C_n$. For $w \in \mathcal{M}$, there is a representation $c_{i_1} \ldots c_{i_k} w = c_{j_1} \ldots c_{j_l}$, where w is a proper postfix of c_{j_l}. We show by induction on $k+l$ that $w \in C_n$ for some $n \geq 1$. For $k+l = 2$, we have $k = l = 1$, and $c_{i_1} w = c_{j_1}$ shows that $w \in C_1$. Now let $k + l > 2$. If $l = 1$, we conclude from $c_{i_1} \ldots c_{i_k} w = c_{j_1}$ that $c_{i_2} \ldots c_{i_k} w \in C_1$ and $c_{i_3} \ldots c_{i_k} w \in C_2$, and so on, so finally, $w \in C_k$.

There remains the case $l \geq 2$. We illustrate this with a sketch:

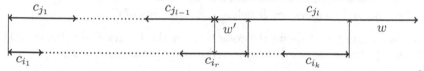

There exists an $r \leq k$ with

$$|c_{i_1} \ldots c_{i_{r-1}}| \leq |c_{j_1} \ldots c_{j_{l-1}}| < |c_{i_1} \ldots c_{i_r}|$$

($c_{j_{l-1}}$ ends with $c_{i_{r-1}}$ or the end of $c_{j_{l-1}}$ is in c_{i_r}).

Let $w' \in Y^* \setminus \{\varepsilon\}$ with

$$c_{j_1} \ldots c_{j_{l-1}} w' = c_{i_1} \ldots c_{i_r}$$

and

$$w' c_{i_{r+1}} \ldots c_{i_k} w = c_{j_l} \in C.$$

If $w' = c_{i_r}$, then we conclude as above that $w \in C_{k-r+1}$. In this case, the assertion is shown.

If w' is a proper postfix of c_{i_r}, then the induction hypothesis applied to $c_{j_1} \ldots c_{j_{l-1}} w' = c_{i_1} \ldots c_{i_k}$ implies that $w' \in C_m$ for some m. Since $w' c_{i_{r+1}} \ldots c_{i_k} w \in C$ (i.e., w' is a prefix of a code word), we conclude that $c_{i_{r+1}} \ldots c_{i_k} w$ is an element of C_{m+1}, and as above, it follows that $w \in C_{m+(k-r)+1}$.

Directly from the definition of $\mathcal{M}$ we conclude that C is uniquely decodable if and only if $C \cap \mathcal{M} = \emptyset$. From $\mathcal{M} = \bigcup_{n \geq 1} C_n$, it follows that $C \cap \mathcal{M} = \emptyset$ if and only if $C \cap C_n = \emptyset$ for all $n \in \mathbb{N}$. $\square$

Corollary 4.34. *Unique decodability is decidable, i.e., there is an algorithm which decides whether C can be uniquely decoded.*

Proof. Let $C \subset Y^* \setminus \{\varepsilon\}$ be a code. We design an algorithm to decide unique decodability with the criterion of the previous proposition. Let $m = \max_{c \in C} |c|$. We have $|w| \leq m$ for all $w \in C_n$, $n \in \mathbb{N}$. Therefore, $C_n \subset Y^m$ for all $n \in \mathbb{N}$. Since Y^m has only a finite number of subsets, the sequence $(C_n)_{n \in \mathbb{N}}$ becomes periodic. We have to check condition 2 of Proposition 4.33 for only finitely many n. $\square$

Definition 4.35 *(graphical representation of a code).*

1. Let $Y = \{y_1, \ldots, y_n\}$ be an alphabet. We assign to all messages $Y^* = \bigcup_{k=0}^{\infty} Y^k$ over Y a tree B:
    a. The root of the tree is the empty word $\{\varepsilon\}$.
    b. Let $y = y_{i_1} \ldots y_{i_k}$ be a node in B. The node y has the n successors
       $y_{i_1} \ldots y_{i_k} y_1, \ldots, y_{i_1} \ldots y_{i_k} y_n$.
2. Let $C \subset Y^*$ be a code over Y.
    In the tree B of Y^*, we mark the root, all code words from C and all paths leading from the root to code words.
    The marked elements of B define the *code tree* of C.

Example. Figure 4.33 shows the code tree for the binary code $\{00, 001, 110, 111, 0001\}$. The code words are located in the rectangular nodes.

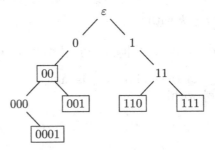

Fig. 4.33: A code tree example.

Definition 4.36. A code $C = \{c_1, \ldots, c_m\} \subset Y^* \backslash \{\varepsilon\}$ is called *instantaneous* or a *prefix-condition code* or a *prefix code*[6] if c_i is not a prefix of c_j for $i \neq j$.

The code words of prefix-condition codes are located in the leaves of the code tree. Prefix-condition codes can therefore be uniquely decoded. Each path in the code tree from the root to a leaf corresponds to a code word. We use the code tree as a parser to split $c = c_{i_1} \ldots c_{i_n}$ into code words. The table *tab* assigns a code word to the corresponding message.

Algorithm 4.37.
```
Decode(code c[1..n])
1   l ← 1, m ← ε
2   while l ≤ n do
3       node ← root, j ← l
4       while node ≠ leaf do
5           if c[j] = 0 then node ← node.left
6           else node ← node.right
7           j ← j + 1
8       m ← m‖tab[c[l..j − 1]], l ← j
```

---

[6] Actually a prefix-free code.

Prefix-Condition Codes for Natural Numbers – the Elias Codes.
Natural numbers are often represented by their corresponding binary representation. However, this does not yield a uniquely decodable code. We get a prefix-condition code, for example, if we encode the numbers in the unary alphabet $\{0\}$ and use 1 to mark the end of a code word ($1 = 1, 2 = 01, 3 = 001$, etc.). For the representation of z, we need z bits. The Elias[7] codes are prefix-condition codes for the natural numbers, which manage with considerably fewer bits. The basic idea of the Elias codes is to precede a binary representation with an encoding of its length. This leads to prefix-condition codes.

The *Elias gamma code* C_γ precedes the binary representation of z with $\lfloor \log_2 z \rfloor$ 0-bits. The length of the binary representation is calculated with the formula $\lfloor \log_2 z \rfloor + 1$. From the $\lfloor \log_2 z \rfloor$ prefixed 0-bits, we calculate the length of the code word for z. For example, 31 has the binary representation 11111. four 0-bits must be prefixed. We get 000011111. The code word length of the code for z is $2\lfloor \log_2 z \rfloor + 1$. Figure 4.34 shows part of the code tree for C_γ.

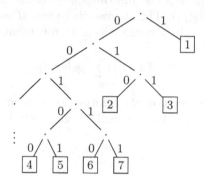

Fig. 4.34: Elias gamma code.

The *Elias delta code* C_δ builds on C_γ. In the case of C_δ, we prefix the binary representation of z with the length of the binary representation of z, coded with C_γ. Since every binary representation of a number starts with 1, we omit the leading 1 in the encoding of z. For example, 31 has binary representation 11111. $C_\gamma(\lfloor \log_2 z \rfloor + 1) = C_\gamma(5) = 00101$. We get 001011111.

Algorithm for decoding:

1. Count the leading zeros. Let n be the number of leading zeros. The first $2n + 1$ bits encode the length l of the binary representation of z.
2. We precede the $l - 1$ following bits by 1 and get the binary representation of z.

---

[7] Peter Elias (1923 – 2001) was an American information theorist.

Since C_γ is a prefix-condition code, C_δ is also a prefix-condition code. The code word length is $|C_\delta(z)| = 2\lfloor\log_2(\lfloor\log_2 z\rfloor + 1)\rfloor + 1 + \lfloor\log_2 z\rfloor$. For $z \geq 32$, we get $|C_\delta(z)| < |C_\gamma(z)|$.

4.6.2 Huffman Codes

Huffman[8] codes use a statistical model of the data to be compressed. The statistical model is derived from the frequency of occurrence of the code words in the message to be compressed. The decoder reconstructs the original data from the compressed data. No information is lost during encoding. It is a *lossless coding*.

Definition 4.38. A *(memoryless) source* (X, p) consists of an alphabet $X = \{x_1, \ldots, x_m\}$ and a probability distribution $p = (p_1, \ldots, p_m)$, i.e., $p_i \in \,]0, 1]$, $i = 1, \ldots, m$, and $\sum_{i=1}^m p_i = 1$ (see Definition A.1).
The source sends the symbol x_i with the probability $\mathrm{p}(x_i) = p_i$.

1. In information theory, *the information content* of x_i is defined as $\log_2\left(1/p_i\right) = -\log_2(p_i)$. The *information content* or the *entropy* $H(X)$ of a source (X, p) is the average information content of its messages, i.e.,

$$\mathrm{H}(X) := -\sum_{i=1}^m p_i \log_2(p_i).$$

   The unit of measurement of the information content is the bit.

2. Let $C : X \longrightarrow Y^* \setminus \{\varepsilon\}$ be an encoding of X over Y, then we call

$$l(C) := \sum_{i=1}^m p_i |C(x_i)|$$

   the *average code word length* of the code C.

3. A uniquely decodable encoding $C : X \longrightarrow Y^* \setminus \{\varepsilon\}$ is said to be *compact or minimal* if the average code word length $l(C)$ is minimal for all uniquely decodable encodings $C : X \longrightarrow Y^* \setminus \{\varepsilon\}$.

   The term entropy is defined independently of the encoding of the source. The connection to the encoding of the source is established by the Noiseless Coding Theorem of Shannon[9].

Proposition 4.39. *Let (X, p) be a source and $C : X \longrightarrow \{0, 1\}^* \setminus \{\varepsilon\}$ a uniquely decodable encoding. Then*

$$\mathrm{H}(X) \leq l(C).$$

Furthermore, there exists a prefix-condition code C for X with $l(C) < \mathrm{H}(X) + 1$. This is especially true for every compact code.

---

[8] David A. Huffman (1925 – 1999) was an American computer scientist.
[9] Claude Elwood Shannon (1916 – 2001) was an American mathematician. He is the founder of information theory and is famous for his fundamental work on coding theory ([Shannon48]) and cryptography ([Shannon49]).

A proof of the proposition can be found, for example, in [HanHarJoh98].

The *Huffman algorithm*, published in [Huffman52], constructs for a source a compact prefix-condition code and the corresponding code tree. First we assign to each message a node, more precisely a leaf, and weight this node with the probability of occurrence of the message.

The construction of the code tree now takes place in two phases. In the first phase, we construct a binary tree from the leaves up to the root. In each step, the algorithm creates a new node n and selects from the existing nodes without predecessor two nodes n_1 and n_2 with the least weights as successors of n. The weight of n is the sum of the weights of n_1 and n_2. In the source, we replace the messages corresponding to n_1 and n_2 with a message corresponding to n. The probability of this message is the sum of the probabilities it replaces. In each step the number of elements of the source decreases by one. The first phase starts with the leaves associated with the messages and terminates if the source contains only one element. This element has a probability of 1 and stands for the root of the code tree.

In the second phase, we calculate the code words from the root down to the leaves. We assign the empty code word ε to the root. The codes of the two successors of a node n result from the extension of the code of n with 0 and 1. This results in longer codes for messages with low probability of occurrence and shorter codes for messages with a high probability. The Huffman algorithm thus implements the greedy strategy.

Example. Let $X = \{a, b, c, d, e, f\}$, $p = (0.4, 0.25, 0.1, 0.1, 0.1, 0.05)$. In Figure 4.35 the leaf nodes contain the messages and the occurrence probabilities. The code of each message is derived from the labels on the edges of the path connecting the root to the message: $C(a) = 0$, $C(b) = 10$, $C(c) = 1100$, $C(d) = 1101$, $C(e) = 1110$, $C(f) = 1111$.

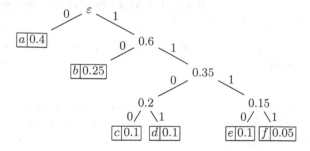

Fig. 4.35: The code tree of a Huffman code.

Now, we describe the general case of the construction of the Huffman encoding

$$C : X \longrightarrow \{0,1\}^* \setminus \{\varepsilon\}$$

of a source (X, p), $X = \{x_1, \ldots, x_m\}$, $p = (p_1, \ldots, p_m)$. We assume without loss of generality that $m \geq 2$ and $p_i > 0$ for $1 \leq i \leq m$.

1. $m = 2$:
   $X = \{x_1, x_2\}$. Set $C(x_1) := 0$ and $C(x_2) := 1$.
2. Let $m > 2$:
   Sort the symbols x_i of the source by descending probabilities $p_1 \geq p_2 \geq \ldots \geq p_m$.
   Let $(\tilde{X}, \tilde{p})$ be defined by

$$\tilde{X} = \{x_1, \ldots, x_{m-2}, \tilde{x}_{m-1}\},$$
$$\mathrm{p}(x_i) := p_i \text{ for } 1 \leq i \leq m - 2,$$
$$\mathrm{p}(\tilde{x}_{m-1}) := p_{m-1} + p_m.$$

$\tilde{X}$ contains $m - 1$ symbols. Choose a Huffman encoding

$$\tilde{C} : \tilde{X} \longrightarrow \{0,1\}^* \setminus \{\varepsilon\}$$

and get the Huffman encoding

$$C : X \longrightarrow \{0,1\}^* \setminus \{\varepsilon\}$$

by setting

$$C(x_i) := \tilde{C}(x_i) \text{ for } 1 \leq i \leq m - 2,$$
$$C(x_{m-1}) := \tilde{C}(\tilde{x}_{m-1})0,$$
$$C(x_m) := \tilde{C}(\tilde{x}_{m-1})1.$$

Before we show that the construction provides a compact code, we formulate two lemmas.

Lemma 4.40. *Let $C : X \longrightarrow \{0,1\}^* \setminus \{\varepsilon\}$ be a compact encoding of (X, p). If $p_i > p_j$, then $|C(x_i)| \leq |C(x_j)|$.*

Proof. Suppose that $p_i > p_j$ and $|C(x_i)| > |C(x_j)|$. Swapping the encodings of x_i and x_j results in a shorter average code word length. A contradiction. $\square$

Lemma 4.41. *Let $C = \{c_1, \ldots, c_m\}$ be a compact prefix-condition code. Then for each code word w of maximum length, there is a code word which matches w up to the last digit.*

Proof. Suppose the assertion of the lemma is not valid. Then a code word could be shortened and, hence, the code is not compact. $\square$

Proposition 4.42. *The Huffman construction provides a compact prefix-condition code.*

Proof. It is immediate from the construction that C is a prefix-condition code. We shall prove our assertion that C is compact by induction on the number m of elements of the source. The assertion follows at once for $m = 2$.

Let $m > 2$ and assume that the assertion is proved for $m - 1$. Let (X, p), C, $(\tilde{X}, \tilde{p})$ and $\tilde{C}$ be given as above. By the induction hypothesis, $\tilde{C}$ is compact. We show that C is compact. Let $C' = \{c'_1, \ldots, c'_m\}$ be a compact code for X. By Lemma 4.40 we get $|c'_1| \leq |c'_2| \leq \ldots \leq |c'_m|$. According to Lemma 4.41, we arrange the code words of maximum length in such a way that $c'_{m-1} = \tilde{c}0$ and $c'_m = \tilde{c}1$ for a $\tilde{c} \in \{0, 1\}^*$. Let $\tilde{C}'$ be the following code for $\tilde{X}$:

$$\tilde{C}'(x_i) := C'(x_i) \text{ for } 1 \leq i \leq m - 2,$$
$$\tilde{C}'(\tilde{x}_{m-1}) := \tilde{c}.$$

Since $\tilde{C}$ is compact, $l(\tilde{C}) \leq l(\tilde{C}')$. From this we conclude:

$$l(C) = l(\tilde{C}) + p_{m-1} + p_m \leq l(\tilde{C}') + p_{m-1} + p_m = l(C').$$

Thus $l(C) = l(C')$. It follows that C is compact.   □

Remark. The Huffman tree is not uniquely defined. Not even the lengths of the code words are unique (Exercise 20). Only the average code word length is unique.

We now describe the Huffman procedure by pseudo-code. The Huffman method assumes that we access the probability distribution $prob[1..m]$ in descending order. We can do this by using the heap data structure without sorting $prob[1..m]$ (see Section 2.2). The heap is built by calling BuildHeap($prob[1..m]$) (Algorithm 2.13) and must be done before calling Huff-manCode. We assign each message $x_i \in X$ a node which represents a leaf in the Huffman tree and weight it with $p(x_i)$.

Algorithm 4.43.
HuffmanCode(int $prob[1..m]$)
```
1   if m ≥ 2
2      then p ← prob[1], prob[1] ← prob[m]
3           DownHeap(prob[1..m − 1])
4           q ← prob[1], prob[1] ← p + q
5           DownHeap(prob[1..m − 1])
6           CreatePredecessor(p, q)
7           HuffmanCode(prob[1..m − 1])
```

The function CreatePredecessor(p, q) is used to build the Huffman tree. It creates a new node, assigns the probability $p + q$, adds the node with probability p as left successor and the node with probability q as right successor and marks the edge to the left successor with 0 and the edge to the right successor with 1. After executing DownHeap, the heap condition is established if it was only violated at the root (see Algorithm 2.12). Therefore, we choose the two lowest probabilities in lines 2 and 4.

Proposition 4.44. *Algorithm 4.43 computes a Huffman code for the source* (X, p). *The running time is* $O(m \log(m))$.

Proof. The running time of BuildHeap is $O(m)$ and the running time of DownHeap is $O(\log(m))$ (Proposition 2.17 and Lemma 2.16). CreatePredecessor can be implemented with constant running time. The number of (recursive) calls to HuffmanCode is $m - 1$. Thus, the running time is $O(m + (m - 1) \log(m)) = O(m \log(m))$. □

Coding and Decoding. For encoding, we use the table $(x_i \to c_i)$ defined by the code tree. In this table, we look up how to encode the individual symbols. To encode $x = x_{i_1} \ldots x_{i_n} \in X^*$, we replace x_{i_j} with c_{i_j}.

The source messages are located in the leaves of the code tree (Figure 4.35). The Huffman code is a prefix-condition code. We decode with Algorithm 4.37. In particular, the running time for coding and decoding is linear in the length of the input.

An Adaptive Huffman Procedure – the Algorithm of Faller, Gallager and Knuth. The Huffman method requires a statistical model of the data to be compressed. With the adaptive Huffman method, the statistical analysis is performed concurrently with the coding of the data. The data to be compressed are read only once. Thus, it is possible to simultaneously generate a compressed output stream from an input stream. After each processed message, we adjust the source frequencies and with it the Huffman code. Updating the source frequencies is easy. Using the Huffman procedure to redefine a Huffman code after each update of the source frequencies would be inefficient. The adaptive Huffman procedure modifies the existing Huffman code with each new message sent by the source.

The adaptive Huffman method was published by Faller[10] in [Faller73]. Later it was extended by Gallager[11] and Knuth[12]. First we characterize Huffman codes by an equivalent property, the Gallager order. With this, we show that the procedure delivers a compact code.

Definition 4.45.

1. A binary tree is called a *binary code tree* if every node that is not a leaf has two successors.
2. A binary code tree with a weight function w on the set of nodes is called a *weighted code tree* if for each node n with the successors n_1 and n_2 the following holds: $w(n) = w(n_1) + w(n_2)$.

Lemma 4.46. *A binary code tree with m leaves has $2m - 1$ nodes.*

---

[10] Newton Faller (1947 – 1996) was a Brazilian computer scientist.
[11] Robert G. Gallager (1931 –) is an American information theorist.
[12] Donald E. Knuth (1938 –) is an American computer scientist.

Proof. We shall prove our assertion by induction on m. For $m = 1$ there is nothing to prove. Let $m > 1$ and assume the assertion proved for $m - 1$. Let T be a code tree with m leaves, $m \geq 2$. We remove two leaves with the same predecessor, so we get a code tree with $m - 1$ leaves. According to the induction hypothesis it has $2(m - 1) - 1$ nodes. Therefore, T has $2(m - 1) + 1 = 2m - 1$ nodes. □

Definition 4.47. Let T be a weighted code tree with m leaves and the nodes $\{n_1, \ldots, n_{2m-1}\}$.

1. T is a *Huffman tree* if there is an instance of the Huffman algorithm that generates T.
2. $n_1, \ldots, n_{2m-1}$ is a Gallager order of the nodes of T if
   a. $w(n_1) \leq w(n_2) \leq \ldots \leq w(n_{2m-1})$.
   b. n_{2l-1} and n_{2l}, $1 \leq l \leq m - 1$, are sibling nodes.

The nodes of the weighted code trees in Figures 4.36 and 4.37 are numbered consecutively: (1), (2), ...

Example. The weighted code tree T in Figure 4.36 has multiple arrangements of nodes by ascending weights which fulfill the sibling condition. For example, the arrangements 5, 6, 8, 9, 13, 14, 16, 17, 4, 7, 12, 15, 3, 10, 11, 2, 1 and 13, 14, 16, 17, 5, 6, 8, 9, 12, 15, 4, 7, 3, 10, 11, 2, 1 fulfill the sibling condition. The code tree T has several Gallager orders.

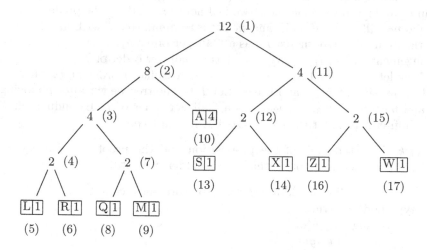

Fig. 4.36: Code tree with several Gallager orders.

Example. The weighted code tree in Figure 4.37 has no Gallager order. There are only two possible arrangements of the nodes according to ascending weights: 4, 5, 7, 8, 3, 10, 11, 6, 2, 9, 1 and 4, 5, 7, 8, 3, 10, 11, 6, 9, 2, 1. For both arrangements the sibling condition is violated.

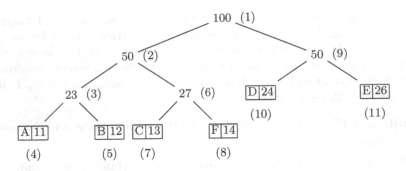

Fig. 4.37: A code tree with no Gallager order.

Proposition 4.48. *Let T be a weighted code tree with $w(n) > 0$ for all nodes n. Then the following statements are equivalent:*

1. *T is a Huffman tree.*
2. *T has a Gallager order.*

Proof. We show the statement by induction on the number m of leaves of T. For $m = 1$ the statements are obviously equivalent. Let $m \geq 2$ and T be a Huffman tree with m leaves and n_1 and n_2 be the nodes that were combined in the first step of the construction of the Huffman tree. n_1 and n_2 are sibling nodes with $w(n_1) \leq w(n_2) \leq w(n)$, where n is any node other than n_1 and n_2. If we remove the two leaf nodes n_1 and n_2, the predecessor of n_1 and n_2 will be a leaf node, and we get a Huffman tree $\tilde{T}$ with $m-1$ leaves. By the induction hypothesis, $\tilde{T}$ has a Gallager order $\tilde{n}_1, \ldots, \tilde{n}_{2(m-1)-1}$. The arrangement $n_1, n_2, \tilde{n}_1, \ldots, \tilde{n}_{2(m-1)-1}$ is a Gallager order of T.

Now let $m \geq 2$ and $n_1, n_2 \ldots, n_{2m-1}$ be a Gallager order of T. Then n_1 and n_2 are sibling nodes and leaves. Let $\tilde{T}$ be the tree we get after removing n_1 and n_2 from T. $n_3, \ldots, n_{2m-1}$ is a Gallager order of $\tilde{T}$. By induction, $\tilde{T}$ is a Huffman tree. But then T is also a Huffman tree.   □

Remark. The statement of the proposition and the proof are also correct under the weaker assumption that one node has weight 0.

We use the following data structure to represent a code tree:
      type node = struct
            string   *symbol*
            int   *weight*
            node   *parent, left, right, prev, next*

A node can store a message in the variable *symbol*. We only use this in leaf nodes. The variable *weight* stores the weight of the node. The variable *parent* references the predecessor, *left* the left and *right* the right successor in the tree, and *prev* the predecessor and *next* the successor in the Gallager order. A tree is then represented by a linked structure of nodes.

Let n_1 and n_2 be nodes in a weighted code tree T. By $\tilde{m}_1$ and $\tilde{m}_2$, we denote the predecessors of n_1 and n_2 in T and by m_1 and m_2 the predecessors of n_1 and n_2 regarding the Gallager order. By swapping the variables $n_1.parent$ and $n_2.parent$, $n_1.prev$ and $n_2.prev$, $n_1.next$ and $n_2.next$, $m_1.next$ and $m_2.next$ as well as $\tilde{m}_1.left$ or $\tilde{m}_1.right$ with $\tilde{m}_2.left$ or $\tilde{m}_2.right$ a new code tree $\tilde{T}$ is created. The tree $\tilde{T}$ results from T by exchanging the subtrees with roots n_1 and n_2. We say $\tilde{T}$ is created from T by *exchanging the nodes n_1 and n_2*. If n_1 and n_2 have the same weight, i.e., $n_1.weight = n_2.weight$, then $\tilde{T}$ is a weighted code tree.

Lemma 4.49. *Let $n_1, \ldots, n_\ell, \ldots, n_k, \ldots, n_{2m-1}$ be a Gallager order of the nodes of T, n_ℓ and n_k be nodes with $w(n_\ell) = w(n_k)$, and $\tilde{T}$ result from T by exchanging the nodes n_ℓ and n_k. Then*

$$n_1, \ldots, n_{\ell-1}, n_k, n_{\ell+1}, \ldots, n_{k-1}, n_\ell, n_{k+1}, \ldots, n_{2m-1}$$

is a Gallager order of the nodes of $\tilde{T}$.

Proof. Because of $w(n_\ell) = w(n_k)$, the weights of the sequence $n_1, \ldots, n_{\ell-1}$, $n_k, \ n_{\ell+1}, \ldots, n_{k-1}, n_\ell, n_{k+1}, \ldots, n_{2m-1}$ are sorted in ascending order. The condition concerning the sibling nodes is also fulfilled. □

Figure 4.38 shows the exchange of the node $\boxed{A\,2}$ with the subtree with root 2 and its successors $\boxed{F\,1}$ and $\boxed{E\,1}$.

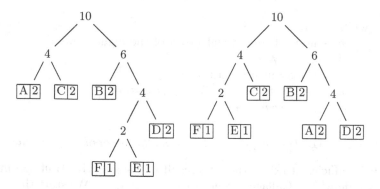

Fig. 4.38: Exchanging two nodes.

We now describe the algorithm of Faller, Gallager and Knuth. The algorithm starts with the NULL node. We depict the NULL node with

$$\boxed{\,0}.$$

It represents the messages from the source that have not yet been sent. At the beginning of the algorithm, all messages of the source are represented by the NULL node. The NULL node is a leaf, has weight 0, is present in every code tree and is the first node in the Gallager order.

If the source sends a symbol m for the first time, we call the function *InsertNode*(m). *InsertNode* generates two new nodes n_1 and n_2 and adds them to the NULL node. The left successor of NULL becomes n_1 – it represents the new NULL node – and the right successor n_2. It represents m. The old NULL node is now an inner node. We call it n. *InsertNode* initializes the nodes n, n_1 and n_2. In the Gallager order n_1 comes first, then n_2 and finally n. Figure 4.39 shows the code trees for the empty message and for a message A.

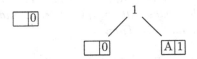

Fig. 4.39: Code tree for a single element.

After receiving a symbol m, the TreeUpdate algorithm updates the Huffman tree.

Algorithm 4.50.
  void TreeUpdate(message m)
  1   $n \leftarrow$ leaf node corresponding to m
  2   if n is the NULL node
  3   then *InsertNode*(m)
  4         $n \leftarrow n.parent$
  5   while $n \neq$ root node do
  6       $\tilde{n} \leftarrow$ node of equal weight to n of the highest order
  7   if $n.parent \neq \tilde{n}$
  8   then exchange n with $\tilde{n}$
  9       $n.weight \leftarrow n.weight + 1$, $n \leftarrow n.parent$
  10 $n.weight \leftarrow n.weight + 1$

Proposition 4.51. *The adaptive Huffman method generates a compact code.*

Proof. It is sufficient to show that the result of the adaptive Huffman procedure is a code with a Gallager order (Proposition 4.48). We start the procedure with a tree with a Gallager order. Therefore, it is sufficient to show that the Gallager order is preserved when executing Algorithm 4.50. According to Lemma 4.49, if two nodes of the same weight are swapped, the Gallager order is maintained. If we increase the weight of a node by one, it is possible that we violate the Gallager order. We therefore swap the node with the node of the same weight and highest Gallager order. At this position we can increase the weight of n by one without violating the Gallager order. □

Example. Figures 4.40 and 4.41 show the insertion of the message F: First we add a new NULL node and a node representing F (see the second code tree).

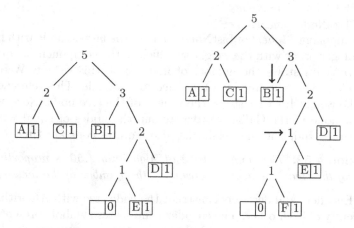

Fig. 4.40: Inserting F.

We swap the two nodes marked with an arrow and get the first code tree of the following figure. Then we increment the weights along the path from the node representing F up to the root. The result is the second code tree in Figure 4.41.

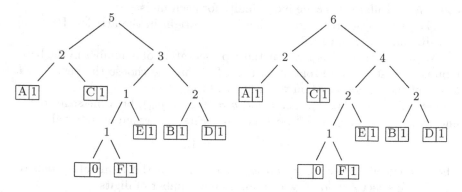

Fig. 4.41: Swap two nodes and update weights.

To implement line 6 of Algorithm 4.50 efficiently, we introduce an additional data structure, the *weight list*. This allows us to execute line 6 of the algorithm in constant time. The weight list contains all weights that are present in the tree. We organize the list as a double linked list, sorted by weights.

```
type ListNode = struct
     int         weight
     node        highest
     int         nrNodes
     ListNode    next, prev
```
The component *highest* of ListNode refers to the largest node with respect to the Gallager order with the weight specified in the component *weight*; the variable *nrNodes* stores the number of nodes with this weight. We extend the node element of the tree by a reference to ListNode. This references the node in the weight list that stores the weight of the tree node. Now, we find the largest node in the Gallager order among the nodes of equal weight in constant time. Updating the weight list also requires constant time.

Proposition 4.52. *The running time of Algorithm 4.50 is proportional to the depth of the tree. The depth is always $\leq$ the number of the messages - 1.*

Remark. Encoders and decoders construct the code tree with Algorithm 4.50 independently of each other. The encoder compresses symbols present in the Huffman tree. The first time a symbol occurs, it is sent uncompressed to the decoder. The decoder can therefore extend the code tree in the same way as the encoder.

4.6.3 Arithmetic Codes

Arithmetic coding does not use code tables to encode single symbols or blocks of symbols of fixed length. It assigns a complete message of any length to a code. We calculate this code individually for each message.

The method of arithmetic coding has its origin in the articles [Pasco76] and [Rissanen76] from 1976.

An arithmetic code is given by the representation of a number in the base-b numeral system (see Proposition B.2). For this, we choose the base $b \in \mathbb{N}$, $b > 1$, of the numeral system which we will use.

Let (X, p), $X = \{x_1, \ldots, x_m\}$ and $p = (p_1, \ldots, p_m)$, be a message source and let $x := x_{i_1} \ldots x_{i_n} \in X^n$ be a message. First we assign an interval to x:

$$x \longmapsto [\alpha, \beta[\subset [0, 1[.$$

Then we encode x with $c = .c_1 c_2 c_3 \ldots \in [\alpha, \beta[$ in the numeral system to base-b. We select c in $[\alpha, \beta[$ with a minimum number of digits.
Then the code word is $c_1 c_2 \ldots \in \{a_0, \ldots, a_{b-1}\}^*$. For $b = 2$ we get codes in $\{0, 1\}^*$, and for $b = 10$ we get codes in $\{0, 1, 2, 3, 4, 5, 6, 7, 8, 9\}^*$.

Interval assignment. We now describe how to assign a message to an interval. We assign a subinterval of the unit interval $[0, 1[$ to each symbol. The length of the subinterval is the probability with which the symbol occurs. The subintervals obtained in the first step are further subdivided according to the same procedure in order to obtain the intervals for messages of length 2.

Example. Let $X = \{a, b, c, d, e\}$, $p = (0.3, 0.3, 0.2, 0.1, 0.1)$. Figure 4.42 shows the intervals assigned to the messages $a, b, c, d, e, ba, bb, bc, bd$ and be.

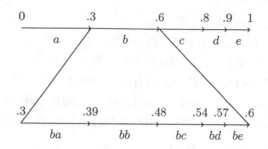

Fig. 4.42: Interval assignment.

We now describe the general case for a message source (X, p), $X = \{x_1, \ldots, x_m\}$ and $p = (p_1, \ldots, p_m)$.

We introduce the following notations for an interval $I = [\alpha, \beta[$.

$$t + I := [t + \alpha, t + \beta[,$$
$$lI := [l\alpha, l\beta[.$$

Let $\mathcal{I} := \{[\alpha, \beta[\mid [\alpha, \beta[\subset [0, 1[\}$ be the set of all subintervals of the interval $[0, 1[$ which are closed to the left and open to the right. Recursively, we describe the map which assigns a message to an element of $\mathcal{I}$.

$$I : X^* \setminus \{\varepsilon\} \longrightarrow \mathcal{I}$$

is defined by

$$I(x_i) := \left[\sum_{j=1}^{i-1} p_j, \sum_{j=1}^{i} p_j \right[,$$
$$I(x_{i_1} \ldots x_{i_n}) := \alpha + (\beta - \alpha)I(x_{i_n}), \text{ where } [\alpha, \beta[= I(x_{i_1} \ldots x_{i_{n-1}}).$$

Remark. The length of $I(x_i)$ equals p_i and the length of $I(x_{i_1} \ldots x_{i_n})$ is $l = \prod_{j=1}^{n} p_{i_j}$. The length of the interval is therefore equal to the probability with which the message $x_{i_1} \ldots x_{i_n}$ occurs. Further, we get

$$[0, 1[= \dot{\bigcup}_{1 \leq i \leq m} I(x_i) \text{ and } [0, 1[= \dot{\bigcup}_{i_1 \ldots i_n} I(x_{i_1} \ldots x_{i_n}).$$

Consequently, the representation of c in the numeral system with base b for a prescribed n is within exactly one interval $I(x_{i_1} \ldots x_{i_n})$. Therefore, c and n uniquely define $x_{i_1} \ldots x_{i_n}$, i.e., the arithmetic coding is uniquely decodable.

Example. Let $X = \{a, b, c, d, e\}$, $p = (0.3, 0.3, 0.2, 0.1, 0.1)$.
$I(a) = [.0, .3[$, $I(b) = [.3, .6[$, $I(c) = [.6, .8[$, $I(d) = [.8, .9[$ and $I(e) = [.9, 1[$.

1. Calculate $I(adeeba)$:

$$I(a) = [.0, .3[,$$
$$I(ad) = .0 + .3\, I(d) = [.24, .27[,$$
$$I(ade) = .24 + .03\, I(e) = [.267, .27[,$$
$$I(adee) = .267 + .003\, I(e) = [.2697, .27[,$$
$$I(adeeb) = .2697 + .0003\, I(b) = [.26979, .26988[,$$
$$I(adeeba) = .26979 + .00009\, I(a) = [.26979, .269817[.$$

Represent $I(adeeba)$ by $.2698$.

2. Calculate $I(adeebb)$:

$$I(adeebb) = .26979 + .00009\, I(b) = [.269817, .269844[.$$

Represent $I(adeebb)$ by $.26982$.

Remark. Let (X, p) be a message source. We consider the arithmetic coding of X^n. As the example from above shows, we generally do not get a prefix-condition encoding of the product source X^n.

Calculation of the Representative. We now describe the algorithm that determines the representative of an interval for given interval endpoints. We consider the interval $[\alpha, \beta[$ with $\alpha = .\alpha_1 \alpha_2 \alpha_3 \ldots$ and $\beta = .\beta_1 \beta_2 \beta_2 \beta_3 \ldots$.
Let $\alpha_i = \beta_i$, for $i = 1, \ldots, t-1$ and $\alpha_t < \beta_t$.
For all $\gamma = .\gamma_1 \gamma_2 \ldots \in [\alpha, \beta[$, we have $\gamma_i = \alpha_i$, $i = 1, \ldots, t-1$, i.e., each representative has $.\alpha_1 \ldots \alpha_{t-1}$ as prefix.
When determining the representative r with the shortest representation, we consider the following cases:

1. If $\alpha = .\alpha_1 \ldots \alpha_k$, $\alpha_k \neq 0$ and $k \leq t$, then $.\alpha_1 \ldots \alpha_k$ is the shortest representative.
2. If $.\alpha_1 \ldots \alpha_{t-1}(\alpha_t + 1)$ is still $< \beta$, we increment α_t by 1.
3. There remains the case $.\alpha_1 \ldots \alpha_{t-1}(\alpha_t + 1) = \beta$, i.e., $\alpha_t + 1 = \beta_t$ and $\beta_{t+1} = \beta_{t+2} = \ldots = 0$.
   Let τ be the first position after position t with $\alpha_\tau < b - 1$, i.e., $\alpha_{t+1} = \alpha_{t+2} = \ldots = \alpha_{\tau-1} = b - 1$ and $\alpha_\tau < b - 1$. Then we set

$$r = \begin{cases} .\alpha_1 \ldots \alpha_{\tau-1} & \text{if } 0 = \alpha_\tau = \alpha_{\tau+1} = \ldots, \\ .\alpha_1 \ldots (\alpha_\tau + 1) & \text{otherwise.} \end{cases}$$

Proposition 4.53. *Let* $r(x_{i_1} \ldots x_{i_n})$ *be the encoding of* $x_{i_1} \ldots x_{i_n}$ *over* $\{0, \ldots, b-1\}$. *Then*

$$|r(x_{i_1} \ldots x_{i_n})| \leq \log_b \left(\prod_{j=1}^{n} p_{i_j}^{-1} \right) + 1,$$

i.e., the length of an encoded message is bounded by the logarithm to base b of the reciprocal occurrence probability $\mathrm{p}(x_{i_1} \ldots x_{i_n})^{-1} = \prod_{j=1}^{n} p_{i_j}^{-1}$ *of the message plus 1, thus by the information content of the message plus 1 (see Definition 4.38).*

Proof. Let $r = r(x_{i_1} \ldots x_{i_n})$. We have $|r| \leq \log_b \left(\prod_{j=1}^{n} p_{i_j}^{-1} \right) + 1$ if and only if $\log_b \left(\prod_{j=1}^{n} p_{i_j} \right) \leq -(|r| - 1)$. Since $\beta - \alpha = \prod_{j=1}^{n} p_{i_j}$, it is sufficient to show

$$\beta - \alpha \leq b^{-(|r|-1)}. \qquad (*)$$

Let $I(x_{i_1}, \ldots, x_{i_n}) = [\alpha, \beta[$, $\alpha = .\alpha_1 \alpha_2 \alpha_3 \ldots$ and $\beta = .\beta_1 \beta_2 \beta_3 \ldots$, $\alpha_1 = \beta_1, \alpha_2 = \beta_2, \ldots, \alpha_{t-1} = \beta_{t-1}, \alpha_t < \beta_t$.
$\alpha_{t+1} = \ldots = \alpha_{\tau-1} = b - 1$, $\alpha_\tau < b - 1$, for some $\tau \geq t + 1$.

$$\begin{aligned}
\beta - \alpha &= \beta - .\beta_1 \ldots \beta_{t-1} - (\alpha - .\alpha_1 \ldots \alpha_{t-1}) \\
&= .0 \ldots 0 \beta_t \ldots \qquad - \\
&\quad .0 \ldots 0 \alpha_t \alpha_{t+1} \ldots \alpha_{\tau-1} \alpha_\tau \ldots .
\end{aligned}$$

Since $\beta - \alpha$ has a digit $\neq 0$ for the first time at the tth position after the point, we conclude $\beta - \alpha \leq b^{-(t-1)}$.

If $\alpha = 0$ then $r = 0$ and $|r| = 1$, hence $(*)$ is fulfilled.

Now let $\alpha > 0$. Finally, we consider the remaining cases to determine r (see page 186). In the cases of points 1 and 2, we have $|r| \leq t$ and therefore $\beta - \alpha \leq b^{-(t-1)} \leq b^{-(|r|-1)}$.

In the third case $\beta - \alpha \leq \beta - .\alpha_1 \ldots \alpha_{\tau-1} = b^{-(\tau-1)}$. $|r| = \tau - 1$ or $|r| = \tau$. In all cases $\beta - \alpha \leq b^{-(|r|-1)}$ is true. $\qquad \square$

Proposition 4.54. *Let X be a message source, let C be an arithmetic encoding of X^* over $\{0, 1\}$, and let l_n be the average code word length, averaged over all encodings of messages from X^n.[13] Then*

$$l_n \leq n\mathrm{H}(X) + 1,$$

where $\mathrm{H}(X)$ denotes the entropy of the source X (Definition 4.38).

Proof. Let $X = \{x_1, \ldots, x_m\}$ and $p = (p_1, \ldots, p_m)$. By Proposition 4.53

$$|r(x_{i_1} \ldots x_{i_n})| \leq \log_2 \left(\prod_{j=1}^{n} p_{i_j}^{-1} \right) + 1.$$

Hence,

---

[13] X^n equipped with the product probability, which is defined by $\mathrm{p}(x_{i_1} \ldots x_{i_n}) = \mathrm{p}(x_{i_1}) \cdot \ldots \cdot \mathrm{p}(x_{i_n}) = p_{i_1} \cdot \ldots \cdot p_{i_n}$, is a source. We call it the *nth power of X*.

$$l_n = \sum_{(i_1,\ldots,i_n)} p(x_{i_1} \ldots x_{i_n}) |r(x_{i_1} \ldots x_{i_n})|$$

$$\leq \sum_{(i_1,\ldots,i_n)} p(x_{i_1} \ldots x_{i_n}) \left(\log_2 \left(\prod_{j=1}^{n} p_{i_j}^{-1} \right) + 1 \right)$$

$$= \sum_{(i_1,\ldots,i_n)} p(x_{i_1} \ldots x_{i_n}) \sum_{j=1}^{n} \log_2(p_{i_j}^{-1}) + \sum_{(i_1,\ldots,i_n)} p(x_{i_1} \ldots x_{i_n})$$

$$= \sum_{j=1}^{n} \sum_{i_j=1}^{m} \sum_{(i_1,\ldots,\hat{i}_j,\ldots,i_n)} p(x_{i_1} \ldots x_{i_n}) \log_2(p_{i_j}^{-1}) + 1$$

$$= \sum_{j=1}^{n} \sum_{i_j=1}^{m} p_{i_j} \log_2(p_{i_j}^{-1}) + 1 = n\,H(X) + 1.$$

We used $\sum_{(i_1,\ldots,\hat{i}_j,\ldots i_n)} p(x_{i_1} \ldots x_{i_j} \ldots x_{i_n}) = p(x_{i_j}) = p_{i_j}$.   □

Remark. We get $l_n/n \leq H(X) + 1/n$ for the average code word length per symbol (Proposition 4.54). The comparison with the Noiseless Coding Theorem (Proposition 4.39), which says $H(X) \leq l_n/n$, shows that the upper bound of l_n/n differs only by $1/n$ from the lower bound, which is determined by the Noiseless Coding Theorem. This shows that the arithmetic coding has good compression properties.

Rescaling. If the endpoints of the interval have a common prefix, we decrement the number of digits in the display of the endpoints of the interval by rescaling. Further calculations are then carried out with the interval given by the shortened representations. For rescaling, replace $[\alpha, \beta[$ with

$$[\alpha', \beta'[:= [\{b^{t-1}\alpha\}, \{b^{t-1}\beta\}[\,.$$

Here $\{x\} := x - [x]$ is the fractional part of x.
Because every number in $[\alpha, \beta[$ has $\alpha_1 \ldots \alpha_{t-1}$ as prefix, $\alpha_1 \ldots \alpha_{t-1} = \beta_1 \ldots \beta_{t-1}$ is a prefix of the code word to be calculated.

Example. Let $X = \{a, b, c, d, e\}$, $p = (0.3, 0.3, 0.2, 0.1, 0.1)$.
$I(a) = [.0, .3[, I(b) = [.3, .6[, I(c) = [.6, .8[, I(d) = [.8, .9[$ and $I(e) = [.9, 1[$.
    We calculate the interval I associated with *adeeba*, the representative of I and the code for the compressed message.

$$I(a) = [.0, .3[,$$
$$I(ad) = .0 + .3\,I(d) = [.24, .27[\longrightarrow 2$$
$$= [.4, .7[,$$
$$I(ade) = .4 + .3\,I(e) = [.67, .7[,$$
$$I(adee) = .67 + .03\,I(e) = [.697, .7[,$$

$$I(adeeb) = .697 + .003\, I(b) = [.6979, .6988[\longrightarrow 69$$
$$= [.79, .88[,$$
$$I(adeeba) = .79 + .09\, I(a) = [.79, .817[.$$

Represent $[.79, .817[$ by $.8$ and $I(adeeba)$ by $.2698$.

Remark. If rescaling is used, parts of the code word are already available during the encoding process. Rescaling reduces the required amount of computing.

Example. Let $X = \{a, b, c, d, e\}$, $p = (0.3, 0.3, 0.2, 0.1, 0.1)$.
$I(a) = [.0, .3[$, $I(b) = [.3, .6[$, $I(c) = [.6, .8[$, $I(d) = [.8, .9[$ and $I(e) = [.9, 1[$.
We calculate the interval $I(baaaa)$ for the message $baaaa$.

$$I(b) = [.3, .6[,$$
$$I(ba) = .3 + .3\, I(a) = [.3, .39[\longrightarrow 3$$
$$= [.0, .9[,$$
$$I(baa) = .0 + .9\, I(a) = [.0, .27[$$
$$I(baaa) = .0 + .27\, I(a) = [.0, .081[\longrightarrow 0$$
$$= [.0, .81[,$$
$$I(baaaa) = .0 + .81\, I(a) = [.0, .243[.$$

Represent $[.0, .243[$ by $.0$ and therefore $I(baaaaaa)$ by $.300$. Without rescaling, $I(baaaa) = [0.3, 0.30243[$ and $r = 0.3$. The code word is extended by rescaling.

Remark. With and without rescaling, the same code word is calculated in most cases. There is only one exception: If the word w to be encoded ends with the first element of the alphabet (let's call it a as in the examples), superfluous zeros can occur at the end of the code word during rescaling (as in the second example). Whether it happens depends on the concrete probabilities of the symbols, but the more a's there are at the end, the more likely it is. Of course, you could simply delete the superfluous zeros at the end. But this does not work anymore if we code an input stream and send the digits of the code word as soon as they are available (without waiting for the encoding of the whole message). The phenomenon of superfluous zeros does not occur if we terminate messages to be encoded with a special character "EOF" for the end of the message (and EOF is not the first character of the alphabet). The use of an EOF symbol is helpful for decoding; then a separate transmission of the message length is no longer necessary (see below).

Underflow. Underflow can occur when the interval endpoints are close together and rescaling is not possible. In this situation the representation of the interval endpoints increases with each step. We speak of underflow and discuss the underflow problem first with an example.

Example. Let $X = \{a, b, c, d, e\}$, $p = (0.3, 0.3, 0.2, 0.1, 0.1)$.
$I(a) = [.0, .3[$, $I(b) = [.3, .6[$, $I(c) = [.6, .8[$, $I(d) = [.8, .9[$ and $I(e) = [.9, 1[$.
We calculate the interval for $I(bbabacb)$.

$$I(b) = [.3, .6[,$$
$$I(bb) = .3 + .3\, I(b) = [.39, .48[,$$
$$I(bba) = .39 + .09\, I(a) = [.39, .417[,$$
$$I(bbab) = .39 + .027\, I(b) = [.3981, .4062[,$$
$$I(bbaba) = .3981 + .0081\, I(a) = [.3981, .40053[,$$
$$I(bbabac) = .3981 + .00243\, I(c) = [.399558, .400044[,$$
$$I(bbabacb) = .399558 + .000464\, I(b) = [.3997038, .3998496[.$$

Represent $I(bbabacb)$ by .3998.

The interval $I(bbab) = [.3981, .4062[$. Now it can happen that during the processing of the further symbols, after each symbol the interval contains the number 0.4, i.e., $\alpha = .39\ldots$ $\beta = .40\ldots$. Then rescaling is not possible. The interval $[\alpha, \beta[$ becomes shorter with each step. The number of digits required to represent α and β increases with each step. This is a problem if we use in our computations only finitely many digits. The underflow treatment, which we now explain, provides a solution to this problem.

Let $\alpha = .\alpha_1\alpha_2\alpha_3\ldots$ and $\beta = .\beta_1\beta_2\beta_3\ldots$,
We say *underflow* occurs if

$$\beta_1 = \alpha_1 + 1, \alpha_2 = b - 1 \text{ and } \beta_2 = 0.$$

In the case of underflow, $r = .r_1 r_2 \ldots \in [\alpha, \beta[$ satisfies

$$r_2 = \begin{cases} b - 1 & \text{if } r_1 = \alpha_1, \\ 0 & \text{if } r_1 = \beta_1, \end{cases}$$

i.e., r_2 depends functionally on r_1.

Now we describe the algorithm to handle underflow.
We cancel α_2, β_2 and r_2 in the representation of α, β and r. We get $\alpha = .\alpha_1\alpha_3\ldots$, $\beta = .\beta_1\beta_3\ldots$ and $r = .r_1 r_3 \ldots$.
This operation is translation by $.\alpha_1(b - 1 - \alpha_1)$ followed by stretching with factor b. For $x \in [\alpha, \beta[$, we get

$$.x_1 x_2 x_3 \to b(.x_1 x_2 x_3 - \alpha_1(b - 1 - \alpha_1)) = .x_1 x_3.$$

If underflow occurs, $|\beta - \alpha| < \frac{1}{b^2}$.

The encoding procedure is as follows:

1. While $\alpha_1 \neq \beta_1$:
   i. As long as there is underflow, we perform the underflow treatment, i.e., we remove the second digit after the point from α and β and increment the variable *count* (it counts how often the second digit has been removed).
   ii. Process the next symbol from the input, i.e., apply the algorithm to divide the interval based on the next symbol from the input.
2. Output $r_1 = \alpha_1$ (here $\alpha_1 = \beta_1$ holds) and *count* times r_2 depending on r_1.

During underflow treatment, α_1 and β_1 do not change. If α_1 or β_1 change when processing the next symbol from the input, the case $\alpha_1 = \beta_1$ occurs. Therefore, the digits removed from r during the underflow treatment are all the same.

Example. Let $X = \{a, b, c, d, e\}$, $p = (0.3, 0.3, 0.2, 0.1, 0.1)$.
$I(a) = [.0, .3[$, $I(b) = [.3, .6[$, $I(c) = [.6, .8[$, $I(d) = [.8, .9[$ and $I(e) = [.9, 1[$.
We calculate the interval for $I(bbabacb)$.

$$I(b) = [.3, .6[,$$
$$I(bb) = .3 + .3\,I(b) = [.39, .48[,$$
$$I(bba) = .39 + .09\,I(a) = [.39, .417[,$$
$$I(bbab) = .39 + .027\,I(b) = [.3981, .4062[\longrightarrow [.381, .462[, \text{ count} = 1,$$
$$I(bbaba) = .381 + .081\,I(a) = [.381, .4053[,$$
$$I(bbabac) = .381 + .0243\,I(c) = [.39558, .40044[\longrightarrow [.3558, .4044[, \text{ count} = 2,$$
$$I(bbabacb) = .3558 + .0486\,I(b) = [.37038, .38496[$$
$$\longrightarrow 399, \text{ count} = 0, \; [.7038 + .8496[\longrightarrow 8.$$

Represent $I(bbabac)$ by .3998.

Rescaling and underflow treatment shorten the representation of the interval limits. This makes it possible to perform the calculations with a fixed number of digits. In the application an integer arithmetic with 32 bits is sufficient. Floating-point arithmetic is not suitable due to the limited accuracy and memory that floating-point formats allow.

Decoding. Input is a compressed message c_m and its length n. The original message $x_{i_1} \ldots x_{i_n}$ is searched for. We calculate $x_{i_1} \ldots x_{i_n}$ recursively:

1. We have $i_1 = j$ if and only if $c_m \in I(x_j)$.
2. Let $x_{i_1} \ldots x_{i_{k-1}}$ and $I(x_{i_1} \ldots x_{i_{k-1}}) = [\alpha, \beta[$ and $l = \beta - \alpha$ be calculated. Then $i_k = j$ if $c_m \in \alpha + l\,I(x_j)$. This again is equivalent to $(c_m - \alpha)/l \in I(x_j)$.

Calculate α and l from $I(x) = [\alpha_x, \beta_x[$ and $l_x = \beta_x - \alpha_x$:

$$\alpha_{new} = \alpha_{old} + l_{old}\alpha_x,$$
$$l_{new} = l_{old}l_x.$$

Example. Let $X = \{a, b, c, d, e\}$, $p = (0.3, 0.3, 0.2, 0.1, 0.1)$.
$I(a) = [.0, .3[$, $I(b) = [.3, .6[$, $I(c) = [.6, .8[$, $I(d) = [.8, .9[$ and $I(e) = [.9, 1[$.
Given: .2697, 4.

α	l	$(c_m - \alpha)_{/l}$	x
0	1	.2697	a
0	.3	.899	d
.24	.03	.99	e
.267	.003	.9	e

Decoding with Rescaling. In order to simplify the calculation when decoding a message, we apply rescaling. We describe the algorithm using an example.

Example. Let $X = \{a, b, c, d, e\}$, $p = (0.3, 0.3, 0.2, 0.1, 0.1)$.
$I(a) = [.0, .3[$, $I(b) = [.3, .6[$, $I(c) = [.6, .8[$, $I(d) = [.8, .9[$ and $I(e) = [.9, 1[$.
Given code: .2698, 6.

c_m	α	l	$(c_m - \alpha)_{/l}$	x
.2698	.0	1	.2698	a
	.0	.3	.8993333	d
	.24	.03	.9933333	e
.698	.4	.3		
	.67	.03	.99333333	e
.98	.7	.3		
	.97	.03	.3333337	b
.8	.7	.3		
	.79	.09	.1111111	a

We perform rescaling as soon as common leading digits appear in α and β. A necessary condition for this is that leading zeros are produced in l. We multiply α, l and c_m by b^k, where k is equal to the number of common leading digits.

Coding the Length of the Message. For decoding, the length n of the message must be known. We provide the decoder with the length n outside the encoded message, or we agree on a special symbol "EOF" for the end of the message. The source sends EOF with a very small probability. The decoder then recognizes the end of the message. Of course, this additional symbol slightly lengthens the encoded message.

Adaptive Arithmetic Coding. With *adaptive arithmetic coding*, the statistical model is developed with the encoding of the message, just as with adaptive Huffman coding. In contrast to Huffman coding, the effects of changing the statistical model on the encoder and decoder are small. The further division of an already calculated subinterval is simply carried out according to the newly determined probabilities. We make this clear with an example.

Example. Let $X = \{a, b, c, d, e\}$, $p = (\frac{1}{5}, \frac{1}{5}, \frac{1}{5}, \frac{1}{5}, \frac{1}{5})$.
$I(a) = [.0, .2[$, $I(b) = [.2, .4[$, $I(c) = [.4, .6[$, $I(d) = [.6, .8[$ and $I(e) = [.8, 1[$.
We calculate the interval I associated with *adeeba*.

Source	Calculation of the Interval
$(\frac{1}{5}, \frac{1}{5}, \frac{1}{5}, \frac{1}{5}, \frac{1}{5})$	$I(a) = [.0, .2[$
$(\frac{1}{3}, \frac{1}{6}, \frac{1}{6}, \frac{1}{6}, \frac{1}{6})$	$I(ad) = .0 + .2\,I(d) = [.132, .166[\quad \longrightarrow 1$
	$= [.32, .66[$
$(\frac{2}{7}, \frac{1}{7}, \frac{1}{7}, \frac{2}{7}, \frac{1}{7})$	$I(ade) = .32 + .34\,I(e) = [.61, .64[\quad \longrightarrow 1$
	$= [.2, .4[$
$(\frac{1}{4}, \frac{1}{8}, \frac{1}{8}, \frac{1}{4}, \frac{1}{4})$	$I(adee) = .2 + .2\,I(e) = [.35, .7[$
$(\frac{2}{9}, \frac{1}{9}, \frac{1}{9}, \frac{2}{9}, \frac{1}{3})$	$I(adeeb) = .35 + .35\,I(b) = [.427, .4655[\longrightarrow 1$
	$= [.27, .655[$
$(\frac{1}{5}, \frac{1}{5}, \frac{1}{10}, \frac{1}{5}, \frac{3}{10})$	$I(adeeba) = .27 + .385\,I(a) = [.27, .347[$

Represent $I(adeeba)$ by $.1113$.

Remark. We have discussed two methods of source coding, Huffman coding and arithmetic coding. With the Huffman method, we create code tables and use them for encoding and decoding. Arithmetic coding does not use code tables. Compared to Huffman coding, however, it requires considerable computational effort. When implementing the procedure, we use integer arithmetic (in floating-point arithmetic, the coded message is limited by the number of bytes of the number format and is therefore too small). The compression efficiency of the two methods is closely related.

4.6.4 Lempel-Ziv Codes

Lempel[14] and Ziv[15] introduced new techniques for data compression in [ZivLem77] and [ZivLem78]. In contrast to Huffman or arithmetic coding, these methods do not require a statistical model.

The methods of Lempel and Ziv are called *dictionary methods*. The idea is to store frequently occurring text segments in a dictionary. In the text to be compressed, we replace the text segments with references to the text segments. If the reference requires fewer bits than the replaced text segment, compression occurs.

There are many variants of the two original algorithms, which are called LZ77 and LZ78 after the year of their origin. These variants are used by popular compression applications, such as GNU zip or Unix compress, for data transmission, such as V.42bis, and for compression of graphics formats, such as Graphics Interchange Format (GIF), Portable Network Graphics (PNG) or Adobe PDF.

---

[14] Abraham Lempel (1936 –) is an Israeli computer scientist.
[15] Jacob Ziv (1931 –) is an Israeli information theoretician.

Lempel-Ziv Algorithm with Sliding Window. The LZ77 algorithm lets a window of constant size slide over the character string $x_1 \ldots x_n$ to be encoded. The window consists of two parts, the text buffer and the preview buffer. The text buffer contains characters that have already been encoded; the characters from the preview buffer are still to be encoded. Let w be the length of the text buffer and v the length of the preview buffer. See Figure 4.43.

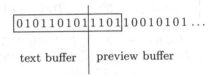

text buffer | preview buffer

Fig. 4.43: LZ77 compression.

We recursively explain the encoding and assume that the characters $x_1 \ldots x_{i-1}$ are already encoded. The text buffer contains the characters $x_{i-w} \ldots x_{i-1}$ and the preview buffer the characters $x_i x_{i+1} \ldots x_{i+v-1}$. The main idea now is to find a string that starts in the text buffer and has the longest match with the string $x_i x_{i+1} \ldots x_{i+v-1}$ in the preview buffer.

For k with $i - w \le k \le i - 1$, let

$$\ell_k = \max\{j \mid j \le v \text{ and } x_k \ldots x_{k+j-1} = x_i \ldots x_{i+j-1}\}$$

and

$$m = \max\{\ell_k \mid i - w \le k \le i - 1\}.$$

The longest match consists of m characters and starts in the text buffer with x_{i-j}, where $\ell_{i-j} = m$. It can extend into the preview buffer.

If $m \ge 1$, we encode

$$x_i \ldots x_{i+m-1} \longmapsto (j, m).$$

We move the window m positions to the right.

If we do not find a match, i.e., $m = 0$, then we encode

$$x_i \longmapsto x_i$$

and move the window one position to the right.

The output stream contains the two different data types, characters and references, i.e., pairs (j, m), where j indicates the index of the first character of the match relative to the end of the text buffer, and m indicates the length of the match. We code both data types with a fixed number of bits and distinguish them by a leading bit, for example, 0 if a character follows and 1 if a reference follows. If we represent j with 8 bits and m with 4 bits, we get a text buffer with 256 bytes and a preview buffer with 16 bytes. To encode a character we need 7 bits and to encode a reference we need 13 bits.

In particular, the start of the induction is now explained. At the beginning of the encoding the text buffer is empty. We cannot find any matching segments; the output stream contains the individual characters.

When implementing, we encode short matching segments through the individual characters if this results in a shorter output stream. If m is the number of matching characters, s the number of bits for encoding a character, t the number of bits for encoding a pair (j, m) and if $ms < t$, then we encode the individual characters.

The complex part of encoding is finding the longest matching segment. Greedy parsing determines the length of a match with each character in the text buffer as a starting point. Then a longest match is used. However, this does not ensure that we get the best compression rate overall. This cannot be achieved due to the complexity of the problem.

Variants of the LZ77 algorithm implement methods that allow matching segments to be accessed faster. They use a hash method or a binary search tree to address matching segments. In the text buffer, we no longer check for matches at every position, but only at positions where earlier matching segments were found.

Example. We execute the algorithm with the input $x = 01101101101$, $w = 6$ and $v = 3$. Each row of the following matrix corresponds to one step in the execution of the algorithm. The three characters of the preview buffer are limited by "|" in the first five lines. In the second column the resulting codes are noted.

$$
\begin{array}{l|l}
|011|01101101 & 0 \\
0|110|1101101 & 1 \\
01|101|101101 & (1,1) \\
011|011|01101 & (3,3) \\
011011|011|01 & (3,3) \\
011|011011|01 & (3,2)
\end{array}
$$

While compression involves a lot of computation, decompression is easy to perform. Either the codes of the individual characters are available or links are provided that are easy to evaluate.

If the encoding match extends into the preview buffer, we extend the text buffer step by step. We will now explain this point in more detail with an example. Let $w = 12$, $v = 6$ and $\ldots 111110|101010$ be the string that was encoded. The output is then $(2,6)$. We assume that $\ldots 111110|$ is already decoded and $(2,6)$ has to be decoded in the next step. We get one after the other

$$\ldots |111110|10, \ldots |111110|1010, \ldots |111110|101010.$$

The dictionary is represented by the text buffer. The sliding window technique and the constant length of the text buffer ensure that only segments that have occurred in the recent past are in the dictionary. The adaptation of the dictionary to changes in the patterns of the data to be compressed is therefore done automatically.

Lempel-Ziv Algorithms with Digital Search Tree. We study LZ78 and a variant of LZ78, the LZW method, in more detail. In both algorithms, we read the data to be compressed only once. We compress the data and generate the dictionary. In contrast to LZ77, the dictionary is explicitly constructed. We implement LZ78 with a digital search tree. The encoder generates this digital search tree while analyzing the source code. The decoder generates an identical search tree from the compressed data. We do not have to transmit any data other than the compressed data from the encoder to the decoder.

The Algorithm LZ78.

Definition 4.55. Let $X = \{x_1, \ldots, x_n\}$ be a message source and $y \in X^n$. A Lempel-Ziv decomposition of y,

$$y = y_0 \| y_1 \| \cdots \| y_k,$$

consists of pairwise distinct y_j, $0 \le j \le k$, and is defined by:

1. $y_0 := \varepsilon$.
2. For each y_i, $1 \le i \le k$, there is exactly one y_j in the sequence $y_0, \ldots, y_{i-1}$ and one $x \in X$ with $y_i = y_j \| x$.

We call the substrings y_i *phrases* of y.

We specify an algorithm for constructing a Lempel-Ziv decomposition. The algorithm uses a *digital search tree*. First we explain the data structure of a digital search tree.

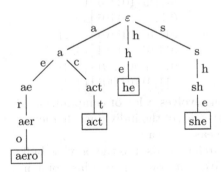

Fig. 4.44: A digital search tree.

A digital search tree is based on an alphabet X. A node of the digital search tree can have up to $|X|$ successors. Each edge is labeled with a symbol from X. No two edges starting from the same node are labeled with the same symbol. See Figure 4.44.

Each node corresponds to a string from X^*. The string results from the edge labels on the path from the root to the corresponding node. The root corresponds to the empty word ε. There are two functions associated with the digital search tree.

1. *Searching* for $x \in X^*$ is done from the root by comparing the first character of x with the edge labels of the edges starting at the root. If there is a match with an edge label, we recursively continue the search in the corresponding successor.

2. When *inserting* characters into a digital search tree, we add new nodes. If a string x is to be inserted, we perform a search with x starting from the root. If x is not in the search tree, the search ends in a node without consuming all characters of x. We call this node k. For each character of x which was not used in the search, we add another node, and label the necessary edge with the corresponding character. We append the first node to k, the second to the first appended node, and the next to the previously appended node, until all characters of x are used.

   In our application, we only add one new leaf at a time.

Example. We demonstrate the algorithm LZ78 with $x = 01011010101\ldots$, starting with a tree only consisting of the root. See Figure 4.45. The root gets the number 0. In each step, we add a leaf to the tree. We number the nodes in the order of their creation.

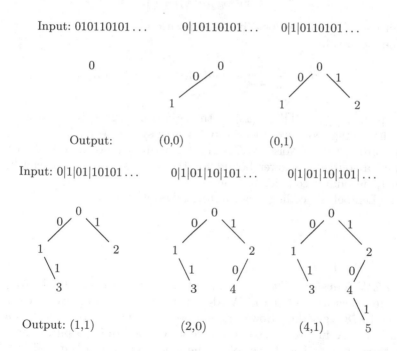

Fig. 4.45: Encoding with LZ78.

In each step, we determine a phrase of the Lempel-Ziv decomposition. It results from digital searching starting at the root. In the last node k in the search path, we extend the tree with an additional leaf. We label the edge to this leaf with the next character of the input. The phrase found corresponds to the new node.

The output consists of the last node k in the search path together with the label of the newly inserted edge. The compressed file consists of the outputs. The outputs provide the data necessary for the construction of the tree. Therefore, we can extract the code tree from the compressed file and then the original data from the code tree.

Processing the tail of the string to be compressed, the search can end at an inner node. We do not go into the technical details that are then necessary.

Remark. Let p be a probability distribution on X. By $a(x)$ we denote the number of phrases that occur in a decomposition of $x \in X^n$. The compressed data then consists of a sequence of length $a(x)$ of pairs (k, c), consisting of the number k of a node in the code tree and a symbol c. The number of nodes is then also $a(x)$. The representation of a node k requires $\log_2(a(x))$ bits and the representation of a pair (k, c) requires $\log_2(a(x)) + e$ bits (e is a constant). Altogether we need

$$a(x)(\log_2(a(x)) + e)$$

bits for encoding the Lempel-Ziv decomposition.

The mean value

$$\ell_n = \frac{1}{n} \sum_{x \in X^n} \mathrm{p}(x)a(x)(\log_2(a(x)) + e),$$

where $\mathrm{p}(x_1 \ldots x_n) = \prod_{i=1}^{n} \mathrm{p}(x_i)$ is the occurrence probability of $x_1 \ldots x_n$, gives the average code word length per source symbol from X.

According to the Noiseless Coding Theorem (Proposition 4.39), the entropy of a source is a lower bound for the average code word length of a uniquely decodable code for the source.

The Lempel-Ziv coding is asymptotically optimal, i.e.,

$$\lim_{n \to \infty} \ell_n = \mathrm{H}(X)$$

(see [ZivLem78]).

The LZW Version. The LZW variant was published in 1984 by Welch[16]. The implementation of the LZW algorithm uses a digital search tree, just like the LZ78 algorithm. However, here we start with a tree that has a leaf for each $x \in X$ in level 1 next to the root. We determine a phrase again by digital search, starting at the root. The search ends in a leaf node n. Now there are two actions.

1. Output the number of the node n.

---

[16] Terry A. Welch (1939 – 1988) was an American computer scientist.

2. Add a new leaf node to n. Label the new edge with the next character x from the input. x is the first character of the next phrase.

Now, phrases found no longer uniquely correspond to the nodes in the code tree. There can be nodes for which no phrases exist, and the phrases found are no longer necessarily pairwise distinct.

Compared to LZ78 the advantage of LZW is that the output only consists of the number of the attached node. It conserves one symbol compared to the output of LZ78.

Example. We demonstrate the operation of the encoder with the input $x =$ 010110101... in Figure 4.46.

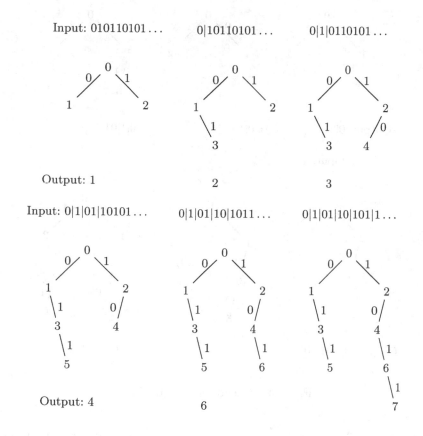

Fig. 4.46: Encoding with LZW.

The example shows that LZ78 and LZW provide different code trees.

When decoding, we reconstruct the code tree from the node numbers. This requires further consideration if the encoder uses the last inserted leaf to determine the phrase, as in the example for determining the phrase 101 with the output of node number 6.

Figure 4.47 shows the code trees constructed by the decoder. The input is the node number which is outputted by the encoder. The decoder outputs the phrase corresponding to the node. After the decoder receives the node number 6, it first reconstructs the tree that was created in the previous step. This tree does not contain a node with the number 6.

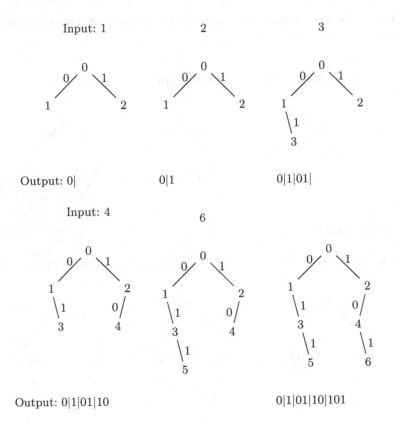

Fig. 4.47: Decoding with LZW.

By the *exceptional case*, we understand the case where the decoder has to decode a node which is not contained in its code tree. The exceptional case arises from the fact that the decoder can only construct the code tree with a delay of one step.

We now specify a procedure for handling the exceptional case. Let $y_1 \| \ldots \| y_i$ be the phrases that the encoder has found so far. The encoder inserts a node into the code tree for each phrase. So it has added a total of i nodes. We assume that the decoder has decoded the phrases $y_1 \| \ldots \| y_{i-1}$. The decoder can only reconstruct $i-1$ nodes. The only node that the decoder does not know is the node that the encoder added when it found the ith phrase y_i, that is, the node with the number i.

Let us further assume that in the next step the encoder uses the node with the number i. The node is the successor of the node that the encoder last used, the node belonging to y_{i-1}.

The node with the number i has the phrase y_i, but also the phrase $y_{i-1} \| x$, where x is the first character of y_i. Hence, $y_i = y_{i-1}x$, i.e., y_{i-1} and y_i match in the first character. The decoder can find the "unknown" node by appending a leaf to the node transmitted in the previous step and labeling the edge with the first character of y_{i-1}.

Only limited memory is available for the dictionary, which we implemented with a digital search tree. Therefore, strategies have to be implemented to adapt the dictionary to changing patterns in the text to be compressed and to prevent the dictionary from becoming full and not being able to add entries anymore. Possible strategies are to delete the dictionary completely after a limit of the occupied memory is exceeded or if the compression rate falls below a given limit. Another option is to monitor the usage of the entries and remove the entry that has not been used for the longest time.

Exercises.

1. The elements a, b, c, d, e, f, h, j are stored in the nodes of a binary tree. Pre-order output creates the list c, a, h, f, b, j, d, e, post-order output the list h, f, a, d, e, j, b, c. How can the binary tree be constructed from these data? Display the binary tree. Describe your procedure and justify the individual steps. Under what circumstances is the tree uniquely identified by the pre-order and post-order outputs?

2. Specify all binary search trees for $\{1, 2, 3, 4\}$.

3. A binary tree can be assigned to each arithmetic expression with the operators + and *. Develop a function that generates an arithmetic expression with parentheses and postfix notation when traversing the assigned tree.

4. Let v be a node in a binary search tree. By pv we denote the node that occurs immediately before v in the in-order output (if any). Show: If v has a left successor (in the tree), pv has no right successor. What is the equivalent statement for the node sv that occurs immediately after v in the in-order output?

5. Develop and implement an algorithm that determines whether a given sequence of nodes of a binary search tree with the keys $s_1, s_2, \ldots, s_n = s$ can occur as a search path for s.

6. Let T be a binary search tree, x a leaf of T and y the predecessor of x. The element e is stored in x and the element f is stored in y. Show that f is either the smallest element in T that is greater than e, or the largest element in T that is less than e.

7. Let $n \in \mathbb{N}$. Show that there is a binary search tree with n nodes of height $\lfloor \log_2(n) \rfloor + 1$.

8. Prove or refute with a counterexample the following statement: For each AVL tree, there is a sequence of keys that leads to this tree when inserted, without rotations.

9. The set $\{1, \ldots, n\}$ is stored in an empty AVL tree in ascending order. Determine the height of the tree.

10. Let T be a binary search tree. We get $\overline{T}$ by replacing the null references with external nodes in T. In $\overline{T}$ each node that is not a leaf has two successors and the leaves are the external nodes. A *red-black tree* is a binary search tree in which each edge is colored red or black, and in $\overline{T}$ the following properties are satisfied:
    a. The input edges of leaves are black.
    b. In a path, a red edge is always followed by a black edge.
    c. All paths from the root to a leaf contain the same number of black edges.

    The red-black conditions guarantee good balance characteristics. Let T be a red-black tree with n nodes. Show that the height of T is limited by $2 \log_2(n + 1)$.

11. Let $(f_i)_{i \geq 0}$ be the sequence of Fibonacci numbers. In the *Fibonacci search* the division of the sorted array $a[1..n]$, which contains the element to be searched for, is done with the help of the Fibonacci numbers. First, we assume that $n = f_k - 1$ holds. The array is then divided into the sections $a[1..f_{k-1} - 1], a[f_{k-1}]$ and $a[f_{k-1} + 1..f_k - 1]$ of lengths f_{k-1}, 1 and f_{k-2}. If the wanted element is not at position f_{k-1}, the search is continued recursively with $a[1..f_{k-1} - 1]$ or $a[f_{k-1} + 1..f_k - 1]$. If $n + 1$ is not a Fibonacci number, set the upper limit equal to the smallest Fibonacci number greater than $n + 1$.

    Work out the details of the Fibonacci search. Establish the connection to Fibonacci trees (see Definition 4.12) and analyze the running time of the algorithm.

12. Let S be the set consisting of key-priority pairs
    $S = \{(1, 4), (2, 1), (3, 8), (4, 5), (5, 7), (6, 6), (8, 2), (9, 3)\}$.
    a. Construct a treap by inserting the key-priority pairs in the following order:
       $(8, 2), (9, 3), (2, 1), (5, 7), (3, 8), (1, 4), (4, 5), (6, 6)$.
    b. Insert the new element $(7, 0)$ and specify all relevant intermediate steps.
    c. Delete the element $(8, 2)$ and specify all relevant intermediate steps.

   d. Which treap is created if $(7,0)$ had been inserted instead of $(8,2)$?

13. Show that there are $c_n := \frac{1}{n+1} \binom{2n}{n}$, $n \geq 0$, binary trees with n nodes. The numbers c_n are called *Catalan numbers*[17].

14. A B-tree B stores in alphabetical order in the root j and w, and in the first level a, c, f, i, o, r, u, v, y and z.
   a. Display B graphically.
   b. Specify the possible orders of B.
   c. Insert the elements x, p, k, q, e and l one after the other and sketch the tree after each step.

15. A B-tree B stores in alphabetical order the element m in level 0, the elements e, h, t and x in level 1 and the elements b, f, l, r, u, v, w and y in level 2.
   a. Sketch B and state the order of B.
   b. Delete h and l one after the other from B, then delete b from the tree you get after you have completed the preceding deletion. Describe the essential steps.

16. Prove or disprove the following statement: For a given set S, the number of nodes of a B-tree that stores S is unique.

17. We construct a binary search tree from a B-tree of order 4. We map the B-tree pages as follows:

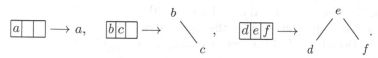

In order to obtain a binary search tree, we add the edges of the B-tree. We color the input edges of a, b, e black and the input edges of c, d, f red. Assign a red-black tree to the B-tree from Figure 4.24 (see Exercise 10). Using the defined mapping rule, show that red-black trees and fourth-order B-trees are equivalent structures. Specify the inverse transformation of the above mapping rule that assigns to each red-black tree a B-tree of order four.

18. Which of the two codes
   (a) $C_1 = \{c, bb, bbd, dea, bbaa, abbd, aacde\}$,
   (b) $C_2 = \{c, bb, bbd, dea, abbe, baad, bbaa, aacde\}$
is uniquely decodable? Justify your answer and give a counterexample if possible.

19. Let $n_1, \ldots, n_\ell \in \mathbb{N}$ and C a prefix code over Y of order n. C has n_i words of length i, $i = 1, \ldots, \ell$. Show that $n_i \leq n^i - n_1 n^{i-1} - \cdots - n_{i-1} n$, $i = 1, \ldots, \ell$.

---

[17] Eugène Charles Catalan (1814 – 1894) was a Belgian mathematician.

20. A source has the elements $\{x_1, x_2, x_3, x_4, x_5, x_6, x_7\}$ and the probabilities $p_1 = \frac{2}{7}, p_2 = p_3 = p_4 = p_5 = \frac{1}{7}, p_6 = p_7 = \frac{1}{14}$.

    a. Is the code $c_1 = 00, c_2 = 11, c_3 = 010, c_4 = 100, c_5 = 101, c_6 = 0110, c_7 = 0111$ (c_i encodes x_i for $i = 1, \ldots, 7$) compact?

    b. Are there compact codes over $\{0,1\}$ for the above source with different word lengths? Specify such a code if possible.

21. The Huffman algorithm can be extended to any alphabet Y. How to construct the code?

22. Let (X, p) be a message source. $X = \{x_1, \ldots, x_{256}\}$ and $p_i = \frac{1}{256}$. Is $C = \{c_1 c_2 c_3 c_4 c_5 c_6 c_7 c_8 | c_i \in \{0,1\}\}$ a compact code for (X, p)?

23. Given is a message source (X, p). $p = (p_1, \ldots, p_k)$ and $p_i = \frac{1}{2^{\nu_i}}$, $\nu_i \in \mathbb{N}, i = 1, \ldots, k$. Specify a compact code C for (X, p) and the average code word length $l(C)$.

24. Let (X, p) be a source. $\ell_1, \ldots, \ell_n$ are the lengths of the code words of a compact code over $\{0,1\}$. Show:

$$\sum_{i=1}^{n} \ell_i \leq \frac{1}{2}(n^2 + n - 2).$$

25. A source has the elements $\{a,b,c,d,e,f,g\}$ and the probabilities $(0.3, 0.14, 0.14, 0.14, 0.14, 0.07, 0.07)$. Messages from $\{a,b,c,d,e,f,g\}^*$ are arithmetically encoded over $\{0, 1, \ldots, 9\}$.

    a. Compute the code for the message acfg.

    b. Decode 1688 if the message length is 6.

26. Let $k = 2^l, l \in \mathbb{N}$, $X = \{x_1, \ldots, x_k\}$ and $p_i = \frac{1}{k}$, $i = 1, \ldots, k$. Which word lengths occur for messages of length n when encoded by arithmetic codes over $\{0, 1\}^*$.

27. Given is a message source $(X = \{a, b\}, p = (1 - \frac{1}{2^k}, \frac{1}{2^k}))$. Provide an arithmetic code for $b^n a$, $n \in \mathbb{N}$, over $\{0, 1\}^*$.

28. An LZ77 procedure is implemented with a text buffer of length r. Specify an alphabet X and a message $x \in X^*$ where the compression rate $|C(x)|/|x|$ of the LZ77 encoding $C(x)$ of x is maximum.

5. Graphs

Graph theory is part of discrete mathematics. As a mathematical discipline, it has an extensive, abstract, theoretical part. But it also has interesting, application-relevant, algorithmic aspects.

Many everyday problems, such as the search for a short route in a traffic or communication network, the representation of the World Wide Web (www), consisting of the web pages and their interconnections by means of links, the description of the timing of assembly operations by priority graphs, the design of electronic circuits, semantic networks to represent knowledge or the modeling of the dependencies of work packages in a project lead to a representation with graphs. The structural characteristics of algorithmic problems can often be described using graphs. This enables the solution of these problems by graph algorithms.

We study graph algorithms in the following two chapters. We cover the basic algorithms breadth-first search and depth-first search for systematically searching a graph. These two algorithms are used in many other graph algorithms. We use them to compute spanning trees, the distances between nodes, the connected components of a graph and the strongly connected components of a directed graph, test for cycles and sort acyclic directed graphs topologically. A randomized algorithm for the computation of a minimal cut completes the chapter.

5.1 Modeling Problems with Graphs

In this section, we will formulate a series of popular problems by using graphs.

Königsberg Bridge Problem. We explain the Königsberg[1] bridge problem with the sketch in Figure 5.1, which shows the river Pregel in the city of Königsberg. Seven bridges are drawn between the banks and the two islands. A bridge connects the two islands. One of the islands is connected by a bridge with the suburb and the old town. From the other island there are two bridges leading to each of the suburb and the old town. The question of whether it is possible to choose a walk that returns to the starting point and

---

[1] The former German town Königsberg, today Kaliningrad, was the capital of Ostpreußen.

© Springer Nature Switzerland AG 2020
H. Knebl, *Algorithms and Data Structures*, https://doi.org/10.1007/978-3-030-59758-0_5

crosses each bridge exactly once, is said to have served as entertainment for the citizens of Königsberg.

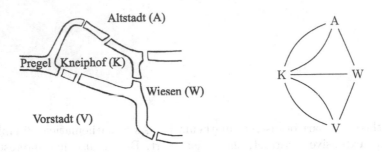

Fig. 5.1: Königsberg bridge problem.

The figure on the right shows the facts of the sketch as a multigraph.[2] Here we abstracted from the topographical properties, which are irrelevant for the problem. We consider only two object types, nodes and relations between nodes, which we call edges. We represent the four areas by the nodes {A,K,V,W}. Two nodes are related if they are connected by a bridge. So there are seven edges, which we represent by the two nodes that are related to each other. The edges are given by {A,K}, {A,K}, {K,V}, {K,V}, {A,W}, {K,W}, {V,W}. The mathematical notation reduces the problem to its essentials and thus facilitates its solution.

The solution to the problem was published by Euler[3] in 1736. This work in which Euler presented the Königsberg bridge problem in mathematical notation is regarded as the first work on graph theory. In honor of Euler, we call a closed path in a graph which contains each edge exactly once an *Eulerian cycle*. Euler's work gives a necessary and sufficient condition for the existence of an Eulerian cycle. A graph has an Eulerian cycle if and only if all nodes have even degrees[4] (to show this is Exercise 1). This condition is not fulfilled for the Königsberg bridge problem.

House-Utility Problem. The house-utility problem consists of three houses H_1, H_2, H_3 and three Utilities, one each for gas (G), water (W) and electricity (E). The graph representing this situation in Figure 5.2 is a *bipartite graph*. In a bipartite graph, the set of nodes is divided into two parts (disjoint subsets). The two endpoints of an edge are located in different parts. A bipartite graph where each part has three elements and where each node from the first part is connected to each node from the second part is called $K_{3,3}$.

---

[2] Multigraphs permit multiple edges between two nodes.
[3] Leonhard Euler (1707 – 1783) was a Swiss mathematician and physicist.
[4] The degree of a node is the number of edges incident on it.

The supply lines intersect in the two arrangements outlined in Figure 5.2. Counted with multiplicity, they intersect in the first figure at nine points; in the second figure there is only one point with multiplicity 3. The question arises whether it is possible to find an arrangement without intersections. This question leads to the concept of a planar graph.

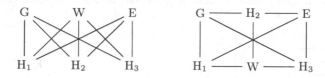

Fig. 5.2: House-utility problem.

Planar Graphs. By a *planar graph* we mean a graph that we can draw in the plane without crossing edges. This works for the complete graph[5] K_4 with four nodes. With K_5, the complete graph with five nodes, this does not seem to be possible, as Figure 5.3 shows.

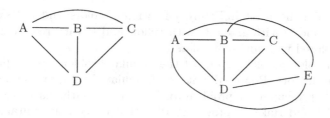

Fig. 5.3: K_4 and K_5.

The Theorem of Kuratowski[6] gives a necessary and sufficient criterion for planar graphs. This criterion shows that K_5 and $K_{3,3}$ are not planar.

The algorithm of Hopcroft[7]-Tarjan[8] serves to test the planarity of a graph and to embed a planar graph into the plane. Planar graphs are treated, for example, by [Jungnickel13] or [Gould88].

Four-Color Problem. The four-color problem is easy to formulate. It reads: Is it possible to color each map with four colors so that neighboring countries have different colors?

---

[5] A graph is called complete if each node is connected to every other node by an edge. It is thus determined by the number of nodes.

[6] Kazimierz Kuratowski (1896 – 1980) was a Polish mathematician and logician.

[7] John Edward Hopcroft (1939 –) is an American computer scientist and Turing Award winner.

[8] Robert Endre Tarjan (1948 –) is an American computer scientist and Turing Award winner.

The problem can be formulated with graphs. The nodes represent the capitals of the countries. We connect the capitals of neighboring countries with an edge. Since neighboring countries have a common border, there is an edge that runs entirely on the territory of the two countries. Thus, it is a planar graph.

Formulated with graphs, the four-color problem is: Can each planar graph be colored with four colors so that neighboring nodes have different colors?

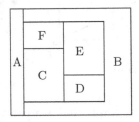 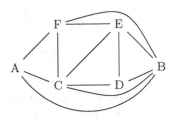

Fig. 5.4: Four-color problem.

We can color the graph in Figure 5.4 with four colors: the nodes A and E with blue, F and D with green, C with yellow and B with red. Neighboring nodes are colored with different colors.

The four-color problem is one of the popular problems of graph theory. It has a long history. Reportedly, it was formulated by Francis Guthrie[9] in 1852. Caley[10] presented the problem to the London Mathematical Society in 1878. Appel[11] and Haken[12] proved in 1976 that every planar graph can be colored with four colors, so that neighboring nodes have different colors.

The proof uses a reduction method developed by Birkhoff[13] and Heesch[14]. This method reduces the general case to 1482 cases, which were solved with extensive use of computers. A more recent proof using the same techniques is published in [RobSanSeyTho97].

Minimum Spanning Trees, Distances, Chinese Postman and Traveling Salesman Problems. We explain the problem of computing minimum spanning trees, the distance problem, the Chinese postman problem and the traveling salesman problem with Figure 5.5.

The nodes v_i in the graph in Figure 5.5 model places (cities or intersections of roads), the edges model connections between places, and the label d_i on an edge indicates the length or cost of that connection.

---

[9] Francis Guthrie (1831 – 1899) was a South African mathematician.
[10] Arthur Cayley (1821 – 1895) was an English mathematician.
[11] Kenneth Appel (1932 – 2013) was an American mathematician.
[12] Wolfgang Haken (1928 –) is a German mathematician.
[13] George David Birkhoff (1884 – 1944) was an American mathematician.
[14] Heinrich Heesch (1906 – 1995) was a German mathematician.

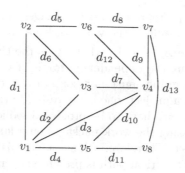

Fig. 5.5: Several graph problems.

1. To construct a minimum spanning tree, all nodes must be connected by edges (see Definition 6.23). The sum of the costs has to be minimized. We study several algorithms for the computation of a minimum spanning tree (Algorithms 6.26, 6.29, 6.34 and 6.50).
2. The distance problem is to find a shortest path between two nodes v_i and v_j or between all pairs of nodes. We solve this problem in Section 6.2 and Section 6.7.
3. A Chinese postman tour is a path which starts and ends at a node v_i and runs through each edge at least once. The Chinese postman problem is: Find a shortest Chinese postman tour in a given graph (see [Schrijver03, Chapters 29.1, 29.11g]).
4. The Traveling Salesman problem reads: We are looking for a shortest path which starts and ends at a node v_i and goes through each node at least once. The traveling salesman problem is also discussed in [Schrijver03, Chapter 58]. It is important in operations research and theoretical computer science.

Non-Symmetric Relationships. In the previous problems, we used graphs for modeling. They represent symmetrical relationships. Non-symmetric relationships are modeled by directed graphs. We explain such a problem with Figure 5.6.

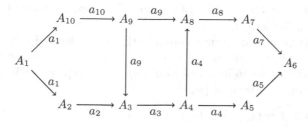

Fig. 5.6: Non-symmetric relationships – dependencies.

The nodes of the graph represent work packages of a project. If the work package A_i requires the result of the work package A_j, A_j must precede A_i. We draw a directed edge $A_j \xrightarrow{a_j} A_i$, where a_j is the time effort required to process A_j. This gives us the dependency graph of the work packages. Of course, the dependency graph must not contain any cycles (see Definition 5.3). When carrying out a project, one is interested in the longest paths in G. The work packages on a path have to be processed sequentially, one after the other. A delay in processing the work packages on a longest path delays the completion of the project. Therefore, a longest path is also called a *critical path*. The calculation of a critical path is presented as an exercise in Chapter 6 (Exercise 3).

5.2 Basic Definitions and Properties

The basic concepts of graph theory are clear and easy to understand. We now present the basic definitions and properties that we need in the following. A graph consists of nodes or vertices and edges that represent relationships between nodes. We specify the terms in the definition below.

Definition 5.1.

1. A *directed graph* is a pair $G = (V, E)$, where V is a non-empty finite set and $E \subset V \times V \setminus \{(v, v) \mid v \in V\}$. V is the set of *nodes* and E is the set of *(directed) edges*.
   A node w is called a *neighbor* of v or *adjacent* to v if $(v, w) \in E$.
   v is called the *start node* and w the *end node* of the edge (v, w).
2. For an *(undirected) graph*, the edges have no direction. $E \subset \mathcal{P}_2(V)$, the set of the two-element subsets of V. The nodes $v, w \in V$ are *neighbors* or *adjacent* if $\{v, w\} \in E$; v and w are called *end nodes* of the edge $e = \{v, w\}$. The edge $\{v, w\}$ is called *incident* to v and w.
3. Let $v \in V$. $U_v := \{w \in V \mid w \text{ adjacent to } v\}$ is called the *environment* of v. The number $|U_v|$ of the elements of U_v is called the *degree* of v, or $\deg(v)$ for short. The number $|V|$ of nodes is called the *order* of G.

Remarks:

1. $|V|$ and $|E|$ measure the size of a graph. The running time of algorithms depends on $|V|$ and $|E|$.
2. A directed graph can be associated with an (undirected) graph, the *underlying graph*, by associating the edge (v, w) with the edge $\{v, w\}$. We get the *directed graph assigned to a graph* if we replace each edge $\{v, w\}$ with the edges (v, w) and (w, v).

Definition 5.2. Let $G = (V_G, E_G)$ be a (directed) graph.

1. A graph $H = (V_H, E_H)$ is said to be a *subgraph* of G if $V_H \subset V_G$ and $E_H \subset E_G$.

2. Let H be a subgraph of G. H is called a G *spanning subgraph* if $V_H = V_G$ holds.
3. Let $S \subset V_G$, and let E_S be the set of edges in E whose end nodes (or start and end nodes in the directed case) are in S. The graph $\langle S \rangle := (S, E_S)$ is called the *subgraph generated by S*.

Examples: Figure 5.7 shows subgraphs H and I of G, I is the subgraph of G generated by {A, B, C, D}, and H is a spanning subgraph (tree) of G.

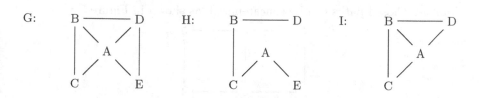

Fig. 5.7: Various graphs.

Paths. Paths are special subgraphs of a graph. With paths, we define important terms for graphs such as connectivity and distance.

Definition 5.3.

1. Let $G = (V, E)$ be a graph. A *path* P is a sequence of nodes $v_0, v_1, \ldots, v_n$, where $\{v_i, v_{i+1}\} \in E, i = 0, \ldots, n - 1$. v_0 is called the *start node* and v_n the *end node* of P. n is called the *length* of P.
   w is *accessible* from v if there is a path P with start node v and end node w. If there is a path from v to w for every pair of nodes $v, w \in V$, then G is said to be *connected*.
   A path P is *simple* if $v_i \neq v_j$ for $i \neq j$ and $0 \leq i, j \leq n$. A path P is *closed* if $v_0 = v_n$. A closed path P is *simple* if $v_i \neq v_j$ for $i \neq j$ and $0 \leq i, j \leq n-1$.
   A simple closed path of *length* ≥ 3 is called a *cycle* or *circle*. A graph G without cycles is called *acyclic*.
2. For a directed graph G, we explain the terms analogously. In a path P, the edges have the appropriate direction, i.e., $(v_i, v_{i+1}) \in E, i = 0, \ldots, n - 1$. For a cycle it is required that the length is ≥ 2.
   The nodes v, w are *mutually accessible* if v is accessible from w and w from v. If each two nodes v, w are mutually accessible in V, G is called *strongly connected*.

Remarks: Let $G = (V, E)$ be a graph.

1. Let $\{v, w\} \in E$. The path v, w, v is a simple closed path, but no cycle.
2. Let $v \in V$. v is a (closed) path from v to v. In particular, v is accessible from v.

3. The relation "accessible" defines an equivalence relation[15] on V. For a directed graph $G = (V, E)$, the relation "mutually accessible" is an equivalence relation on V ("accessible" is not symmetric for a directed graph).

4. Two closed paths $P = v_0, \ldots, v_n$ and $P' = w_0, \ldots, w_n$ with:

$$w_i = v_{(i+j) \bmod (n+1)}, \text{ for fixed } j \text{ and } i = 0, \ldots, n,$$

define the same cycle. The condition states that P and P' differ only in the selection of the start node.

Example. Closed paths can be concatenated, as shown in Figure 5.8.

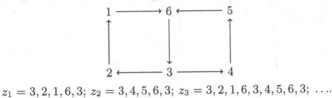

$$z_1 = 3, 2, 1, 6, 3; \ z_2 = 3, 4, 5, 6, 3; \ z_3 = 3, 2, 1, 6, 3, 4, 5, 6, 3; \ \ldots$$

Fig. 5.8: Many closed paths.

With the help of paths, we explain the distance of nodes.

Definition 5.4. Let $G = (V, E)$ be a (directed) graph and $v, w \in V$. The *distance* $d(v, w)$ between the nodes v and w is the length of a shortest path connecting v and w, i.e., a path with the minimum number of edges. If there is no path from v to w, we set $d(v, w) = \infty$.

Remark. For a connected graph $G = (V, E)$, the definition of the distance d of nodes obviously fulfills the axioms of a metric (see Definition B.24). For a strongly connected directed graph, the "axiom of symmetry" $d(u, v) = d(v, u)$, $u, v \in V$, may be violated.

Definition 5.5.

1. Let G be a graph, and let C be an equivalence class[16] of the relation "accessible". The graph $\langle C \rangle$ generated by C is called *a connected component* of G.

2. Let G be a directed graph, and let C be an equivalence class of the equivalence relation "mutually accessible". The graph $\langle C \rangle$ generated by C is called a *strongly connected component* of G.

Remark. Let $K_i = (V_i, E_i)$, $i = 1, \ldots, l$, be the connected components of $G = (V, E)$. Then $V = \cup_{i=1}^l V_i$, $V_i \cap V_j = \emptyset$ for $i \neq j$, and $E = \cup_{i=1}^l E_i$, $E_i \cap E_j = \emptyset$ for $i \neq j$.

---

[15] A relation $\sim$ on V which is reflexive ($v \sim v, v \in V$), symmetrical ($v \sim w$ implies $w \sim v$) and transitive ($u \sim v$ and $v \sim w$ implies $u \sim w$) is called an *equivalence relation*.

[16] An *equivalence class* of an equivalence relation $\sim$ consists of all elements equivalent to a given element v ($\{w \, | w \sim v\}$).

Trees. We already met rooted trees in Chapter 4. Trees are a special class of graphs. They occur in most of the algorithms which we study in the two chapters on graphs.

Definition 5.6. An acyclic connected graph G is called a *(free) tree*. If G has more than one connected component, we speak of a *forest*.

Remark. A free tree can be assigned to a rooted tree. To do this, we mark a node as root and provide each edge with an orientation in the direction away from the root. The ith level of the tree consists of the nodes which have distance i from the root. See Figure 5.9.

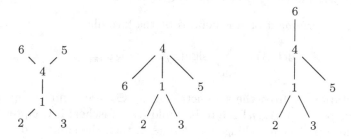

Fig. 5.9: Miscellaneous trees.

Proposition 5.7. *For a graph $T = (V, E)$ the following statements are equivalent:*

1. *T is a tree.*
2. *T is connected and $|E| = |V| - 1$.*

Proof. Let $n = |V|$ and $m = |E|$. First we show that statement 2 follows from statement 1. A tree T is by definition connected. By induction on n, we conclude that $m = n - 1$. The base case is for $n = 1$. When $n = 1$, we have $m = 0$. Let $n > 1$ and assume the assertion proved for $< n$. Let T be a tree of order n and $e = \{v, w\}$ an edge in T. Let $T \setminus \{e\}$ be the graph that results from T when we remove the edge e in T. Since T is acyclic, there is no path in $T \setminus \{e\}$ that connects v with w. After removing an edge, the number of connected components increases by a maximum of 1. Therefore, $T \setminus \{e\}$ breaks down into two components (trees) $T_1 = (V_1, E_1)$ and $T_2 = (V_2, E_2)$. We have $m = |E| = |E_1| + |E_2| + 1 = |V_1| - 1 + |V_2| - 1 + 1 = |V| - 1 = n - 1$.

To show the other direction, let T be connected and $m = n - 1$. Suppose T has a cycle Z. Let $e \in Z$. Then $T \setminus \{e\}$ is connected and has $n - 2$ edges, a contradiction, because in order to connect n nodes, you need at least $n - 1$ edges.   □

Bipartite Graphs. A graph $G = (V, E)$ is said to be *bipartite* if the set of nodes V splits into parts V_1 and V_2, i.e., $V = V_1 \cup V_2$, $V_1 \cap V_2 = \emptyset$, such that each edge of G has one end node in V_1 and the other in V_2.

A *perfect matching* for G consists of a set of edges that define a bijective map from V_1 to V_2. The following proposition specifies for a bipartite graph with $|V_1| = |V_2|$ a criterion for the existence of a perfect matching.

Proposition 5.8. *Let* $G = (V, E)$ *be a bipartite graph with parts* $V_1 = \{v_1, \ldots, v_n\}$ *and* $V_2 = \{w_1, \ldots, w_n\}$, *and let the* X_{ij}, $1 \leq i, j \leq n$, *be indeterminates. The matrix* $A = (a_{ij})_{1 \leq i,j \leq n}$ *is defined by*

$$a_{ij} = \begin{cases} X_{ij} & \text{if } \{v_i, w_j\} \in E, \\ 0 & \text{otherwise.} \end{cases}$$

G *has a perfect matching if and only if* $\det(A) \neq 0$.

Proof. The determinant of A is defined by the formula

$$\det(A) = \sum_{\pi \in \mathfrak{S}_n} \text{sign}(\pi) a_{1\pi(1)} \cdots a_{n\pi(n)}.$$

All permutations π from the symmetric group $\mathfrak{S}_n$ are summed up, i.e., all bijective maps on $\{1, \ldots, n\}$ are to be build (see [Fischer14, Chapter 3]). If G has a perfect matching that defines π, then the summand

$$a_{1\pi(1)} \cdots a_{n\pi(n)} = X_{1\pi(1)} \cdots X_{n\pi(n)} \neq 0. \qquad (*)$$

Since the summands in $\det(A)$ are pairwise distinct, $\det(A)$ is also $\neq 0$. If vice versa $\det(A) \neq 0$, it follows that at least one summand $a_{1\pi(1)} \cdots a_{n\pi(n)} \neq 0$. Then $(*)$ follows; in other words: π defines a perfect matching. $\square$

Remarks:

1. $\det(A)$ is a polynomial with the coefficients $+1$ or -1 and the indeterminates X_{ij}, $1 \leq i, j \leq n$. In Section 1.6.3, we developed a Monte Carlo algorithm to test the identity of two polynomials (see Corollary 1.55). We can use this algorithm to test $\det(A) = 0$. The efficiency of the method which results from Proposition 5.8 is dominated by the algorithm used to calculate the determinant. The calculation according to the defining formula based on Leibniz[17] or by the expansion theorem of Laplace[18] is of order $O(n!)$ and therefore unsuitable. Modern methods have a running time of order $O(n^3)$ or better.

2. Let $G = (V, E)$ be a graph and $Z \subset E$. Z is called a perfect matching if each node of V is incident to exactly one edge of Z. The question of whether any graph $G = (V, E)$ with the node set $V = \{v_1, \ldots v_n\}$, where

---

[17] Gottfried Wilhelm Leibniz (1646 – 1716) was a German philosopher, mathematician and polymath. He is the co-founder of the infinitesimal calculus and is considered to be the most important universal scholar of his time.

[18] Pierre-Simon Laplace (1749 – 1827) was a French mathematician, physicist and astronomer.

n is even, has a perfect matching can be answered with a *Tutte*[19] *matrix*. Let X_{ij} be indeterminates. The Tutte matrix $A = (a_{ij})_{1 \le i,j \le n}$ of G is defined by

$$a_{ij} = \begin{cases} X_{ij} & \text{if } \{v_i, v_j\} \in E \text{ and } i < j, \\ -X_{ji} & \text{if } \{v_i, v_j\} \in E \text{ and } i > j, \\ 0 & \text{otherwise.} \end{cases}$$

A graph has a perfect matching if and only if the determinant of its Tutte matrix $\det(A)$ is not zero. The proof of this fact, however, is not as simple as with bipartite graphs. There are randomized algorithms not only for testing the existence of a perfect matching, but also for determining a perfect matching (see [MotRag95, Chapter 12.4]).

5.3 Representations of Graphs

For a graph $G = (V, E)$ we consistently write $n = |V|$ for the number of nodes and $m = |E|$ for the number of edges of G. For a graph, it holds that $0 \le m \le \binom{n}{2}$, and for a directed graph, it holds that $0 \le m \le n(n-1)$. In the following, we often assume that $V = \{1, \ldots, n\}$. This does not restrict the generality of the algorithms.

Definition 5.9.

1. A (directed) graph $G = (V, E)$ is called *complete* if each node is connected to every other node by an edge.
2. If G has many edges (m large compared to $\binom{n}{2}$ or $n(n-1)$), then G is called *dense*.
3. If G has few edges (m small compared to $\binom{n}{2}$ or $n(n-1)$), then G is called *sparse*.

Remark. Let $G = (V, E)$ be a complete (directed) Graph. Then $|E| = n(n-1)$ if G is directed, and $|E| = \binom{n}{2}$ if G is undirected.

Definition 5.10. Let $G = (V, E)$ be a directed graph with $V = \{1, \ldots, n\}$.

1. The *adjacency matrix adm* is an $n \times n$–matrix,

$$adm[i, j] := \begin{cases} 1 & \text{for } (i, j) \in E, \\ 0 & \text{otherwise.} \end{cases}$$

2. The *adjacency list adl*$[1..n]$ is an array of lists. For each node $j \in V$, the list *adl*$[j]$ is defined by

$$i \in adl[j] \text{ if and only if } (j, i) \in E.$$

The list *adl*$[j]$ contains the nodes that are adjacent to j.
3. The *parent array* $p[1..n]$ is used if G is a rooted tree or a forest of rooted trees. $p[i]$ stores the predecessor of i or the value 0 if i is a root of a

---

[19] William Thomas Tutte (1917 – 2002) was a British-Canadian cryptologist and mathematician.

component of G.

4. A graph is represented by the adjacency matrix or adjacency list of the associated directed graph.

Example. Adjacency matrix. See Figure 5.10.

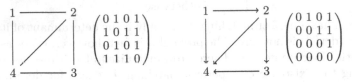

Fig. 5.10: Graph and directed graph – each with adjacency matrix.

Remarks:

1. The adjacency matrix adm of a graph is symmetric and it needs n^2 memory locations. This is also true if G has only a few edges, i.e., if G is sparse.
2. There are $2m$ entries in the adjacency list of a graph. A directed graph has m entries.
3. An entry in an adjacency matrix requires less memory than an entry in the equivalent adjacency list. Therefore, an adjacency matrix is more suitable for dense graphs, whereas the adjacency list is more suitable for sparse graphs. See Figure 5.11.

Example. Adjacency list.

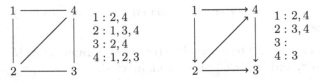

Fig. 5.11: Graph and directed graph – each with adjacency list.

We implement an adjacency list by a linked list of list items. The variable $adl[j]$, $j = 1, \ldots, n$, contains a reference to the first element of the linked list or null. The null reference specifies that $adl[j]$ does not reference a list element, i.e., we assign the empty list to the node j. A list element is defined by

      type vertex $= 1..n$
      type node $=$ struct
          vertex v
          node   *next*

The definition specifies that a vertex of the graph can take the values from the set $\{1, \ldots, n\}$. A list element has variables v of type vertex and *next* of type node. v stores a node of the graph and *next* a reference to a list element of type node or null. The null reference indicates that the end of the list is reached. The access to v and *next* is done with the structure member operator "." (see Section 1.7).

5.4 Basic Graph Algorithms

Depth-first search and breadth-first search provide two different methods for traversing a graph. Traversing means systematically running through the edges of the graph in order to visit all nodes of the graph. Depth-first search and breadth-first search are applied to graphs and directed graphs. They are fundamental to many further graph algorithms.

5.4.1 Breadth-First Search

First, we describe the algorithm *breadth-first search*, BFS for short, informally.

(1) Select a start node.
(2) Starting from this node, visit all neighbors $n_1, n_2, \ldots$ and then
(3) all neighbors of the first neighbor n_1 and then
(4) all neighbors of the second neighbor n_2,
(5) and so on ......
(6) If we do not reach all nodes of the graph, we continue breadth-first search with another start node, a node that has not yet been reached. We repeat this until all nodes are visited.

Example. In Figure 5.12, the sequence of visits is along the dashed path that begins at the center, orbits it twice and ends at the outer node at northeast. The starting node of the path is explicitly selected.

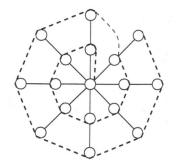

Fig. 5.12: Breadth-first search.

The visit sequence results in levels for each start node. Level 0 consists of the start node. Level i, $i \geq 1$, consists of the nodes that are adjacent to a node at level $i - 1$, but not to a node at levels $0, \ldots, i - 2$.

We divide the nodes $V = \{1, \ldots, n\}$ of the graph into three disjoint groups:

V_T: visited nodes,
V_{ad}:   nodes adjacent to nodes from V_T, but not in V_T,
V_R: $V \setminus (V_T \cup V_{ad})$.

Nodes from V_{ad} are marked for visiting. The assignment of a node to V_T, V_{ad} and V_R changes during the execution of BFS:
Start: $V_T = \emptyset, V_{ad} = \{startnode\}, V_R = V \setminus \{startnode\}$.
When visiting $j \in V_{ad}$, we set

$$V_T = V_T \cup \{j\},$$
$$V_{ad} = (V_{ad} \setminus \{j\}) \cup (U_j \cap V_R),$$
$$V_R = V \setminus (V_T \cup V_{ad}),$$

where the environment U_j of j consists of the nodes adjacent to j.

Construction of a Breadth-First Forest. For each start node, we get a rooted tree inductively.
Start: $T = (\{startnode\}, \emptyset)$.
Let $T = (V_T, E_T)$ be constructed. When visiting j, we set

$$T = (V_T \cup (U_j \cap V_R), E_T \cup \{\{j, k\} \mid k \in U_j \cap V_R\}).$$

The node j becomes the parent node for all nodes $k \in U_j \cap V_R$. These nodes change from V_R to V_{ad}. Since for each connected component the number of edges is equal to the number of nodes minus 1, the construction results in a tree for each connected component.

Example. Figure 5.13 shows a graph with its breadth-first tree. The superscripts at the nodes indicate the visit order.

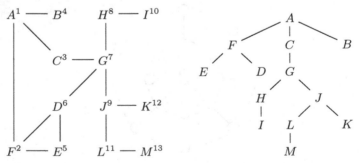

Fig. 5.13: Breadth-first search with breadth-first tree.

Altogether, we get a spanning forest. This is not unique. It depends on the choice of starting nodes and the order in which we treat adjacent nodes.

Managing the Nodes from V_{ad} with a Queue. We use a queue to cache elements from V_{ad}. Elements stored in the queue cannot be accessed at random. The principle "first in, first out" (FIFO principle) is applied. This means that we can remove the elements in the order in which they were saved i.e., we can remove the element that has been in the queue for the longest time.

We define a queue by the access functions:

1. ToQueue(vertex k) stores k in the queue.
2. FromQueue returns and removes the element from the queue that has been longest in the queue.
3. QueueEmpty checks the queue for elements.

We implement V_T, V_{ad} and V_R using the array $where[1..n]$ and the breadth-first forest by the array $parent[1..n]$.

$$where[k] \begin{cases} > 0 & \text{if } k \in V_T, \\ < 0 & \text{if } k \in V_{ad}, \\ = 0 & \text{if } k \in V_R. \end{cases}$$

$parent[k] = j$ if j is the predecessor of k.
Our pseudo-code follows [Sedgewick88].

Algorithm 5.11.
   vertex $parent[1..n]$; node $adl[1..n]$; int $where[1..n]$, nr

   BFS()
   1   vertex k
   2   for $k \leftarrow 1$ to n do
   3       $where[k] \leftarrow 0$, $parent[k] \leftarrow 0$
   4   $nr \leftarrow 1$
   5   for $k \leftarrow 1$ to n do
   6   if $where[k] = 0$
   7   then Visit(k), $nr \leftarrow nr + 1$

   Visit(vertex k)
   1   node no
   2   ToQueue(k), $where[k] \leftarrow -1$
   3   repeat
   4       $k \leftarrow$ FromQueue, $where[k] \leftarrow nr$
   5       $no \leftarrow adl[k]$
   6   while $no \neq$ null do
   7   if $where[no.v] = 0$
   8   then ToQueue($no.v$), $where[no.v] \leftarrow -1$
   9                   $parent[no.v] \leftarrow k$
   10          $no \leftarrow no.next$
   11 until QueueEmpty

Remarks:

1. Calling Visit(k) in BFS (line 7) results in visiting all previously unvisited nodes that can be reached from k, because starting from k all neighbors of k are visited and then all neighbors of the neighbors, and so on, that is, all nodes from V_R that are accessible from k.
2. The while loop in Visit examines the environment of k.
3. After the termination of BFS, *where*[k] contains the number of the component of the spanning forest in which k lies.
4. A node k is the root of a component of the spanning forest if after termination *parent*[k] $= 0$ is valid.

BFS with an Adjacency Matrix. We delete the variable *no* and replace in Visit the lines 5–10 with:

> for $j \leftarrow 1$ to n do
>   if *where*[j] $= 0$ and *adm*[k, j]
>   then ToQueue(j), *where*[j] $\leftarrow -1$, *parent*[j] $\leftarrow k$

Now, breadth-first search works if the graph is given by an adjacency matrix.

Running Time Analysis of BFS. Let $G = (V, E)$ be a graph, $n = |V|$, $m = |E|$ and $T(n, m)$ the running time of BFS. Since we fetch each node exactly once from the queue, the repeat-until loop (lines 3 – 11 of Visit) is repeated n times. When represented by an adjacency list, the while loop for each node k (lines 6 – 10 of Visit) is passed through $\deg(k)$ times. In particular, the number of iterations of while is equal to $\sum_k \deg(k) = 2m$ for all nodes. The total running time for an adjacency list is $T(n, m) = O(n + m)$[20].

When represented by an adjacency matrix, the number of iterations of the first statement of the for loop is n^2. For the running time, it follows that $T(n, m) = O(n^2)$.

More Benefits of BFS.

1. Test for cycles on graphs. If we find a node j with *where*[j] $\neq 0$ and *parent*[j] $\neq k$ (in line 7 of Visit), while investigating the environment of a node k, the edge $\{k, j\}$ leads to a cycle because j is already in the tree. We can find the corresponding cycle by looking for the lowest common ancestor of k and j in the breadth-first subtree represented by the parent array. We study a solution to this problem in Section 6.1.3.
2. Determination of distances. Using the algorithm BFS, the distances for all nodes to the root of the respective subtree can be determined. The following modification is necessary:
   a. We define a global array *int dist*[$1..n$].
   b. In BFS *dist* is initialized. We insert *dist*[k] $\leftarrow 0$ in line 3.
   c. In Visit, line 9, we insert *dist*[*no.v*] $\leftarrow$ *dist*[k] $+ 1$.
   After termination, the distances to the respective roots are stored in *dist*.

---

[20] By Definition 1.12, this means that there exist $n_0, m_0, c \in \mathbb{N}$ such that $T(n, m) \leq c(n + m)$ for $n \geq n_0$ or $m \geq m_0$.

5.4.2 Depth-First Search

First, we describe the algorithm *depth-first search*, DFS for short, informally.

(1) Select a start node.
(2) Starting from this node, visit the first neighbor n_1 and then
(3) the first neighbor n_2 of n_1 and then
(4) the first neighbor n_3 of n_2,
(5) and so on ... until all first neighbors are visited.
(6) Visit the second neighbor from the last visited node,
(7) and so on ....
(8) If we do not reach all nodes, we continue depth-first search with another start node, a node that has not yet been reached. Now, we visit all the nodes from the set of unvisited nodes that can be reached from this node. We repeat this until all nodes are visited.

Example. Figure 5.14 shows the sequence of visits along the dashed path, which starts at the center, rounds it once and ends at the outer node at northeast.

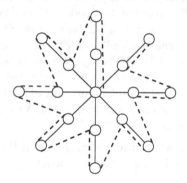

Fig. 5.14: Depth-first search.

For a graph with node set $V = \{1, \ldots, n\}$ we specify our procedure as follows.

Algorithm 5.12.
    vertex $parent[1..n]$, node $adl[1..n]$, boolean $visited[1..n]$
    int $btime[1..n]$, $etime[1..n]$, $time$
    DFS()
1   vertex k
2   for $k \leftarrow 1$ to n do
3        $visited[k] \leftarrow$ false , $parent[k] \leftarrow 0$
4    $time \leftarrow 0$
5   for $k \leftarrow 1$ to n do
6   if not $visited[k]$
7   then Visit(k)

Visit(vertex k)
1   node no
2    $btime[k] \leftarrow time, \ time \leftarrow time + 1$
3    $visited[k] \leftarrow$ true
4    $no \leftarrow adl[k]$
5   while $no \neq$ null do
6   if $visited[no.v] =$ false
7   then $parent[no.v] \leftarrow k, \ \text{Visit}(no.v)$
8        $no \leftarrow no.next$
9    $etime[k] \leftarrow time, \ time \leftarrow time + 1$

Remarks:

1. The call Visit(k) in line 7 of DFS causes Visit to be called recursively for all nodes accessible from k that have not yet been visited. In total, for each node of G exactly one call of Visit is made.
2. We only need the arrays *btime* and *etime* to analyze the algorithm.
3. **Construction of a *depth-first forest*.** For each node k for which Visit is called by DFS, Visit constructs a rooted tree. The node k is the predecessor of the node v if the call of Visit(v) is made while the environment of k is inspected. All calls to Visit in DFS generate a spanning forest for G, which is represented by the array *parent*. If $parent[k] = 0$, k is the root of one of the subtrees of the depth-first forest.

   This forest depends on the implementation of DFS. The degrees of freedom are the selection of the node used to call Visit in DFS and the order of the nodes in the adjacency list.

Example. Figure 5.15 shows a directed graph with its depth-first tree. The superscripts at each node indicate the visit order.

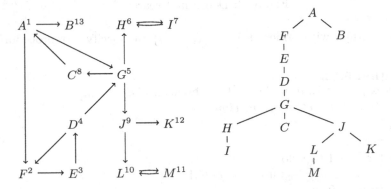

Fig. 5.15: Depth-first search with depth-first tree.

For a node k of G, we set $t_b(k) := btime[k]$ (begin time – call time) and $t_e(k) := etime[k]$ (end time – termination time) with respect to a depth-first traversal. The *activation interval*

$$I(k) := [t_b(k), t_e(k)]$$

specifies the time period in which the (recursive) call of Visit(k) is active.

Proposition 5.13. *Let $G = (V, E)$ be a (directed or undirected) graph and let $j, k \in V$.*

1. *If $I(j) \cap I(k) \neq \emptyset$, then $I(j) \subset I(k)$ or $I(k) \subset I(j)$.*
2. *$I(j) \subset I(k)$ if and only if k is an ancestor of j in the corresponding depth-first tree.*

Proof.

1. Let $I(j) \cap I(k) \neq \emptyset$. We assume without loss of generality $t_b(j) < t_b(k)$ and $t_b(k) < t_e(j)$. Then we visit k during the recursive descent from j. Consequently, Visit must first terminate in node k and then in node j. Thus, it follows that $I(k) \subset I(j)$.
2. We have $I(j) \subset I(k)$ if and only if $t_b(k) < t_b(j)$ and $t_e(j) < t_e(k)$. This in turn is equivalent to the condition k is an ancestor of j in the corresponding depth-first tree.

The assertions of the proposition are proven. □

Definition 5.14. Let $G = (V, E)$ be a directed graph, and let T be a depth-first forest of G. An edge $e = (v, w) \in E$ is called a *tree edge* if e is also an edge in T. It is called a *backward edge* if w is an ancestor of v in T and it is called a *forward edge* if w is a descendant of v in T. All other edges from E are called *cross edges*.

Example. Figure 5.16 shows a directed graph and a depth-first tree with drawn cross, backward and forward edges.

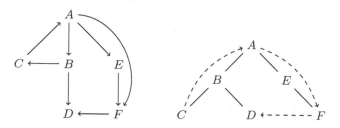

Fig. 5.16: Cross, backward and forward edges.

Remark. An edge (v, w) with $t_b(w) < t_b(v)$ is a cross edge if $t_e(w) < t_b(v)$. The end node w is located in another part of the graph that has already been traversed.

Running Time Analysis of the Algorithm DFS. Let $G = (V, E)$ be a graph, $n = |V|$, $m = |E|$ and $T(n, m)$ be the running time of DFS. Then we have $T(n, m) = O(n + m)$.

The computational effort for lines 3 and 6 in DFS is of order $O(n)$. Since Visit is called exactly once for each node, the number of calls to Visit is n. The number of iterations of while in Visit is given by the degree of the corresponding node. The sum of the degrees of all nodes is $2m$. Overall, it follows that $T(n, m) = O(n + m)$.

Remark. In depth-first search, the sequence of visits is determined by the recursive calls. The call stack is implicitly linked to this. If the recursion is replaced by an (explicit) stack, the visit sequence is determined by the LIFO principle (last in first out) in contrast to the FIFO principle (first in first out), which we use for breadth-first search. Here you can see that the area of visited nodes during depth-first search goes into the depths of the graph. In breadth-first search, the range of visited nodes extends evenly along the boundary between already visited and not yet visited nodes.

5.5 Directed Acyclic Graphs

We use a directed acyclic graph (DAG) to model the individual steps of production processes, the dependencies between the chapters of a book or of files in include mechanisms. Another example is the representation of the structure of arithmetic expressions.

Example. Figure 5.17 shows the structure of an arithmetic expression with repeated partial expressions:

$$(a + b) * c * ((a + b) * c + (a + b + e) * (e + f)).$$

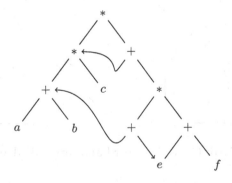

Fig. 5.17: Syntax graph of an arithmetic expression.

You can use the depth-first algorithm to test a directed graph for cycles.

Proposition 5.15. *A directed graph is acyclic if and only if DFS does not produce backward edges.*

Proof. Each backward edge closes a cycle. Conversely, if $v_1, \ldots, v_n$ is a cycle and v_i is the first node for which DFS is called, then $I(v_{i-1}) \subset I(v_i)$, i.e., v_{i-1} is a descendant of v_i in the corresponding depth-first tree (Proposition 5.13). Thus, the edge (v_{i-1}, v_i) is a backward edge in the depth-first forest. $\square$

Topological Sorting. The nodes of a directed acyclic graph are partially ordered. We can arrange a partially ordered set linearly, in accordance with the partial order. This is captured by the following proposition.

Definition 5.16.

1. $(M, \leq)$ is called a *partially ordered set* if for $m_1, m_2, m_3 \in M$ we have
   a. $m_1 \leq m_1$ (reflexivity).
   b. If $m_1 \leq m_2$ and $m_2 \leq m_1$, then follows $m_1 = m_2$ (antisymmetry).
   c. If $m_1 \leq m_2$ and $m_2 \leq m_3$, then follows $m_1 \leq m_3$ (transitivity).
2. By a *topological sort* of a partially ordered set M, we understand a linear ordering that respects the partial order, that is, if $w \leq v$, then w precedes v in the linear ordering.

Remarks:

1. Let $G = (V, E)$ be a directed acyclic graph and $v_1, v_2 \in V$. We define $v_1 \leq v_2$ if and only if v_2 is accessible from v_1. This defines a partial order on V.
2. If we complete a linear ordering of the nodes with all edges of the graph, then the linear ordering is a topological sorting if and only if all edges are directed from left to right.

Example. Topological sortings of the nodes of the graph in Figure 5.18 are J,K,L,M,A,C,G,H,I,B,F,E,D and A,B,C,F,E,D,J,K,L,M,G,H,I.

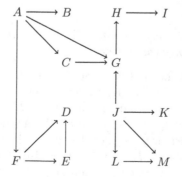

Fig. 5.18: Topological sortings.

Figure 5.19 shows that J,K,L,M,A,C,G,H,I,B,F,E,D is indeed a topological sorting of the nodes of the graph in Figure 5.18.

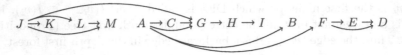

Fig. 5.19: Topological sorting – linear ordering.

The following algorithm, a modification of DFS, sorts the nodes $V = \{1, \ldots, n\}$ of a directed acyclic graph topologically.

Algorithm 5.17.

vertex $sorted[1..n]$; node $adl[1..n]$; boolean $visited[1..n]$; index j

```
TopSort()
1   vertex k
2   for k ← 1 to n do
3       visited[k] ← false
4   j ← n
5   for k ← 1 to n do
6       if not visited[k]
7           then Visit(k)

Visit(vertex k)
1   node no
2   visited[k] ← true
3   no ← adl[k]
4   while no ≠ null do
5       if not visited[no.v]
6           then Visit(no.v)
7       no ← no.next
8   sorted[j] := k, j := j − 1
```

Proposition 5.18. *After termination of* TopSort, *the array* sorted *contains the nodes of* G *in a topological sorting.*

Proof. Let $w < v$. This means that there is a path from w to v. We show that w is placed before v in the array *sorted*. Let us first consider the case $t_b(w) < t_b(v)$. Since there is a path from w to v, $I(v) \subset I(w)$ (Proposition 5.13). Therefore, $t_e(v) < t_e(w)$. Since we fill the array *sorted* from the end in the order of termination, w is placed before v in *sorted*. In the case of $t_b(v) < t_b(w)$, we have $I(v) \cap I(w) = \emptyset$. Otherwise, if $I(v) \cap I(w) \neq \emptyset$, then $I(w) \subset I(v)$ would follow (loc. cit.). Therefore, w would be accessible from v. A contradiction to G acyclic. Thus, $t_e(v) < t_e(w)$, and w is placed before v in the array *sorted*.   □

5.6 The Strongly Connected Components

A strongly connected component of a directed graph G is a maximum subgraph of G with respect to the equivalence relation "mutually accessible" (see Definition 5.5). We discuss two algorithms for determining the strongly connected components. Both algorithms are based on depth-first search, applied to a directed graph. The first algorithm is named after Tarjan. The second algorithm was developed by Kosaraju[21], but not published. Independently of Kosaraju's discovery, the algorithm was published by Sharir[22] in [Sharir81].

In this section, T denotes a depth-first forest of G (Section 5.4.2). The graph T depends on the order of the nodes k in which Visit(k) is called by Algorithm 5.12. Let v be a node of G. By T_v we denote the subtree of T which consists of the nodes that we discover during the recursive descent from v. These are the nodes w with $t_b(w) \in I(v)$.

The Algorithm of Tarjan. The algorithm of Tarjan results from a modification of the Visit function in Algorithm 5.12. It computes successively the strongly connected components of a directed graph. The strongly connected components result as subtrees of T. If C is a strongly connected component of G, and if u is the first node of C in which we call Visit, then all nodes of C are in the subtree T_u, the subtree with root u. We call u the *root of the strongly connected component C*. Tarjan's algorithm determines the roots of the strongly connected components and thus also the strongly connected components. Let $G = (V, E)$ be a graph with the node set $V = \{1, \ldots, n\}$.

Algorithm 5.19.
    vertex $component[1..n]$, $adl[1..n]$; boolean $visited[1..n]$
    int $where[1..n]$, $dfs[1..n]$, $low[1..n]$, num

    TarjanComponents()
    1   vertex k
    2   for $k \leftarrow 1$ to n do
    3       $visited[k] \leftarrow$ false , $component[k] \leftarrow 0$, $where[k] = 0$
    4   $num \leftarrow 1$
    5   for $k \leftarrow 1$ to n do
    6   if not $visited[k]$
    7   then Visit(k)

---

[21] Sambasiva R. Kosaraju is an Indian and American computer scientist.
[22] Micha Sharir (1950 –) is an Israeli mathematician and computer scientist.

Visit(vertex k)
```
 1   node no
 2   dfs[k] ← num, low[k] ← num, num ← num + 1
 3   Push(k), where[k] ← −1, visited[k] ← true
 4   no ← adl[k]
 5   while no ≠ null do
 6       if visited[no.v] = false
 7       then Visit(no.v)
 8            low[k] = min(low[k], low[no.v])
 9       else  if where[no.v] = −1
10            then low[k] = min(low[k], dfs[no.v])
11       no ← no.next
12   if low[k] = dfs[k]
13   then repeat
14            k′ ← Pop, where[k′] ← 1, component[k′] ← k
15        until k′ ≠ k
```

Remarks:

1. In line 3 of Visit, we push the node k with Push(k) on a stack. We note this in the variable $where[k]$ (line 3: $where[k] \leftarrow -1$). The variable $where[k]$ is defined by

$$
where[k] = \begin{cases} 0 & \text{if } k \text{ has not yet been visited,} \\ -1 & \text{after } k \text{ has been pushed on the stack,} \\ 1 & \text{after } k \text{ has been removed from the stack.} \end{cases}
$$

2. The while loop (line 5 of Vist) inspects the environment of k. For nodes that have not yet been visited, the recursive call of Visit is performed. After the call terminates, $low[k]$ is updated (line 8). If there is a node on the stack that is adjacent to k and has already been visited, an update of $low[k]$ (line 10) is also performed.

3. After the completion of the inspection of the environment of k (the while loop terminates), we check whether k is the root of a strongly connected component. If this is the case (line 12: $low[k] = dfs[k]$), the nodes of this strongly connected component are on the stack in the reverse order of the recursive descent. In the repeat-until loop, for each of the nodes of this strongly connected component, we enter the root of the strongly connected component into the array *component*.

For a node v, the subtree $T_v \subset T$ with root v and the set of backward edges

$$
R_v = \{(u, w) \mid u \in T_v \text{ and } w \text{ is an ancestor of } v \text{ in } T\}
$$

are defined.

Let v be a node of G, and let $t_e(v)$ be the termination time of Visit regarding v. Let $C_1, \ldots, C_l$ be the strongly connected components discovered at this time, i.e., those connected components whose roots have already been determined. At this point we define for a node v of G and the subtree $T_v \subset T$ with root v the subset Q_v of *active cross edges*

$$Q_v = \{(u, w) \mid u \in T_v, w \notin T_v, w \notin C_1 \cup \ldots \cup C_l \text{ and } (u, w) \notin R_v\}.$$

We number each node v of the graph during the depth-first traversal with $t_b(v)$ and set

$$low(v) = \begin{cases} \min\{t_b(w) \mid (v, w) \in Q_v \cup R_v\} & \text{if } Q_v \cup R_v \neq \emptyset, \\ t_b(v) & \text{otherwise.} \end{cases}$$

In line 9, Visit detects end nodes of active cross edges and end nodes of backward edges starting from v. In line 10, the value $low[v]$ is updated for these nodes.

If $low[v]$ results from a backward edge or an active cross edge that starts from a descendant of v, we calculate $low[v]$ recursively from the low value of the successor (line 8).

Example. Figure 5.20 shows a directed graph and an associated depth-first tree with drawn backward and cross edges. Cross edges are (D, A) and (K, F). The last edge is an active cross edge at the time of its discovery. Next to each node k is superscripted $t_b(k), low(k)$.

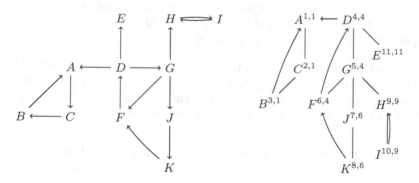

Fig. 5.20: Strongly connected components with Tarjan's algorithm.

In the depth-first forest, we remove any edge entering a root of a strongly connected component. The resulting subtrees form the strongly connected components $\{A, B, C\}$, $\{D, F, G, J, K\}$, $\{H, I\}$ and $\{E\}$.

Lemma 5.20. *Let $v \in V$ and T_v be the subtree of T with root v. Then v is the root of a strongly connected component of G if and only if $Q_v \cup R_v = \emptyset$. We consider the set Q_v after Visit(v) has completed the inspection of the environment U_v.*

Proof. If $Q_v \cup R_v = \emptyset$, v cannot belong to a strongly connected component whose root is an ancestor of v. For this reason, the node v is the root of a strongly connected component.

If $R_v \neq \emptyset$, there is a backward edge from a descendant of v to an ancestor w of v. v and w belong to the same strongly connected component. We have $t_b(z) \leq t_b(w) < t_b(v)$ for the root z of this strongly connected component. Because of this, the node v is not the root of its strongly connected component.

If $Q_v \neq \emptyset$ is valid, there is a cross edge (u, w). Let z be the root of the strongly connected component of w. Then $t_b(z) \leq t_b(w)$. The call of Visit(z) is not yet terminated when the cross edge (u, w) is inspected, because otherwise the strongly connected component with root z would be discovered as a strongly connected component. The node z is therefore an ancestor of v. Hence, the node v belongs to the strongly connected component with root z.
$\square$

Lemma 5.21. *A node k is the root of a strongly connected component if and only if $low(k) = t_b(k)$.*

Proof. A node k is the root of a strongly connected component if and only if $Q_k \cup R_k = \emptyset$ (Lemma 5.20). This in turn is equivalent to $low(k) = t_b(k)$. $\square$

Proposition 5.22. *Let G be a directed graph, and let n be the number of nodes and m the number of edges. The algorithm* TarjanComponents *computes the strongly connected components of G. The running time $T(n, m)$ of* TarjanComponents *satisfies $T(n, m) = O(n + m)$.*

Proof. From Lemmas 5.20 and 5.21, it follows that the algorithm TarjanComponents is correct. The running time of DFS is $O(n + m)$ and the additional running time for the repeat-until loop in Visit is $O(n)$, accumulated over all calls of Visit. In total, TarjanComponents runs in time $O(n + m)$. $\square$

The Algorithm of Kosaraju-Sharir. Let G be a directed graph and G_r be the assigned *reverse graph*, the graph with the same nodes but inverted edges. The algorithm uses the fact that the strongly connected components of G and G_r match. Let $t_e(v)$ be the numbering of the nodes of G with respect to the termination of Visit. Then the node v with the highest t_e number is the root of the component last entered by DFS. In the reverse graph, we determine the strongly connected component containing v by calling DFS with v as start node. We get the following algorithm:

Algorithm 5.23.
1. Execute DFS in G and number each node v with $t_e(v)$.
2. Construct the graph $G_r = (V, E_r)$ from G.
3. Perform depth-first search in G_r; start Visit with the node v with the highest number $t_e(v)$. The first strongly connected component of G consists of all nodes which we reach from v. If we do not reach all nodes, we start Visit again with the node v with the highest number $t_e(v)$ of the remaining nodes. The nodes that we now access form the second strongly connected component of G. We repeat this until all nodes in G_r are visited.

Steps 1 and 3 run in time $O(n + m)$; the running time for step 2 is $O(m)$. Overall, it follows that the running time is of order $O(n + m)$.

Example. Figure 5.21 shows a graph G and the assigned reverse graph G_r. Start depth-first search DFS in the node A of G. The superscripts indicate the depth-first numbering. We get the strongly connected components $\{A, C, G\}$, $\{B\}$, $\{H, I\}$, $\{J\}$, $\{K\}$, $\{L, M\}$ and $\{F, D, E\}$ by executing DFS in G_r.

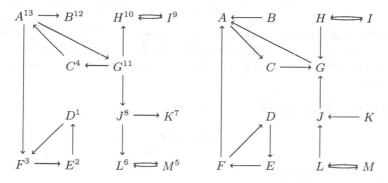

Fig. 5.21: Strongly connected components with Kosaraju-Sharir.

Proposition 5.24. *The nodes of the components of G_r, computed by Algorithm 5.23, correspond to the nodes of the strongly connected components of G.*

Proof. If v and w are in a strongly connected component of G, there is a path from w to v and from v to w in G and thus also in G_r. For this reason, v and w are also in the same component of G_r.

Let v be the root of the spanning tree of a component of G_r and w be another node in that component. Then we have a path from v to w in G_r, thus also a path from w to v in G. We show that v and w are mutually accessible in G. Without restriction, we assume $v \neq w$. Suppose that $t_b(w) < t_b(v)$. Since there is a path from w to v in G, it follows that $t_e(v) < t_e(w)$. A contradiction, because the root v has the highest number $t_e(v)$. So $t_b(v) < t_b(w)$. Since $t_e(w) < t_e(v)$, it follows that $I(w) \subset I(v)$. Hence, v is an ancestor of w in the corresponding depth-first tree of G (see Proposition 5.13). Thus, there is a path from v to w in G. v and w are mutually accessible. Consequently, any two nodes v and w from a component of G_r are mutually accessible in G. By definition, v and w belong to the same strongly connected component of G. □

5.7 A Randomized Min-Cut Algorithm

The following algorithm MinCut (Algorithm 5.33) is a Monte Carlo algorithm (see Definition 1.49). It is based on a simple idea. The algorithm SimpleMin-Cut, which follows immediately from this idea, has a low success probability. With a remarkable idea, we can considerably increase the success probability. Through independent repetitions, a standard procedure for randomized algorithms, the probability of success is further increased. The algorithm was first published in [Karger93]. Our presentation follows [KarSte96]. We study another method for computing a minimal cut in Section 6.8 (see Proposition 6.67).

Definition 5.25. Let $G = (V, E)$ be a connected multigraph.[23] A subset $C \subset E$ is called a *cut* of G if the graph $\tilde{G} = (V, E \setminus C)$ splits into at least two connected components. A cut C is called a *minimal cut* if $|C|$ is minimal for all cuts of G.

Remark. Let C be a minimal cut of G. Then

$$|C| \leq \min_{v \in V} \deg(v).$$

C can also be $< \min_{v \in V} \deg(v)$.

Definition 5.26. Let $G = (V, E)$ be a connected multigraph. Let $e = \{v, w\} \in E$. The multigraph G/e results from G by *contraction* of e if all edges between v and w are removed and the nodes v and w are identified.

The following algorithm RandContract randomly selects an edge e in a graph $G = (V, E)$ with $n = |V|$ and $m = |E|$ and calculates G/e. G is given by an integer adjacency matrix $adm[1..n, 1..n]$. $adm[i, j] = k$ if and only if there are k edges between i and j. Additionally, there is an array $a[1..n]$ with $a[i] = \deg(i)$. It holds that $\sum_{i=1}^{n} a[i] = 2m$. We think of the edges starting from each of the nodes 1 to n numbered in this order from 1 to $2m$. Each edge has two end nodes and thus also two numbers. The following algorithm randomly selects the number $r \in \{1, \ldots, 2m\}$ of the edge to be contracted and performs the contraction of the edge.

---

[23] Multiple edges are allowed between two nodes.

Algorithm 5.27.
  graph RandContract(graph G)
  1   int $i \leftarrow 0$, $j \leftarrow 0$, $s \leftarrow 0$, $t \leftarrow 0$
  2   choose $r \in \{1, \ldots, 2m\}$ at random
  3   while $s < r$ do
  4        $i \leftarrow i + 1$, $s \leftarrow s + a[i]$
  5   $s \leftarrow r - s + a[i]$
  6   while $t < s$ do
  7        $j \leftarrow j + 1$, $t \leftarrow t + adm[i, j]$
  8   $s \leftarrow 0$
  9   for $k \leftarrow 1$ to n do
  10       $adm[i, k] \leftarrow adm[i, k] + adm[j, k]$
  11       $adm[k, i] \leftarrow adm[i, k]$, $s \leftarrow s + adm[i, k]$
  12 $a[i] \leftarrow s - adm[i, i]$, $a[j] \leftarrow 0$, $adm[i, i] \leftarrow 0$

Remarks:

1. In line 2, we randomly select a number $r \in \{1, \ldots, 2m\}$. Then we determine the node from which the rth edge originates (lines 3 and 4).
2. After line 5 has been executed, s contains the number of the rth edge in the sequence of the edges which leave node i.
3. In lines 6 and 7, we determine the other end node of the rth edge.
4. The ith and jth rows (and columns) are to be "merged" (lines 9, 10 and 11) and $a[i]$ and $a[j]$ are to be recalculated.
5. The running time of RandContract is of order $O(n)$.
6. $a[k] = 0$ means that node k was identified with another node during contraction. The kth row and the kth column of the adjacency matrix are invalid. We think of the kth row and the kth column as deleted. RandContract can repeatedly operate on adm and a. adm describes a multigraph. The valid rows and columns of adm are noted in a.
7. RandContract can easily be adapted for a representation of the multigraph by an adjacency list. The union of the adjacency lists of the nodes i and j is possible in time $O(n)$ if these lists are sorted.

The idea of the algorithm SimpleMinCut is to contract edges one after the other until only two nodes v and w are left. Let C be a minimal cut of G. C survives the contractions of SimpleMinCut if we do not contract an edge from C. Then the edges from C remain as edges between v and w. If a graph with two nodes is the result of repeated contractions, and no edge of a certain minimal cut is contracted, then SimpleMinCut computes a minimal cut. But the probability of success of SimpleMinCut is very small (Proposition 5.29).

Example. SimpleMinCut calculates a minimal cut if in Figure 5.22 the edge $\{C, G\}$ is not contracted.

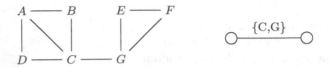

Fig. 5.22: SimpleMinCut.

Algorithm 5.28.

edgeset SimpleMinCut(graph G)

1   graph $I \leftarrow G$
2   while I has more than two vertices do
3       $I \leftarrow$ RandContract(I)
4   return E_I

Proposition 5.29. *Let G be a graph with n nodes. The success probability of* SimpleMinCut *satisfies*

$$\text{p(SimpleMinCut } \textit{calculates a minimal cut }) \geq \frac{2}{n(n-1)}.$$

Proof. Let C be a minimal cut of G, $k = |C|$, and let

$$G = I_0 = (V_0, E_0), I_1 = (V_1, E_1), \dots, I_{n-2} = (V_{n-2}, E_{n-2})$$

be the sequence of multigraphs that results from contractions by SimpleMin-Cut, where I_i is the result after the ith iteration.

$$pr := \text{p(SimpleMinCut computes a minimal cut)}$$
$$\geq \text{p(SimpleMinCut returns } C).$$

The last probability is equal to the probability that RandContract in line 3 does not choose an edge from C.

$$\text{p(SimpleMinCut returns } C) = \prod_{i=0}^{n-3} \frac{|E_i| - k}{|E_i|} = \prod_{i=0}^{n-3} 1 - \frac{k}{|E_i|}.$$

If we do not select an edge from C in the first i iterations, the cardinality of a minimal cut of I_i is equal to k. The degree of every node in I_i is $\geq k$. For this reason, $|E_i| \geq \frac{(n-i)k}{2}$, or, equivalently, $1 - \frac{k}{|E_i|} \geq 1 - \frac{2}{n-i}$. Thus,

$$pr \geq \prod_{i=0}^{n-3} \left(1 - \frac{2}{n-i}\right) = \prod_{i=0}^{n-3} \frac{n-i-2}{n-i} = \frac{2}{n(n-1)},$$

thereby proving the assertion of the proposition. $\square$

Remark. Each minimal cut in K_3, the full graph with three nodes (and three edges), consists of a pair of edges. The lower bound for the probability that SimpleMinCut calculates a given minimal cut is attained by K_3.

The probability that the selected edge is not in C is highest for the first selected edge and decreases for every further edge. In order to increase the success probability, we apply the following idea. Perform only so many contractions that about $\frac{n}{\sqrt{2}}$ nodes are left (instead of $n-2$ contractions with two nodes left) and continue the procedure recursively. Perform a total of two independent repetitions. As we will see in a moment, this will considerably increase the likelihood of success.

Algorithm 5.30.
    edgeset L(graph G)
    1   graph $I \leftarrow \tilde{I} \leftarrow G$
    2   int $t \leftarrow \left\lceil \frac{n}{\sqrt{2}} + \left(\sqrt{2} - 1\right) \right\rceil$
    3   if $t \leq 10$
    4   then enumerate all cuts and return a minimal cut
    5   while $|V_I| \geq t+1$ do
    6            $I \leftarrow$ RandContract(I)
    7   while $|V_{\tilde{I}}| \geq t+1$ do
    8            $\tilde{I} \leftarrow$ RandContract($\tilde{I}$)
    9    $E_I \leftarrow$ L(I), $E_{\tilde{I}} \leftarrow$ L($\tilde{I}$)
    10   if $|E_I| \leq |E_{\tilde{I}}|$
    11   then return E_I
    12   else return $E_{\tilde{I}}$

Proposition 5.31. *Let G be a graph with n nodes, and let $T(n)$ denote the running time of* L. *Then*

$$T(n) = O\left(n^2 \log_2(n)\right).$$

Proof. The running time $T(n)$ of L is defined by the recurrence

$$T(n) = 2T\left(\left\lceil \frac{n}{\sqrt{2}} + \left(\sqrt{2} - 1\right) \right\rceil\right) + cn^2.$$

We have $\left\lceil \frac{n}{\sqrt{2}} + \left(\sqrt{2} - 1\right) \right\rceil < \frac{n+2}{\sqrt{2}}$. We consider

$$\tilde{T}(n) = 2\tilde{T}\left(\frac{n+2}{\sqrt{2}}\right) + cn^2.$$

Set $\alpha = \frac{2}{\sqrt{2}-1}$, $n = \sqrt{2^k} + \alpha$ and $x_k = \tilde{T}\left(\sqrt{2^k} + \alpha\right)$. Then

$$x_k = \tilde{T}\left(\sqrt{2^k} + \alpha\right)$$
$$= 2\tilde{T}\left(\sqrt{2^{k-1}} + \alpha\right) + c\left(\sqrt{2^k} + \alpha\right)^2$$
$$= 2x_{k-1} + c\left(\sqrt{2^k} + \alpha\right)^2,$$
$$x_1 = b.$$

By Proposition 1.15 and formula (F.5) in Appendix B, we get

$$x_k = 2^{k-1}\left(b + c\sum_{i=2}^{k} \frac{2^i + 2\alpha\sqrt{2^i} + \alpha^2}{2^{i-1}}\right)$$
$$= b2^{k-1} + c(k-1)2^k + c\alpha^2\left(2^{k-1} - 1\right) + \frac{2\alpha c}{\sqrt{2} - 1}\sqrt{2^k}\left(\sqrt{2^{k-1}} - 1\right)$$
$$= O(k2^k).$$

Let $k = 2\log_2(n - \alpha)$. Then by Lemma B.23

$$\tilde{T}(n) = O\left(2\log_2(n - \alpha)2^{2\log_2(n-\alpha)}\right) = O\left(n^2\log_2(n)\right).$$

Because $T(n) \leq \tilde{T}(n)$, $T(n)$ is also of order $O\left(n^2\log_2(n)\right)$.   □

Proposition 5.32. *Let G be a graph with n nodes. The success probability of L satisfies*

$$p(L \text{ computes a minimal cut }) \geq \frac{1}{\log_2(n)}.$$

Proof. Let C be a minimal cut of G, $k = |C|$, $t = \left\lceil \frac{n}{\sqrt{2}} + (\sqrt{2} - 1)\right\rceil$, and let

$$(V_i, E_i) \text{ be } I_i \text{ or } \tilde{I}_i, \ i = 0, \ldots, n - t,$$

be the sequence of multigraphs created by contraction while L is executed. Let pr be the probability that C is a minimal cut of I or $\tilde{I}$. Then

$$pr = \prod_{i=0}^{n-t-1} \frac{|E_i| - k}{|E_i|} = \prod_{i=0}^{n-t-1}\left(1 - \frac{k}{|E_i|}\right) \geq \prod_{i=0}^{n-t-1}\left(1 - \frac{2}{n-i}\right)$$
$$= \prod_{i=0}^{n-t-1} \frac{n-i-2}{n-i} = \frac{t(t-1)}{n(n-1)} \geq \frac{1}{2}$$

(see the proof of Proposition 5.29).

The probability of success of L is determined by two independent phases. The first phase consists of the repeated contractions. The probability that a cut C with $|C| = k$ will survive the contractions is $\geq 1/2$. The second phase consists of the recursive executions of L.

Let $pr_G := p(\text{L computes a minimal cut of G})$. Since the probability that L computes a minimal cut of G with I or $\tilde{I}$ is greater than or equal to $\frac{1}{2}pr_I$ or $\frac{1}{2}pr_{\tilde{I}}$, and the two events are independent, we get

$$pr_G \geq 1 - \left(1 - \frac{1}{2}pr_I\right)\left(1 - \frac{1}{2}pr_{\tilde{I}}\right).$$

Actually, this formula depends only on $n = |V_G|$ and on $t = |V_I| = |V_{\tilde{I}}|$. We replace pr_G by pr_n, pr_I and $pr_{\tilde{I}}$ by pr_t and get

$$pr_n \geq pr_t - \frac{1}{4}pr_t^2.$$

As above, we set $\alpha = \frac{2}{\sqrt{2}-1}$, $n = \sqrt{2^k} + \alpha$ and $x_k = pr_{(\sqrt{2^k}+\alpha)}$. Algorithm 5.30 computes a minimal cut for small n, thus $x_1 = 1$.

$$x_k = x_{k-1} - \frac{1}{4}x_{k-1}^2.$$

We set $y_k := \frac{4}{x_k} - 1$. Then $x_k = \frac{4}{y_k+1}$ and

$$y_k = y_{k-1} + \frac{1}{y_{k-1}} + 1.$$

This is a simple non-linear first-order difference equation.[24]

We show by induction on k that

$$k < y_k < k + H_{k-1} + 3.$$

For $y_1 = 3$ the inequality is fulfilled. Further, according to the induction hypothesis for $k - 1$

$$y_k = y_{k-1} + \frac{1}{y_{k-1}} + 1 > k - 1 + \frac{1}{k + H_{k-2} + 3} + 1 > k$$

and

$$y_k = y_{k-1} + \frac{1}{y_{k-1}} + 1 < k - 1 + H_{k-2} + 3 + \frac{1}{k-1} + 1 = k + H_{k-1} + 3.$$

Then $x_k = \frac{4}{y_k+1} > \frac{4}{k+H_{k-1}+4}$ and

$$pr_n = x_{2\log_2(n-\alpha)} > \frac{4}{2\log_2(n-\alpha) + H_{\lceil 2\log_2(n-\alpha)-1\rceil} + 4} > \frac{1}{\log_2(n)}.$$

---

[24] This is a special case of the *logistic difference equation* for which (except in special cases) no closed solution can be specified (see [Elaydi03, page 13]).

□

In order to increase the success probability, we now use a standard procedure for randomized algorithms. Through independent repetitions of L we can make the error probability arbitrarily small. We repeat L $l = k\lceil \log_2(n)\rceil$ times. k is a constant and determines the success probability (see Proposition 5.34).

Algorithm 5.33.
```
edgeset MinCut(graph G; int l)
 1   edgeset Ẽ, E ← E_G
 2   for i = 1 to l do
 3       Ẽ ← L(G)
 4       if |Ẽ| < |E|
 5           then E ← Ẽ
 6   return E
```

Proposition 5.34. *Let $T(n)$ be the running time of* MinCut. *Then $T(n) = O(n^2 \log_2(n)^2)$ and the probability of success of* MinCut *satisfies*

$$p(\text{MinCut } calculates\ a\ minimal\ cut\,) > 1 - e^{-k}.$$

Proof. The statement about the running time follows immediately from Proposition 5.31. The error probability p_{err} of L satisfies $p_{err} < 1 - \frac{1}{\log_2(n)}$. The probability pr that L is wrong in every iteration satisfies

$$pr < \left(1 - \frac{1}{\log_2(n)}\right)^{k\lceil \log_2(n)\rceil} \leq \left(1 - \frac{1}{\log_2(n)}\right)^{k\log_2(n)}.$$

Since the sequence $\left(1 - \frac{1}{n}\right)^n$ converges strictly increasing to e^{-1} (Proposition B.18),

$$\left(1 - \frac{1}{\log_2(n)}\right)^{k\log_2(n)}$$

converges strictly increasing to e^{-k}. Hence, $pr < e^{-k}$ follows. L always calculates a cut. However, this need not necessarily be minimal. If one of the executions of L calculates a minimal cut, it is the execution that returns the result with the least number of edges. The probability that at least one calculation is correct is $> 1 - e^{-k}$.   □

Exercises.

1. Show that a graph contains an Eulerian cycle if and only if it is connected and all nodes have even degree.

2. Let G be a connected planar graph, v be the number of nodes of G and e be the number of edges of G. By f we denote the number of regions into which G divides the plane. Show Euler's polyhedron formula for planar graphs:

$$v - e + f = 2.$$

The unrestricted region must also be counted.

3. Let $G = (V, E)$ be a graph. $\Delta = \max_{v \in V} \deg(v)$ denotes the maximum degree of G. Show that G can be colored with $\Delta + 1$ colors so that neighboring nodes have different colors.

4. Show that in a graph, the number of nodes of odd degree is even.

5. Let $[x], [y] \in \mathbb{Z}_{21}$. We define $[x] \sim [y]$ if and only if $x \equiv y \bmod 7$. Show that this defines an equivalence relation. Display it with a graph and characterize the equivalence classes.

6. Let $G = (V, E)$ be a graph, $n = |V|$, $m = |E|$. Show:
   a. If G is connected, then $m \geq n - 1$.
   b. Whenever $m \geq \binom{n-1}{2} + 1$, it follows that G is connected.

7. Let $G = (V, E)$ be a graph with $|V| \geq 2$. Show that the following statements are equivalent:
   a. G is a tree.
   b. G is acyclic and has exactly $|V| - 1$ edges.
   c. G is acyclic and adding an edge always results in a cycle.
   d. G is connected and $G \setminus \{e\} := (V, E \setminus \{e\})$ splits up into exactly two components for all $e \in E$.
   e. For every two nodes k and l, there is exactly one path that connects k and l.

8. Let $G = (V, E)$ be a graph and $|V| = 6$. Show that there are three nodes so that the subgraph generated by them is complete, or there are three nodes so that the subgraph generated by them consists of isolated nodes.

9. Let $G = (V, E)$ be a graph and $n = |V| \geq 3$. For each two nodes k and l which are not adjacent, we have $\deg(k) + \deg(l) \geq n$. Show that G has a Hamiltonian[25] circuit, i.e. a cycle that contains each node exactly once. This result is attributed to Ore ([Gould88, Theorem 5.2.1]). In particular, a graph with $\deg(v) \geq \frac{n}{2}$ for $v \in V$ has a Hamiltonian circuit.

10. Let $V = \{I_1, \ldots, I_n\}$ be a set of intervals. We assign to V the *interval graph* $G = (V, E)$: $\{I_i, I_j\} \in E, 1 \leq i, j \leq n, i \neq j$, if and only if $I_i \cap I_j \neq \emptyset$. Specify an efficient algorithm that generates the interval graph G for a given V. Analyze your algorithm.

---

[25] William Rowan Hamilton (1805 – 1865) was an Irish mathematician and physicist, known primarily for his contributions to mechanics and for his study of quaternions.

11. Alcuin was a scholar at the court of Charlemagne and one of his most important advisers. A collection of mathematical problems attributed to Alcuin contains the following task [Herrmann16, page 259]: A man wants to cross a river with a wolf, a goat and a head of cabbage. He has a boat at his disposal in which only an animal or the head of cabbage can be placed besides himself as a rower. If goat and wolf are alone, the wolf eats the goat. If goat and head of cabbage are alone, the goat eats the head of cabbage. How can the man bring the wolf, goat and head of cabbage safely to the other shore?

12. Develop a non-recursive version of DFS.

13. We classify the edges of a graph analogously to Definition 5.14. Which types of edges (tree, forward, backward or cross edges) are caused by the type of traversing (BFS or DFS) of graphs and directed graphs?

14. Which of the linear arrangements (1) A,G,H,I,B,F,D,E,J,C,K,L,M (2) A,B,J,K,L,M,C,G,H,I,F,E,D (3) A,B,J,K,L,M,G,C,H,I,F,E,D are topological sortings of the graph from the example on page 225. Specify the calls of Visit for the topological sortings. Can every topological sorting of V be created by TopSort?

15. Show that a directed acyclic graph G has at least one node into which no edge enters, and further show that there is exactly one node into which no edge enters if G is a directed tree, i.e., there is one node from which all other nodes can be reached.

16. Let $G = (V, E)$ be a directed graph, $V_1, \ldots, V_r$ its strongly connected components. $G_{red} = (V_{red}, E_{red})$, where $V_{red} = \{V_1, \ldots, V_r\}$, $E_{red} = \{(V_i, V_j) \mid i \neq j$ and there exists $v \in V_i, w \in V_j : (v, w) \in E\}$, the reduced graph associated with G. Show that G_{red} is acyclic.

17. Let A be the adjacency matrix of a directed graph G and A^r the rth power of A, $r \geq 1$.
    a. Show that G has $A^r[i,j]$ different directed paths from i to j of length r. In particular, G is a directed acyclic graph if there is an $r \in \mathbb{N}$ with $A^r = 0$ (i.e., A is *nilpotent*).
    b. Let $A \in M(n \times n, \{0, 1\})$, $A[i, i] = 0, i = 1, ..., n$. Specify an efficient algorithm that decides whether A is nilpotent.

18. Let $(M, \leq)$ be a finite partially ordered set, i.e., for $a, b, c \in M$ holds: $a \leq a$, from $a \leq b$ and $b \leq a$ it follows that $a = b$, from $a \leq b$ and $b \leq c$ it follows that $a \leq c$. Because of the transitivity of the $\leq$ relation, all relations can be obtained from relations of the form $a < b$, $a \neq b$ and there is no c with $a < c < b$. We assign $(M, \leq)$ to a directed graph $G = (V, E)$: $V = M, E = \{(a, b) | a < b, a \neq b$ and there is no c with $a < c < b\}$.

a. Let $M = \{a, b, c, d, e, f\}$ and $a < b$, $a < c$, $a < d$, $a < e$, $a < f$, $b < c$, $b < f$, $c < e$, $c < f$, $e < d$, $e < f$.

Draw the directed graph associated with $(M, \leq)$.

For the following subtasks, $(M, \leq)$ is an arbitrary finite partially ordered set.

b. Does the directed graph associated with $(M, \leq)$ have cycles? What are its strongly connected components?

c. How do you determine for $a \in M$ all $b \in M$ with $b > a$ and all $b \in M$ with $b < a$ using the directed graph associated with $(M, \leq)$?

19. Let $G = (V, E)$ be a connected graph, $|V| \geq 3$ and T a DFS tree of G with root r. R denotes the set of backward edges. A node $v \in V$ is called an *articulation point* if $G \backslash \{v\} := (V \backslash \{v\}, E \backslash \{e \in E \mid v \text{ end node of } e\})$ is not connected. A graph without articulation points is called *bi-connected* or *not separable*. A *block* of a graph G is a maximal non-separable subgraph of G.

a. Use a sketch to figure out the terms.

b. Show that v is an articulation point of G if there are $u, w \in V \backslash \{v\}$ such that every simple path from u to w goes through v.

c. Show that r is an articulation point if r has at least two successors.

d. Let $v \in V, v \neq r$. Show that v is an articulation point if there is a successor v' of v and for all $(u, w) \in R$ w is not an ancestor of v if u is a descendant of v' or v'.

e. $low(v) := min(\{t_b(v)\} \cup \{t_b(w) | (u, w) \in R \text{ and } u \text{ is a descendant of } v \text{ or } u = v\})$.

Show that $v \in V, v \neq r$, is an articulation point if there is a successor v' of v with $low(v') \geq t_b[v]$.

f. Specify an algorithm to calculate $low(v)$ for all $v \in V$ and find the articulation points.

20. Let $G = (V, E)$ be a connected graph, $|V| \geq 3$. Show that G is biconnected if and only if for every two nodes there is a cycle that contains both.

6. Weighted Graphs

In this chapter, we discuss weighted graphs, that is, graphs for which each edge has an associated positive weight. In detail, we deal with minimum spanning trees, the distance problem and the computation of the maximum flow in a network.

In the first section, we study algorithms that we will apply later. Among these are priority queues, the union-find data type, the LCA problem and a more efficient procedure for the RMQ problem from the first chapter. Priority queues are implemented applying binary heaps. We use the Ackermann function to analyze the union-find data type. The LCA problem is to determine the lowest common ancestor of two nodes in a rooted tree. Solving this problem in linear running time is a prerequisite for the algorithm of King for verifying a minimum spanning tree in linear running time.

The algorithms of Borůvka, Kruskal and Prim construct minimum spanning trees, and the algorithm of Dijkstra solves the single-source distance problem. The algorithms of Prim and Dijkstra generalize breadth-first search from Chapter 5. In its implementation, the priority queue replaces the queue that we use for breadth-first search. The union-find data type is used in Kruskal's algorithm.

The randomized algorithm of Karger, Klein and Tarjan computes a minimum spanning tree in linear time. An algorithm that performs the verification of a minimum spanning tree in linear time is essential for this.

Warshall's algorithm determines the transitive closure of a graph and Floyd's algorithm the distance matrix. The algorithms of Ford-Fulkerson and Edmonds-Karp solve the flow problem in networks.

First, we clarify the concept of a weighted graph.

Definition 6.1. A graph $G = (V, E)$ with a map $w : E \longrightarrow \mathbb{R}_{>0}$ is called a *weighted graph*. The map w is called the *weight function*. For $e \in E$, $w(e)$ is said to be the *weight of e*. The *weight of G* is the sum of the weights of all edges, $w(G) = \sum_{e \in E} w(e)$.

To describe weighted graphs, we use the adjacency list and adjacency matrix data structures – as with the description of graphs. We only need to extend the definitions slightly.

1. An adjacency matrix adm is an $n \times n$–matrix with coefficients from $\mathbb{R}_{\geq 0}$,

$$adm[i,j] := \begin{cases} w(\{i,j\}) \text{ if } \{i,j\} \in E, \\ 0 \text{ otherwise.} \end{cases}$$

2. In the list elements of the adjacency list, we will save the weight of an edge. Therefore, we extend the list element for graphs on page 216 with the component *weight*.

6.1 Basic Algorithms

In this section, we study basic algorithms which we will apply in the rest of the chapter. These are priority queues and the union-find data type, which belong to the advanced data structures and can be applied in many situations.

We treat the LCA problem, which is linearly equivalent to the RMQ problem (see Section 1.5.4), as an independent problem. It is a basic algorithmic problem that has been intensively studied. The computation of the lowest common ancestor (LCA) of two nodes in a rooted tree is an essential input into a linear-time verification algorithm for minimum spanning trees, which we study in Section 6.5.

6.1.1 The Priority Queue

The priority queue generalizes the abstract data type queue. With a queue, the elements leave the queue in the same order in which they were stored (first in, first out – FIFO principle). With a priority queue, we assign a priority to each element when it is saved. Our later application requires the priority of a stored element to be lowered. The element with the lowest priority leaves the queue next. A priority queue is defined by the following functions:

1. PQInit(int *size*) initializes a priority queue for *size* elements.
2. PQUpdate(element k, priority n) inserts k with priority n into the priority queue. If k is already in the priority queue and k has a higher priority than n, then PQUpdate lowers the priority of k to n. PQUpdate returns true if an insert or update operation has occurred, otherwise false.
3. PQRemove returns the element with the lowest priority and removes it from the priority queue.
4. PQEmpty checks the priority queue for elements.

When implementing the priority queue, we use the following data types: type element = $1..n$, type index = $0..n$ and
type queueEntry = struct

      element   *elem*

      int   *prio*   .

We implement a priority queue by using the two arrays $prioQu[1..n]$ and $pos[1..n]$ and organize the array $prioQu$ – ordered by priority – as a heap (Section 2.2.1), i.e., with $a[i] := prioQu[i].prio$ we have

$$a[i] \leq a[2i] \text{ for } 1 \leq i \leq \left\lfloor \frac{n}{2} \right\rfloor \text{ and } a[i] \leq a[2i+1] \text{ for } 1 \leq i \leq \left\lfloor \frac{n-1}{2} \right\rfloor.$$

In order that an element k in $prioQu$ can be reached with one access (and does not need to be searched for), we require the array $pos[1..n]$. The variable $pos[k]$ contains the position of the element k in $prioQu$. If the element k is not stored, $pos[k]$ contains the value 0.

A change of the priority of element k requires the priority of the $queueEntry$ in $prioQu$ at the position $r = pos[k]$ to be changed. This may violate the heap condition at position $\lfloor r/2 \rfloor$ and further places. The function UpHeap operates on the array $prioQu[1..n]$ and restores the heap condition.

Algorithm 6.2.
UpHeap(index r)
1   index : i, j; item : x
2   $i \leftarrow r$, $j \leftarrow \lfloor \frac{i}{2} \rfloor$, $x \leftarrow prioQu[i]$
3   while $j \geq 1$ do
4   if $x.prio \geq prioQu[j].prio$
5   then break
6       $prioQu[i] \leftarrow prioQu[j]$, $i \leftarrow j$, $j \leftarrow \lfloor \frac{i}{2} \rfloor$
7   $prioQu[i] \leftarrow x$

The organization of $prioQu[1..n]$ as a heap underlays $prioQu[1..n]$, the structure of a binary tree of minimum height with n nodes (see Section 2.2.1). The number of iterations of the while loop in UpHeap and in DownHeap is limited by $\lfloor \log_2(n) \rfloor$ (Lemma 2.16).

UpHeap is implemented analogously to DownHeap (Algorithm 2.12). UpHeap and DownHeap operate on the arrays $prioQu$ and pos. If elements are rearranged in $prioQu$, the new positions must be entered in pos. An actual implementation of UpHeap must be supplemented by this point.

We first insert new elements after the last element of the queue. UpHeap then brings the element to the right place in the heap. If we remove the element of minimum priority, we put the last element in the first place. With DownHeap we restore the heap condition. We now specify the algorithms PQUpdate and PQRemove more precisely.

Algorithm 6.3.
int $nrElem$; queueEntry $prioQu[1..n]$; index $pos[1..n]$
element PQRemove()
1   element ret
2   $ret \leftarrow prioQu[1].elem$
3   $pos[prioQu[1].elem] \leftarrow 0$
4   $prioQu[1] \leftarrow prioQu[nrElem]$
5   $pos[prioQu[nrElem].elem] \leftarrow 1$
6   $nrElem \leftarrow nrElem - 1$
7   DownHeap(1)
8   return ret

boolean PQUpdate(element k; int $prio$)

```
 1   if pos[k] = 0
 2      then nrElem ← nrElem + 1
 3           prioQu[nrElem].elem ← k, prioQu[nrElem].prio ← prio
 4           UpHeap(nrElem)
 5           return true
 6      else if prioQu[pos[k]].prio > prio
 7              then prioQu[pos[k]].prio ← prio
 8                   UpHeap(pos[k])
 9                   return true
10   return false
```

Remark. The running time $T(n)$ of PQUpdate and of PQRemove is of the same order as the running time of UpHeap and of DownHeap, that is $T(n) = O(\log_2(n))$.

6.1.2 The Union-Find Data Type

The *union-find data type*, also known as the *disjoint-set data structure*, supports dynamic partitioning of a set $V = \{v_1, \ldots, v_n\}$ in subsets $V_i \subset V$, $i = 1, \ldots, l$, i.e.,

$$V = \bigcup_{i=1}^{l} V_i, V_i \cap V_j = \emptyset \text{ for } i \neq j.$$

For each subset V_i, a representative $r_i \in V_i$ is chosen, $i = 1, \ldots, l$.

The union-find data type provides the following operations:

1. Find(element x) returns for $x \in V_i$ the representative r_i of V_i.
2. Union(element x, y) returns false if x and y are in the same subset V_i and otherwise true. If x and y are in distinct subsets V_i and V_j, Union replaces V_i and V_j with $V_i \cup V_j$ and chooses a representative for $V_i \cup V_j$.
3. FindInit(element $v_1, \ldots, v_n$) initializes subsets $V_i = \{v_i\}, i = 1, \ldots, n$. The representative of V_i is v_i.

The union-find data type and its implementations have been studied intensively. A significant part is attributed to Tarjan. We follow [Tarjan99] and [HopUll73].

We assume without loss of generality that $V = \{1, \ldots, n\}$. We implement $V_1, \ldots, V_l$ using rooted trees. Each V_i corresponds to a rooted tree T_i. The elements of V_i are stored in the nodes of T_i. The representative of V_i is the element stored in the root. Let $T := \cup_{i=1}^{l} T_i$ be the forest that the T_i form. We describe T by the array $parent[1..n]$. Then:

1. The elements i and j belong to the same V_i if i and j belong to the same tree, i.e., have the same root. Each root w is encoded by $parent[w] = 0$.
2. Two components with roots i and j are combined into one component by $parent[j] \leftarrow i$ (or $parent[i] \leftarrow j$).

3. FindInit(n) allocates memory for the *parent* array and initializes each cell of *parent* to 0.

We are going to present pseudo-code for Find and Union.

Algorithm 6.4.

```
int Find(int i)
1   while parent[i] > 0 do
2       i ← parent[i]
3   return i
```

```
boolean Union(int i, j)
1   ret ← false
2   i ← Find(i)
3   j ← Find(j)
4   if i ≠ j
5       then parent[i] ← j, ret = true
6   return ret
```

With this implementation of Union, trees can degenerate. In the worst case, linear lists are the result. We now discuss two techniques – union by height and path compression – that prevent this.

Union by Height. When applying *union by height*, we make the node with the greater height the new root. In the following algorithm, this is done in lines 5 – 10, which replace line 5 in Algorithm 6.4. The height only increases by 1 if both trees have the same height. We use the array $rank[1..n]$ to store the height of a node. In FindInit, we set $rank[i] = 0$, $i = 1, \ldots, n$.

Algorithm 6.5.

```
boolean Union(int i, j)
1    ret ← false
2    i ← Find(i)
3    j ← Find(j)
4    if i ≠ j
5        then ret = true
6             if rank[i] > rank[j]
7                 then parent[j] ← i
8                 else parent[i] ← j
9                      if rank[i] = rank[j]
10                         then rank[j] = rank[j] + 1
11   return ret
```

Remark. After a node i has become the successor of a node j, $rank[i]$ remains unchanged. This also holds when we apply path compression. But then $rank[i]$ no longer stores the height of i.

Path Compression. The idea behind *path compression* is to replace the parent node of a node with the root of the tree. If we apply this idea consistently, we have to completely reorganize one of the two trees at union. This is too time-consuming. Therefore, we only change the branching in Find along the path from i to the root. We use path compression along with union by height. Path compression can change the height of a tree. Now, $rank[i]$ no longer stores the height of the node i. The number $rank[i]$ is called the *rank* of the node i. The rank of the node i approximates the logarithm of the number of nodes in the subtree with root i (Lemma 6.7, statement 2). We use the rank as a criterion for balancing the tree. We call the procedure union by rank. Additionally, we extend Find by path compression. We first demonstrate this as shown in Figure 6.1.

Example. Using path compression, we replace the parent node of a node with the root of the tree.

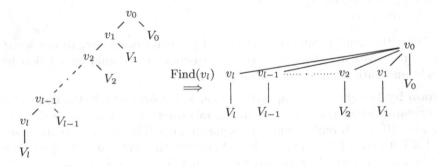

Fig. 6.1: Path compression.

Algorithm 6.6.
    int Find(int i)
    1   int $k \leftarrow i$
    2   while $parent[k] > 0$ do
    3        $k \leftarrow parent[k]$
    4   while $parent[i] > 0$ do
    5        $m \leftarrow i$, $i \leftarrow parent[i]$, $parent[m] \leftarrow k$
    6   return i

Remark. The algorithm Union only needs the rank of the root nodes. We can store the rank k of the root i as $-k$ in $parent[i]$. We can now recognize roots by negative entries or by the value 0. Thus, we can save the array $rank$. In the following, we write $rank[u] = \text{rank}(u)$ as a function.

We now consider the union-find algorithm after $n-1$ Union and m Find calls. One step consists of calling one of the two functions above. Altogether there are $n - 1 + m$ steps. After l steps of the algorithm have been executed, i.e., after the lth call terminates, for a node u we denote by T_u the subtree with root u, by $\operatorname{rank}(u)$ the rank of the node u and by $U_r := \{u \mid \operatorname{rank}(u) = r\}$. The value $\operatorname{rank}(u)$ increases with the number of steps.

Lemma 6.7. *We have for $0 \le l \le n - 1 + m$:*

1. *The function* $\operatorname{rank}(u)$ *is strictly increasing along the path from a node to the root of the subtree.*
2. *We have* $\operatorname{rank}(u) \le \lfloor \log_2(|T_u|) \rfloor \le \lfloor \log_2(n) \rfloor$. *In particular, the height of the tree is at most* $\log_2(n)$.
3. $|U_r| \le n/2^r$.

Proof.

1. If u is followed by v in the ascending path, v was defined as the root of the subtree T_u. Then $\operatorname{rank}(v) > \operatorname{rank}(u)$. In the further progress, the rank of u remains constant, while the rank of v can increase. Since path compression does not change the rank of a node, and since after path compression a node can only become the child of a node with a higher rank, the statement also holds after path compression has been performed.
2. We show the assertion by induction on l. For $l = 0$ (after FindInit) $\operatorname{rank}(u) = 0$ and $\log_2(|T_u|) = 0$; the assertion is therefore correct. After a call to Union, when the union of components is carried out either the rank remains the same, in which case the inequality also holds after the union of the trees, or the rank increases by one. Then

$$\operatorname{rank}(u)_{new} = \operatorname{rank}(u) + 1 = \log_2(2^{\operatorname{rank}(u)+1})$$

$$= \log_2(2 \cdot 2^{\operatorname{rank}(u)}) = \log_2(2^{\operatorname{rank}(u)} + 2^{\operatorname{rank}(v)})$$

$$\le \log_2(|T_u| + |T_v|) = \log_2(|\tilde{T}_u|),$$

where v is the root of the second tree and $\tilde{T}_u$ is the union of T_u and T_v. From $|T_u| \le n$ follows the second inequality from statement 2. With the first statement, we get the statement about the height.
3. If $\operatorname{rank}(u) = \operatorname{rank}(v)$, then by statement 1 $T_u \cap T_v = \emptyset$. Hence,

$$n \ge |\bigcup_{u \in U_r} T_u| = \sum_{u \in U_r} |T_u| \ge \sum_{u \in U_r} 2^r = |U_r| \cdot 2^r.$$

The lemma is therefore proven.   □

Running Time Analysis. The running time analysis of the union-find algorithm (see Proposition 6.10) uses the Ackermann function (Algorithm 1.5). Therefore, we derive properties of the Ackermann function. First, we show that the Ackermann function

$$A(m,n) = \begin{cases} n+1 & \text{if } m = 0, \\ A(m-1,1) & \text{if } n = 0, \\ A(m-1, A(m, n-1)) & \text{otherwise}, \end{cases}$$

is increasing and give an equivalent definition for this purpose. We define a family of functions $A_m(n)$ by

$$A_0(n) = n+1,$$
$$A_m(n) = A_{m-1}^{n+1}(1) = \underbrace{A_{m-1} \circ \ldots \circ A_{m-1}}_{n+1}(1).$$

Lemma 6.8. *We have:*

1. *$A_m(n) = A(m,n)$ for $m, n \geq 0$.*
2. *$A_m(n) \geq n+1$ for $m, n \geq 0$.*
3. *$A_m(n+1) > A_m(n)$ for $m, n \geq 0$.*
4. *$A_m^n(1) \geq n+1$ for $n \geq 0$.*

Proof.

1. We set $A(m,n) = \tilde{A}_m(n)$. Then

$$\tilde{A}_m(n) = \tilde{A}_{m-1}(\tilde{A}_m(n-1)) = \tilde{A}_{m-1}(\tilde{A}_{m-1}(\tilde{A}_m(n-2)))\ldots =$$

$$\tilde{A}_{m-1}^n(\tilde{A}_m(0)) = \tilde{A}_{m-1}^n(\tilde{A}_{m-1}(1)) = \tilde{A}_{m-1}^{n+1}(1).$$

Since A_m and $\tilde{A}_m$ satisfy the same recursion, and since $A_0(n) = \tilde{A}_0(n)$ is valid, $A_m(n)$ and $\tilde{A}_m(n) = A(m,n)$ agree for all $m, n \geq 0$.

2. We show the assertion by induction on m. For $m = 0$, we have $A_0(n) = n+1$. The induction hypothesis is $A_{m-1}(n) \geq n+1$ for $m \geq 1$ and all $n \geq 0$. We have to show that $A_m(n) \geq n+1$ for all $n \geq 0$. We shall prove this by induction on n. For $n = 0$, according to the induction hypothesis for m, we have $A_m(0) = A_{m-1}(1) \geq 2$. Let $m \geq 1$ and assume the assertion proved for $m - 1$.
   Then $A_m(n) = A_{m-1}(A_m(n-1)) \geq A_m(n-1) + 1 \geq n+1$. The first inequality follows by the induction hypothesis for m and the second by the induction hypothesis for n.

3. For $m = 0$, we have $A_0(n+1) = n+2 > A_0(n) = n+1$. For $m \geq 1$, it holds that $A_m(n+1) = A_{m-1}(A_m(n)) \geq A_m(n) + 1 > A_m(n)$ (with point 2).

4. $A_m^n(1) = A_m(A_m^{n-1}(1)) \geq A_m^{n-1}(1) + 1 \geq \ldots \geq A_m^0(1) + n = n+1.$

The lemma is shown. □

Lemma 6.9. *The function $A(m,n)$ is strictly increasing in both arguments and grows faster in the first than in the second. More precisely*

$$A_{m+1}(n) \geq A_m(n+1) \geq A_m(n) + 1$$

for all $m, n \geq 0$.

Proof. Let $m \geq 0$.

$$A_{m+1}(n) = A_m(A_m^n(1)) \geq A_m(n+1) = A_{m-1}(A_m(n)) \geq A_m(n) + 1.$$

This shows the assertion of the lemma. □

Now we introduce some functions that we will use when analyzing the union-find data type. Let u be a node different from a root. We define

(1) $\qquad \delta(u) = \max\{k \mid \text{rank}(\text{parent}(u)) \geq A_k(\text{rank}(u))\}.$

Since $\text{rank}(\text{parent}(u)) \geq \text{rank}(u) + 1 = A_0(\text{rank}(u))$ (Lemma 6.7), $\delta(u)$ is welldefined, and we conclude that $\delta(u) \geq 0$.

(2) $\qquad r(u) = \max\{r \mid \text{rank}(\text{parent}(u)) \geq A_{\delta(u)}^r(\text{rank}(u))\}.$

Because of Lemma 6.7, we have

(3) $\qquad \lfloor \log_2(n) \rfloor \geq \text{rank}(\text{parent}(u)) \geq A_{\delta(u)}(\text{rank}(u)).$

If $\delta(u) \geq 2$, we conclude with Lemma 6.9 that

(4) $\quad \lfloor \log_2(n) \rfloor \geq A_{\delta(u)}(\text{rank}(u)) \geq A_{\delta(u)-2}(\text{rank}(u) + 2) \geq A_{\delta(u)-2}(2).$

Let $\alpha(n)$ be defined by

$$\alpha(n) = \min\{k \mid A_k(2) \geq n\}.$$

Since $A_{\delta(u)-2}(2) \leq \lfloor \log_2(n) \rfloor < n$ (see (4)), it follows immediately with the definition of α that

(5) $\qquad \delta(u) \leq \alpha(\lfloor \log_2(n) \rfloor) + 2.$

The function $\alpha(n)$ is essentially the inverse function of $A_m(2)$. It is an extremely slow-increasing function. We have

$$A_0(2) = 3, A_1(2) = 4, A_2(2) = 7, A_3(2) = 2^5 - 3 = 29, A_4(2) = 2^{65536} - 3.$$

Therefore,

$$\alpha(0) = \ldots = \alpha(3) = 0, \alpha(4) = 1, \alpha(5) = \alpha(6) = \alpha(7) = 2,$$

$$\alpha(8) = \ldots = \alpha(29) = 3, \alpha(30) = \ldots = \alpha(2^{65536} - 3) = 4.$$

The number 2^{65536} is a binary number with 65,537 bits. This is about 20,000 decimal digits. The function α takes a value ≤ 4 for all practically occurring inputs.

Proposition 6.10. *The union-find algorithm, with union by rank and path compression, has a worst-case running time of order $O((m+n) \cdot \alpha(n))$ for $n - 1$ Union and m Find calls.*

Proof. The running time for a Union call is constant, except for the two Find calls. There are $n - 1$ Union calls. The time complexity t_U for all executions of the function Union (without the Find calls) is therefore $O(n)$.

We now estimate the running time for all Find executions. We first look at the call Find(u) for a u. Let $P : u = u_1, \ldots, u_r = v$ be the path from u to the root v before the lth execution of Find. The running time of Find is distributed equally among the individual nodes on P. The effort is constant for each node. We assume a time unit for it. We now set up time counters: for each node u the counter t_u and for the function Find the counter t_F. With these counters we record the effort for all executions of Find. We consider the lth step and the nodes u_i on P, $i = 1, \ldots, r$.

1. We increase t_{u_i} by one if $u_i \neq u$ and $u_i \neq v$ (i.e., u_i is neither leaf (rank(u_i) ≥ 1) nor root) and if some $j > i$ exists with $\delta(u_j) = \delta(u_i)$.
2. We increase t_F by one if (a) u_i is a leaf or a root, or if (b) $\delta(u_j) \neq \delta(u_i)$ for all $j > i$.

The running time for all Find executions is $t_F + \sum_u t_u$.

We consider the first case. Let $i < j$ with $\delta(u_i) = \delta(u_j) = k$. Then

$$\text{rank}(v) \geq \text{rank}(\text{parent}(u_j)) \geq A_k(\text{rank}(u_j))$$
$$\geq A_k(\text{rank}(\text{parent}(u_i))) \geq A_k(A_k^{r(u_i)}(\text{rank}(u_i)))$$
$$= A_k^{r(u_i)+1}(\text{rank}(u_i)).$$

The first inequality uses the monotonicity of rank along paths, the second inequality follows by the definition of $\delta(u_i)$, the third inequality by the monotonicity of rank along paths and the monotonicity of A_k, and the fourth inequality uses (2) and the monotonicity of A_k. After terminating Find, parent(u_i) = v and

$$(6) \qquad\qquad \text{rank}(\text{parent}(u_i)) \geq A_k^{r(u_i)+1}(\text{rank}(u_i)).$$

Each time the first condition for u_i occurs and t_{u_i} is increased by one, the exponent of A_k in (6) increases by at least one. If the case $r(u_i) = \text{rank}(u_i)$ occurs, then

$$\text{rank}(\text{parent}(u_i)) \geq A_k^{\text{rank}(u_i)+1}(\text{rank}(u_i)) \geq A_k^{\text{rank}(u_i)+1}(1) = A_{k+1}(\text{rank}(u_i)).$$

The first inequality follows from (6), the second uses the monotonicity of A_k. Consequently,

$$\text{rank}(\text{parent}(u_i)) \geq A_{k+1}(\text{rank}(u_i)).$$

From the definition of $\delta(u_i)$, we conclude that $\delta(u_i) \geq k+1$ (see (1)). Further, $\delta(u_i) \leq \alpha(\lfloor \log_2(n) \rfloor) + 2$ (see (5)). Thus,

$$t_{u_i} \leq \text{rank}(u_i)(\alpha(\lfloor \log_2(n) \rfloor) + 2).$$

We sum up all t_u and summarize nodes with the same rank. With Lemma 6.7 and the formula for the derivative of the geometric series (Appendix B (F.8)), we conclude that

$$\sum_u t_u \le \sum_{r=0}^{\infty} r \cdot (\alpha(\lfloor \log_2(n) \rfloor) + 2) \frac{n}{2^r}$$

$$= n(\alpha(\lfloor \log_2(n) \rfloor) + 2) \sum_{r=0}^{\infty} \frac{r}{2^r}$$

$$= 2n(\alpha(\lfloor \log_2(n) \rfloor) + 2).$$

We now consider the second case. For the nodes u and v together, we increase t_F by 2. Each node u satisfies $\delta(u) \le \alpha(\lfloor \log_2(n) \rfloor) + 2$ (see (5)).

We are looking at a $k \le \alpha(\lfloor \log_2(n) \rfloor) + 2$. Then condition 2 (b) is only fulfilled for the last node $\tilde{u}$ in path P with $\delta(\tilde{u}) = k$ (case 1 occurs for all preceding nodes). Thus, for each value $k \le \alpha(\lfloor \log_2(n) \rfloor) + 2$ there is at most one node which satisfies case 2 (b). Accordingly, t_F increases by a maximum of $\alpha(\lfloor \log_2(n) \rfloor) + 4$ when Find is executed. For m executions follows $t_F \le m(\alpha(\lfloor \log_2(n) \rfloor) + 4)$. We get

$$t_U + t_F + \sum_u t_u \le c(m+n)\alpha(\lfloor \log_2(n) \rfloor) = O((m+n) \cdot \alpha(n)),$$

thereby proving the proposition.   □

6.1.3 The LCA and the RMQ Problem

We first consider the problem of computing the lowest common ancestor (LCA) of two nodes in a rooted tree. Let u and v be nodes in a rooted tree. The *lowest common ancestor* of u and v is the common ancestor of u and v that has the greatest distance from the root.

Figure 6.2 shows the lowest common ancestor (filled) of the two filled leaf nodes.

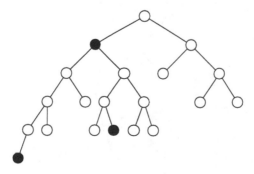

Fig. 6.2: Lowest common ancestor.

Tarjan's Algorithm for Computing the Lowest Common Ancestor.
The following algorithm LCA, published in [Tarjan79], computes for each
node pair $\{u, v\}$ from a list Q having m elements the lowest common ancestor in a rooted tree T. We describe T with node set $\{1, \ldots, n\}$ by the
adjacency list $adl[1..n]$. In the implementation of LCA, we demonstrate a
first application of the union-find data type.

The user calls LCA with the root of the tree as parameter and provides
a union-find data type initialized with FindInit(n). LCA uses the boolean
array $marked[1..n]$, which is predefined with "false".

Algorithm 6.11.

   node $adl[1..n]$; boolean $marked[1..n]$
   vertex $ancestor[1..n]$, $lca[1..n, 1..n]$
   LCA(vertex k)
   1   node no
   2   $ancestor[k] \leftarrow k$, $no \leftarrow adl[k]$
   3   while $no \neq$ null do
   4   LCA($no.v$)
   5   Union($k, no.v$), $ancestor[\text{Find}(k)] \leftarrow k$
   6      $no \leftarrow no.next$
   7   $marked[k] \leftarrow$ true
   8   for each $\{u, k\}$ from Q do
   9   if $marked[u]$
   10   then $lca[u, k] \leftarrow ancestor[\text{Find}(u)]$

Remarks:

1. LCA traverses T using depth-first search (Algorithm 5.12). Let k be a
   node of T and $v_0, v_1, \ldots, v_l = k$ the path P in T from the root v_0 to the
   node k. P consists of the ancestors of k. Figure 6.3 reflects the moment t
   at which the processor has executed for the call LCA(k) all instructions
   including line 7.

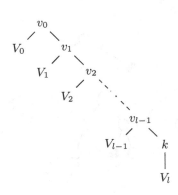

Fig. 6.3: LCA computation.

Let $L = \{v \in T \mid$ the call $\text{LCA}(v)$ terminated up to the moment $t\}$. These are the nodes to the left of the path $v_0, \ldots, v_{l-1}$ and below $v_l = k$. Let

$$V_i = \{v \in L \mid v \text{ is a descendant of } v_i\}, \quad i = 0, \ldots, l.$$

For the nodes $v \in V_i$, v_i is the last common ancestor of v and k.

2. At the moment t, the nodes from $\{v_i\} \cup V_i$ form a Union-Find partition. $\text{Find}(v)$ returns the root of the partition where v is located. Since v_i is the ancestor of the nodes of this partition, $ancestor[\text{Find}(v)] = v_i$ was previously set (line 5).

3. For all node pairs $\{u, k\}$ from Q where the node u is already marked, we determine the lowest common ancestor (lines 9 and 10). Since $lca[u, v]$ is only set if u and v are marked, line 10 is executed exactly once for each node pair $\{u, v\} \in Q$.

4. Depth-first search runs in time $O(n)$ for a tree. This also holds for lines $1 - 7$ of LCA, because the Union and Find calls can be assumed to run in total time $O(n)$ (see Proposition 6.10). We have to add the running time for lines $8 - 10$, which is $O(m)$ in total, if Q is represented so that for each k the pair $\{u, k\}$ can be retrieved in constant time. So the time complexity is $O(n + m)$.

Summarizing, we get the following.

Proposition 6.12. *For each pair of nodes from Q, the algorithm LCA computes the lowest common ancestor in time $O(n + m)$.*

We now discuss another method to solve the LCA problem; we follow the presentation in [BeFa00].

Reduction Algorithm for the LCA Problem. We reduce the LCA problem to the calculation of the minimum in an array. More precisely, let $a[1..n]$ be an array of numbers. An algorithm for the range minimum query (RMQ) problem (Section 1.5.4) computes for indices i and j with $1 \leq i \leq j \leq n$ an index k with $i \leq k \leq j$ and

$$a[k] = \min\{a[l] \mid i \leq l \leq j\}.$$

The following algorithm reduces the LCA problem for a rooted tree T with node set $\{1, \ldots, n\}$ to the RMQ problem by a depth-first search in T.

Algorithm 6.13.
    vertex $parent[1..n]$, $no[1..2n - 1]$; node $adl[1..n]$; index $ino[1..n]$
    int $depth[1..n]$, $de[1..2n - 1]$

Init()
  1   index $i \leftarrow 1$, $parent[1] \leftarrow 0$, $depth[0] \leftarrow -1$
  2   Visit(1)

Visit(vertex k)

1   node no
2    $depth[k] \leftarrow depth[parent[k]] + 1$
3    $de[i] \leftarrow depth[k],\ no[i] \leftarrow k,\ ino[k] \leftarrow i,\ i := i + 1$
4    $node \leftarrow adl[k]$
5   while $node \neq$ null do
6        $parent[node.v] \leftarrow k$
7   Visit($node.v$)
8        $de[i] \leftarrow depth[k],\ no[i] \leftarrow k,\ i := i + 1$
9        $node \leftarrow node.next$

Remarks:

1. The tree T with the node set $\{1, \ldots, n\}$ is given by the adjacency list adl. The list stores the successors for each node. The algorithm Visit performs a depth-first search in T.

2. After calling Visit, for each node an entry is added to the arrays de, no and ino. The variable $de[i]$ stores the depth of the node $no[i]$ and $ino[k]$ stores the index of the first occurrence of k in no. Therefore, $no[ino[k]] = k$ is valid. For each node, there is an additional entry in the arrays de and no for each of its successors (see line 8).

3. The arrays de, no and ino require one entry for each node and the arrays de and no another entry for each successor. Since there are n nodes and a total of $n - 1$ successors, de and no require $2n - 1$ places.

    Visit traverses each edge twice, shown in the following example by the path that starts and ends at node A. For each pass of an edge, an entry is entered in de and no, with an additional entry for the start node.

Example. Figure 6.4 shows an example of reduction of the LCA problem to the RMQ problem by depth-first search.

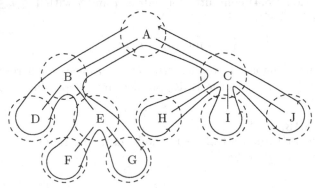

i :	1	2	3	4	5	6	7	8	9	10	11	12	13	14	15	16	17	18	19
de :	0	1	2	1	2	3	2	3	2	1	0	1	2	1	2	1	2	1	0
no :	A	B	D	B	E	F	E	G	E	B	A	C	H	C	I	C	J	C	A

$node$:	A	B	C	D	E	F	G	H	I	J
ino :	1	2	12	3	5	6	8	13	15	17

Fig. 6.4: Reduction of the LCA problem to the RMQ problem.

Proposition 6.14. *Let k and l be nodes of T with $ino[k] < ino[l]$. The LCA computation in T is traced back to the RMQ computation in the array de:*

$$lca(k, l) = no[rmq_{de}(ino[k], ino[l])].$$

Proof. Let k and l be nodes of T with $ino[k] < ino[l]$. Let v be the lowest common ancestor of k and l. The nodes k and l are located in T_v, the sub-tree of T with root v. The depth of v is minimal for all nodes in T_v. Since these are all nodes that lie between the first and last occurrences of the node v in the array no, the depth d_v of v is minimal in $[de[ino[k]..ino[l]]]$, i.e., $no[rmq_{de}(ino[k], ino[l])] = v$. □

Proposition 6.15. *Let T be a rooted tree with n nodes. After preprocessing with running time of order $O(n)$, m LCA requests referring to T can be answered in time $O(m)$. In total, we get an algorithm to solve the LCA problem that runs in time $O(n + m)$.*

Proof. Algorithm 6.13, which reduces the RMQ problem to the LCA problem, runs in time $O(n)$. It computes an array of length $2n - 1$. To solve the RMQ problem, we apply the linear-time algorithm from the following section. It has a preprocessing time of order $O(n)$ (Proposition 6.16). Then an RMQ request and thus also an LCA request can be answered in constant time. Altogether, we get an algorithm that answers m requests in time $O(m)$, after a preprocessing time of order $O(n)$. □

The array $de[1..2n-1]$ has the property that two consecutive entries differ only by $+1$ or -1. Such arrays are called *incremental arrays*. We specify an algorithm to solve the RMQ problem for such arrays.

A Linear-Time Algorithm for the Incremental RMQ Problem. Let $a[0..n-1]$ be an incremental array of numbers and $k := \lceil \log_2(n)/2 \rceil$. We split a into partial arrays of length k. We get $m = \lceil n/k \rceil$ partial arrays, where the last partial array can have length $\leq k$. In order to simplify the following explanations, we assume that the decomposition works without remainder, i.e., all partial arrays have length k. The resulting partial arrays are designated starting from the left by $a_0, \ldots, a_{m-1}$.

Let $i < j$ be indices for a, $\gamma = \lfloor i/k \rfloor$, the index of the partial array in which i is located and $\delta = \lfloor j/k \rfloor$, the index of the partial array in which j lies, as shown in Figure 6.5. Then $i \bmod k$ is the position of i in a_γ and $j \bmod k$ the position of j in a_δ.

Fig. 6.5: Decomposition into sub-arrays.

The minimum $m_{i,j}$ in $a[i..j]$ is

$$m_{i,j} = \min\{m_\alpha, m_\mu, m_\omega\},$$

where

$$m_\alpha = \min a_\gamma[i \bmod k..k-1],$$
$$m_\omega = \min a_\delta[0..j \bmod k] \text{ and}$$
$$m_\mu = \min_{l=\gamma+1}^{\delta-1} a_l[0..k-1].$$

The partial arrays $a_0, \ldots, a_{m-1}$ are incremental arrays. Therefore, we specify an algorithm for the RMQ problem for an incremental array $b[0..k-1]$. Without loss of generality, we may assume that $b[0] = 0$ (otherwise, replace $b[i]$ with $b[i] - b[0]$, $i = 0, \ldots, k-1$). Since $b[0]$ and the sequence of the differences $-1, +1$ of two successive entries determine the array $b[0..k-1]$, there are 2^{k-1} assignments (with $-1, +1$) for an incremental array b of length k with $b[0] = 0$. We consecutively number the assignments. For the lth assignment, we store in a table T_l for all index pairs $i < j$ the position of the minimum of $b[i..j]$. There are $(k-1)k/2$ index pairs $i < j$. Thus, T_l is an array of length $(k-1)k/2$. We get the sequence $T_a = (T_1, \ldots, T_{2^{k-1}})$. Using T_a we can now look up requests. The assignment of b determines l and thus T_l, and the indices i, j determine the entry in T_l. The table T_a depends only on k. Therefore, we can use it for all partial arrays $a_0, \ldots, a_{m-1}$ of a. In particular, we can now look up the positions of m_α and m_ω.

To calculate m_μ we use an array $c[0..m-1]$ and an array $p[0..m-1]$. We look up the position of the minimum of a_l in T_a and store the minimum in $c[l]$ and its position in $p[l]$. Then

$$m_\mu = \min c[\gamma+1..\delta-1].$$

Using the table T_c we can determine $\mathrm{rmq}_c(\gamma+1, \delta-1)$ by looking up T_c twice (Proposition 1.37).

Figure 6.6 visualizes the tables for the calculation of

$$\mathrm{rmq}_a(i,j) = \min\{\mathrm{rmq}_a(i \bmod k, k-1), \mathrm{rmq}_a(0, j \bmod k), \mathrm{rmq}_c(\gamma+1, \delta-1)\}.$$

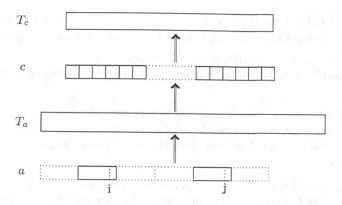

Fig. 6.6: The incremental RMQ Problem.

We now discuss the running time needed to calculate T_a and T_c. The calculation of each of the components T_l from $T_a = (T_1, \ldots, T_{2k-1})$ can be done by an algorithm, in $k \log_2(k)$ steps (Proposition 1.37). For the calculation of the running time T_a, we get the result:

$$c \cdot 2^{k-1} \cdot k \cdot \log_2(k) = c \cdot 2^{\lceil \log_2(n)/2 \rceil - 1} \cdot \left\lceil \frac{\log_2(n)}{2} \right\rceil \cdot \log_2 \left(\left\lceil \frac{\log_2(n)}{2} \right\rceil \right)$$
$$< c \cdot \sqrt{n} \log_2(n)^2 = O(n).$$

The effort to calculate T_c is $m \log_2(m)$, where m is the length of the array c (Proposition 1.37).

$$m = \left\lceil \frac{n}{k} \right\rceil = \left\lceil \frac{n}{\left\lceil \frac{\log_2(n)}{2} \right\rceil} \right\rceil$$

and therefore

$$m \log_2(m) = O\left(\frac{n}{\log_2(n)} \log_2 \left(\frac{n}{\log_2(n)} \right) \right) = O(n).$$

Thus, we can also calculate T_c by an algorithm that runs in time $O(n)$. We summarize the result in the following proposition.

Proposition 6.16. *Let $a[0..n-1]$ be an incremental array of length n. Every RMQ request for a can be answered in constant time, after preprocessing with running time of order $O(n)$.*

Reducing the RMQ Problem to the LCA Problem. We reduce the RMQ problem for any integer array $a[1..n]$ to the LCA problem. To do this, we assign a cartesian tree B to the array a. RMQ requests for a are then traced back to LCA requests for B. The construction of B from a is done in time $O(n)$. We define the term cartesian tree and describe the individual steps of the reduction.

Definition 6.17. Let $a[1..n]$ be an array of integers. A binary tree B which stores the elements $a[1], \ldots, a[n]$ is called the *cartesian tree* assigned to a if

1. B meets the heap condition (see Definition 2.11).
2. The result of the in-order output of B is $a[1], \ldots, a[n]$ (see Definition 4.4).

Remark. The cartesian tree B assigned to a is uniquely determined. The heap condition uniquely determines the root, and the in-order output uniquely determines the left and right subtree of the root. The uniqueness of B follows by recursion.

We use linked lists of node elements of type node to implement B (see page 131). The following algorithm creates the cartesian tree assigned to an array.

Algorithm 6.18.

```
tree BuildCartesianTree(int a[1..n])
 1   node rnode, nd, b
 2   b ← new(node)
 3   b.element ← a[1], b.left ← null
 4   b.right ← null, rnode ← b
 5   for i ← 2 to n do
 6       nd ← new(node)
 7       nd.element ← a[i]
 8       nd.right ← null
 9       rnode ← UpHeap(rnode, a[i])
10       if rnode ≠ null
11          then nd.left ← rnode.right
12               rnode.right ← nd
13          else  nd.left ← b, b ← nd
14       rnode ← nd
15   return b
```

Remarks:

1. The code of lines 2-4 creates the root node and stores $a[1]$ in the root node.
2. The for loop iterates over the elements of a. At the beginning of the ith iteration the cartesian tree for $a[1..i-1]$ is constructed. In the ith iteration, we store the element $a[i]$ in the allocated tree node nd (line 7).
3. Here, the implementation of Upheap (called in line 9) requires the adaptation of Algorithm 6.2 to the changed representation of the tree. The input of Upheap is the last-inserted node $rnode$ (line 4, line 14). Upheap determines the lowest node on the path from $rnode$ to the root for which $rnode.element \leq a[i]$ is valid. If all elements stored on the path are $> a[i]$, UpHeap returns null. In this case, the new node nd becomes the root of the tree (line 13). The previous tree becomes the left subtree of the new root (line 13).

4. Otherwise, we add the new tree node as the right successor of *rnode* (line 12). The node *rnode.right* becomes the left successor of *nd* (line 11).
5. After each insertion of a node into the tree, the heap condition is retained. The condition for the in-order output is fulfilled because we insert the node *nd* into the tree in such a way that after insertion, it is the rightmost node.

Proposition 6.19. *The running time of Algorithm 6.18 is $O(n)$.*

Proof. The running time of BuildCartesianTree is proportional to the number of comparisons which we make in Upheap over all iterations of the for loop. We anchor the next node in line 12 or 14 as the last node in the path P which consists of the nodes lying furthest to the right. UpHeap traverses the path P until the insertion position is found. For each comparison made in UpHeap, we insert a node into P or remove a node from P. Each node is inserted only one time into P and removed only one time from P. Therefore, the number of comparisons in UpHeap over all iterations of the for loop is of order $O(n)$. □

To reduce the RMQ problem to the LCA problem, we assign the array a to a cartesian tree B. A node of B now stores the pair $(i, a[i])$. The sort order of these elements is defined by the order on the second component.

In order to be able to access the node k that stores $(i, a[i])$ for an index i in constant time, we introduce the array *pos*: *pos[i]* stores a reference to k. The implementation of BuildCartesianTree and Upheap must update *pos*.

Example. The cartesian tree assigned to $a = \{7, 4, 5, 11, 3, 6\}$ is shown in Figure 6.7.

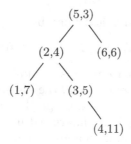

Fig. 6.7: The assigned cartesian tree.

Proposition 6.20. *Let $a[1..n]$ be an array of integers, and let $i, j \leq n$ be indices. Let B be the cartesian tree assigned to a.*

1. *Then*

$$rmq_a(i, j) = lca(pos[i], pos[j]),$$

where $lca(pos[i], pos[j])$ denotes the first component of the element stored in the lowest common ancestor of the nodes referenced by $pos[i]$ and $pos[j]$.

2. *Our investigations show that we can implement an algorithm that answers*
   m RMQ requests for an integer array of length n in time of order $O(m)$,
   after preprocessing in time $O(n)$.

Proof. The node that stores $(k, a[k])$ is an ancestor of the nodes that store
$(i, a[i])$ and $(j, a[j])$ if and only if $a[k] < a[i]$, $a[k] < a[j]$ and $i \leq k \leq j$, and it
is the lowest common ancestor if and only if $a[k] = \min(a[i..j])$ and $i \leq k \leq j$.
This shows the first statement.

   We first trace RMQ requests back to LCA requests (Section 6.1.3) and
then trace LCA requests back to incremental RMQ requests (Proposition
6.14). Both reductions run in time $O(n)$. The statement about the running
time now follows from Proposition 6.19 and Proposition 6.15.   □

6.2 The Algorithms of Dijkstra and Prim

The algorithm of Dijkstra, published in [Dijkstra59], solves the single-source
distance problem for a node in a weighted graph, i.e., the algorithm computes
the distances from a fixed node to all other nodes. The algorithm of Prim[1]
constructs a minimum spanning tree (see [Prim57]). Before we explain the
algorithms, we specify the first problem.

Definition 6.21. Let $G = (V, E)$ be a weighted graph and let $v, w \in V$. Let
$v = v_1, \dots, v_{n+1} = w$ be a path P from v to w. The *length* of P is

$$l(P) := \sum_{i=1}^{n} w(\{v_i, v_{i+1}\}).$$

The *distance* $d(v, w)$ of v and w is defined by

$$d(v, w) := \min\{l(P) \mid P \text{ is a path from } v \text{ to } w\}.$$

Remark. A shortest path from v to w is a simple path. Since there are only
finitely many simple paths from v to w, the distance $d(v, w)$ is defined. One
can easily check that for a connected graph the map d fulfills the axioms of
a metric (Definition B.24). We are interested in an algorithm that not only
computes the distances $d(v, w)$ from a given node v to all other nodes w, but
also stores together with $d(v, w)$ a shortest path from v to w.

The Algorithm of Dijkstra. Let $G = (V, E)$ be a connected weighted
graph and $v \in V$. Dijkstra's algorithm finds a path of minimum length from
v to w for all $w \in V$. It constructs a G spanning tree $T = (V_T, E_T)$ with root
v. The path from v to w in T is a path of minimum length from v to w in
G, i.e., $d_T(v, w) = d(v, w)$ for all $w \in V$, where d_T denotes the distance in T.
Such a tree is called a *shortest-path tree*, or SPT for short.

---

[1] In the literature the algorithm is referred to as the algorithm of Prim, although
   it was already published in 1930 in a paper by Vojtěch Jarník (1897 – 1970), a
   Czech mathematician working in the field of number theory and analysis.

Algorithm. Let $G = (V, E)$ be a connected weighted graph and $v \in V$. Dijkstra's algorithm computes the distances $d(v, w)$ for all nodes w of G and a shortest-path tree for G:

1. Start: Set $T := (\{v\}, \emptyset)$.
2. Construction step: Let $T = (V_T, E_T)$ be constructed.
   Choose $w \in V \setminus V_T$ with $d(v, w)$ minimum for all $w \in V \setminus V_T$ and a path P of minimum length $v = v_1, \ldots, v_{k-1}, v_k = w$ from v to w in G. Set $T := (V_T \cup \{w\}, E_T \cup \{v_{k-1}, w\})$.
3. Repeat step 2 until $V_T = V$ is valid.

We now perform the algorithm on the graph in Figure 6.8.

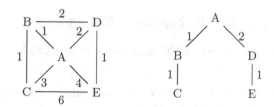

Fig. 6.8: SPT computation with Dijkstra's algorithm.

Remark. Dijkstra's algorithm searches in each step for a solution that seems optimal at the moment. We choose a node that has a minimum distance from the start node v. A locally optimal solution should result in an optimal solution. Dijkstra's algorithm refers to the knowledge available at the time of the choice. These are the distances to the nodes of the already constructed tree and to nodes adjacent to tree nodes.

This strategy does not always succeed. With Dijkstra's algorithm this works if all edges have a positive weight. If negatively weighted edges are allowed, this strategy fails (Exercise 2).

Algorithms that work according to this strategy are called greedy algorithms (see Section 1.5.3). Further greedy algorithms are the algorithms of Kruskal and Borůvka (Algorithms 6.3 and 6.4) and the algorithm of Prim (Algorithm 6.2), which we will study subsequently.

Proposition 6.22. *Let G be a connected weighted graph. Dijkstra's algorithm computes a shortest-path tree for G.*

Proof. We show the assertion by induction on the number j of iterations. Let T_j be the tree constructed in the first j iterations. We show that T_j is a shortest-path tree for the subgraph of G which is generated by T_j. For $j = 0$ the assertion is valid. Let P be the path $v = v_1, \ldots, v_{k-1}, v_k = w$ of minimum length selected in the jth iteration. We show that $v_2, \ldots, v_{k-1} \in V_{T_{j-1}}$. Suppose for the purpose of contradiction that there exists an $i \in$

$\{2,\ldots,k-1\}$ with $v_i \notin V_{T_{j-1}}$. Then, it follows that $d(v,v_i) < d(v,w)$, a contradiction to the choice of w. Since $v_2,\ldots,v_{k-1} \in V_{T_{j-1}}$, it follows from the induction assumption that $d_{T_{j-1}}(v,v_{k-1}) = d(v,v_{k-1})$. After the choice of P, we have $d_{T_j}(v,w) = d(v,w)$, i.e., T_j is a shortest-path tree for the subgraph of G generated by the nodes of T_j. This shows the assertion. $\square$

Remark. The algorithm of Dijkstra also computes for a directed graph the distances from a fixed node v to all other nodes that are accessible from v. The implementation we will discuss also works for directed graphs.

The Algorithm of Prim. We explain the concept of a minimum spanning tree[2] for a connected weighted graph $G = (V,E)$. For this purpose we consider the set of all spanning subgraphs

$$SP := \{S = (V,E_S) \mid E_S \subset E, S \text{ connected}\}.$$

We are looking for an $S \in SP$ with minimum weight $w(S)$ for $S \in SP$. Such an S is a tree.

Definition 6.23. A tree that spans G and has minimum weight is called a *minimum spanning tree* (MST) for G.

Remark. If identical weights occur, a minimum spanning tree is not necessarily uniquely determined. Figure 6.9 shows two minimum spanning trees of a graph.

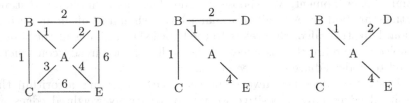

Fig. 6.9: The MST is not uniquely determined.

Algorithm. Let $G = (V,E)$ be a connected weighted graph. The algorithm of Prim computes a minimum spanning tree $T = (V_T, E_T)$ for a connected G in the following steps:

1. Start: Choose $v \in V$ and set $T := (\{v\}, \emptyset)$.
2. Construction step: Let $T = (V_T, E_T)$ be constructed.
   Choose an edge $e = \{v,w\}$ with $w(e)$ minimum for all nodes $v \in V_T$ and $w \notin V_T$. Set $T := (V_T \cup \{w\}, E_T \cup \{e\})$.
3. Repeat step 2 until $V_T = V$ holds.

---

[2] "Minimum spanning tree" is shortened from "minimum-weight spanning tree", also called a "minimum-cost spanning tree".

We now perform the algorithm on the graph in Figure 6.10.

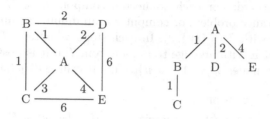

Fig. 6.10: MST computed with Prim's algorithm.

Lemma 6.24 *(cut property). Let $G = (V, E)$ be a connected weighted graph, $U \subset V$, $U \neq V$ and*

$$E_U = \{\{v, w\} \in E \mid v \in U, w \notin U\}.$$

For each edge $e \in E_U$ of minimum weight, there is a minimum spanning tree $T = (V, E_T)$ for G with $e \in E_T$.

Proof. Let $e \in E_U$ be an edge of minimum weight, T be a minimum spanning tree for G and $e = \{u, v\} \notin E_T$. The graph $T \cup \{e\}$ has a cycle Z. Beside e there is another edge $e' = \{r, s\} \in Z$ with $r \in U$ and $s \notin U$. $T' = (T \cup \{e\}) \setminus \{e'\}$ is a tree and spans G. Since e is of minimum weight in E_U, $w(T') = w(T) + w(e) - w(e') \leq w(T)$. Since T is a minimum spanning tree for G, we conclude that $w(T') = w(T)$. Thus, T' is a minimum spanning tree for G which contains the edge e. □

Remark. The graph G splits into two components when we remove all edges from E_U. Therefore, we say E_U defines a *cut* in G. The statement of Lemma 6.24 in this notation is: For each edge e of minimum weight in a cut, there is a minimum spanning tree containing e.

Proposition 6.25. *Let $G = (V, E)$ be a connected weighted graph. Prim's algorithm computes a minimum spanning tree for G.*

Proof. Let T be the spanning tree constructed with Prim's algorithm. $T = (\{v_1, \ldots, v_n\}, \{e_1 \ldots, e_{n-1}\})$, $U_i = \{v_1, \ldots, v_i\}$, $i = 1, \ldots, n$. The U_i form an ascending chain $U_1 \subset U_2 \subset \ldots \subset U_n = V$. We have $U_i \neq U_j$ for $i \neq j$ because e_i has one end node in U_i and the other in $U_{i+1} \setminus U_i$.
Let $T_{\min}$ be a minimum spanning tree for G. As in the proof of Lemma 6.24, construct for $i = 1, \ldots, n - 1$ for every U_i and e_i an edge $f_i \in E$. The edge e_i is an edge of minimum weight for the cut E_{U_i}. Set $T_0 = T_{\min}$ and $T_i = (T_{i-1} \cup \{e_i\}) \setminus \{f_i\}$, $i = 1, \ldots, n-1$. Since an end node of f_i is in $U_{i+1} \setminus U_i$, but both end nodes of e_j are in U_i for $j = 1, \ldots, i-1$, $f_i \notin \{e_1, \ldots, e_{i-1}\}$. It holds that $w(T_i) = w(T_{\min})$, $i = 1, \ldots, n-1$. Since $T = T_{n-1}$ holds, T is also a minimum spanning tree for G. □

The Implementation of the Algorithms of Dijkstra and Prim. The following implementation of the two algorithms does not assume that the graph G is connected. For each connected component of G, it solves the single-source distance problem or computes a minimum spanning tree. Both algorithms start with $T = (\{v\}, \emptyset)$. In each step, we extend T. We select a node and connect it with an edge to a node from T if it is possible.

We divide the nodes $V = \{1, \ldots, n\}$ of G into three disjoint groups:

V_T : nodes of T.

$V_{ad} := \{w \notin V_T \mid$ there's a $u \in V_T : \{u, w\} \in E\}$.

$V_R : V \setminus (V_T \cup V_{ad})$.

For both algorithms, the selected node is a node from V_{ad} that satisfies a minimum condition or the start node for the next connected component. We call this element an element of minimum priority.

In Dijkstra's algorithm, we choose a path P starting from a root node v which has minimum length over all nodes $w \notin V_T$ as end node. Then $w \in V_{ad}$ and $d(v, w)$ is the priority of w (see the proof of Proposition 6.22). In Prim's algorithm, it is the weight $w(\{u, w\})$ of an edge $\{u, w\}$ for which $u \in V_T$ and $w \notin V_T$. Both algorithms select a node $w \in V_{ad}$ of minimum priority.

We get an implementation of the algorithms when we replace the queue in Algorithm 5.11 with a priority queue. We replace the principle "first in, first out" with the principle "priority first". The priority queue identifies the element of minimum priority at any time. During the execution of the algorithm, the priority of nodes from V_{ad} can be lowered. In this case, a priority update must take place.

While we actually use the priority queue from Section 6.1.1 if the graph is represented by an adjacency list, it is only conceptually present if the representation is by an adjacency matrix. We determine the element of minimum priority explicitly in the algorithm. Here, this is done without reducing the efficiency of the algorithm.

We realize both algorithms, essentially by one implementation. Our pseudo-code follows the presentation in [Sedgewick88].

1. First all nodes are in V_R. During the execution of the algorithm they first move to V_{ad} and then to V_T.

2. Construction step:
   Either select a node k of minimum priority *prio* from V_{ad}, where

   $$prio := prio(k) := \begin{cases} \min\{w(\{v, k\}) \mid v \in V_T\} & \text{for Prim,} \\ d(v, k) \text{ with a starting node } v & \text{for Dijkstra,} \end{cases}$$

   if $V_{ad} \neq \emptyset$, or the start node for the next component.

3. We mark in the array *priority* to which of the sets V_T, V_{ad} or V_R a node k belongs:

$priority[k] \geq 0$ if $k \in V_T$.

$-\text{infinite} < priority[k] = -prio(k) < 0$ if $k \in V_{ad}$.

$priority[k] = -\text{infinite}$ if $k \in V_R$.

The constant infinite is greater than any occurring value for $prio(k)$.

4. The forest T is implemented by the array $parent[1..n]$.

We first specify an implementation if the graph is given by an adjacency matrix.

Matrix Priority-First Search. MatrixPriorityFirst implements both algorithms.

Algorithm 6.26.

int $adm[1..n, 1..n]$, $priority[1..n]$;   vertex $parent[1..n]$

const infinite $=$ maxint -1

Init()

1   vertex k

2   for $k \leftarrow 1$ to n do

3       $priority[k] \leftarrow -\text{infinite}$, $parent[k] \leftarrow 0$

4   $priority[0] \leftarrow -(\text{infinite} + 1)$

MatrixPriorityFirst()

1   vertex k, t, min

2   $Init()$, $min \leftarrow 1$

3   repeat

4       $k \leftarrow min$, $priority[k] \leftarrow -priority[k]$, $min \leftarrow 0$

5   if $priority[k] = \text{infinite}$

6   then $priority[k] = 0$

7   for $t \leftarrow 1$ to n do

8   if $priority[t] < 0$

9   then if $(adm[k, t] > 0)$ and $(priority[t] < -prio)$

10   then $priority[t] \leftarrow -prio$

11                    $parent[t] \leftarrow k$

12   if $priority[t] > priority[min]$

13   then $min \leftarrow t$

14   until $min = 0$

$prio := adm[k, t]$ (Prim) or $prio := priority[k] + adm[k, t]$ (Dijkstra).

Remarks:

1. Init initializes the arrays *priority* and *parent*. The value infinite cannot occur as a true priority. $priority[0]$ serves as a marker. We access $priority[0]$ in line 12 with $min = 0$. Each value in the array $priority[1..n]$ is $> -(\text{infinite} + 1)$.

2. The start node is node 1 (line 2: $min \leftarrow 1$). We first solve the problem for the connected component which contains node 1. The next connected component is defined by the first node t for which $priority[t] = -$infinite is valid (line 12).
3. repeat-until loop: In line 4, we set $min = 0$. The variable min specifies the element of minimum priority if $min \neq 0$. In each iteration of the repeat-until loop, we include a node k in V_T (line 4: $priority[k]$ turns positive). At this point, in the case of Dijkstra, we have $d(v, k) = d_T(v, k)$, where v is the corresponding root of T, i.e., T is a shortest-path tree for the subgraph of G generated by the nodes of T.
   Lines 5 and 6 are only needed for the algorithm of Dijkstra. We accumulate distances in $priority[k]$. Therefore, in line 6 we set $priority[k] = 0$.
   In line 13, we set $min = t$ as long as there is a $t \in \{1, \ldots, n\}$ with $priority[t] < 0$. If this is not the case, the repeat-until loop terminates. So we repeat it n times.
4. for loop: In the for loop (lines 12 and 13), we determine the element of minimum priority for the elements from V_{ad} ($-$infinite $< prio < 0$) or V_R ($prio = -$infinite). We include the element of minimum priority as the next node in V_T. The mark $priority[0] = -($infinite $+ 1)$, which is smaller than any other element in the $priority$ array, gives a simpler code.
5. In the for loop (lines 9, 10 and 11), for a node t which is adjacent to k but not in V_T we update priority and parent (priority update) if this is necessary (lines 10 and 11).
6. The array $priority$ satisfies after termination of MatrixPriorityFirst:

$$priority[k] = \begin{cases} w(\{k, parent[k]\}) & \text{for Prim,} \\ d(r, k) & \text{for Dijkstra,} \\ 0 & \text{if } parent[k] = 0, \end{cases}$$

where r is the root of the component of k.
7. The running time of MatrixPriorityFirst is $O(n^2)$.

List Priority-First Search. ListPriorityFirst implements both algorithms if G is represented by an adjacency list.
We keep the nodes from V_{ad} in a priority queue.

Algorithm 6.27.
    int $priority[1..n]$; vertex $parent[1..n]$; node $adl[1..n]$
    const infinite $=$ maxint $- 1$

```
ListPriorityFirst()
1   vertex k
2   for k ← 1 to n do
3       priority[k] ← −infinite
4   for k ← 1 to n do
5       if priority[k] = −infinite
6           then Visit(k)
```

Visit(vertex k)
```
1   node no
2   if PQUpdate(k, infinite)
3      then parent[k] ← 0
4   repeat
5         k ← PQRemove, priority[k] ← −priority[k]
6         if priority[k] = infinite
7            then priority[k] ← 0
8         no ← adl[k]
9         while no ≠ null do
10           if priority[no.v] < 0
11              then if PQUpdate(no.v, prio)
12                 then priority[no.v] ← −prio
13                      parent[no.v] ← k
14           no ← no.next
15  until PQEmpty
```

$prio = no.weight$ (Prim) or $prio = priority[k] + no.weight$ (Dijkstra).

Remarks:

1. The return value of PQUpdate(k, infinite) in line 2 is true if k is the root of a tree.
2. The call Visit(k) creates a spanning tree T for the connected component of k. The first start node is node 1. For a connected G, there is only this start node.
3. repeat-until loop: In each iteration of the repeat-until loop, we include a node k in V_T (line 5: $priority[k]$ becomes positive). At this point, in the case of Dijkstra we have $d(r, k) = d_T(r, k)$, where r is the corresponding root of T, i.e. T is a shortest-path tree for the subgraph of G generated by the nodes of T.
4. while loop: In the while loop (lines 10-13), we add a node t which is adjacent to k but not from V_T to the priority queue. We update the *priority* and *parent* arrays for all adjacent nodes $\notin V_T$ (priority update) if this is necessary (lines 12, 13).
5. After termination of ListPriorityFirst, the array *priority* satisfies

$$priority[k] = \begin{cases} w(\{k, parent[k]\}) & \text{for the algorithm of Prim,} \\ d(r, k) & \text{for the algorithm of Dijkstra,} \\ 0 & \text{if } parent[k] = 0, \end{cases}$$

   where r is the root of k's component.
6. PQUpdate and PQRemove run in time $O(\log_2(n))$ (Section 6.1.1). Therefore, the running time of ListPriorityFirst is of order $O((n + m)\log_2(n))$.
7. If instead of binary heaps, Fibonacci heaps were used to implement a priority queue, the operations PQInit and PQUpdate can be implemented with constant running time and PQRemove with running time $O(\log_2(n))$ (see [CorLeiRivSte09, Chapter 20]), and the order of the running time of Algorithm 6.27 improves to $O(m + n\log_2(n))$.

6.3 The Algorithm of Kruskal

The algorithm of Kruskal[3], published in [Kruskal56], computes for a connected weighted graph $G = (V, E)$ a minimum spanning tree $T = (V, E_T)$. First we describe the algorithm informally.

1. Start: Let $T := (V, \emptyset)$.
2. Construction step: Let $T = (V, E_T)$ be constructed.
   Find an edge $e \in E \setminus E_T$ so that $T \cup \{e\}$ is acyclic and $w(e)$ is minimal.
   Set $T := (V, E_T \cup \{e\})$.
3. Repeat step 2 until $|E_T| = |V| - 1$ holds.

Figure 6.11 shows the result of the algorithm on an example graph.

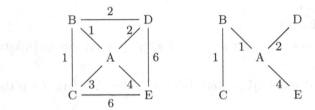

Fig. 6.11: MST computed with Kruskal's algorithm.

Proposition 6.28. *Let $G = (V, E)$ be a connected weighted graph. Kruskal's algorithm computes a minimum spanning tree for G.*

Proof. Directly from the construction it results that the algorithm creates a spanning tree for G. Let $T = (V, E_T)$ be the tree created with Kruskal's algorithm. $E_T = \{e_1, \ldots, e_{n-1}\}$, $w(e_i) \leq w(e_{i+1})$ for $i = 1, \ldots, n - 2$. Let $T_{\min} = (V, E_{\min})$ be a minimum spanning tree for G with $|E_{\min} \cap E_T|$ is maximum. We assume $T_{\min} \neq T$. There is an i with $1 \leq i \leq n - 1$, $e_1, \ldots, e_{i-1} \in E_{\min}$ and $e_i \notin E_{\min}$. The graph $H = T_{\min} \cup \{e_i\}$ is not acyclic. Let Z be a cycle of H and $e \in Z \setminus E_T$. $H \setminus \{e\}$ is a tree. Since $T_{\min}$ is a minimum spanning tree, $w(H \setminus \{e\}) = w(T_{\min}) + w(e_i) - w(e) \geq w(T_{\min})$. Consequently, $w(e_i) - w(e) \geq 0$. The edge e_i is chosen in Kruskal's algorithm with the property $w(e_i)$ is minimal and $(V, \{e_1, \ldots, e_i\})$ is acyclic. Since $(V, \{e_1, \ldots, e_{i-1}, e\})$ is acyclic, $w(e) \geq w(e_i)$ holds. In total, $w(e) = w(e_i)$ and $w(H \setminus \{e\}) = w(T_{\min})$ follows. Thus, $H \setminus \{e\}$ is also a minimum spanning tree. The number of common edges of $H \setminus \{e\}$ and E_T is greater than $|E_{min} \cap E_T|$. This is a contradiction to the assumption $T_{\min} \neq T$. Hence, T is a minimum spanning tree for G. $\square$

---

[3] Joseph B. Kruskal (1928 – 2010) was an American mathematician.

Implementation of Kruskal's Algorithm. We sort the edges in ascending order by weight. Then we process the sorted list. Let V be the set of nodes of G. T has the components $T_1, \ldots, T_l$. V_i is the set of nodes of T_i, $i = 1, \ldots, l$.

We use the union-find data type to decide whether $T \cup \{e\}$, $e = \{v, w\}$, is acyclic. This is true if the end nodes v and w of e are in different components. So it must be decided whether $v, w \in T_i$ for an i. If this is not the case, i.e., $v \in T_i$ and $w \in T_j$ for $i \neq j$, connect the components T_i and T_j with e, in other words form $T_i \cup T_j$. The union-find data type provides a solution to this problem (see Section 6.1.2).

As noted before, Kruskal's algorithm requires all edges of the graph. We define the data structure of an edge by

type edge = struct
    vertex v_1, v_2
    weight w

Algorithm 6.29.
  edge $ed[1..m]$
  Kruskal()
  1   int i
  2   Sort(ed), FindInit(n)
  3   for $i \leftarrow 1$ to m do
  4   if Union($ed[i].v_1, ed[i].v_2$) = true
  5   then Insert($ed[i]$)

The procedure Insert inserts the edge $ed[i]$ into the tree.

Remark. Sort runs in time $O(m \log_2(m))$ (Chapter 2), FindInit in time $O(n)$, the effort for all Union calls is of order $O(m)$ (Proposition 6.10) and Insert runs in constant time (with a suitable data structure for trees). Altogether, we get that Kruskal's algorithm runs in time $O(n + m \log_2(m))$.

6.4 The Algorithm of Borůvka

The algorithm of Borůvka[4] is another deterministic algorithm for computing a minimum spanning tree for a weighted graph. Borůvka formulated the MST problem in 1926 in connection with the design of a network for the electrification of Moravia, a part of today's Czech Republic ([Borůvka26]). His algorithm is regarded as the first algorithm for the solution of the MST problem.

Let $G = (V, E)$ be a weighted graph. If the weights $w(e)$, $e \in E$, are pairwise distinct, there is only one sequence of edges, sorted descending by weights. In this case, the minimum spanning tree is uniquely determined.

---

[4] Otakar Borůvka (1899 – 1995) was a Czech mathematician.

If some weights are identical, we introduce the min-max order on the set of edges, which is explained analogously to the length-lexicographical order. We define

$\{u, v\} < \{\tilde{u}, \tilde{v}\}$ if and only if

$$w(\{u, v\}) < w(\{\tilde{u}, \tilde{v}\}) \text{ or}$$
$$w(\{u, v\}) = w(\{\tilde{u}, \tilde{v}\}) \text{ and } \min\{u, v\} < \min\{\tilde{u}, \tilde{v}\} \text{ or}$$
$$w(\{u, v\}) = w(\{\tilde{u}, \tilde{v}\}) \text{ and } \min\{u, v\} = \min\{\tilde{u}, \tilde{v}\} \text{ and}$$
$$\max\{u, v\} < \max\{\tilde{u}, \tilde{v}\}.$$

Since the algorithms in Sections 6.4 – 6.6 do not depend on the actual weights of the edges, we can always consider the min-max order on E. Therefore, we assume in the following that two edges have different weights. A minimum spanning tree with respect to the min-max order is uniquely determined and a spanning tree with minimal weight (in the usual order).

Let $v \in V$ and $e = \{v, w\}$. The edge e is called a *minimal incident edge*[5] of v if e is the smallest incident edge of v. The minimal incident edge of v is uniquely determined and leads to the nearest neighbor of v. An edge $e \in E$ is called a *minimal incident edge of G* if e is a minimal incident edge for a $v \in V$. By E_{MI} we denote the *set of all minimal incident edges of G*. E_{MI} is uniquely determined. Since an edge can only be a minimal incident edge for two nodes, it follows that $n > |E_{\mathrm{MI}}| \geq {}^n/_2$.

Contraction of the Minimal Incident Edges. The basic idea of Borůvka's algorithm is the contraction of all minimal incident edges. Let $G = (V, E)$ be a connected graph with at least two nodes and $e = \{v, w\} \in E$. To *contract* the edge e means to identify the end nodes v and w, i.e., to combine them into one node. This identification can result in loops and multiple edges. We remove all loops and for multiple edges we remove all but the smallest edge. Let $\tilde{G} = (\tilde{V}, \tilde{E})$ be the graph that results from $G = (V, E)$ when we contract all edges of E_{MI} in G. We write $\tilde{G} = G/E_{\mathrm{MI}}$ for the result. When contracting all minimal incident edges, we identify the nodes that are in a connected component C of (V, E_{MI}). We select a representative $R(C) \in V$ for each connected component C and define $\tilde{V}$ as the set of these selected representatives. So we regard $\tilde{V} \subset V$. The transition from G to $\tilde{G}$ is called the *contraction* of G.

Lemma 6.30. *The contraction of a connected graph $G = (V, E)$ with at least two nodes reduces the number of nodes by at least half.*

Proof. The contraction identifies the nodes in each connected component of (V, E_{MI}). Since each component contains at least two nodes, after the contraction there will remain at most ${}^n/_2$ nodes. The number of nodes is therefore at least halved.   □

---

[5] "Minimal incident edge" is shortened from "incident minimal-weight edge".

Example. Figure 6.12 shows a weighted graph with its minimal incident edges (drawn solid) and the resulting contraction.

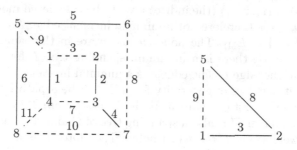

Fig. 6.12: Contraction of the minimal incident edges.

We are going to specify an algorithm for the contraction.

Algorithm 6.31.
(graph,edges) Contract(graph G)
1   $E_{MI} \leftarrow$ set of minimal incident edges of G
2   $\tilde{V} \leftarrow \{R(C_1),\ldots,R(C_k)\} \leftarrow \{$connected components of $(V, E_{MI})\}$
3   $\tilde{E} \leftarrow$ edges of $\tilde{V}$
4   return $((\tilde{V}, \tilde{E}), E_{MI})$

Remarks: We will take a closer look at the implementation of Contract if the graph G is described by an adjacency list.

1. The determination of the minimal incident edges E_{MI} requires an inspection of the adjacency list. The effort is of order $O(m)$.
2. We determine the connected components of (V, E_{MI}) by breadth-first search in (V, E_{MI}). The effort is of order $O(n)$. The roots of the resulting spanning trees serve as representatives of the corresponding connected components. For each node, we add a reference to the root of the tree of its connected component.
3. Determining the edges of $\tilde{V}$ requires another inspection of the adjacency list of V. If the end nodes of an edge are in different connected components, we insert an edge between the roots of the two spanning trees into the adjacency list of $\tilde{V}$. If an edge already exists, the weight will be updated if the new edge has a lower weight.

The addition of the running times under point 1 – point 3 shows that Contract runs in time $O(n + m)$.

Lemma 6.32. *Let $G = (V, E)$ be a weighted graph and E_{MI} be the set of minimal incident edges. Then*

1. *There is no cycle that only consists of minimal incident edges.*
2. *The edges of E_{MI} are edges of every minimum spanning forest of G.*

Proof.

1. We assume a cycle $Z = v_0, v_1, \ldots, v_l = v_0$ consisting of minimal incident edges. Let (v_i, v_{i+1}) be the largest edge. Then $(v_{i-1}, v_i) < (v_i, v_{i+1})$ and $(v_{i+1}, v_{i+2}) < (v_i, v_{i+1})$ (the indices have to be calculated modulo l). The edge (v_i, v_{i+1}) is therefore not a minimal incident edge. A contradiction.

2. Let $e = \{u, v\} \in E_{\mathrm{MI}}$. The nodes u and v are in the same component C of G. Suppose there is a minimum spanning tree T for C that does not contain the edge e. The edge e is a minimal incident edge for u or v, suppose without loss of generality for u. Let P be a path from u to v in T. Let e' be the first edge in this path. T' arises from T by adding e and removing e'. Then T' is also a spanning tree of C and since all edges have different weights, $w(T') < w(T)$ holds. Therefore, T is not a minimum spanning tree. A contradiction.

This shows the assertions. □

Remark. Borůvka's algorithm implements a greedy strategy. This follows from statement 2 of Lemma 6.32. Start with n nodes and select the minimal incident edges for the edge set. Apply this recursively to the graph that results from the contraction of all minimal incident edges. More precisely we have the following.

Proposition 6.33. *Let $G = (V, E)$ be a weighted graph, E_{MI} be the set of minimal incident edges, and $\tilde{T}$ be a minimum spanning forest of $\tilde{G} = G/E_{\mathrm{MI}}$. Then*

$$T = (V, E_{\tilde{T}} \cup E_{\mathrm{MI}})$$

is a minimum spanning forest of G. If G is connected, then T is a minimum spanning tree.

Proof. Lemma 6.32 shows that T is acyclic. If G is connected, then the construction of T immediately implies that T is also connected. □

Borůvka's algorithm starts with $T = (V, \emptyset)$ and $G = (V, E)$. Let $T = (V, E_T)$ and $G = (V, E)$ be constructed. In the next step we consider the components $V_1, \ldots, V_l$ of (V, E_{MI}). If V has only one component left, we are done. Otherwise, we choose for each component V_i the smallest edge t_i which has an end node in V_i and the other end node in the complement of V_i. We continue the procedure recursively with $T = (V, E_T \cup \{t_1, \ldots, t_l\})$ and $G = G/E_{\mathrm{MI}}$.

We now implement this idea for a connected weighted graph using the discussed contraction technique.

Algorithm 6.34.

```
edges Boruvka(graph G)
1   if |V| ≥ 2
2      then (G, E_MI) = Contract(G)
3         return E_MI ∪ Boruvka(G)
4   return E
```

Proposition 6.35. *Borůvka's algorithm computes a minimum spanning tree. The number of (recursive) calls of* Boruvka *is at most* $\lfloor \log_2(n) \rfloor + 1$ *and the running time is* $O((n+m)\log_2(n))$.

Proof. By applying Proposition 6.33 inductively, we conclude that Boruvka computes a minimum spanning tree. Contract reduces the number of nodes by more than a half (Lemma 6.30). Let $T(n)$ be the number of calls of the function Boruvka, depending on n. Then

$$T(1) = 1, \ T(n) \leq T\left(\left\lfloor \frac{n}{2} \right\rfloor\right) + 1, n \geq 2.$$

By Proposition 1.28, it follows that $T(n) \leq \lfloor \log_2(n) \rfloor + 1 = O(\log_2(n))$. Since the running time of Contract is $O(n+m)$, it follows that Boruvka runs in time $O((n+m)\log_2(n))$. □

Example. In the graph in Figure 6.13, the first call of Boruvka contracts the (incident minimal-weight) edges $\{1,4\}, \{2,3\}, \{3,7\}, \{5,6\}$ and $\{5,8\}$. In the resulting graph, the recursive call contracts the edges $\{1,2\}$ and $\{6,7\}$. The resulting MST is shown on the right of the figure.

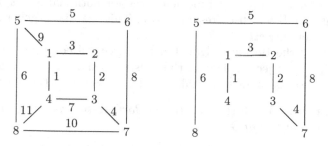

Fig. 6.13: MST with Borůvka's algorithm.

Construction of the Borůvka Tree. Let Boruvka$_i$, $i = 1, \ldots, l$, be the ith execution of Boruvka (Algorithm 6.34). We set $G_0 = G$ and denote by $G_i = (V_i, E_i)$ the value of the variable G and by $E_{\mathrm{MI}}^i \subset E_{i-1}$ the value of the variable E_{MI} after the execution of line 2 in Boruvka$_i$. The nodes V_i of G_i are the components of $(V_{i-1}, E_{\mathrm{MI}}^i)$. A component C of G_{i-1} can also be interpreted as a subset of V:

1. The components of G_0 are the nodes V of G, i.e., single-element subsets.
2. We assume that the components of G_{i-1} are identified with nodes from V. A component $C_i = \{c_1, \ldots, c_k\}$ of G_i consists of nodes c_i of V_i, $i = 1, \ldots, k$. The nodes c_i are components of G_{i-1}. Therefore, we can identify them by recursion with nodes from V. We identify C_i with $\cup_{j=1}^k c_j \subset V$.

In this view, Borůvka's algorithm combines two or more components into a new component in one step.

Let $v \in V$, and let $C_i(v)$ be the component of V_i that contains v, $i = 1, \ldots, l$. Then $C_0(v) = \{v\} \subset C_1(v) \subset \ldots \subset C_l(v) = V$. In the following, we consider a component $C_i(v)$ of G_i as a subset of V_i or as a subset of V, without distinguishing in its naming.

Using Algorithm 6.34, we assign to G the following weighted tree B:

1. The nodes of the ith level of B are the nodes V_{l-i} of G_{l-i}, $i = 0, \ldots, l$. In particular, the leaves of B are the nodes V of G.

2. A node u in level $i - 1$ is the predecessor of a node v in level i if $u = R(C(v))$ is a representative of the component $C(v)$, $i = 1, \ldots, l$. Each node in the $(i-1)$th level has at least two successors in the ith level. Let e_v be the minimal incident edge in the ith execution of Boruvka with end node v. The weight of the edge $(u, v) \in B$ is $w_B(u, v) := w(e_v)$.

3. The edges between levels $i - 1$ and i in the Borůvka tree, including their weights, correspond to the minimal incident edges contracted in the ith execution of Boruvka. We get a map

$$\varepsilon : E_B \longrightarrow E_G,$$

which assigns an edge in E_B to the corresponding edge in E_G. If a contracted edge e is a minimal incident edge for both end nodes, there are two edges in B which correspond to e. This map is in general neither injective nor surjective.

4. If we apply the Borůvka algorithm to a tree, all edges are contracted. The map ε is surjective. During the construction of the Borůvka tree, we save the description of ε in a table for later use (in Section 6.6).

Definition 6.36. We call the tree B the *Borůvka-tree assigned to G* or for short the *Borůvka tree of G*.

Example. Figure 6.14 shows a weighted graph with assigned Borůvka tree.

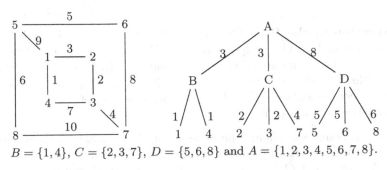

$B = \{1, 4\}$, $C = \{2, 3, 7\}$, $D = \{5, 6, 8\}$ and $A = \{1, 2, 3, 4, 5, 6, 7, 8\}$.

Fig. 6.14: A graph with assigned Borůvka tree.

Definition 6.37. A rooted tree T is said to be *full branching*[6] if all leaves of T are on the same level and each node that is not a leaf has at least two successors.

Remark. The Borůvka tree assigned to a graph is full branching.

Lemma 6.38. *Let T be a full branching tree with levels $0, \ldots, l$, and let n be the number of leaves of T. Then*

1. *The number n_i of nodes in the ith level satisfies $n_i \leq n/2^{l-i}$.*
2. *The number of nodes of T is $\leq 2n$.*
3. *The depth l of T satisfies $l \leq \lfloor \log_2(n) \rfloor$.*

Proof. Since $n_l = n$ and $n_i \leq n_{i+1}/2$, we get $n_i \leq n/2^{l-i}$, $i = 0, \ldots, l$. From $n_0 \leq \frac{n}{2^l}$, we conclude that $l \leq \lfloor \log_2(n) \rfloor$. The number of nodes is

$$\sum_{i=0}^{l} n_i \leq \sum_{i=0}^{l} \frac{n}{2^{l-i}} = n \sum_{i=0}^{l-1} \frac{1}{2^i} = n \left(2 - \frac{1}{2^l} \right) \leq 2n$$

(Appendix B (F.5)).   □

6.5 Verification of Minimum Spanning Trees

Let $G = (V, E)$ be a connected weighted graph and $T = (V, E_T)$ be a spanning tree for G. To decide whether T is a minimum spanning tree for G, we use the following criterion: If each edge $e \notin T$ is the edge of maximum weight on the cycle which results in $T \cup \{e\}$, then T is a minimum spanning tree. This can be computed with one comparison if for each path in T which results in a cycle by adding an edge from $E \setminus E_T$, the edge of maximum weight is known. Consequently, it is sufficient to develop an algorithm for this problem, the so-called tree-path-maximum problem.

Let T be a weighted tree, let l be a list of pairs of distinct nodes u and v in T. The *tree-path-maximum problem* is to find for each pair (u, v) on the list l an edge of maximum weight on the (unique) path which connects u and v in T. An algorithm that solves this problem with linear running time can be used to implement a linear running time algorithm to verify whether a given spanning tree is a minimum spanning tree.

First, we reduce the solution of the tree-path-maximum problem to the class of full branching trees.

---

[6] János Komlós (1942–), a Hungarian-American mathematician, introduced this term in [Komlós85].

Reduction of the Tree-Path-Maximum Problem to Full Branching Trees. The following proposition, published in [King97], reduces the tree-path-maximum problem for a tree T to the problem of computing the maximum weight edge on a path in the Borůvka tree assigned to T. First, let's consider the running time needed to compute the associated Borůvka tree.

Lemma 6.39. *Let T be a weighted tree with n nodes. Borůvka's algorithm applied to T runs in time $O(n)$. In particular, the running time for computing the Borůvka tree of T is $O(n)$.*

Proof. In the case of a tree T, we have $n + m = 2n - 1 = O(n)$. If we apply Contract to a tree, the result is again a tree. Let $T_0 = T$, and let $T_1, \ldots, T_l$ be the trees that arise during the execution of Boruvka. Let n_i be the number of nodes and $m_i = n_i - 1$ the number of edges of T_i, $i = 0, \ldots, l$. The running time for depth-first search to determine the components of T_i and thus also the running time of Contract and the running time of an iteration of Boruvka is cn_i, where c is constant. We sum over all iterations and get that

$$\sum_{i=0}^{l} cn_i \leq c \sum_{i=0}^{l} \frac{n}{2^i} \leq 2cn = O(n)$$

is valid because $n_i \leq n/2^i$ (see Appendix B (F.8)).   □

Example. Figure 6.15 shows a tree with the assigned Borůvka tree:

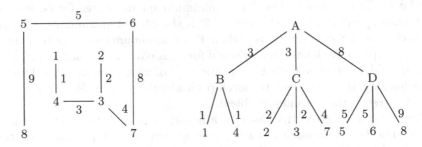

Fig. 6.15: A tree with assigned Borůvka tree.

Proposition 6.40. *Let $T = (V, E)$ be a weighted tree (with pairwise distinct weights) and $u, v \in V$. By $P_T(u, v)$ we denote the path from u to v in T and by $P_B(u, v)$ the (undirected) path connecting the leaves u and v in the Borůvka tree B assigned to T. Then*

$$\max_{e \in P_T(u,v)} w(e) = \max_{\tilde{e} \in P_B(u,v)} w_B(\tilde{e}).$$

Proof. Let $P_T(u, v) : u = u_0, \ldots, u_r = v$ be the path connecting u and v in T and $f = \{u_i, u_{i+1}\}$ the edge with maximum weight on $P_T(u, v)$. We assume that the contraction of f occurs in the jth execution of Boruvka. Let $C \subset T_{j-1}$ be the component containing u_i and $C' \subset T_j$, the component containing the nodes u_i and u_{i+1} after the contraction of f (see the section Construction of the Borůvka tree, page 275). Without loss of generality, we may assume that f is a minimal incident edge of the component C (otherwise, consider the component which contains $u_{i+1}, \ldots, u_r = v$). Since the edges of the sub-path $P_T(u, u_i)$ that connects u to u_i have a lower weight than $w(f)$, it follows that $P_T(u, u_i) \subset C$. So there is a path from u to C in B. The edge (C', C) corresponds to f and lies on the path $P_B(u, v)$. Therefore, it follows that $\max_{e \in P_T(u,v)} w(e) \leq \max_{\tilde{e} \in P_B(u,v)} w_B(\tilde{e})$.

It remains to show that the reverse inequality also holds. Let $\tilde{f} = (\tilde{x}, \tilde{y})$ be an edge of $P_B(u, v)$, let $\tilde{x}$ be the end node of $\tilde{f}$ with the greater depth, and let f be the image of $\tilde{f}$ under the map $\varepsilon : E_B \longrightarrow E_T$ (see page 276). We show that f is an edge of $P_T(u, v)$. Since the lowest common ancestor of u and v in B is not equal to $\tilde{x}$, it follows that $u \in \tilde{x}$ and $v \notin \tilde{x}$ holds ($\tilde{x}$ now denotes the component corresponding to $\tilde{x}$ in T). $T \setminus \{f\}$ breaks down into two components $T_1 = T \cap \tilde{x}$ and $T_2 = T \cap \overline{\tilde{x}}$. Since $u \in T_1$ and $v \in T_2$, the path $P_T(u, v)$ also breaks down into two components. Thus, $f \in P_T(u, v)$. From this we conclude that $\max_{e \in P_T(u,v)} w(e) \geq \max_{\tilde{e} \in P_B(u,v)} w_B(\tilde{e})$. $\square$

To solve the tree-path-maximum problem for a tree, it is sufficient to determine the edge of maximum weight in a non-directed path connecting two leaves v and w in a full branching tree B. Then, we compute the lowest common ancestor u of the two nodes v and w in B with the algorithms underlying Proposition 6.15. This is done, with preprocessing of order $O(n)$, in constant time (Section 6.1.3). Now, we trace the computation of the edge of maximum weight of the undirected path from v to w back to the computation of the edge of maximum weight on the two directed paths from u to v and from u to w. In total, the tree-path-maximum problem for a tree can be reduced to directed paths in the assigned Borůvka tree in preprocessing time $O(n)$. Then a query will be answered in constant time.

Tree-Path-Maximum Problem for Full Branching Trees. Let $T = (V, E)$ be a full branching tree with root r, and let $(u_1, v_1), \ldots, (u_m, v_m)$ be pairs of nodes, where v_i is a leaf and u_i is an ancestor of v_i, $i = 1, \ldots, m$. Let p_i be the path that connects u_i with v_i and $Q = \{p_1, \ldots, p_m\}$ the set of these paths.

We develop an algorithm that determines an edge of maximum weight on each path from Q. The solution outlined here is based on work by King ([King97]) and Komlós ([Komlós85]).

In a first step, for each node v we store in a list $M[v]$ the start nodes of the paths from Q which go through v, i.e., those paths which start at an ancestor of v and contain v. Each node $u \in M[v]$ defines a path, namely the path from u to v. We identify the start nodes with these paths and therefore also speak of the paths in $M[v]$. We compute $M[v]$ from bottom to top, starting with the leaves.

The list $M[v_i]$, $i = 1, \ldots, m$, contains the start nodes of all paths from Q that end in v_i. For all other nodes v, we set $M[v]$ equal to the empty list.

Starting from $M[v_1], \ldots, M[v_m]$, we compute $M[v]$ for all v lying on one of the paths from Q. Let $w_1, \ldots, w_k$ be the successors of v, and let $M'[w_i]$ be the list which we get when we remove all elements v from $M[w_i]$. We define $M[v]$ to be the concatenation of the lists $M'[w_i]$,

$$ M[v] := M'[w_1] \| \ldots \| M'[w_k]. $$

We compute the list $M[v]$ by a modified depth-first search in T (Algorithm 5.4.2).

In a second step, we compute further lists, starting from the root r. For a node v and a path $p \in Q$, we consider the restriction $p|_v$ from p to the levels $0, \ldots, d(v)$ from T, where $d(v)$ is the depth of v. We designate the set of these paths as

$$ P[v] = \{ p|_v \mid p \in Q \text{ and } p \text{ goes through } v \}. $$

The start nodes of these paths are in $M[v]$. We first describe properties of the list $L[v]_{v \in V}$ and then specify how we compute this list.

The list $L[v]$ contains one entry for each node that is an ancestor of v and the start node of a path $p|_v$ from $P[v]$. This entry consists of the end node of an edge of maximum weight of $p|_v$. The list $L[v]$ is sorted in descending order with respect to the following order on the set V, defined by $v < w$ if and only if the weight of (parent$(v), v$) is less than the weight of (parent$(w), w$). parent(v) denotes the predecessor of a node v in T.

We compute the list $L[v]_{v \in V}$ top-down starting from the root (e.g., on the basis of breadth-first search, Algorithm 5.11). For the root r, $L[r]$ is the empty list.

Let u be the predecessor of v. We compute the list $L[v]$ from $L[u]$. The edge (u, v) is an element of $P[v]$ if u is the start node of a path from $P[v]$ that consists only of one edge. All other paths in $P[v]$ are the paths from $P[u]$ that branch to v in the node u, in other words, these paths from $P[v]$ are formed from a path $\tilde{p} \in P[u]$ by extending it with the edge (u, v). Let $\tilde{P}[u] \subset P[u]$ be the subset of those paths and $\tilde{L}[v] \subset L[u]$ be the list of the end nodes of edges of maximum weight of the paths from $\tilde{P}[u]$. $\tilde{L}[v]$ can be computed from $L[u]$ with the help of $M[u]$ and $M[v]$. Using $M[u]$ and $M[v]$, we identify the paths from $M[u]$ that go through v. We need these to determine $\tilde{L}[v]$. The list $\tilde{L}[v]$ is sorted in descending order. We now describe in detail how the calculation is performed.

Using binary search we determine the elements in $\tilde{L}[v]$ that are less than v. These represent the end nodes of edges of maximum weight, whose weights are smaller than the weight of the edge (u, v). Therefore, they have to be replaced by v.

Now the paths only consisting of one edge (u, v) have to be considered. For each $u \in M[v]$, we extend $\tilde{L}[v]$ by one v. The result is the list $L[v]$. With $\tilde{L}[v]$, $L[v]$ is also sorted in descending order.

The list $L[v_i]$, $i = 1, \ldots, m$, contains for each of the paths from $P[v_i]$, the set of paths from Q ending in v_i, the lower end node of an edge of maximum weight. We can answer a path maximum query with the lists $M[v]$ and $L[v]$ in constant time.

Example. We compute the lists $M[v]_{v \in V}$ and $L[v]_{v \in V}$ for the example tree shown in Figure 6.16. The query paths are given by their start and end nodes: $(A, 8)$, $(A, 14)$, $(A, 17)$, $(B, 5)$, $(C, 13)$, $(C, 17)$ and $(H, 17)$.

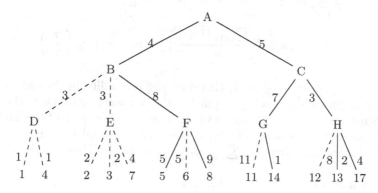

Fig. 6.16: Tree-path-maximum problem for a full branching tree.

We specify the list elements from $M[v]_{v \in V}$, $\tilde{L}[v]_{v \in V}$ and $L[v]_{v \in V}$ for nodes on query paths. The entries in the list $\tilde{L}[v]$ stem from entries in the list $L[\text{parent}(v)]$.

$$
\begin{array}{lll}
M[5] : B & M[8] : A & M[13] : C \\
M[14] : A & M[17] : A, C, H & \\
M[F] : B, A & M[G] : A & M[H] : C, A, C \\
M[B] : A & M[C] : A, A & \\
M[A] : & &
\end{array}
$$

$$
\begin{array}{lll}
L[A] : & & \\
L[B] : \binom{A}{B} & L[C] : \binom{A}{C}, \binom{A}{C} & \\
\tilde{L}[F] : \binom{A}{B} & \tilde{L}[G] : \binom{A}{C} & \tilde{L}[H] : \binom{A}{C} \\
L[F] : \binom{A}{F}, \binom{B}{F} & L[G] : \binom{A}{G} & L[H] : \binom{A}{C}, \binom{C}{H}, \binom{C}{H} \\
\tilde{L}[5] : \binom{A}{F} & \tilde{L}[8] : \binom{A}{F} & \tilde{L}[13] : \binom{C}{H} \\
\tilde{L}[14] : \binom{A}{G} & \tilde{L}[17] : \binom{A}{C}, \binom{C}{H} & \\
L[5] : \binom{B}{F} & L[8] : \binom{A}{8} & L[13] : \binom{C}{H} \\
L[14] : \binom{A}{G} & L[17] : \binom{A}{C}, \binom{C}{17}, \binom{H}{17} &
\end{array}
$$

For the remaining nodes, the list elements are empty. Here, the list L stores the end node of the maximum-weight edge in the second component and in the first component the start node of the query path.

Lemma 6.41. *For a full branching tree with n leaves, the list $L[v]_{v \in V}$ to answer m maximum weight edge queries can be generated with $O(n + m)$ comparisons.*

Proof. We denote by V_i the set of nodes v of B at the ith level which fulfill $\tilde{L}[v] \neq \emptyset$, and we set $n_i = |V_i|$, $i = 0, \ldots, l$. The number N_i of comparisons using Algorithm 2.36 for binary search for all nodes of level i satisfies

$$N_i \leq \sum_{v \in V_i} (\log_2(|\tilde{L}[v]|) + 1) \leq n_i + n_i \sum_{v \in V_i} \frac{\log_2(|\tilde{L}[v]|)}{n_i}$$

$$\leq n_i + n_i \log_2 \left(\frac{\sum_{v \in V_i} |\tilde{L}[v]|}{n_i} \right) \leq n_i + n_i \log_2 \left(\frac{m}{n_i} \right).$$

We have $\sum_{v \in V_i} \frac{1}{n_i} = |V_i| \frac{1}{n_i} = 1$, therefore the inequality in the second line follows from Jensen's inequality, applied to the concave function $\log_2$ (Lemma B.22). Since each query path passes through exactly one node of the ith level and the number of elements of $\tilde{L}[v]$ is less than or equal to the number of query paths passing through v, $\sum_{v \in V_i} |\tilde{L}[v]| \leq m$ holds. Therefore, the fourth inequality follows.

We then sum up all levels $i = 0, \ldots, l$

$$\sum_{i=0}^{l} n_i \leq \sum_{i=0}^{l} \frac{n}{2^{l-i}} \leq n \sum_{i=0}^{l} \frac{1}{2^l} \leq 2n$$

(using Lemma 6.38 and Appendix B (F.8)).

$$\sum_{i=0}^{l} n_i + n_i \log_2 \left(\frac{m}{n_i} \right) \leq 2n + \sum_{i=0}^{l} n_i \log_2 \left(\frac{m}{n} \cdot \frac{n}{n_i} \right)$$

$$= 2n + \sum_{i=0}^{l} n_i \log_2 \left(\frac{m}{n} \right) + n_i \log_2 \left(\frac{n}{n_i} \right)$$

$$\leq 2n + 2n \log_2 \left(\frac{m}{n} \right) + \sum_{i=0}^{l} n_i \log_2 \left(\frac{n}{n_i} \right)$$

$$\leq 2n + 2m + 3n = O(n + m).$$

The function

$$x \mapsto x \log_2 \left(\frac{n}{x} \right)$$

is increasing for $x \leq \frac{n}{4}$. Hence,

$$\sum_{i=0}^{l} n_i \log_2\left(\frac{n}{n_i}\right) = n_l \log_2\left(\frac{n}{n_l}\right) + n_{l-1} \log_2\left(\frac{n}{n_{l-1}}\right) + \sum_{i=0}^{l-2} n_i \log_2\left(\frac{n}{n_i}\right)$$

$$\leq n + \sum_{i=0}^{l-2} \frac{n}{2^{l-i}} \log_2\left(2^{l-i}\right)$$

$$\leq n + n \sum_{i\geq 0} \frac{i}{2^i} \leq 3n \text{ (Appendix B (F.8))}.$$

This shows the second inequality.   □

Remark. By skillfully encoding the vectors $M[v]_{v\in V}$ and $L[v]_{v\in V}$ as bit vectors, the complete calculation of $L[v]_{v\in V}$ is possible using bit operations in time $O(n+m)$. For the details, we refer to an article by King ([King97]). As a result, for a full branching tree with n leaves we get an algorithm which computes an edge of maximum weight for m paths with a running time of order $O(n+m)$.

Let $G = (V, E)$ be a connected weighted graph with n nodes and m edges. The verification of a minimum spanning tree $T = (V, E_T)$ for G is done as follows.

Algorithm 6.42.

```
    boolean MSTVerify(graph (V, E),  tree (V, E_T))
1   B ← BoruvkaTree(V, E_T)
2   Q₁ ← E \ E_T
3   Q₂ ← LCA(B, Q₁)
4   MaxEdgeInit(B, Q₂)
5   for  each edge e = {u, v} ∈ Q₁ do
6       if e.weight < MaxEdge(u, v).weight
7           then return false
8   return true
```

Remarks:

1. $\text{LCA}(B, Q_1)$ reduces the calculation of the lowest common ancestors of the end nodes of the edges from Q_1 in the tree B to the solution of the RMQ problem and executes
   a. Algorithm 6.13 to reduce the LCA problem to the RMQ problem.
   b. The algorithms to initialize the tables for the solution of the RMQ problem (page 257).
   c. LCA queries for all $\{u, v\} \in Q_1$. For $\{u, v\} \in Q_1$ the list Q_2 contains the lowest common ancestor $\text{LCA}(u, v)$ of u and v in B.
2. MaxEdgeInit computes the lookup table L from this section (page 280).
3. For an edge $\{u, v\} \in Q_1$ MaxEdge computes the edge of maximum weight on the path connecting u and v in T. For nodes u and v in B, the maximum weights of the resulting sub-paths from u to $\text{LCA}(u, v)$ and from

LCA(u,v) to v are looked up in the table L and the edge of maximum weight of the complete path is computed. With the map $\varepsilon : E_B \longrightarrow E_T$, which is defined on page 276, the edge in T is determined which corresponds to the edge of maximum weight in B.

4. We can modify Algorithm 6.42 and record for all edges e from Q_1 whether the comparison for e in line 6 is fulfilled or not.

Proposition 6.43. *Let $G = (V,E)$ be a connected weighted graph with n nodes and m edges. The verification of a minimum spanning tree T for G is done by Algorithm 6.42 in time $O(n+m)$.*

Proof. The generation of the Borůvka tree B (Lemma 6.39), the reduction of the LCA problem to the RMQ problem by Algorithm 6.13 and the creation of the tables for the solution of the RMQ problem (Proposition 6.16) is done with running time of order $O(n)$. All LCA queries are executed in time $O(m)$ (Proposition 6.15). The Algorithm MaxEdgeInit initializes the table L in time $O(n+m)$ (see Lemma 6.41 and the following remark). We perform a query MaxEdge in constant time (loc. cit.). The number of edges $|E \setminus E_T|$ is $< m$. The running time of Algorithm 6.42 is therefore of order $O(n+m)$.   □

6.6 A Randomized MST Algorithm

The running time of Prim's and Borůvka's algorithm is of order $O((n + m) \log_2(n))$. Kruskal's algorithm runs in time $O(n + m \log_2(m))$. By using probabilistic methods, it is possible to specify an algorithm to solve the problem which has a better running time.

The algorithm of Karger, Klein and Tarjan – we call it KKT-MST – computes a minimum spanning tree for a connected graph (see [KarKleTar95]). The expected value of the running time of the algorithm is $O(n + m)$. To achieve this, we use the function Contract from Borůvka's algorithm and a probabilistic method that samples a subgraph using random bits. This step is used to identify edges that cannot occur in a minimum spanning tree.

First, we prove a property of minimum spanning trees and introduce notations that we will need later.

Lemma 6.44 *(circle property). Let G be a connected graph, Z a cycle in G and $e \in Z$ an edge with $w(e) > w(e')$ for all $e' \in Z$, $e' \neq e$. Then e cannot be an edge of a minimum spanning tree.*

Proof. Let T be a minimum spanning tree for G and $e = \{u,v\}$ an edge of maximum weight in Z. Suppose $e \in T$. If we remove e, T breaks down into two components T_u and T_v. Because Z is a cycle, there is an edge $e' = \{u',v'\} \in Z$ with $u' \in T_u$ and $v' \in T_v$. Then $T' = (T \setminus \{e\}) \cup \{e'\}$ is a spanning tree and $w(T') = w(T) - w(e) + w(e') < w(T)$, a contradiction.   □

Definition 6.45. Let $G = (V, E)$ be a weighted graph, $F \subset G$ an acyclic spanning subgraph. For nodes u, v from the same component of F, the $F-$ *path* between u and v is the (uniquely determined) path between u and v that runs entirely in F.

$$
w_F(u, v) := \begin{cases} \infty \text{ if } u \text{ and } v \text{ lie in different components of } F, \\[2mm] \max_{1 \leq i \leq l} w(\{v_{i-1}, v_i\}), \text{ with the } F\text{--path} \\[1mm] \qquad\qquad P : u = v_0, \dots, v_l = v \text{ connecting } u \text{ and } v. \end{cases}
$$

An edge $e = \{u, v\} \in E$ is said to be F–*heavy* if $w(e) > w_F(u, v)$ and F–*light* if $w(e) \leq w_F(u, v)$.

Remark. An edge $e = \{u, v\}$ is F–heavy if all edges of the F–path connecting u and v have weight $< w(e)$. Edges connecting different components of F and edges of F are all F–light.

Lemma 6.46. *Let $G = (V, E)$ be a weighted connected graph, $F \subset G$ be an acyclic subgraph and $e \in E$ be an F–heavy edge. Then e does not occur as an edge in a minimum spanning tree for G.*

Proof. Let the edge $e = \{u, v\}$ be F–heavy, and let $P : u = v_0, \dots, v_l = v$ be the path from u to v in F. The weight $w(e)$ is greater than the weight of each edge on the path P. According to Lemma 6.44, e cannot be an edge of a minimum spanning tree.   □

Since an F–heavy edge e in a graph G does not occur in any minimum spanning tree for G, G and $G \setminus \{e\}$ have the same minimum spanning tree. Therefore, when computing an MST, we may first remove the F–heavy edges of the graph.

We now describe how to identify the F–heavy edges of a graph G with n nodes and m edges.

Let $F \subset G$ be a spanning acyclic subgraph, and let $T_1, \dots, T_l$ be the connected components of F. By n_i we denote the number of nodes of T_i and by m_i the number of edges $e = (u, v)$ of $G \setminus F$ whose end nodes lie in the same tree T_i. For all these edges, we can compute an edge of maximum weight on the path connecting u with v in T_i with running time in $O(n_i + m_i)$ (see remarks to Algorithm 6.42). We run the modified algorithm MSTVerify for each component T_i and get the F–heavy edges of G in time $O(\sum_{i=1}^{l} n_i + \sum_{i=1}^{l} m_i) = O(n + m)$.

The probabilistic part of the algorithm of Karger, Klein and Tarjan is the algorithm SampleSubgraph, which randomly generates a subgraph H of $G = (V, E)$.

Algorithm 6.47.
  graph SampleSubgraph(graph G)
  1   $H \leftarrow (V, \emptyset)$
  2   for each $e \in E$ do
  3   if coinToss = heads
  4   then $H \leftarrow H \cup \{e\}$
  5   return H

The subgraph H of G is not necessarily connected. The expectation is that the (uniquely determined) minimum spanning forest F of H is a good approximation of a minimum spanning tree for G, i.e., only a few edges of G that do not lie in F are F–light.

Proposition 6.48. Let $G = (V, E)$ be a graph with n nodes and m edges, H the result of SampleSubgraph(G) and let F the minimum spanning forest of H. Then the expected number of edges of H is $m/2$ and the expected number of F–light edges in G is at most $2n$.

Proof. Let X denote the number of edges of H and let Y denote the number of F–light edges in G. The random variable X is binomially distributed with parameter $(m, 1/2)$. Therefore, $\mathrm{E}(X) = m/2$ (Proposition A.16).

In order to estimate the expected value of Y, we modify SampleSubgraph and simultaneously calculate from H the minimum spanning forest of H according to Kruskal's method (Algorithm 6.29). The modified algorithm decides like SampleSubgraph for each edge e, based on a coin toss, whether e is taken as an edge of H.

Algorithm 6.49.
  SampleSubgraphMSF(graph G)
  1   $H \leftarrow (V, \emptyset)$, $F \leftarrow (V, \emptyset)$, $Y \leftarrow 0$
  2   $\{e_1, \ldots, e_m\} \leftarrow \mathrm{sort}(E)$
  3   for $i \leftarrow 1$ to m do
  4   if e_i is F–light
  5   then $Y \leftarrow Y + 1$
  6   if coinToss = heads
  7   then $H \leftarrow H \cup \{e_i\}$
  8                  $F \leftarrow F \cup \{e_i\}$
  9   else if coinToss = heads
  10   then $H \leftarrow H \cup \{e_i\}$

Kruskal's algorithm requires that the edges of G are sorted in ascending order. For each F–light edge of G, we decide on the basis of a coin toss (with a penny) in line 6 whether to choose it for H and F. The variable Y counts the number of F–light edges and, after termination, contains their overall number. If the end nodes of the edge e_i which we consider in the ith step, are in the same component of F, e_i is F–heavy (since the edges are sorted in ascending order, all edges of E_F have weight $< w(e_i)$). If e_i has its end nodes

in different components of F, e_i is F–light (note $w_F(e_i) = \infty$). We compute
– analogously to the method of Kruskal's algorithm (Algorithm 6.3) – the
minimum spanning forest F of H. In line 9, we decide for an F–heavy edge
e_i based on a coin toss (with a nickel) whether we choose e_i for H. An edge
e_i which we select in line 7 is also F–light after terminating SampleSubgraph,
since the weight of an edge that will later be added to F is $> w(e_i)$.

Our random experiment consists of two phases. In phase 1, we run the
algorithm SampleSubgraphMSF. Since F is acyclic and has n nodes, after
termination of SampleSubgraphMSF we have $|E_F| \leq n - 1$. In phase 2, we
continue tossing the penny and also denote by Y the random variable which
counts all penny-flips. We end phase 2 as soon as the event "heads" occurs
n times (together in phase 1 and phase 2).

The random variable Y counts the number of repetitions until the event
"heads" occurs n times. It is negative binomially distributed with parameter $(n, 1/2)$. The expected value of Y satisfies $E(Y) = 2n$ (Proposition A.22).
Since the number of F–light edges is bounded by Y, the expected value of
the number of F–light edges in G is $\leq E(Y)$, thus also $\leq 2n$. $\square$

The input of the algorithm KKT-MST is a weighted (not necessarily connected) graph $G = (V, E)$. The result is a minimum spanning forest for G.
KKT-MST reduces the size of the graph G in two steps. In the first step,
we consecutively apply Contract (Algorithm 6.31) three times. The result is
$G_1 = (V_1, E_1)$. In the second step, we delete edges in G_1 that cannot occur
in any minimum spanning tree. We call the result $G_3 = (V_3, E_3)$.

Algorithm 6.50.
    edgeset KKT-MST(graph G)
  1    $F_1 \leftarrow \emptyset$
  2   for $i \leftarrow 1$ to 3 do
  3        $(G_1, E_{\mathrm{MI}}) \leftarrow$ Contract(G)
  4        $F_1 \leftarrow F_1 \cup E_{\mathrm{MI}}, \ G \leftarrow G_1$
  5   if $|V_1| = 1$ then return F_1
  6    $G_2 \leftarrow$ SampleSubgraph(G_1)
  7    $F_2 \leftarrow$ KKT-MST(G_2)
  8    $G_3 \leftarrow$ DeleteHeavyEdges(F_2, G_1)
  9   return $F_1 \cup$ KKT-MST(G_3)

Proposition 6.51. *Let G be a weighted connected graph with n nodes and m
edges. The algorithm KKT-MST returns the edges of a minimum spanning
tree for G and it's expected running time is $O(n + m)$.*

Proof. Let $G_i = (V_i, E_i)$, $i = 1, 2, 3$. First we show that KKT-MST computes
a minimum spanning tree. From Proposition 6.33, it follows that the edges
of F_1 belong to the minimum spanning tree of G. If G_1 has only one node,
the edges of F_1 form the minimum spanning tree. F_2 is acyclic and therefore
also an acyclic subgraph of G. According to Lemma 6.46, the F_2–heavy edges

do not belong to a minimum spanning tree for G_1. Therefore, the minimum spanning trees for G_1 and G_3 match. Since $|V_2|, |V_3| < n$ and $|E_2|, |E_3| < m$, the recursive calls of KKT-MST terminate. According to the induction hypothesis, the call KKT-MST(G_3) computes a minimum spanning tree for G_3. In Proposition 6.33, we have learned that $F_1 \cup$ KKT-MST(G_3) is a minimum spanning tree for G.

It remains to be shown that the expected value of the running time of KKT-MST is $O(n + m)$. The following holds: $|V_1| \leq {}^n\!/_8$ (Lemma 6.30) and $|E_1| < m$, $|V_1| = |V_2| = |V_3|$, $\mathrm{E}(|E_2|) = {}^m\!/_2$ (Proposition 6.48) and $\mathrm{E}(|E_3|) \leq 2 \cdot {}^n\!/_8 = {}^n\!/_4$ (loc. cit.). The running time for Contract, SampleSubgraph and DeleteHeavyEdges is of order $O(n + m)$. Consequently, the expected value $T(n, m)$ of the running time of KKT-MST fulfills

$$T(n, m) \leq T\left(\frac{n}{8}, \frac{m}{2}\right) + T\left(\frac{n}{8}, \frac{n}{4}\right) + c(n + m)$$

for a constant c. We consider the recurrence that we get when we replace "$\leq$" with "$=$". It is easy to verify that $2c(n + m)$ is the solution of this equation. Consequently, $T(n, m) \leq 2c(n + m)$.   □

Remark. Algorithm 6.50 is a minor modification of the original algorithm, which goes back to [MotRag95]. It leads to the recurrence above, for which a solution is easy to specify.

6.7 Transitive Closure and Distance Matrix

The set of edges E of a directed graph $G = (V, E)$ defines a relation $\sim$ on the set of nodes V: $u \sim v$ if and only if $(u, v) \in E$. This relation is generally not transitively closed.[7] The algorithm of Warshall[8] computes the transitive closure of this relation. The transitive closure describes for each node $v \in V$ which nodes w are accessible from v.

The algorithm of Floyd[9] determines the distances for all pairs (v, w) of nodes in a directed graph.

Both algorithms, published in 1962 in [Floyd62] and [Warshall62], have the same structure. They are summarized as the Floyd-Warshall algorithm and are inspired by an algorithm for regular expressions by Kleene[10] from 1956.

The Floyd-Warshall algorithm is designed according to the design method of dynamic programming (see Section 1.5.4).

---

[7] Transitively closed means if $u \sim v$ and $v \sim w$, then $u \sim w$.

[8] Stephen Warshall (1935 – 2006) was an American computer scientist.

[9] Robert W. Floyd (1936 – 2001) was an American computer scientist and Turing Award winner.

[10] Stephen Cole Kleene (1909 – 1994) was an American mathematician and logician. He is known for the Kleene closure of a formal language and the Kleene operator
    *.

Definition 6.52. Let $G = (V, E)$ be a directed graph. The graph

$$G_c = (V, E_c) \text{ with } E_c := \{(v, w) \mid w \text{ accessible from } v \text{ and } w \neq v\}$$

is called the *transitive closure* or *transitive envelope* of G.

Remarks:

1. G is a subgraph of G_c and G_c is the smallest transitively closed graph that contains G.
2. For graphs, the transitive closure is defined by the connected components: w is accessible from v, i.e., $(v, w) \in E_c$, if v and w are in the same connected component of G. We compute with breadth-first search (Algorithm 5.11) all connected components and thus the transitive closure with running time of order $O(n + m)$ or $O(n^2)$.
3. For directed graphs, the node w is accessible from v if w is in C_v, the connected component of v. The determination of E_c corresponds to the determination of C_v for all $v \in V$. The effort is of order $O(n^3)$ or $O(n(n + m))$ if we use depth-first search (Algorithm 5.12) or breadth-first search (Algorithm 5.11).

The Algorithm of Warshall. Let $G = (V, E)$ be a directed graph, and let a be the adjacency matrix of G. Warshall's algorithm computes a sequence of matrices $a_0, a_1, \ldots, a_n$, $n = |V|$, with coefficients from $\{0, 1\}$. This sequence is defined by the recurrence

$$a_0 := a,$$
$$a_k[i, j] := a_{k-1}[i, j] \text{ or } (a_{k-1}[i, k] \text{ and } a_{k-1}[k, j]) \text{ for } k = 1, \ldots, n.$$

The matrices a_k have a descriptive interpretation by means of the following definition and the following proposition.

Definition 6.53. A simple path from i to j which contains except i and j only nodes $\leq k$ is called a k-*path*.

Proposition 6.54. *For the matrix* $a_k, 1 \leq k \leq n$, *the following statements are equivalent:*

1. $a_k[i, j] = 1$ for $i \neq j$.
2. There is a k-path from i to j for $i \neq j$.

In particular, a_n *describes the transitive closure of* G.

Proof. We show the assertion by induction on k. For $k = 0$ we have $a_0[i, j] = 1$ if and only if there is a 0-path (an edge) from i to j. Let $k \geq 1$ and assume the assertion proved for $k - 1$. $a_k[i, j] = 1$ if and only if $a_{k-1}[i, j] = 1$ or $(a_{k-1}[i, k] = 1$ and $a_{k-1}[k, j] = 1)$. This in turn is true if there is a $(k - 1)$-path from i to j, or there is a $(k - 1)$-path from i to k and from k to j. The last statement holds if and only if there is a k-path from i to j.

Since the set of n-paths includes all paths, we get the last statement of the proposition. □

Example. Figure 6.17 shows the calculation of the transitive closure by dynamic programming with the algorithm of Warshall.

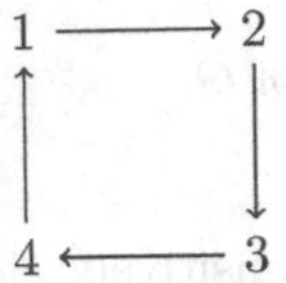

$$
a_0 = \begin{pmatrix} 0\,1\,0\,0 \\ 0\,0\,1\,0 \\ 0\,0\,0\,1 \\ 1\,0\,0\,0 \end{pmatrix}, \ a_1 = \begin{pmatrix} 0\,1\,0\,0 \\ 0\,0\,1\,0 \\ 0\,0\,0\,1 \\ 1\,1\,0\,0 \end{pmatrix},
$$

$$
a_2 = \begin{pmatrix} 0\,1\,1\,0 \\ 0\,0\,1\,0 \\ 0\,0\,0\,1 \\ 1\,1\,1\,0 \end{pmatrix}, \ a_3 = \begin{pmatrix} 0\,1\,1\,1 \\ 0\,0\,1\,1 \\ 0\,0\,0\,1 \\ 1\,1\,1\,0 \end{pmatrix}, \ a_4 = \begin{pmatrix} 0\,1\,1\,1 \\ 1\,0\,1\,1 \\ 1\,1\,0\,1 \\ 1\,1\,1\,0 \end{pmatrix}.
$$

Fig. 6.17: Transitive closure with Warshall's algorithm.

Remarks:

1. Ones remain ones in subsequent matrices (because of the or operator), therefore we consider for an iteration only zeros outside the diagonal.
2. By definition $a_k[i,k] = a_{k-1}[i,k]$ or $(a_{k-1}[i,k]$ and $a_{k-1}[k,k])$. Since $a_{k-1}[k,k] = 0$, we get $a_k[i,k] = a_{k-1}[i,k]$. Analogously, it follows that $a_k[k,j] = a_{k-1}[k,j]$. Therefore, we can perform the calculation with one matrix (memory).

Algorithm 6.55.
Warshall(boolean $a[1..n, 1..n]$)
1   vertex i, j, k
2   for $k \leftarrow 1$ to n do
3   for $i \leftarrow 1$ to n do
4   for $j \leftarrow 1$ to n do
5                $a[i,j] = a[i,j]$ or $(a[i,k]$ and $a[k,j])$

Remark. The outer for loop computes the matrices $a_1, a_2, \ldots, a_n$. Then we calculate the matrix a_k for fixed k by the two inner for loops. The running time of Warshall is of order $O(n^3)$.

The Algorithm of Floyd. We can calculate the distances for all pairs of nodes in positively weighted graphs by applying Dijkstra's algorithm with every node as start node (Section 6.2). The following algorithm of Floyd does this also for graphs with negative weights if no cycles with negative weights occur.

Let $G = (V, E)$ be a weighted directed graph. We represent G with the adjacency matrix a.

$$
a[i,j] := \begin{cases} w(i,j) & \text{if } (i,j) \in E, \\ \infty & \text{if } (i,j) \notin E, i \neq j, \\ 0 & \text{if } i = j. \end{cases}
$$

The distance matrix a_d of G is defined by

$$a_d[i,j] := d(i,j) := \begin{cases} \text{length of a shortest path from } i \text{ to } j, \\ \infty \text{ if no path exists.} \end{cases}$$

To calculate the distance matrix a_d from a, we define a sequence of matrices $a_0, \ldots, a_n$ by the recurrence

$$a_0 = a,$$
$$a_k[i,j] = \min\{a_{k-1}[i,j], a_{k-1}[i,k] + a_{k-1}[k,j]\} \text{ for } k = 1, \ldots, n.$$

Proposition 6.56. *For the matrix a_k, we get that $a_k[i,j]$ is the length of a shortest k–path from i to j or $a_k[i,j] = \infty$ if no k–path from i to j exists. In particular, a_n defines the distance matrix for G.*

Proof. We shall prove our assertion by induction on k. For $k = 0$, $a_0[i,j]$ is the length of a 0–path (an edge) from i to j. Let $k \geq 1$ and assume the assertion proved for $k-1$. Let $M_k[i,j]$ be the set of k–paths from i to j, and let $P \in M_k[i,j]$ be a path of minimum length. We consider two cases.

1. If $k \notin P$, then $P \in M_{k-1}[i,j]$ and P is of minimal length, so according to the induction hypothesis $l(P) = a_{k-1}[i,j]$. Since P is a k–path of minimal length, $l(P) \leq a_{k-1}[i,k] + a_{k-1}[k,j]$, and consequently, $a_k[i,j] = \min\{a_{k-1}[i,j], a_{k-1}[i,k] + a_{k-1}[k,j]\} = a_{k-1}[i,j] = l(P)$.
2. If $k \in P$, decompose P into $P_1 \in M_{k-1}[i,k]$ and $P_2 \in M_{k-1}[k,j]$. P_1 and P_2 are $(k-1)$–paths of minimum length. According to the induction hypothesis $l(P_1) = a_{k-1}[i,k]$ and $l(P_2) = a_{k-1}[k,j]$. Since P is a k–path of minimum length, $l(P) = a_{k-1}[i,k] + a_{k-1}[k,j]$. There is no shorter $(k-1)$–path, so $a_{k-1}[i,k] + a_{k-1}[k,j] \leq a_{k-1}[i,j]$, and consequently, $a_k[i,j] = \min\{a_{k-1}[i,j], a_{k-1}[i,k] + a_{k-1}[k,j]\} = a_{k-1}[i,k] + a_{k-1}[k,j] = l(P)$.

This shows the assertion. □

Remarks:

1. Due to $a_k[i,k] = a_{k-1}[i,k]$ and $a_k[k,j] = a_{k-1}[k,j]$ we can perform the calculation with one matrix (memory).
2. If negative weights are allowed but no cycles with negative lengths occur, Floyd works correctly because then the path of shortest length is a simple path.

Example. Figure 6.18 shows the calculation of the distance matrix with Floyd's algorithm using the dynamic programming method.

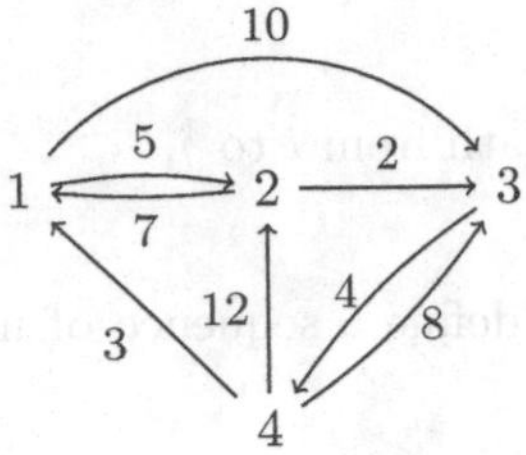

$$a_0 = \begin{pmatrix} 0 & 5 & 10 & \infty \\ 7 & 0 & 2 & \infty \\ \infty & \infty & 0 & 4 \\ 3 & 12 & 8 & 0 \end{pmatrix}, \ a_1 = \begin{pmatrix} 0 & 5 & 10 & \infty \\ 7 & 0 & 2 & \infty \\ \infty & \infty & 0 & 4 \\ 3 & 8 & 8 & 0 \end{pmatrix},$$

$$a_2 = \begin{pmatrix} 0 & 5 & 7 & \infty \\ 7 & 0 & 2 & \infty \\ \infty & \infty & 0 & 4 \\ 3 & 8 & 8 & 0 \end{pmatrix}, \ a_3 = \begin{pmatrix} 0 & 5 & 7 & 11 \\ 7 & 0 & 2 & 6 \\ \infty & \infty & 0 & 4 \\ 3 & 8 & 8 & 0 \end{pmatrix}, \ a_4 = \begin{pmatrix} 0 & 5 & 7 & 11 \\ 7 & 0 & 2 & 6 \\ 7 & 12 & 0 & 4 \\ 3 & 8 & 8 & 0 \end{pmatrix}.$$

Fig. 6.18: The distance matrix computed with Floyd's algorithm.

Algorithm 6.57.

Floyd(real $a[1..n, 1..n]$)

1   vertex i, j, k
2   for $k \leftarrow 1$ to n do
3   for $i \leftarrow 1$ to n do
4   for $j \leftarrow 1$ to n do
5   if $a[i, k] + a[k, j] < a[i, j]$
6   then $a[i, j] \leftarrow a[i, k] + a[k, j]$

Remark. The outer for loop computes the matrices $a_1, a_2, \ldots, a_n$ one after the other. Then we calculate the matrix a_k for fixed k in the two inner for loops. The running time $T(n)$ of Floyd is of order $O(n^3)$.

Computing the Shortest Paths. We modify Floyd's algorithm to allow the reconstruction of all shortest paths. For this purpose we use an $n \times n$— matrix P. In $P[i, j]$ we store the largest node on a shortest path from i to j. Again we proceed iteratively. We initialize $P_0[i, j] = 0$. In $P_k[i, j]$ we store the largest node of a shortest k–path from i to j. In $P[i, j] = P_n[i, j]$ the largest node on a shortest path from i to j is stored. We replace line 6 in Floyd with

$$a[i, j] \leftarrow a[i, k] + a[k, j]; P[i, j] \leftarrow k.$$

We can get all shortest paths from P.

Algorithm 6.58.

Path(vertex i, j)

1   vertex k
2    $k \leftarrow P[i, j]$
3   if $k > 0$
4   then Path(i, k), print(k), Path(k, j)

For i, j with $a_d[i, j] \neq \infty$, the procedure Path returns all nodes k of a shortest path from i to j which are between i and j. An upper limit on the number of nodes in all simple paths is n^3. The method used here only requires an $n \times n$–matrix to store all shortest paths.

6.8 Flow Networks

We will study the problem of computing a maximum flow in a flow network. We discuss the algorithm of Ford[11]-Fulkerson[12] in the variant of Edmonds[13]-Karp[14]. The original algorithm was published in [FordFulk56] and the optimization in [EdmoKarp72]. Our presentation is based on [CorLeiRivSte09]. There are many real situations that can be modeled using a flow network. Examples are networks for the distribution of electrical energy or the pipe system of a city's canalization. Both have in common that the capacity of the pipelines is limited and that the nodes do not have storage. In a power grid, this is Kirchhoff's[15] first law. First, we clarify the problem with an example.

Example. In Figure 6.19, there are pumping stations n_1, n_2, s_1, s_2, s is an oil well, t is a refinery and the edges are oil pipes that transport the oil from the oil well to the refinery. The labeling on the edges indicates the capacity of each line.

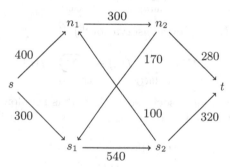

Fig. 6.19: A flow network.

The problem to be solved is: How much do we have to pump through the individual pipes so that the amount transported from s to t becomes maximum?

The following constraints for the flow have to be considered:

1. No more can be pumped through a pipe than the capacity allows.

---

[11] Lester Randolph Ford (1927 – 2017) was an American mathematician.
[12] Delbert Ray Fulkerson (1924 – 1976) was an American mathematician.
[13] Jack R. Edmonds (1934 –) is a Canadian mathematician and computer scientist.
[14] Richard Manning Karp (1935 –) is an American computer scientist.
[15] Gustav Robert Kirchhoff (1824–1887) was a German physicist.

2. For a node n, different from s and from t, all that flows into n must also flow out again.

We state the situation of the previous example more precisely in the following

Definition 6.59.

1. A *flow network* or *network* $N = (V, E, s, t)$ consists of a weighted directed graph (V, E). The weight function

$$c : E \longrightarrow \mathbb{R}_{>0}$$

is called the *capacity*. $s \in V$ denotes the *source*, $t \in V$ denotes the *sink*.
2. Let $S \subset V$.

$$\text{In}(S) := \{(v, w) \in E \mid v \notin S, w \in S\}.$$
$$\text{Out}(S) := \{(v, w) \in E \mid v \in S, w \notin S\}.$$

3. A flow for N is a map $f : E \longrightarrow \mathbb{R}_{\geq 0}$ with
   a. $f(e) \leq c(e)$ for $e \in E$ (capacity constraint).
   b.
   $$\sum_{e \in \text{In}(v)} f(e) = \sum_{e \in \text{Out}(v)} f(e)$$

   for $v \in V \setminus \{s, t\}$ (flow conservation[16]).
4.
$$F = \sum_{e \in \text{In}(t)} f(e) - \sum_{e \in \text{Out}(t)} f(e)$$

is called the *total flow* associated with f. It is the flow from s to t.
5. A subset S of V is said to be a *cut* of N if $s \in S$ and $t \notin S$.

$$C(S) := \sum_{e \in \text{Out}(S)} c(e)$$

is called the *capacity of the cut defined by* S.
S defines a *cut of minimum capacity* if $C(S)$ is minimum for all cuts S.

Example. In the network in Figure 6.20, $S = \{s, n_1\}$ defines a cut of minimum capacity with $C(S) = 600$.

---

[16] Flow conservation is also called Kirchhoff's first law.

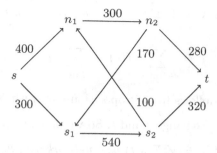

Fig. 6.20: $\{s, n_1\}$ is a cut of minimum capacity.

Remarks:

1. For the source s and sink t, we do not require that $\text{In}(s) = \emptyset$ or $\text{Out}(t) = \emptyset$. However, we do not maintain flow conservation in s and t.
2. Since nodes that do not lie on a path from s to t do not contribute to the total flow, we assume that each node in N lies on a path from s to t. In particular, N is connected and t is accessible from s.
3. A cut S defines a disjoint decomposition of the nodes $V = S \cup (V \setminus S)$ into two proper subsets. The following proposition shows that the total flow must flow over every cut.

Proposition 6.60. *Let $N = (V, E, s, t)$ be a network, S a cut of N, f a flow with associated total flow F. Then*

$$F = \sum_{e \in \text{Out}(S)} f(e) - \sum_{e \in \text{In}(S)} f(e).$$

Proof.

$$F = \sum_{v \in V \setminus (S \cup \{t\})} \left(\sum_{e \in \text{In}(v)} f(e) - \sum_{e \in \text{Out}(v)} f(e) \right) + \sum_{e \in \text{In}(t)} f(e) - \sum_{e \in \text{Out}(t)} f(e)$$

$$= \sum_{v \in V \setminus S} \sum_{e \in \text{In}(v)} f(e) - \sum_{v \in V \setminus S} \sum_{e \in \text{Out}(v)} f(e)$$

$$= \sum_{e \in \text{In}(V \setminus S)} f(e) - \sum_{e \in \text{Out}(V \setminus S)} f(e) = \sum_{e \in \text{Out}(S)} f(e) - \sum_{e \in \text{In}(S)} f(e).$$

We explain the individual steps of the calculation above. In line 2, there is no edge $e = (x, y)$ with $x, y \in S$. For edges $e = (x, y) \in E$ with $x, y \notin S$, it holds that $e \in \text{Out}(x)$ and $e \in \text{In}(y)$. As a result, the flows along these edges cancel each other and make no contribution to the sum. The remaining edges are $\text{In}(V \setminus S)$ and $\text{Out}(V \setminus S)$. Let $e = (x, y) \in E$ with $x \in S$, $y \notin S$. Then $e \in \text{In}(V \setminus S) \cap \text{Out}(x)$. If $e = (x, y) \in E$ with $x \notin S$, $y \in S$ then $e \in \text{Out}(V \setminus S) \cap \text{In}(y)$. The assertion is thus shown.   □

Corollary 6.61. *Let $N = (V, E, s, t)$ be a network, f a flow with associated total flow F. Then*

$$F = \sum_{e \in \text{Out}(s)} f(e) - \sum_{e \in \text{In}(s)} f(e).$$

Proof. The corollary follows from Proposition 6.60 with $S = \{s\}$.   □

Remark. If $F < 0$, we exchange s and t. So we may always assume $F \geq 0$.

Corollary 6.62. *Let $N = (V, E, s, t)$ be a network with flow f and associated total flow F. Then for a cut S*

$$F \leq C(S).$$

Proof. We have

$$F = \sum_{e \in \text{Out}(S)} f(e) - \sum_{e \in \text{In}(S)} f(e) \leq \sum_{e \in \text{Out}(S)} f(e) \leq \sum_{e \in \text{Out}(S)} c(e) = C(S).$$

This shows the corollary.   □

Algorithm of Ford-Fulkerson. The algorithm of Ford-Fulkerson constructs a flow f for N such that the total flow F associated with f is maximum. The algorithm starts with the zero flow and increases the flow step by step.

The method of increasing the total flow is to find a path from s to t that allows us to increase the flow for each of its edges. Edges with flow > 0 can also be included in the path in the reverse direction to the edge direction. An increase of the flow along an edge is possible if the current flow is less than the capacity constraint, or if the edge has the reverse direction (and the flow is decreased). We will first show the procedure using an example.

Example. In Figure 6.21 the first number in the edge labels is the capacity, the second the flow. Augmenting paths are $P = s, s_1, s_2, t$ (augmentation = 50) and $P = s, n_1, s_2, t$ (augmentation = 100).

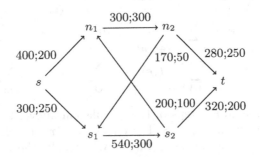

Fig. 6.21: Augmenting paths.

The residual graph is used to model augmenting paths.

Definition 6.63. Let $N = (V, E, s, t)$ be a network and $f : E \longrightarrow \mathbb{R}_{\geq 0}$ a flow for N. The directed graph $G_f := (V, E_f)$, where

$$E_f := \{(v, w) \in V^2 \mid ((v, w) \in E \text{ and } f(v, w) < c(v, w))$$
$$\text{or } ((w, v) \in E \text{ and } f(w, v) > 0)\},$$

is called the *residual* Graph of N relative to f.
$c_f : E_f \longrightarrow \mathbb{R}^+$,

$$c_f(v, w) := \begin{cases} c(v, w) - f(v, w) & \text{for } (v, w) \in E, (w, v) \notin E, \\ f(w, v) & \text{for } (v, w) \notin E, (w, v) \in E, \\ c(v, w) - f(v, w) + f(w, v) & \text{for } (v, w) \in E, (w, v) \in E, \end{cases}$$

is called the *residual capacity* of N relative to f.

Remark. An edge $(v, w) \in E$ can lead to the edges (v, w) and (w, v) in the residual graph. If neither (v, w) nor (w, v) are edges in G, then there is also no edge between v and w in the residual graph. Therefore, $|E_f| \leq 2|E|$.

Example. In Figure 6.22 we explain the construction of the residual graph using an example of a network with edge labeling "capacity, flow":

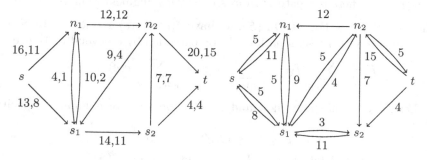

Fig. 6.22: Network with flow and residual graph.

Definition 6.64. Let $N = (V, E, s, t)$ be a network, f be a flow for N and G_f be the residual graph of N relative to f. Let $v_0, v_1, \ldots, v_k$ be a (directed) path P in G_f.

$$\Delta := \min\{c_f(v_i, v_{i+1}) \mid i = 0, \ldots, k - 1\}.$$

P is called a *path P in N with augmentation Δ* if $\Delta > 0$.

Proposition 6.65. *Let P be a path with augmentation Δ from s to t and $e = (v, w) \in E$. $\bar{e} = (w, v)$. $\Delta_e = \min\{c(e) - f(e), \Delta\}$.*

$$g : E \longrightarrow \mathbb{R}_{\geq 0}, \begin{cases} w(e) := f(e) & \text{for } e \notin P, \\ w(e) := f(e) + \Delta & \text{for } e \in P, e \in E, \bar{e} \notin E, \\ w(\bar{e}) := f(\bar{e}) - \Delta & \text{for } e \in P, e \notin E, \bar{e} \in E, \\ w(e) := f(e) + \Delta_e, & \\ w(\bar{e}) := f(\bar{e}) - (\Delta - \Delta_e) & \text{for } e \in P, e \in E, \bar{e} \in E. \end{cases}$$

g is a flow for N and $F_g = F_f + \Delta$.

Proof. The assertion follows directly from the construction.   □

Remark. Let $v_0, \dots, v_k$ be a path P with augmentation Δ. After computing g, the edges (v_i, v_{i+1}) of P with $c_f(v_i, v_{i+1}) - \Delta$ no longer appear as edges in the residual graph G_g.

Proposition 6.66. *Let $N = (V, E, s, t)$ be a network, f a flow with associated total flow F. The following statements are equivalent:*

1. *F is maximum.*
2. *For every path P from s to t, the augmentation $\Delta = 0$.*

Proof. If for a path P the augmentation $\Delta > 0$, then F can be increased and is therefore not maximum. This shows that the second statement is a consequence of the first statement.

To show the reverse conclusion, let

$$S = \{w \in V \mid \text{there is a path } P \text{ from } s \text{ to } w \text{ with augmentation } \Delta > 0\} \cup \{s\}.$$

Then $s \in S$, $t \notin S$. For $e \in \text{Out}(S)$, we have $f(e) = c(e)$ and for $e \in \text{In}(S)$ we get $f(e) = 0$. Otherwise, a path could be extended by e beyond S. Hence,

$$F = \sum_{e \in \text{Out}(S)} f(e) - \sum_{e \in \text{In}(S)} f(e) = \sum_{e \in \text{Out}(S)} c(e) = C(S).$$

Let F^* be a maximum flow and $S^* \subset V$ be a cut of minimum capacity. Then

$$F \leq F^* \leq C(S^*) \leq C(S).$$

From $F = C(S)$, it follows that $F = F^*$ and $C(S^*) = C(S)$.   □

The proof shows the following in addition.

Proposition 6.67 *(theorem of maximum flow – cut of minimum capacity). The value of the maximum total flow is equal to the value of a cut of minimum capacity. The connected component of the source s in the residual graph of the network with maximum flow is a cut of minimum capacity.*

The algorithm of Ford-Fulkerson increases the total flow by means of augmenting paths. The algorithm consists of the following steps:

1. Look for an augmenting path P from s to t.
2. Increase the flow along P with the formulas of Proposition 6.65.
3. Repeat step 1 and step 2 as long as an augmenting path exists.

If no augmenting path exists, the total flow is maximum.

Example. In Figure 6.23 the first number in the edge labeling indicates the capacity, the following number the flow at the start of the algorithm. The next numbers indicate the flows after flow expansion using the paths

$$P = s, s_1, s_2, t \text{ with } \Delta = 5,$$
$$P = s, n_1, s_2, t \text{ with } \Delta = 7,$$
$$P = s, n_1, s_2, n_2, t \text{ with } \Delta = 3.$$

$F = 60$ is the maximum total flow. $S = \{s, n_1\}$ is a cut of minimum capacity.

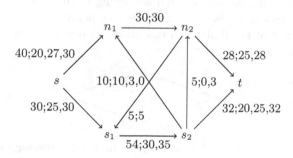

Fig. 6.23: Maximal flow – cut of minimal capacity.

Algorithm 6.68.

real $adm[1..n, 1..n]$, $flow[1..n, 1..n]$; vertex $path[1..n]$
FordFulkerson()
1   vertex j, k; real $delta$, $delta1$
2   for $k = 1$ to n do
3   for $j = 1$ to n do
4           $flow[k, j] \leftarrow 0$
5   while $delta = \text{FindPath}() \neq 0$ do
6       $k \leftarrow n$, $j \leftarrow path[k]$
7   while $j \neq 0$ do
8           $delta1 \leftarrow min(delta, adm[j, k] - flow[j, k])$
9           $flow[j, k] \leftarrow flow[j, k] + delta1$
10          $flow[k, j] \leftarrow flow[k, j] - (delta - delta1)$
11          $k \leftarrow j$, $j \leftarrow path[k]$

Remarks:

1. If an augmenting path P from s $(= 1)$ to t $(= n)$ exists (return value $delta > 0$), FindPath finds the path and stores it in the array $path$, where $path[k]$ stores the predecessor of k in the path P. The while loop in line 7 passes P starting from t and updates the flow for the edges of P.

2. If the capacity c is assumed to have values in $\mathbb{N}$, then the residual capacity c_f will also only take values in $\mathbb{N}$. If we perform a flow increase for a flow with values in $\mathbb{N}$ using an augmenting path, the resulting flow has values in $\mathbb{N}$. For a path with augmentation Δ, we get $\Delta \geq 1$. Since in each iteration of the while loop in line 5 the flow is increased by at least one, the while loop and thus the algorithm terminates.

3. Ford and Fulkerson give in [FordFulk62] a (theoretical) example with irrational capacities, so that for finitely many iterations of the construction with an augmenting path no termination occurs. The construction uses powers of $\frac{1}{g}$, where g is the ratio of the golden mean (Definition 1.22). If the augmenting path is selected according to the method of Edmonds-Karp, the algorithm always terminates (see below).

4. The efficiency of FordFulkerson essentially depends on the choice of the augmenting path.

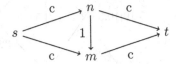

If we alternately choose s, n, m, t and s, m, n, t for the augmenting path, Ford-Fulkerson terminates after $2c$ iterations (independent of $|V|$ and $|E|$).

Algorithm of Edmonds-Karp. Algorithm 6.68 does not specify which method is to be used to determine an augmenting path. This step has a significant influence on the running time. The suggestion of Edmonds and Karp for the choice of the augmenting path is: At each step of Ford-Fulkerson, select an augmenting path from s to t with a minimum number of edges.

The augmenting paths from s to t in N are the directed paths from s to t in the residual graph G_f. A shortest directed path (minimum number of edges) can be determined by breadth-first search in G_f (Algorithm 5.11). The running time is $O(n + m)$ if the graph is given by an adjacency list and of order $O(n^2)$ if the graph is defined by an adjacency matrix ($n = |V|$, $m = |E|$).

We now determine the number of iterations of the while loop in line 5 of Algorithm 6.68, when choosing an augmenting path according to the suggestion of Edmonds and Karp. Let $N = (V, E, s, t)$ be a network with flow f and let $v, w \in V$.

$$\delta_f(v, w) = \text{ distance between } v \text{ and } w \text{ in } G_f,$$

where all edges in G_f must be weighted by one.

Lemma 6.69. *Let $f_1, f_2, \ldots$ be the flows in a network that we construct using augmenting paths after Edmonds-Karp. Then $\delta_{f_i}(s, v)$ is increasing in i for $v \in V \setminus \{s\}$.*

Proof. Suppose there is a $w \in V \setminus \{s\}$ and $i \in \mathbb{N}$ with

$$\delta_{f_{i+1}}(s, w) < \delta_{f_i}(s, w).$$

Set $f := f_i, f' := f_{i+1}$ and

$$U = \{u \in V \setminus \{s\} \mid \delta_{f'}(s, u) < \delta_f(s, u)\}.$$

Since $w \in U$, it follows that $U \neq \emptyset$.

Let $y \in U$ such that $\delta_{f'}(s, y) \leq \delta_{f'}(s, u)$ for all $u \in U$, and let P' be a shortest path from s to y in $G_{f'}$.

$$P' : s = v_0, \ldots v_{l-1}, v_l = y.$$

Set $x = v_{l-1}$. Since $\delta_{f'}(s, x) = \delta_{f'}(s, y) - 1$, we conclude according to the choice of y that $x \notin U$. First we show that $(x, y) \notin E_f$. Suppose that $(x, y) \in E_f$, then

$$\delta_f(s, y) \leq \delta_f(s, x) + 1 \leq \delta_{f'}(s, x) + 1 = \delta_{f'}(s, y),$$

a contradiction to $y \in U$.

Thus, $(x, y) \notin E_f$. We now show that $(y, x) \in E_f$. We consider two cases:

1. If $(x, y) \in E$, then $f(x, y) = c(x, y)$. It follows that $(y, x) \in E_f$.
2. If $(x, y) \notin E$, then $(y, x) \in E$ and $f(y, x) = 0$. Consequently, $f(y, x) < c(y, x)$ and $(y, x) \in E_f$.

Since $(x, y) \notin E_f$ and $(x, y) \in E_{f'}$, the augmenting path P used to construct f' from f contains (y, x) (in the direction from y to x).

Since P is a shortest path and $x \notin U$, we conclude that

$$\delta_f(s, y) = \delta_f(s, x) - 1 \leq \delta_{f'}(s, x) - 1 = \delta_{f'}(s, y) - 2 < \delta_{f'}(s, y),$$

a contradiction to the choice of $y \in U$. Therefore, $U = \emptyset$ and the assertion of the lemma is shown. $\qquad\square$

Proposition 6.70. *Let* $N = (V, E, s, t)$ *be a network,* $n = |V|$, $m = |E|$ *and* $T(n, m)$ *be the number of iterations of the while loop (line 5) in Ford-Fulkerson when using Edmonds-Karp. Then* $T(n, m) = O(nm)$.

Proof. Let P be a path in G_f with augmentation Δ. An edge e of P is said to be minimal with respect to P if $c_f(e) = \Delta$. Let f' be the flow created from f by adding Δ. The minimal edges of P no longer occur in $E_{f'}$.

We estimate how often an edge $e \in E$ can become a minimal edge. Let $e = (u, v)$ be minimal for an iteration of Ford-Fulkerson (construction of f' from f). Since e is an edge of a shortest path in G_f, it follows that $\delta_f(s, v) = \delta_f(s, u) + 1$.

Before (u, v) can again become an edge of an augmenting path, (v, u) must be an edge of a shortest augmenting path, i.e., $(v, u) \in E_{\tilde{f}}$ with a later-calculated flow $\tilde{f}$. Then it follows from Lemma 6.69 that

$$\delta_{\tilde{f}}(s, u) = \delta_{\tilde{f}}(s, v) + 1 \geq \delta_f(s, v) + 1 = \delta_f(s, u) + 2$$

If the edge e was a minimum edge r times before the calculation of f, we have

$$2r \leq \delta_f(s, u).$$

We have $\delta_f(s, u) \leq n - 2$ because on a shortest path from s to u there can be at most $n - 1$ nodes $(u \neq t)$.

We obtain

$$r \leq \frac{n - 2}{2},$$

i.e., an edge can be at most $\frac{n-2}{2}$ times a minimum edge. From $|E_f| \leq 2|E| = 2m$, it follows that the number of minimum edges is less than or equal to $(n - 2)m$. Since in every iteration of Ford-Fulkerson at least one minimum edge disappears, the assertion is shown. □

Exercises.

1. Recalculate the following formulas for Ackermann's function:
   a. $A(1, n) = n + 2$.
   b. $A(2, n) = 2n + 3$.
   c. $A(3, n) = 2^{n+3} - 3$.
   d. $A(4, n) = \underbrace{2^{2^{2^{\cdot^{\cdot^{\cdot^2}}}}}}_{n+3 \text{ times}} - 3$.

2. Given is a graph G weighted with integers:

   $$1 : (2, 1), (3, 1), (4, 4), (5, 2) \quad 4 : (1, 4), (3, 2), (5, 5)$$
   $$2 : (1, 1), (3, 2), (5, -2) \qquad\quad 5 : (1, 2), (2, -2), (4, 5)$$
   $$3 : (1, 1), (2, 2), (4, 2)$$

   The length of a path in G is the sum of the weights of the edges that belong to the path. The distance between the two nodes i, j is the minimum of the lengths of the paths from i to j.
   a. Does the definition above yield a metric on the set of nodes of G? If this is not the case, then list all axioms of a metric that are violated.
   b. Does Dijkstra's algorithm return a shortest path for every pair of nodes? State the individual steps in the determination of the paths.
   c. Does the algorithm of Kruskal yield a minimum spanning tree of G? If this is the case, does this apply to all graphs with negative weighted edges? Justify your statement.

3. Let G be a directed weighted acyclic graph. Develop an algorithm that determines a longest path between two nodes of G (a critical path).

4. Design an algorithm that calculates for an acyclic directed graph G the distances from one node to all other nodes with the running time $O(n + m)$.

5. With Kruskal's algorithm, the constructed MST depends on the selection of an edge among all edges of the same weight. Is it possible to generate every MST of a graph by appropriately selecting an edge in each step? Justify your answer.

6. a. How are the priorities to be assigned for a priority queue to work as a stack or a queue?
   b. The data type priority queue should support the union of queues in addition to the specified access functions. Specify an algorithm and discuss the running time.

7. Develop a procedure for "updating" an MST for a graph G if
   (1) an edge is added to G,
   (2) a node with several incident edges is added to G.

8. Let G be a weighted graph and T a minimum spanning tree for G. We change the weight of a single edge of G. Discuss the effects on T.

9. We model a communication network with bidirectional connections with a weighted graph $G = (V, E)$. The nodes are nodes in the communication network and the edges are communication links. The weight of an edge (u, v) is the failure probability $p(u, v) \in [0, 1]$ for the connection (u, v). We assume that these probabilities are independent of each other. The probability that a connection $v = v_0, \ldots, v_n = w$ from v to w will fail is $1 - \prod_{i=1}^{n}(1 - p(v_{i-1}, v_i))$. Specify an algorithm to calculate paths with the least probability of failure.

10. Four people P_1, P_2, P_3 and P_4 want to cross a bridge in the dark. The bridge can only be crossed if a torch is carried. The four persons only have one torch and the bridge carries a maximum of two persons. The people run at different speeds. P_1 takes five minutes to cross, P_2 ten minutes, P_3 twenty minutes and P_4 twenty-five minutes. If two people cross the bridge together, the time required depends on the slower runner. In what order do the four people have to cross the bridge in order to get everyone to the other side and to minimize the amount of time needed?
   a. Model the problem with a graph.
   b. What algorithm can be used to solve the problem?
   c. Specify a solution to the problem.

11. Let $G = (V, E)$ be a connected graph.
   $d(G) := \max\{d(i, j) \mid i, j \in V\}$ is called the *diameter* of G.
   $e(i) := \max\{d(i, j) \mid j \in V\}$ is called the *excentricity* of i.
   $r(G) := \min\{e(i) \mid i \in V\}$ is called the *radius* of G.
   $i \in V$ is called the *center* of G if i satisfies $e(i) = r(G)$.
   a. Show: $r(G) \le d(G) \le 2r(G)$
   b. Develop algorithms to calculate $d(G), r(G)$ and determine all centers.

c. What do you do if you are only interested in the centers?

12. All cities in a country are to be connected by magnetic levitation trains. When building the rail network, care should be taken to minimize the length of the rails to be built.
    a. How do you determine those cities that are to be connected by a railway line?
    b. What does the structure look like?
    c. After the rail network has been created, parliament decides to relocate the capital. The sum of the travel times from the new capital to all other cities with the magnetic levitation train should be minimal. Develop an algorithm to identify all cities in the country that meet the above condition. Assume that each route is bidirectional and that the travel times are the same in both directions.
    d. Explain your approach using an example with five cities.

13. Verification of a *shortest path tree* in linear time. Let $G = (V, E)$ be a connected weighted graph, $r \in V$ and T a subtree with root r that spans G. Develop an algorithm with linear running time that checks whether the paths in T are the shortest paths in G.

14. Let $X = \{x_1, \ldots, x_n\}$ be a set of boolean variables. We consider boolean expressions of the form $b = b_1 \wedge \ldots \wedge b_n$ with $b_j = b_{j_1} \vee b_{j_2}$, $j = 1, \ldots, n$, and $b_{j_1}, b_{j_2} \in L = \{x_1, \ldots, x_n, \overline{x}_1, \ldots, \overline{x}_n\}$.
    The term $v \vee w$ is equivalent to $\overline{v} \implies w$ and $\overline{w} \implies v$. Instead of $v \vee w$ we write the implications $\overline{v} \implies w$ and $\overline{w} \implies v$.
    We assign to a boolean expression b a directed graph $G = (V, E)$. We set $V = L$. Each term $v \vee w$ in b defines the edges $(\overline{v}, w)$ and $(\overline{w}, v)$.
    Using G, specify an algorithm that determines whether an expression b is *satisfiable*, that is, whether there is a vector $(x_1, \ldots, x_n) \in \{0, 1\}^n$ so that $b(x_1, \ldots, x_n) = 1$. This is called the *2-SAT problem*.[17]

15. A network is defined by the adjacency list

A: (B,25,15),(F,5,5)	B: (F,15,15), (T,5,0)
D: (H,10,0),(F,30,30)	F: (T,35,35), (J,20,15)
H: (J,20,15)	J: (T,30,30)
S: (A,20,20),(D,50,30),(H,20,15)	T:

    An entry is given by (node, capacity, flow). Determine a maximum flow and a cut of minimum capacity.

16. We consider a system consisting of two processors P, Q and n processes. Communication takes place between two processes. Some of the processes must run on P and some must run on Q. The rest of the processes should

---

[17] The 3-SAT problem is NP complete ([HopMotUll07]). It consists of deciding whether a boolean expression $b = b_1 \wedge \ldots \wedge b_n$ with $b_j = b_{j_1} \vee b_{j_2} \vee b_{j_3}$, $j = 1, \ldots, n$, and $b_{j_1}, b_{j_2}, b_{j_3} \in L$ is satisfiable.

be distributed between the processors in such a way that the effort for information transfer from P to Q is minimized.

  a. How to model the problem?

  b. What algorithm can be used to determine the distribution of processes?

17. We consider a network with n sources $S_1, \ldots, S_n$ and m sinks $T_1, \ldots, T_m$. Solve the maximum flow problem for such a network. Perform your solution using the example in Figure 6.24.

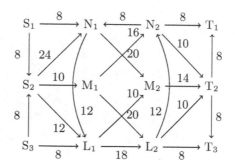

Fig. 6.24: Variant.

18. Let $G = (V \cup W, E)$ be a bipartite graph, and let $Z \subset E$. Z is a *matching* in G if each node is at most the end node of one edge. A *maximum matching* is a matching with a maximum number of edges. Obviously, a flow network N can be assigned to G. Work out the details. Show that the problem of calculating a maximum matching can be reduced to calculating a maximum flow in N.

Determine a maximum matching in the following bipartite graph.

$$
\begin{array}{llll}
1 : 6, 7, 8 & 4 : 8, 9, 10 & 7 : 1, 3 & 10 : 2, 4 \\
2 : 6, 9, 10 & 5 : 6 & 8 : 1, 4 & \\
3 : 6, 7 & 6 : 1, 2, 5, 3 & 9 : 2, 4 &
\end{array}
$$

19. Let $G = (V_1 \cup V_2, E)$ be a bipartite graph, $N = (V, E, s, t)$ the assigned network, Z a matching in G and f the assigned local flow in N. Let $P = s, v_1, \ldots, v_n, t$ be an augmenting path. Show:

  a. P has an odd number of edges.

  b. Let $e_i = (v_i, v_{i+1}), i = 1, \ldots, n-1$. Then $e_{2i-1} \in Z, i = 1, \ldots, \frac{n}{2}$, and $e_{2i} \notin Z, i = 1, \ldots, \frac{n-2}{2}$.

  c. In the algorithm for constructing a maximum matching, the number of edges of the matching increases by one in each step.

  d. Determine the order of the number of iterations of Ford-Fulkerson to compute a maximum matching.

A. Probabilities

We summarize some basic notations and results from probability theory, including probability spaces, random variables and special discrete distributions. We will apply these when analyzing algorithms. An introductory textbook on probability theory is [Feller68].

A.1 Finite Probability Spaces and Random Variables

For the analysis of algorithms, we can usually restrict ourselves to finite probability spaces.

Definition A.1.

1. An n-tuple of real numbers

$$p = (p_1, \ldots, p_n),\ 0 \le p_i \le 1,\ \text{with } \sum_{i=1}^{n} p_i = 1$$

   is called a *probability distribution*, or *distribution* for short.
   If $p_i = \frac{1}{n}$, $i = 1, \ldots, n$, then $(p_1, \ldots, p_n)$ is the *uniform distribution*.
2. A *probability space* $(\mathcal{X}, p_{\mathcal{X}})$ consists of a finite set $\mathcal{X} = \{x_1, \ldots, x_n\}$ with a probability distribution $p = (p_1, \ldots, p_n)$. p_i is the probability of x_i, $i = 1, \ldots, n$. We write $p_{\mathcal{X}}(x_i) := p_i$ and consider $p_{\mathcal{X}}$ as the map $X \to [0, 1]$ which assigns $x_i \in \mathcal{X}$ its probability p_i. We call $p_{\mathcal{X}}$ a *probability measure* on $\mathcal{X}$.
3. An *event* $\mathcal{E}$ is a subset $\mathcal{E}$ of $\mathcal{X}$. We extend the probability measure to events; $p_{\mathcal{X}}(\mathcal{E})$ or for short $p(\mathcal{E})$ is defined by

$$p_{\mathcal{X}}(\mathcal{E}) = \sum_{y \in \mathcal{E}} p_{\mathcal{X}}(y).$$

Remark. Let $(\mathcal{X}, p)$ be a probability space, and let $\mathcal{A}$ and $\mathcal{B}$ be events. Definition A.1 immediately implies

1. $p(\mathcal{X}) = 1$ and $p(\emptyset) = 0$.
2. $p(\mathcal{A} \cup \mathcal{B}) = p(\mathcal{A}) + p(\mathcal{B})$ if $\mathcal{A} \cap \mathcal{B} = \emptyset$.
3. $p(\mathcal{X} \setminus \mathcal{A}) = 1 - p(\mathcal{A})$.

© Springer Nature Switzerland AG 2020
H. Knebl, *Algorithms and Data Structures*, https://doi.org/10.1007/978-3-030-59758-0

Example. A standard example is throwing a die. If you throw a die, then it can fall six ways, each of which is equally likely if the die is fair. Thus, the result set $\mathcal{X} = \{1, \ldots, 6\}$ and $p = \left(\frac{1}{6}, \ldots, \frac{1}{6}\right)$. An event is a subset of $\{1, \ldots, 6\}$. For example, the probability for the event "even number of pips" is $\frac{1}{2}$.

Remark. For our applications, the model for random experiments defined in Definition A.1 is sufficient. Kolmogorov[1] defined a general model that is today common in probability theory.

The set $\mathcal{X}$ of elementary events is not necessarily finite and the set of events is a subset $\mathcal{A}$ of the power set of $\mathcal{X}$, a so-called σ-*algebra*. A probability measure p assigns to each $A \in \mathcal{A}$ a probability $p(A)$ in the interval $[0, 1] \subset \mathbb{R}$ of real numbers. p is *additive*, i.e., $p(A \cup B) = p(A) + p(B)$, if $A \cap B = \emptyset$, and $p(\mathcal{X}) = 1$. A similar property holds for countable disjoint unions, given the additivity property. Our model is a special case of the general model.

Definition A.2. Let $\mathcal{X}$ be a probability space, and let $\mathcal{A}, \mathcal{B} \subseteq \mathcal{X}$ be events with $p(\mathcal{B}) > 0$. The *conditional probability* of $\mathcal{A}$ under the assumption $\mathcal{B}$ is

$$p(\mathcal{A}|\mathcal{B}) := \frac{p(\mathcal{A} \cap \mathcal{B})}{p(\mathcal{B})}.$$

In particular,

$$p(x|\mathcal{B}) = \begin{cases} p(x)/p(\mathcal{B}) & \text{if } x \in \mathcal{B}, \\ 0 & \text{if } x \notin \mathcal{B}. \end{cases}$$

Remark. The conditional probabilities $p(\ |\mathcal{B})$ define a probability distribution on $\mathcal{X}$. It describes the probability of x assuming that the event $\mathcal{B}$ occurs. This concentrates the probability measure p on $\mathcal{B}$. We get $p(\mathcal{B}|\mathcal{B}) = 1$ and $p(\mathcal{X} \setminus \mathcal{B}|\mathcal{B}) = 0$.

Example. Again, we consider the example from above of throwing a die with the probability distribution $p = \left(\frac{1}{6}, \ldots, \frac{1}{6}\right)$. Let $\mathcal{B}$ be the event "even number of pips". Then $p(\mathcal{B}) = \frac{1}{2}$. We get on $\mathcal{X}$ the (conditional) probability distribution $\left(0, \frac{1}{3}, 0, \frac{1}{3}, 0, \frac{1}{3}\right)$ under the assumption $\mathcal{B}$.

Definition A.3. Let $\mathcal{X}$ be a probability space, and let $\mathcal{A}, \mathcal{B} \subseteq \mathcal{X}$ be events. $\mathcal{A}$ and $\mathcal{B}$ are called *independent* if $p(\mathcal{A} \cap \mathcal{B}) = p(\mathcal{A}) \cdot p(\mathcal{B})$. For $p(\mathcal{B}) > 0$ this condition is equivalent to $p(\mathcal{A}|\mathcal{B}) = p(\mathcal{A})$.

Proposition A.4. *Let $\mathcal{X}$ be a finite probability space, and let $\mathcal{X}$ be the disjoint union of the events $\mathcal{E}_1, \ldots, \mathcal{E}_r \subseteq \mathcal{X}$, with $p(\mathcal{E}_i) > 0$ for $i = 1 \ldots r$. Then*

$$p(\mathcal{A}) = \sum_{i=1}^{r} p(\mathcal{E}_i) \cdot p(\mathcal{A}|\mathcal{E}_i)$$

for each event $\mathcal{A} \subseteq \mathcal{X}$.

---

[1] Andrey Nikolaevich Kolmogorov (1903 – 1987) was a Russian mathematician. One of his great contributions was the axiomatization of probability theory.

Proof. We have $\mathcal{A} = \cup_{i=1}^{r}(\mathcal{A} \cap \mathcal{E}_i), (\mathcal{A} \cap \mathcal{E}_i) \cap (\mathcal{A} \cap \mathcal{E}_j) = \emptyset$ for $i \neq j$. Therefore,

$$p(\mathcal{A}) = \sum_{i=1}^{r} p(\mathcal{A} \cap \mathcal{E}_i) = \sum_{i=1}^{r} p(\mathcal{E}_i) \cdot p(\mathcal{A} | \mathcal{E}_i).$$

$\square$

Definition A.5. Let $(\mathcal{X}, p_{\mathcal{X}})$ be a probability space and Y be a finite set. A map $X : \mathcal{X} \longrightarrow Y$ is called a Y–valued *random variable* on $\mathcal{X}$. We say X is a *real random variable* if $Y \subset \mathbb{R}$ and a *binary random variable* if $Y = \{0, 1\}$.

Example. Again, we consider the die experiment from above. The map $X : \{1, \ldots, 6\} \longrightarrow \{0, 1\}$ which assigns to an even result 0 and to an odd result 1 is a binary random variable.

Definition A.6. Let $X : \mathcal{X} \longrightarrow Y$ be a real random variable.

1. The weighted mean value

$$E(X) := \sum_{y \in Y} p(X = y) \cdot y,$$

where $p(X = y) = p(\{x \in \mathcal{X} \mid X(x) = y\})$, is called the *expectation value* of X.
2. The expectation value of the random variable $(X - E(X))^2$ is called the *variance* of X.

$$\text{Var}(X) := E((X - E(X))^2).$$

Variance is a measure of the expected value of the square of the deviation of a random variable from its expected value.[2]
3. The standard deviation of X is

$$\sigma(X) = \sqrt{\text{Var}(X)}.$$

The standard deviation is the measure of the dispersion of a random variable.

Example. We consider the random variable X from the previous example, $X : \{0, \ldots, 6\} \longrightarrow \{0, 1\}$, which assigns to an even result of the die experiment 0 and to an odd result 1. The expectation value is $E(X) = 1/2$. The random variable $(X - 1/2)^2$ has the value $1/4$ for all numbers. Therefore, $\text{Var}(X) = 1/4$ and $\sigma(X) = 1/2$.

Proposition A.7. *Let X and Y be real random variables, $a, b \in \mathbb{R}$. Then*

1. $E(aX + bY) = aE(X) + bE(Y)$.
2. $\text{Var}(X) = E(X^2) - E(X)^2$

---

[2] In fact, we are interested in the expected value $E(|X - E(X)|)$. Since absolute values are difficult to handle, $\text{Var}(X)$ is defined by $E((X - E(X))^2)$.

Proof. Let $x_1, \ldots, x_n$ denote the values of X and $y_1, \ldots, y_m$ the values of Y. Then

$$E(aX + bY) = \sum_{i,j} p(X = x_i \cap Y = y_j) \cdot (ax_i + by_j)$$

$$= a \sum_{i,j} p(X = x_i \cap Y = y_j) \cdot x_i +$$

$$b \sum_{i,j} p(X = x_i \cap Y = y_j) \cdot y_j$$

$$= a \sum_i p(X = x_i) \cdot x_i + \sum_j p(Y = y_j) \cdot y_j$$

$$= aE(X) + bE(Y),$$

(note, $p(X = x_i) = \sum_j p(X = x_i \cap Y = y_j)$ (Proposition A.4)) and

$$E((X - E(X))^2) = E(X^2 - 2XE(X) + E(X)^2) = E(X^2) - E(X)^2.$$

$\square$

Definition A.8. Let X be a random variable and $\mathcal{E}$ be an event in the corresponding probability space. The distribution of the random variable $X \mid \mathcal{E}$ is defined by the conditional probabilities $p(X = x \mid \mathcal{E})$.

Lemma A.9. *Let X and Y be finite random variables. The value set of Y is $\{y_1, \ldots, y_m\}$. Then*

$$E(X) = \sum_{i=1}^{m} E(X \mid Y = y_i)p(Y = y_i).$$

Proof. With Proposition A.4 we conclude

$$p(X = x) = \sum_{i=1}^{m} p(X = x \mid Y = y_i)p(Y = y_i).$$

The value set of X is $\{x_1, \ldots, x_n\}$. Then

$$E(X) = \sum_{j=1}^{n} p(X = x_j)x_j$$

$$= \sum_{j=1}^{n} \left(\sum_{i=1}^{m} p(X = x_j \mid Y = y_i)p(Y = y_i) \right) x_j$$

$$= \sum_{i=1}^{m} \left(\sum_{j=1}^{n} p(X = x_j \mid Y = y_i)x_j \right) p(Y = y_i)$$

$$= \sum_{i=1}^{m} E(X \mid Y = y_i)p(Y = y_i).$$

This shows the assertion.   □

Proposition A.10 *(Markov's Inequality). Let X be a random variable that only has non-negative integers as values. Then for every real number $r > 0$ we get*

$$p(X \geq rE(X)) \leq \frac{1}{r} .$$

Proof. From

$$E(X) = \sum_{i \geq 1} i \cdot p(X = i) \geq \sum_{i \geq rE(X)} i \cdot p(X = i)$$

$$\geq r \cdot E(X) \sum_{i \geq rE(X)} p(X = i)$$

$$= r \cdot E(X) \cdot p(X \geq r \cdot E(X))$$

the assertion follows.   □

A.2 Special Discrete Distributions

In this section, we study examples of random variables that we will use when analyzing algorithms. First, we extend our model for random experiments. We consider the more general situation of a *discrete random variable*. The value set of X consists of the non-negative integers $0, 1, 2 \ldots$. For a random variable X with value set $W \subsetneq \{0, 1, 2 \ldots\}$, we set $p(X = m) = 0$ for $m \notin W$, so finite random variables are also included. We demand that

$$\sum_{i=0}^{\infty} p(X = i) = 1$$

holds true. The probability space associated with X with the distribution $p = (p(X = i))_{i \geq 0}$ is countable and no longer finite. The definitions and propositions from Section A.1 are transferable to the more general situation. If the series

$$E(X) = \sum_{i=0}^{\infty} i \cdot p(X = i)$$

converges, $E(X)$ is the *expectation value of the discrete random variable X*.

Example. The series $\sum_{i=1}^{\infty} \frac{1}{2^i}$ converges to 1 (Appendix B (F.8)). Consequently, $\left(\frac{1}{2^i}\right)_{i \geq 1}$ defines the distribution of a discrete random variable X. The series $\sum_{i=1}^{\infty} i \cdot \frac{1}{2^i}$ converges to 2, so X has the expected value 2 (loc. cit.).

Definition A.11. Let X be a random variable that only takes non-negative integers as values. The power series

$$G_X(z) = \sum_{i=0}^{\infty} p(X = i)z^i$$

is called the *generating function* of the random variable X.[3]

For $|z| \leq 1$ the power series $G_X(z)$ converges and represents within the convergence range an infinitely often differentiable function. The derivation results from differentiating every term separately ([AmannEscher05, Chapter V.3]).

$$G_X(z) = \sum_{i=0}^{\infty} p(X = i)z^i \text{ implies that } p(X = 0) = G_X(0).$$

$$G'_X(z) = \sum_{i=1}^{\infty} ip(X = i)z^{i-1} \text{ implies that } p(X = 1) = G'_X(0).$$

$$G''_X(z) = \sum_{i=2}^{\infty} i(i-1)p(X = i)z^{i-2}$$

$$\text{implies that } p(X = 2) = \frac{1}{2}G''_X(0).$$

$$\vdots$$

$$G_X^{(k)}(z) = \sum_{i=k}^{\infty} i(i-1)\ldots(i-k+1)p(X = i)z^{i-k}$$

$$\text{implies that } p(X = k) = \frac{1}{k!}G_X^{(k)}(0).$$

In addition to the power series representation, often another representation of the generating function is known, for example, as a rational function (proofs of Propositions A.16, A.20 and A.22). Then, from this representation we can obtain formulas for the derivatives and the coefficients of the power series by differentiating this representation of $G_X(z)$. The generating function $G_X(z)$ implicitly contains the complete distribution of X. From an explicit representation of $G_X(z)$, for example, as a rational function, a formula for the expected value and variance of X can be derived.

Proposition A.12. *Let X be a random variable with generating function $G_X(z)$. The first and second left-sided derivatives should exist for $G_X(z)$ at $z = 1$. Then*

$$E(X) = G'_X(1), \ E(X^2) = G''_X(1) + G'_X(1) \ and$$
$$Var(X) = G''_X(1) + G'_X(1) - G'_X(1)^2.$$

---

[3] The random variable z^X takes on the value z^i with the probability $p(X = i)$. So $G_X(z) = E(z^X)$.

Proof. The formulas follow directly from the observation above with state-ment 2 of Proposition A.7, which also applies to discrete random variables. □

We now apply Proposition A.12 to the Bernoulli distribution, the bino-mial distribution, the negative binomial distribution, the Poisson distribution, the geometric distribution, the hyper-geometric distribution and the negative hyper-geometric random variable.

Definition A.13. A random variable X is called *Bernoulli*[4] *distributed* with parameter p, $0 < p < 1$, if X takes on one of the values $0, 1$ and

$$p(X = i) = p^i(1 - p)^{1-i}$$

holds.

Proposition A.14. *Let X be a Bernoulli distributed random variable with parameter p. Then*

$$E(X) = p, \ E(X^2) = p \ and \ Var(X) = p(1 - p).$$

Proof.

$$G_X(z) = pz + (1 - p), \ G'_X(z) = p \ and \ G''_X(z) = 0.$$

The first two assertions follow immediately.

$$Var(X) = E(X^2) - E(X)^2 = p - p^2 = p(1 - p).$$

□

Definition A.15. A random variable X is said to be *binomially distributed* with parameters (n, p), $n > 0$, $0 < p < 1$, if X takes on one of the values $0, 1, 2, \ldots, n$ and

$$p(X = i) = \binom{n}{i} p^i(1 - p)^{n-i}$$

holds.[5]

Example. Figure A.1 shows the distribution of the number X of ones in a random 0-1 sequence that we generate tossing a fair coin (Section 1.6.4). X is binomially distributed with parameters $n = 50$ and $p = 1/2$. The expected value is 25 and the standard deviation is 3.54.

---

[4] Jacob Bernoulli (1655 – 1705) was a Swiss mathematician and physicist.
[5] $\sum_{i=0}^{n} \binom{n}{i} p^i(1 - p)^{n-i} = (p + (1 - p))^n = 1$ (Appendix B (F.3)).

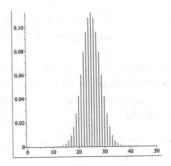

Fig. A.1: Distribution of ones in a random sequence.

Let $\mathcal{E}$ be an event of a random experiment that occurs with the probability $p(\mathcal{E}) = p > 0$. We consider n independent repetitions of the experiment. We call such an experiment a *Bernoulli experiment* with the event $\mathcal{E}$ and *probability* p.

Let X be the random variable that counts how often the event $\mathcal{E}$ occurs. The event occurs with probability $p^i(1-p)^{n-i}$ for n independent repetitions at i given positions of the sequence. There are $\binom{n}{i}$ possible ways to select i positions from n positions. We get $p(X = i) = \binom{n}{i} p^i (1-p)^{n-i}$. X is binomially distributed with parameters (n, p).

Proposition A.16. *Let X be a binomially distributed random variable with parameters (n, p). Then*

$$\mathrm{E}(X) = np, \ \mathrm{E}(X^2) = n(n-1)p^2 + np \ and \ \mathrm{Var}(X) = np(1-p).$$

Proof. The generating function for the binomial distribution follows from the binomial theorem (Appendix B (F.3)) by expanding $(pz + (1-p))^n$.

$$G_X(z) = \sum_{i=0}^{n} \binom{n}{i} p^i (1-p)^{n-i} z^i = (pz + (1-p))^n,$$

$$G_X'(z) = np(pz + (1-p))^{n-1} \ \text{and}$$

$$G_X''(z) = n(n-1)p^2(pz + (1-p))^{n-2}.$$

The first two statements follow immediately.

$$\mathrm{Var}(X) = \mathrm{E}(X^2) - \mathrm{E}(X)^2 = n(n-1)p^2 + np - n^2p^2 = np(1-p).$$

$\square$

Example. Figure A.2 shows the distribution of the number N of keys mapped to a hash value by a random hash function for a hash table with 60 places and 50 records. The variable N is binomially distributed with the parameters $n = 50$ and $p = 1/60$ (Proposition 3.15).

We expect that $\mathrm{E}(N) = 5/6$ keys are mapped to a hash value. The variance $\mathrm{Var}(N) = 250/36 \approx 6.9$ and the standard deviation $\sigma(N) \approx 2.6$.

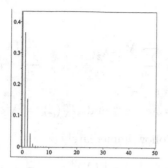

Fig. A.2: Distribution with a random hash function.

For the binomial distribution, we consider the limit for $n \to \infty$ where $n \cdot p = \lambda$ should be kept constant, i.e., we set $p = \lambda/n$:

$$\lim_{n\to\infty} \binom{n}{i} p^i (1-p)^{n-i} = \lim_{n\to\infty} \binom{n}{i} \left(\frac{\lambda}{n}\right)^i \left(1 - \frac{\lambda}{n}\right)^{n-i}$$

$$= \frac{\lambda^i}{i!} \lim_{n\to\infty} \frac{n(n-1)\dots(n-i+1)}{n^i} \left(1 - \frac{\lambda}{n}\right)^{n-i}$$

$$= \frac{\lambda^i}{i!} \lim_{n\to\infty} \left(1 - \frac{\lambda}{n}\right)^n \lim_{n\to\infty} \left(1 - \frac{1}{n}\right)\dots\left(1 - \frac{i-1}{n}\right)\left(1 - \frac{\lambda}{n}\right)^{-i}$$

$$= \frac{\lambda^i}{i!} e^{-\lambda}$$

(for the last "=" see Proposition B.18).

The Poisson distribution approximates for a small occurrence probability $p = \frac{\lambda}{n}$ of an event and for a large number n of repetitions of a Bernoulli experiment the probability with which the event occurs i times. Therefore, the Poisson distribution is sometimes called the *distribution of rare events*.

Definition A.17. A random variable X is called *Poisson distributed*[6] with parameter λ, $\lambda > 0$, if X takes on one of the values $0, 1, 2, \dots$ and

$$p(X = i) = \frac{\lambda^i}{i!} e^{-\lambda}$$

(note, $\sum_{i=0}^{\infty} \frac{\lambda^i}{i!} e^{-\lambda} = e^{-\lambda} \sum_{i=0}^{\infty} \frac{\lambda^i}{i!} = e^{-\lambda} e^{\lambda} = 1$).

Proposition A.18. *Let X be a Poisson distributed random variable with parameter λ. Then*

$$E(X) = \lambda, \ E(X^2) = \lambda^2 \ and \ \mathrm{Var}(X) = \lambda.$$

---

[6] Siméon Denis Poisson (1781 – 1840) was a French mathematician and physicist.

Proof.

$$G_X(z) = \sum_{i=0}^{\infty} \frac{\lambda^i}{i!} e^{-\lambda} z^i = e^{-\lambda} \sum_{i=0}^{\infty} \frac{(\lambda \cdot z)^i}{i!}$$
$$= e^{-\lambda} e^{\lambda z},$$
$$G_X'(z) = \lambda e^{-\lambda} e^{\lambda z} \text{ and } G_X''(z) = \lambda^2 e^{-\lambda} e^{\lambda z}.$$

The first two assertions follow immediately.

$$\mathrm{Var}(X) = \mathrm{E}(X^2) - \mathrm{E}(X)^2 = \lambda^2 + \lambda - \lambda^2 = \lambda.$$

$\square$

Definition A.19. A random variable X is said to be *geometrically distributed* with parameter p, $0 < p < 1$, if X takes on one of the values $1, 2, \ldots$ and

$$p(X = i) = p(1 - p)^{i-1}$$

holds.[7] The name is explained by the fact that the generating function of X is a geometric series (see below).

We consider a Bernoulli experiment with event $\mathcal{E}$ and success probability p. Let X be the random variable that counts the necessary attempts until $\mathcal{E}$ occurs for the first time. $\mathcal{E}$ occurs for the first time at the ith repetition if $\mathcal{E}$ occurs at the ith repetition, but not at the $i - 1$ preceding repetitions. The probability of this is $p(1-p)^{i-1}$, i.e., X is geometrically distributed with parameter p.

Example. The termination of a Las Vegas algorithm often depends on the first occurrence of an event. This is determined by the geometric distribution. Figure A.3 shows for Algorithm 1.50 and for $p = \frac{1}{2}$ the distribution of the number of iterations until the termination condition occurs.

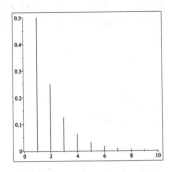

Fig. A.3: Termination of a Las Vegas algorithm.

---

[7] $\sum_{i=1}^{\infty} p(1-p)^{i-1} = p \sum_{i=0}^{\infty} (1-p)^i = 1$ (Appendix B (F.8)).

Proposition A.20. *Let X be a geometrically distributed random variable with parameter p. Then*

$$E(X) = \frac{1}{p}, \ E(X^2) = \frac{2-p}{p^2} \ and \ Var(X) = \frac{1-p}{p^2}.$$

Proof. By the geometric series (Appendix B (F.8)), we get

$$G_X(z) = \sum_{i=1}^{\infty} p(1-p)^{i-1} z^i = \frac{p}{1-p} \sum_{i=1}^{\infty} ((1-p)z)^i$$

$$= \frac{p}{1-p} \cdot \left(\frac{1}{1-(1-p)z} - 1 \right),$$

$$G'_X(z) = \frac{p}{(1-(1-p)z)^2} \ and \ G''_X(z) = \frac{2p(1-p)}{(1-(1-p)z)^3}.$$

The first two assertions follow immediately.

$$Var(X) = E(X^2) - E(X)^2 = \frac{2(1-p)}{p^2} + \frac{1}{p} - \frac{1}{p^2} = \frac{1-p}{p^2}.$$

$\square$

Definition A.21. A random variable X is said to be *negative binomially distributed* with parameters (r, p), $r > 0$, $0 < p < 1$ if X takes on one of the values $r, r+1, \ldots$ and

$$p(X = k) = \binom{k-1}{r-1} p^r (1-p)^{k-r}$$

(note, $\sum_{k \geq r} p(X = k) = G_X(1) = \left(\frac{p}{1-(1-p)} \right)^r = 1$ (see below)).

Remark. Let $k = r + i$. The identity

$$\binom{k-1}{r-1} = \binom{r+i-1}{r-1} = \binom{r+i-1}{i} = (-1)^i \binom{-r}{i}$$

explains the term "negative binomial distribution" (Lemma B.17).

We consider a Bernoulli experiment with event $\mathcal{E}$ and success probability p. Let X be the random variable that counts how many times we have to repeat the experiment until the event $\mathcal{E}$ occurs r times. We get $p(X = k) = p \binom{k-1}{r-1} p^{r-1} (1-p)^{k-r} = \binom{k-1}{r-1} p^r (1-p)^{k-r}$. Consequently, X is negative binomially distributed with parameters (r, p).

The negative binomial distribution with parameters $(1, p)$ gives the geometric distribution. Conversely, we get the negative binomial distribution with parameters (r, p) as the sum of r independent geometrically distributed random variables with parameter p.

Example. The number of F–light edges in a random graph with r nodes is dominated by a negative binomially distributed random variable with the parameters $(r, 1/2)$ (Proposition 6.48). Figure A.4 shows the negative binomial distribution for $r = 50$ and $p = 1/2$.

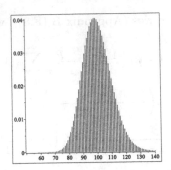

Fig. A.4: The distribution of an upper bound on the number of F–light edges.

Proposition A.22. *Let X be a negative binomially distributed random variable, with parameters (r, p). Then*

$$\mathrm{E}(X) = \frac{r}{p}, \ \mathrm{E}(X^2) = \frac{r^2}{p^2} + \frac{r}{p^2} - \frac{r}{p} \ and \ \mathrm{Var}(X) = \frac{r(1-p)}{p^2}.$$

Proof. From the formula for the binomial series (Appendix B (F.4)) follows with Lemma B.17, $q = 1 - p$ and $r + i = k$

$$(1 - qz)^{-r} = \sum_{i=0}^{\infty} \binom{-r}{i} (-qz)^i = \sum_{i=0}^{\infty} (-1)^i \binom{-r}{i} q^i z^i$$

$$= \sum_{i=0}^{\infty} \binom{r+i-1}{i} q^i z^i = \sum_{i=0}^{\infty} \binom{r+i-1}{r-1} q^i z^i$$

$$= \sum_{k=r}^{\infty} \binom{k-1}{r-1} q^{k-r} z^{k-r}.$$

Multiplying by $(pz)^r$ yields

$$G_X(z) = \sum_{k=r}^{\infty} \binom{k-1}{r-1} p^r q^{k-r} z^k = \left(\frac{pz}{1-qz} \right)^r.$$

Then

$$G'_X(z) = r \left(\frac{pz}{1-qz} \right)^{r-1} \frac{p(1-qz) + pqz}{(1-qz)^2} = rp \left(\frac{(pz)^r}{(1-qz)^{r+1}} \right) \ and$$

$$G''_X(z) = rp^2 \left(\frac{(pz)^{r-2}}{(1-qz)^{r+2}} \right) (r - 1 + 2qz).$$

We obtain

$$E(X) = G'_X(1) = \frac{r}{p},$$

$$E(X^2) = G''_X(1) + G'_X(1) = \frac{r}{p^2}(r + 1 - 2p) + \frac{r}{p} = \frac{r^2}{p^2} + \frac{r}{p^2} - \frac{r}{p},$$

$$\text{Var}(X) = E(X^2) - E(X)^2 = \frac{r^2}{p^2} + \frac{r}{p^2} - \frac{r}{p} - \left(\frac{r}{p}\right)^2 = \frac{r(1-p)}{p^2}.$$

□

Definition A.23. A random variable X is said to be *hyper-geometrically distributed* with the parameters (n, M, N), $n, M \leq N$, if X takes on one of the values $0, 1, 2, \ldots, M$ and

$$p(X = k) = \frac{\binom{M}{k}\binom{N-M}{n-k}}{\binom{N}{n}}$$

holds.

The hyper-geometric distribution describes an urn experiment "drawing without replacement", where the urn contains N balls. Of these N balls, M balls have a certain property $\mathcal{M}$. The probability that k of the drawn balls have the property $\mathcal{M}$ after n draws (without replacement) results from the number of positive cases $\binom{M}{k}\binom{N-M}{n-k}$ divided by the number of possible cases $\binom{N}{n}$. The normalization condition $\sum_k p(X = k) = 1$ follows from

$$\sum_k \binom{M}{k}\binom{N-M}{n-k} = \binom{N}{n}$$

(Lemma B.17).

Example. Figure A.5 shows the distribution of the number E of exchanges in the quicksort partitioning for an array of 100 elements, and with pivot element at position 60. The variable E is hyper-geometrically distributed with the parameters $n = 59$, $M = 40$ and $N = 99$ (Section 2.1.1).

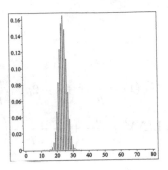

Fig. A.5: A distribution occurring in quicksort partitioning.

Proposition A.24. *Let X be a hyper-geometrically distributed random variable with the parameters (n, M, N). Then*

$$\mathrm{E}(X) = n\frac{M}{N} \text{ and } \mathrm{Var}(X) = n\frac{M}{N}\left(1 - \frac{M}{N}\right)\frac{N-n}{N-1}.$$

Proof.

$$G_X(z) = \sum_k \frac{\binom{M}{k}\binom{N-M}{n-k}}{\binom{N}{n}}z^k.$$

$$G_X'(z) = \sum_k k\frac{\frac{M}{k}\binom{M-1}{k-1}\binom{N-M}{n-k}}{\frac{N}{n}\binom{N-1}{n-1}}z^{k-1}$$

$$= n\frac{M}{N}\sum_k \frac{\binom{M-1}{k-1}\binom{N-M}{n-k}}{\binom{N-1}{n-1}}z^{k-1}.$$

$$G_X''(z) = n\frac{M}{N}\sum_k (k-1)\frac{\frac{M-1}{k-1}\binom{M-1}{k-1}\binom{N-M}{n-k}}{\frac{N-1}{n-1}\binom{N-2}{n-2}}z^{k-2}$$

$$= n(n-1)\frac{M}{N}\frac{M-1}{N-1}\sum_k \frac{\binom{M-2}{k-2}\binom{N-M}{n-k}}{\binom{N-2}{n-2}}z^{k-2}.$$

From

$$G_X'(1) = n\frac{M}{N} \text{ and } G_X''(1) = n(n-1)\frac{M}{N}\frac{M-1}{N-1}$$

follow the formulas for the expected value and variance of X. We used Lemma B.17 for our calculations with binomial coefficients. $\square$

Remark. We consider the limit for $N \to \infty$ and $p = M/N$ constant.

$$\binom{M}{k}\binom{N-M}{n-k} / \binom{N}{n}$$

$$= \frac{M!}{k!(M-k)!} \cdot \frac{(N-M)!}{(n-k)!(N-M-n+k)!} \cdot \frac{(N-n)!n!}{N!}$$

$$= \binom{n}{k} \frac{M}{N} \cdots \frac{M-k+1}{N-k+1} \cdot \frac{N-M}{N-k} \cdots \frac{N-M-(n-k-1)}{N-k-(n-k-1)}.$$

Each of the first k fractions converges for $N \to \infty$ to p and each of the last $n-k$ fractions to $1-p$. Thus, the quotient $\binom{M}{k}\binom{N-M}{n-k}/\binom{N}{n}$ converges for $N \to \infty$ to $\binom{n}{k} p^k (1-p)^{n-k}$, where we keep M/N constant. The binomial distribution describes the independent repetition of the urn experiment "draw with replacement". For large N, replacement has very little impact on the probabilities.

Definition A.25. A random variable X is said to be *negative hyper-geometrically distributed* with the parameters (r, M, N), $r, M, N \in \mathbb{N}$, $0 < r \leq M \leq N$, if X takes on one of the values $r, \ldots, r+N-M$ and

$$p(X = k) = \frac{\binom{k-1}{r-1}\binom{N-k}{M-r}}{\binom{N}{M}}.$$

The negative hyper-geometric distribution describes an urn experiment "drawing without replacement". The urn contains N balls. Of these N balls M balls have a certain property $\mathcal{M}$. Let $r \leq M$. The random variable X counts how often we have to repeat the experiment so that exactly r drawn balls have property $\mathcal{M}$. $X = k$ holds if the rth ball with property $\mathcal{M}$ is drawn in the kth draw, and if in the $k-1$ preceding draws $r-1$ balls have the property $\mathcal{M}$. We call the last event $\mathcal{E}$. Then $p(X = k)$ is the conditional probability that we will draw a ball with $\mathcal{M}$ in the kth draw under the condition $\mathcal{E}$. We get for $k = r, \ldots, r+N-M$

$$p(X = k) = \frac{\binom{M}{r-1}\binom{N-M}{k-r}}{\binom{N}{k-1}} \frac{M-(r-1)}{N-(k-1)}.$$

A simple calculation gives the correspondence with the defining formula in Definition A.25.

Since $p(X = k)$ defines a (conditional) probability distribution, the normalization condition $\sum_k p(X = k) = 1$ is fulfilled, i.e.,

$$\sum_{k=r}^{r+N-M} \binom{k-1}{r-1}\binom{N-k}{M-r} = \binom{N}{M}.$$

Proposition A.26. *Let X be a negative hyper-geometrically distributed random variable with parameters (r, M, N). Then*

$$\mathrm{E}(X) = r\frac{N+1}{M+1} \quad \text{and} \quad \mathrm{Var}(X) = r\frac{(N+1)(N-M)(M+1-r)}{(M+1)^2(M+2)}.$$

Proof. The generating function for X is

$$G_X(z) = \frac{1}{\binom{N}{M}} \sum_{k=r}^{r+N-M} \binom{k-1}{r-1}\binom{N-k}{M-r} z^k.$$

The derivative of $G_X(z)$ is

$$G_X'(z) = \frac{1}{\binom{N}{M}} \sum_{k=r}^{r+N-M} k\binom{k-1}{r-1}\binom{N-k}{M-r} z^{k-1}$$

$$= \frac{r}{\binom{N}{M}} \sum_{k=r}^{r+N-M} \binom{k}{r}\binom{N-k}{M-r} z^{k-1}$$

$$= \frac{r}{\binom{N}{M}} \sum_{k=r+1}^{r+N-M+1} \binom{k-1}{r}\binom{N-(k-1)}{M-r} z^{k-2}.$$

The derivative G_X' evaluates at z=1 to

$$G_X'(1) = \frac{r}{\binom{N}{M}} \sum_{k=r+1}^{r+1+(N+1)-(M+1)} \binom{k-1}{r}\binom{N+1-k}{M+1-(r+1)}$$

$$= \frac{r}{\binom{N}{M}}\binom{N+1}{M+1} = r\frac{N+1}{M+1}.$$

Thus, the formula for the expected value for X is shown.

The second derivative of $G_X(z)$ is

$$G_X''(z) = \frac{r}{\binom{N}{M}} \sum_{k=r+1}^{r+N-M+1} (k-2)\binom{k-1}{r}\binom{N-(k-1)}{M-r} z^{k-3}.$$

Thus, we obtain

$$G_X''(1) = \frac{r}{\binom{N}{M}}\left(\sum_{k=r+1}^{r+N-M+1} k\binom{k-1}{r}\binom{N+1-k}{M-m} \right.$$

$$\left. -2 \sum_{k=m+1}^{m+N-M+1} k\binom{k-1}{m}\binom{N+1-k}{M+1-(m+1)} \right)$$

$$= \frac{m}{\binom{N}{M}} \left((m+1) \sum_{k=m+2}^{m+N-M+2} \binom{k-1}{m+1} \binom{N+2-k}{M+2-(m+2)} \right.$$

$$\left. -2 \binom{N+1}{M+1} \right)$$

$$= \frac{m}{\binom{N}{M}} \left((m+1) \binom{N+2}{M+2} - 2 \binom{N+1}{M+1} \right)$$

$$= m \frac{N+1}{M+1} \left((m+1) \frac{N+2}{M+2} - 2 \right).$$

For the variance of X, we get

$$\mathrm{Var}(X) = r \frac{N+1}{M+1} \left((r+1) \frac{N+2}{M+2} - 1 - r \frac{N+1}{M+1} \right)$$

$$= r \frac{(N+1)(N-M)(M+1-r)}{(M+1)^2(M+2)}.$$

The assertion of the Proposition is therefore shown.   □

Example. Figure A.6 shows the distribution of the number of attempts sl_n necessary to insert the $(n+1)$th key into a hash table with 100 places for $n = 80$. The variable sl_n is negatively hyper-geometrically distributed with the parameters $r = 1$, $M = 20$ and $N = 100$. (Proposition 3.22).

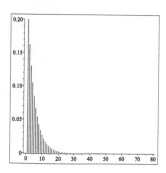

Fig. A.6: Distribution during uniform probing.

Remark. For $N \to \infty$ and $p = M/N$ constant, the negative hyper-geometric distribution converges to the negative binomial distribution:

$$\lim_{\substack{N \to \infty \\ N/M \, const.}} \frac{\binom{k-1}{r-1} \binom{N-k}{M-r}}{\binom{N}{M}} = \binom{k-1}{r-1} p^r (1-p)^{k-r}.$$

Probability theory, especially the binomial distribution, the Poisson distribution and the negative hyper-geometric distribution, are used for the analysis of hash procedures in Section 3.4, for random functions (Proposition 3.19), in the model of uniform probing (Proposition 3.23) and for universal families of hash functions (Corollary 3.21). We also use the binomial distribution to determine the endpoints of random walks (Section 1.6). With the help of the geometric distribution, we determine the expected value of the termination of Las Vegas algorithms (Algorithm 1.50). The hyper-geometric distribution is used in the analysis of quicksort (Section 2.1.1) and the negative binomial distribution in the analysis of random graphs (Proposition 6.48).

B. Mathematical Terminology and Useful Formulas

When analyzing algorithms, we often apply elementary formulas, such as formulas for the geometric series, the binomial coefficients, and the exponential function. In the following section, we will summarize some useful formulas and mathematical notations.

Natural Numbers. We designate by $\mathbb{N} = \{1, 2, \ldots\}$ the set of natural numbers and by $\mathbb{N}_0 = \{0, 1, 2, \ldots\}$ the set of non-negative integers.

Proposition B.1 *(division with remainder). For $z, a \in \mathbb{N}_0, a \neq 0$, there are unique numbers $q, r \in \mathbb{N}_0$ with: $z = q \cdot a + r$, $0 \leq r < a$.*

Proof. We show the existence of the representation by induction on z. If $0 \leq z < a$, $z = 0 \cdot a + z$ is the desired representation. Let $z \geq a$. Then by the induction hypothesis $z - a = q \cdot a + r$, $0 \leq r < a$. We get $z = (q + 1) \cdot a + r$. In order to show the uniqueness, we assume that z has two representations

$$z = q_1 \cdot a + r_1 = q_2 \cdot a + r_2.$$

Then $0 = (q_1 - q_2) \cdot a + (r_1 - r_2)$. Thus, a divides the number $r_1 - r_2$. From $|r_1 - r_2| < a$ we get $r_1 = r_2$ and $q_1 = q_2$. $\square$

Remark. The number q is the integer quotient and $r = z \bmod a$ is the remainder of dividing z by a.

We can represent the natural numbers in a numeral system with respect to any base $b \in \mathbb{N}$, $b > 1$.

Proposition B.2 *(numeral system to base b). Let $b \in \mathbb{N}, b > 1$. Then every number $z \in \mathbb{N}_0$ can be represented by*

$$z = \sum_{i=0}^{n-1} z_i b^i, \ z_i \in \{0, \ldots, b-1\}.$$

The representation of z in the base-b (numeral) system is unique. b is also known as the radix *and the coefficients z_i are called digits of the (numeral) system.*

© Springer Nature Switzerland AG 2020
H. Knebl, *Algorithms and Data Structures*, https://doi.org/10.1007/978-3-030-59758-0

Proof. The existence of the representation is obtained by continued division with remainder.

$$z = q_1 b + r_0, \ q_1 = q_2 b + r_1, \ q_2 = q_3 b + r_2, \ldots, q_{n-1} = 0 \cdot b + r_{n-1}.$$

Set $z_0 := r_0, \ z_1 := r_1, \ldots, z_{n-1} := r_{n-1}$. Then $0 \le z_i < b$, $i = 0, \ldots, n-1$, and $z = \sum_{i=0}^{n-1} z_i b^i$.

To show the uniqueness, let's assume that z has two representations. Then the difference of the representations is a representation of 0 with coefficients $|z_i| \le b - 1$. It is therefore sufficient to show that the representation of 0 is unique. Let

$$z = \sum_{i=0}^{n-1} z_i b^i, |z_i| \le b - 1,$$

be a representation of 0. Then $z \bmod b = z_0 = 0$ and $z/b \bmod b = z_1 = 0$, and so on. Altogether, we get $z_i = 0$, $i = 0, \ldots, n-1$, i.e., the representation of 0, and hence the representation of z is unique. □

If z has the representation $z = \sum_{i=0}^{n-1} z_i b^i$, then we write

$$z = (z_{n-1} \ldots z_0)_b \text{ or simply } z = z_{n-1} \ldots z_0,$$

if the base b is clear from the context.

Lemma B.3. *The maximum value of a number to base b with n digits is $b^n - 1$. The number of digits of a representation of z in base b is $\lfloor \log_b(z) \rfloor + 1$.*

Proof. The maximum value z_{max} of a number with n digits

$$z_{max} = \sum_{i=0}^{n-1}(b-1)b^i = (b-1)\sum_{i=0}^{n-1} b^i = \sum_{i=1}^{n} b^i - \sum_{i=0}^{n-1} b^i = b^n - 1.$$

If z is displayed with n digits and the leftmost is not 0, then $b^{n-1} \le z < b^n$. Then $n - 1 \le \log_b(z) < n$, i.e., $n = \lfloor \log_b(z) \rfloor + 1$. □

Harmonic Numbers. Harmonic numbers often occur in the analysis of algorithms. The following notation has been established.

Definition B.4. The number

$$H_n := \sum_{i=1}^{n} \frac{1}{i}$$

is called the *nth harmonic number.*

The harmonic series $\sum_{i=1}^{\infty} \frac{1}{i}$ diverges. However, it diverges very slowly. The following estimation describes the growth of the harmonic numbers in more detail.

Lemma B.5. $\ln(n + 1) \le H_n \le \ln(n) + 1.$

Proof. From

$$\sum_{i=1}^{n} \frac{1}{i} \geq \int_{1}^{n+1} \frac{1}{x}\, dx = \ln(n+1) \quad \text{and} \quad \sum_{i=2}^{n} \frac{1}{i} \leq \int_{1}^{n} \frac{1}{x}\, dx = \ln(n)$$

the assertion follows.   □

Remark. More precisely:

(F.1) $$H_n = \ln(n) + \gamma + \frac{1}{2n} - \frac{1}{12n^2} + \frac{1}{120n^4} - \varepsilon, \ 0 < \varepsilon < \frac{1}{252n^6}.$$

Where $\gamma = 0.5772156649\ldots$ is *Euler's constant*[1] (see, for example, [Knuth97, page 75]).

Remark. Due to the formula (F.1) we consider $H_n := \sum_{i=1}^{n} \frac{1}{i}$ to be a closed formula, although a sum occurs.

Lemma B.6. *A formula for the sum of the first n harmonic numbers:*

$$\sum_{i=1}^{n} H_i = (n+1)H_n - n.$$

Proof.

$$\sum_{i=1}^{n} H_i = n + (n-1)\frac{1}{2} + \ldots + (n - (n-1))\frac{1}{n}$$

$$= \sum_{i=1}^{n} (n - (i-1))\frac{1}{i} = (n+1)H_n - n.$$

                                                                          □

Residues Modulo n. Next to the ring $\mathbb{Z}$ of the integers, the ring $\mathbb{Z}_n$ of the residues modulo n is also of great importance.

Definition B.7.

1. Let $n \in \mathbb{N}, n \geq 2$. We define an equivalence relation on $\mathbb{Z}$: $a, b \in \mathbb{Z}$ are called congruent modulo n, written as

$$a \equiv b \bmod n,$$

   if n divides $a - b$, i.e., a and b have the same remainder when divided by n.
2. Let $a \in \mathbb{Z}$. The equivalence class $[a] := \{x \in \mathbb{Z} \mid x \equiv a \bmod n\}$ is called the residue class of a and a is called a *representative* for $[a]$.
3. $\mathbb{Z}_n := \{[a] \mid a \in \mathbb{Z}\}$ is called the set of *residue classes*.

---

[1] In contrast to Euler's number e, a transcendent number, it is not even known whether γ is a rational number. The book [Havil07] deals with this question.

Remarks:

1. For each $x \in [a]$ we have $[x] = [a]$.
2. It is easy to show that an equivalence relation is actually given by Definition B.7, point 1. Since division by n with remainder results in the residues $0, \ldots, n-1$, there are n residue classes in $\mathbb{Z}_n$,

$$\mathbb{Z}_n = \{[0], \ldots, [n-1]\}.$$

The numbers $0, \ldots, n-1$ are called *natural representatives*.

Definition B.8. We introduce addition and multiplication on $\mathbb{Z}_n$:

$$[a] + [b] = [a+b], [a] \cdot [b] = [a \cdot b].$$

The independence from the choice of representatives a and b is shown by a simple calculation.

The ring axioms in $\mathbb{Z}$ are inherited by $\mathbb{Z}_n$. $\mathbb{Z}_n$ becomes a commutative ring with the unit element $[1]$. It is called the *residue class ring* of $\mathbb{Z}$ modulo n.

Definition B.9. Let $x \in \mathbb{Z}_n$. x is said to be a *unit* in $\mathbb{Z}_n$ if there is a $y \in \mathbb{Z}_n$ with $xy = [1]$. Obviously, the units in $\mathbb{Z}_n$ form a group together with the multiplication. This group is called the *prime residue class group modulo* n and is denoted by $\mathbb{Z}_n^*$.

Proposition B.10. *Let $[x] \in \mathbb{Z}_n$. $[x]$ is a unit in $\mathbb{Z}_n$ if and only if x and n are relatively prime, i.e., the largest common divisor of x and n is 1.*

Proof. See, for example, [DelfsKnebl15, Proposition A.17]. □

Corollary B.11. *For a prime p, $\mathbb{Z}_p$ is a field.*

Proof. A commutative ring with unit element is a field if every element $\neq 0$ is a unit. Since for a prime number $n = p$ all numbers $1, \ldots, p-1$ are relatively prime to p, the assertion follows from Proposition B.10. □

Remark. We also denote $\mathbb{Z}_p$ by $\mathbb{F}_p$. Another term for a finite field is a Galois[2] field.

Quadratic Residues in $\mathbb{Z}_n$. We apply quadratic residues in hash procedures (see Section 3.3.2).

Definition B.12. A number $j \in \{0, \ldots, n-1\}$ is called a *square number modulo* n if there is an $i \in \mathbb{N}$ with $j \equiv i^2 \bmod n$. If j is a square number modulo n, we call $[j]$ a *square* in $\mathbb{Z}_n$.

---

[2] Évariste Galois (1811 – 1832) was a French mathematician. He is known for his work on the solution of algebraic equations, the so-called Galois theory, which from today's point of view investigates field extensions.

Example. We identify the squares in $\mathbb{Z}_{11}^*$ and $\mathbb{Z}_{13}^*$.

1. $[1], [3], [4], [9], [10], [12]$ are all squares in $\mathbb{Z}_{13}^*$. $-1 \equiv 12$ mod 13, so $[-1]$ is a square and also $[-3], [-4], [-9], [-10], [-12]$ are squares in $\mathbb{Z}_{13}$.
2. $[1], [3], [4], [5], [9]$ are all squares in $\mathbb{Z}_{11}^*$. $2 \ (\equiv -9), 6 \ (\equiv -5), 7 \ (\equiv -4), 8 \ (\equiv -3), 10 \ (\equiv -1)$ modulo 11 are not squares modulo 11.

While in the first case the negatives of squares are again representatives of squares, this does not happen in the second case.

Whether all free cells occur in a probing sequence during quadratic probing (Definition 3.11) is closely related to identifying all squares and the negative squares and their quantities. This is done by the following result.

Proposition B.13. *Let $p > 2$ be a prime. Then*

1. *The numbers i^2 mod p are pairwise distinct, $i = 1, \ldots, \frac{p-1}{2}$. Each square in $\mathbb{Z}_p$ has a representative of this form.*
2. *Let $p = 4k + 3, k \in \mathbb{N}_0$. Then $[-1]$ is not a square in $\mathbb{Z}_p$.*

Proof. 1. Let $0 \leq i < j \leq \frac{p-1}{2}$. If i^2 mod $p = j^2$ mod p, then p divides $j^2 - i^2 = (j-i)(j+i)$. Hence, p also divides $j - i$ or $j + i$. This is a contradiction, as $j - i < p - 1$ and $j + i < p - 1$. Consequently, the numbers i^2 mod p are pairwise distinct, $i = 1, \ldots, \frac{p-1}{2}$. Let $y \in \mathbb{N}, y = kp + x, 0 \leq x \leq p - 1$. Then $y^2 = (kp)^2 + 2kpx + x^2 \equiv x^2$ mod p and $(p - x)^2 = p^2 - 2px + x^2 \equiv x^2$ mod p. Therefore, all squares are of the desired form.
2. Let $p \equiv 3$ mod 4. Then $\frac{p-1}{2}$ is odd. Assume $[-1]$ is a square, i.e., $-1 \equiv n^2$ mod p, then by Fermat's[3] Little Theorem $-1 \equiv (-1)^{(p-1)/2} \equiv n^{p-1} \equiv 1$ mod p. Thus, $2 \equiv 0$ mod p. A contradiction. $\square$

We can now specify all numbers that are suitable as a modulus for quadratic probing.

Corollary B.14. *Let $p = 4k + 3$, then*

$$\mathbb{Z}_p = \{\pm[i^2] \mid i = 0, \ldots, (p-1)/2\}.$$

Proof. The inverse element of a square and the product of two squares is again a square. The elements of $\{[i^2] \mid \in \mathbb{Z}_p \mid i = 1, \ldots, (p-1)/2\}$ are pairwise distinct and squares. If $[-1]$ is not a square, the negative of a square is not a square, i.e., the elements $\{[-i^2] \mid i = 1, \ldots, \frac{p-1}{2}\}$ are also pairwise distinct and not squares. Therefore, the statement of the corollary is shown. $\square$

Remark. The condition $p = 4k + 3, k \in \mathbb{N}_0$ is even equivalent to the fact that $[-1]$ is not a square in $\mathbb{Z}_p$.[4] If prime numbers p are used that do not fulfill the condition, not all table positions are probed with quadratic probing.

---

[3] Pierre de Fermat (1607 – 1665) was a French mathematician. Fermat's Little Theorem: For a prime number p and a number n relatively prime to p, $n^{p-1} \equiv 1$ mod p.

[4] This statement can be proven with the Legendre symbol from elementary number theory (see, for example, [DelfsKnebl15, page 422]).

Finite Sums and Partial Fraction Decomposition. First we compile formulas for special finite sequences.

$$\sum_{i=1}^{n} 1 = n, \qquad\qquad \sum_{i=1}^{n} i = \frac{n(n+1)}{2},$$

$$\sum_{i=1}^{n} 2i = n(n+1), \qquad \sum_{i=1}^{n} (2i-1) = n^2,$$

$$\sum_{i=1}^{n} i^2 = \frac{n(n+1)(2n+1)}{6}, \qquad \sum_{i=1}^{n} i^3 = \left(\frac{n(n+1)}{2}\right)^2.$$

With these formulas we can directly derive formulas for finite sums of polynomial values for polynomials up to degree 3.

The summation of rational functions is analogous to the integration of rational functions by means of partial fraction decomposition. Division with remainder returns for a rational function $f(n) = \frac{p(n)}{q(n)}$ the representation

$$f(n) = s(n) + \frac{r(n)}{q(n)} \text{ with polynomials } r(n) \text{ and } s(n) \text{ and } \deg(r) < \deg(q).$$

We apply *partial fraction decomposition* to $\frac{r(n)}{q(n)}$. We distinguish whether the zeros of the denominator polynomial $q(n)$ are pairwise distinct or whether there are multiple zeros.

1. Simple zeros: $q(n) = \prod_{k=1}^{l} (n - n_k)$, $n_i \neq n_j$, $i \neq j$.
   For different zeros there is a decomposition in the form

(F.2) $$\frac{r(n)}{q(n)} = \sum_{k=1}^{l} \frac{a_k}{n - n_k}.$$

We determine the coefficients a_k by comparing the coefficients. If, for example, $\sum_{i=2}^{n} \frac{1}{i(i-1)}$ is to be calculated, we set $\frac{1}{i(i-1)}$ as

$$\frac{1}{i(i-1)} = \frac{a}{i} + \frac{b}{i-1}.$$

Multiplying both sides by $i(i-1)$ we get

$$1 = a(i-1) + bi = -a + (a+b)i.$$

A coefficient comparison returns $-a = 1$ and $a + b = 0$. So $a = -1, b = 1$, and so we have the partial fraction decomposition

$$\frac{1}{i(i-1)} = \frac{-1}{i} + \frac{1}{i-1}.$$

The result is then

$$\sum_{i=2}^{n} \frac{1}{i(i-1)} = \sum_{i=2}^{n} \left(\frac{-1}{i} + \frac{1}{i-1} \right) = -\sum_{i=2}^{n} \frac{1}{i} + \sum_{i=1}^{n-1} \frac{1}{i} = 1 - \frac{1}{n}.$$

2. Multiple zeros: If n_j is an l-fold zero, then we have to enter for n_j in the partial fractional decomposition l fractions as follows:

$$\frac{a_1}{n - n_j} + \frac{a_2}{(n - n_j)^2} + \ldots + \frac{a_l}{(n - n_j)^l}.$$

If, for example, $\sum_{i=1}^{n} \frac{1}{i^2(i+1)}$ is to be calculated, we take the following approach:

$$\frac{1}{i^2(i+1)} = \frac{a}{i} + \frac{b}{i^2} + \frac{c}{i+1}.$$

The first two fractions come from the double zero. Comparing the coefficients yields $a = -1, b = 1, c = 1$ and thus

$$\frac{1}{i^2(i+1)} = \frac{-1}{i} + \frac{1}{i^2} + \frac{1}{i+1}.$$

A Closed Formula for a Finite Sum of Logarithms.

Lemma B.15.

$$\sum_{r=1}^{n} \lfloor \log_2(r) \rfloor = (n+1) \lfloor \log_2(n) \rfloor - 2 \left(2^{\lfloor \log_2(n) \rfloor} - 1 \right).$$

Proof. We shall prove our assertion by induction on n. For n = 1, both sides of the equation yield 0. Let $n > 1$ and assume the assertion is proved for n - 1. For $\lfloor \log_2(n+1) \rfloor = \lfloor \log_2(n) \rfloor$ follows

$$\sum_{r=1}^{n+1} \lfloor \log_2(r) \rfloor = (n+1) \lfloor \log_2(n) \rfloor - 2 \left(2^{\lfloor \log_2(n) \rfloor} - 1 \right) + \lfloor \log_2(n+1) \rfloor$$

$$= (n+2) \lfloor \log_2(n+1) \rfloor - 2 \left(2^{\lfloor \log_2(n+1) \rfloor} - 1 \right).$$

If $\lfloor \log_2(n+1) \rfloor = \lfloor \log_2(n) \rfloor + 1$, then $(n+1)$ is a power of 2, i.e., $n+1 = 2^{\lfloor \log_2(n+1) \rfloor}$ and

$$\sum_{r=1}^{n+1} \lfloor \log_2(r) \rfloor = (n+1) \lfloor \log_2(n) \rfloor - 2 \left(2^{\lfloor \log_2(n) \rfloor} - 1 \right) + \lfloor \log_2(n+1) \rfloor$$

$$= (n+1)(\lfloor \log_2(n+1) \rfloor - 1)$$
$$\quad -2 \left(2^{\lfloor \log_2(n+1) \rfloor - 1} - 1 \right) + \lfloor \log_2(n+1) \rfloor$$

$$= (n+2) \lfloor \log_2(n+1) \rfloor - (n+1) - 2 \left(2^{\lfloor \log_2(n+1) \rfloor} 2^{-1} - 1 \right)$$

$$= (n+2) \lfloor \log_2(n+1) \rfloor - 2^{\lfloor \log_2(n+1) \rfloor} - 2^{\lfloor \log_2(n+1) \rfloor} + 2$$

$$= (n+2) \lfloor \log_2(n+1) \rfloor - 2 \left(2^{\lfloor \log_2(n+1) \rfloor} - 1 \right).$$

The lemma is shown. □

Binomial Coefficients. If you choose k elements from a set of n elements without replacement, there are $\binom{n}{k}$ ways to do this if you do not consider the order.

Definition B.16. Let $n \in \mathbb{R}$, $k \in \mathbb{Z}$. We set

$$\binom{n}{k} = \begin{cases} \frac{n \cdot (n-1) \cdot \ldots \cdot (n-k+1)}{k \cdot (k-1) \cdot \ldots \cdot 1} & \text{if } k \geq 0, \\ 0 & \text{if } k < 0. \end{cases}$$

$\binom{n}{k}$ is called the *binomial coefficient* and is pronounced "n choose k".

The binomial coefficients occur when $(x+y)^n$ is expanded as a polynomial in x and y. According to the binomial theorem

(F.3)
$$(x+y)^n = \sum_{k=0}^{n} \binom{n}{k} x^k y^{n-k}.$$

Let $\alpha \in \mathbb{R}$. The *binomial series* $\sum_{k=0}^{\infty} \binom{\alpha}{k} x^k$ converges for $|x| < 1$ and

(F.4)
$$(1+x)^\alpha = \sum_{k=0}^{\infty} \binom{\alpha}{k} x^k.$$

The binomial series results from the Taylor series[5] of the general power function $x \mapsto x^\alpha$ at $x = 1$. ([AmannEscher05, Chapter V.3]). The binomial series was discovered by Newton[6].

For $\alpha \in \mathbb{N}$, the binomial coefficients vanish if k is larger than α. The formula (F.4) then results from the binomial theorem. If you replace x with $-x$ you get for $\alpha = -1$ the geometric series because of $\binom{-1}{k} = (-1)^k$ (Appendix B (F.8)).

Lemma B.17. *We state formulas for the binomial coefficients.*

1. *Let $n, k \in \mathbb{N}$, $n < k$. Then*
$$\binom{n}{k} = 0.$$

2. *Let $n \in \mathbb{R}$, $k \in \mathbb{Z}$. Then*
$$\binom{n}{k} + \binom{n}{k+1} = \binom{n+1}{k+1}.$$

3. *Let $r, k \in \mathbb{N}$, $r > k > 1$. Then*
$$\binom{r}{k} = \frac{r}{k} \binom{r-1}{k-1}.$$

---

[5] Brook Taylor (1685 – 1731) was an English mathematician.
[6] Isaac Newton (1642 – 1726) was an English universal scholar. He is the co-founder of the infinitesimal calculus and is famous for his law of gravity.

4. Let $r, s \in \mathbb{N}$, $n \in \mathbb{Z}$. Then

$$\sum_k \binom{r}{k} \binom{s}{n-k} = \binom{r+s}{n}.$$

5. Let $r, s \in \mathbb{N}$, $n \in \mathbb{Z}$. Then

$$\sum_k \binom{r}{k} \binom{s}{n+k} = \binom{r+s}{r+n}.$$

6. Let $r, s \in \mathbb{N}$, $m = \min(r, s)$. Then

$$\sum_{k=1}^{m} k \binom{r}{k} \binom{s}{k} = s \binom{r+s-1}{r-1}.$$

7. Let $k, n \in \mathbb{Z}$. Then

$$\binom{n+k-1}{k} = (-1)^k \binom{-n}{k}.$$

8. Let $n, m \in \mathbb{N}$, $m < n$. Then

$$\sum_{k=0}^{n} \binom{k}{m} = \binom{n+1}{m+1}.$$

Proof.

1. The assertion is immediately obtained from the definition of the binomial coefficients.
2. For $k < 0$ the assertion follows at once. Let $k \geq 0$.

$$
\begin{aligned}
\binom{n}{k} + \binom{n}{k+1} &= \frac{n \cdot (n-1) \cdot \ldots \cdot (n-k+1)}{k \cdot (k-1) \cdot \ldots \cdot 1} + \frac{n \cdot (n-1) \cdot \ldots \cdot (n-k)}{(k+1) \cdot k \cdot \ldots \cdot 1} \\
&= \frac{n \cdot (n-1) \cdot \ldots \cdot (n-k+1)(k+1+n-k)}{(k+1) \cdot k \cdot \ldots \cdot 1} \\
&= \frac{(n+1) \cdot n \cdot (n-1) \cdot \ldots \cdot (n-k+1)}{(k+1) \cdot k \cdot \ldots \cdot 1} \\
&= \binom{n+1}{k+1}.
\end{aligned}
$$

3.

$$\binom{r}{k} = \frac{r!}{k!(r-k)!} = \frac{r}{k} \frac{(r-1)!}{(k-1)!(r-k)!} = \frac{r}{k} \binom{r-1}{k-1}.$$

4. Multiplying $(x+1)^r (x+1)^s = (x+1)^{r+s}$ we get

$$\sum_n \binom{r}{n} x^n \sum_n \binom{s}{n} x^n = \sum_n \sum_k \binom{r}{k} \binom{s}{n-k} x^n = \sum_n \binom{r+s}{n} x^n.$$

Thus

$$\sum_k \binom{r}{k}\binom{s}{n-k} = \binom{r+s}{n}.$$

5. Using point 4 we get

$$\sum_k \binom{r}{k}\binom{s}{n+k} = \sum_k \binom{r}{k}\binom{s}{s-n-k} = \binom{r+s}{s-n} = \binom{r+s}{r+n}.$$

6. From point 3 and point 4, it follows that

$$\sum_k k\binom{r}{k}\binom{s}{k} = s\sum_k \binom{r}{k}\binom{s-1}{k-1} = s\binom{r+s-1}{r-1}.$$

7.

$$\binom{-n}{k} = \frac{-n(-n-1)\cdot\ldots\cdot(-n-k+1)}{k!}$$

$$= (-1)^k \frac{n(n+1)\cdot\ldots\cdot(n+k-1)}{k!}$$

$$= \binom{n+k-1}{k}.$$

8. By induction on n, we see immediately

$$\sum_{k=0}^{n+1}\binom{k}{m} = \sum_{k=0}^{n}\binom{k}{m} + \binom{n+1}{m} = \binom{n+1}{m+1} + \binom{n+1}{m} = \binom{n+2}{m+1}$$

(see point 2).

$\square$

Geometric Series. We state for $x \neq 1$ formulas for the nth partial sum of the geometric series and its derivatives.

(F.5)
$$\sum_{i=0}^{n} x^i = \frac{x^{n+1}-1}{x-1}.$$

We differentiate the nth partial sum, and we get

(F.6)
$$\sum_{i=0}^{n} ix^{i-1} = \frac{nx^{n+1}-(n+1)x^n+1}{(x-1)^2}.$$

If we multiply the equation by x, we get

(F.7)
$$\sum_{i=0}^{n} ix^i = \frac{nx^{n+2}-(n+1)x^{n+1}+x}{(x-1)^2}.$$

We differentiate the last equation and obtain

$$\sum_{i=0}^{n} i^2 x^{i-1} = \frac{n^2 x^{n+2} - (2n^2 + 2n - 1)x^{n+1} - (n+1)^2 x^n - x - 1}{(x-1)^3}.$$

If we multiply the equation by x, we get

$$\sum_{i=0}^{n} i^2 x^{i} = \frac{n^2 x^{n+3} - (2n^2 + 2n - 1)x^{n+2} - (n+1)^2 x^{n+1} - x^2 - x}{(x-1)^3}.$$

From the formulas above, we get for $|x| < 1$

$$(F.8) \qquad \sum_{i=0}^{\infty} x^i = \frac{1}{1-x}, \quad \sum_{i=0}^{\infty} i x^{i-1} = \frac{1}{(1-x)^2} \text{ and } \sum_{i=0}^{\infty} i x^i = \frac{x}{(1-x)^2}.$$

Exponential Function. The exponential function is usually defined by the power series

$$e^x := \sum_{n=0}^{\infty} \frac{x^n}{n!},$$

which converges for all real numbers. But we can also define it as the limit value of an increasing sequence.

Proposition B.18. *For all $x \in \mathbb{R}$ the sequence*

$$\left(\left(1 + \frac{x}{n}\right)^n \right)_{n \in \mathbb{N}}$$

converges strictly increasing to e^x.

Proof. We compute $\ln\left(\left(1 + \frac{x}{n}\right)^n\right) = n \ln\left(1 + \frac{x}{n}\right)$. Then

$$\lim_{n \to \infty} \frac{\ln\left(1 + \frac{x}{n}\right)}{\frac{x}{n}} = \ln'(1) = 1.$$

The sequence $\frac{\ln\left(1+\frac{x}{n}\right)}{\frac{x}{n}} \left(= \frac{\Delta y}{\Delta x}\right)$ is the sequence of the slopes of the secants for $\Delta x = \frac{x}{n} \to 0$. It converges for $x > 0$ strictly increasing and for $x < 0$ strictly decreasing to the slope of the tangent. From this follows that $n \ln\left(1 + \frac{x}{n}\right)$ is strictly increasing and

$$\lim_{n \to \infty} n \ln\left(1 + \frac{x}{n}\right) = \lim_{n \to \infty} \ln\left(\left(1 + \frac{x}{n}\right)^n\right) = x.$$

Hence, $\left(1 + \frac{x}{n}\right)^n$ is strictly increasing and

$$\lim_{n \to \infty} \left(1 + \frac{x}{n}\right)^n = e^x.$$

This shows the assertion. $\qquad\qquad\qquad\qquad\qquad\qquad\qquad\qquad\qquad\qquad\square$

Corollary B.19. *We have $1 - x \le e^{-x}$ for $x \in \mathbb{R}$.*

Proof. For $x \geq 1$ we have $1 - x \leq 0 < e^{-x}$, and for $x < 1$ we have $1 - x \leq 1 - \frac{x}{2} \leq \ldots \leq e^{-x}$. The last inequality follows with Proposition B.18. $\qquad\square$

Jensen's Inequality. Jensen's[7] inequality is an elementary inequality for convex and concave functions.

Definition B.20. Let $f : I \longrightarrow \mathbb{R}$, I be an interval. f is said to be *concave* if there is a map $\lambda : I \longrightarrow \mathbb{R}$ such that

$$f(x) \leq f(x_0) + \lambda(x_0)(x - x_0), \text{ for all } x, x_0 \in I.$$

Lemma B.21. *Let $f : I \longrightarrow \mathbb{R}$ be a function that is twice continuously differentiable and let $f'' < 0$. Then f is concave.*

Proof. We expand f at the point x_0 according to the Taylor formula:

$$f(x) = f(x_0) + f'(x_0)(x - x_0) + R_1(x)$$

with the Lagrange[8] remainder

$$R_1(x) = \frac{(x - x_0)^2}{2!} f''(\xi),$$

where ξ is between x and x_0. Since $f'' < 0$, the assertion follows. $\qquad\square$

Lemma B.22 *(Jensen's inequality). Let $f : I \longrightarrow \mathbb{R}$ be a concave function, $a_1, \ldots, a_n \in \mathbb{R}$, $a_i > 0$, $i = 1, \ldots n$, and $\sum_{i=1}^n a_i = 1$. Then for $x_1, \ldots, x_n \in I$ we get*

$$\sum_{i=1}^n a_i f(x_i) \leq f\left(\sum_{i=1}^n a_i x_i\right).$$

Proof. Set $x_0 = \sum_{i=1}^n a_i x_i$. $x_0 \in I$. Since f is concave, $a_i f(x_i) \leq a_i f(x_0) + a_i \lambda(x_0)(x_i - x_0)$, $i = 1, \ldots, n$. From this follows

$$\sum_{i=1}^n a_i f(x_i) \leq \sum_{i=1}^n a_i f(x_0) + a_i \lambda(x_0)(x_i - x_0)$$

$$= f(x_0) \sum_{i=1}^n a_i + \lambda(x_0) \left(\sum_{i=1}^n a_i x_i - x_0 \sum_{i=1}^n a_i\right)$$

$$= f\left(\sum_{i=1}^n a_i x_i\right).$$

This shows the lemma. $\qquad\square$

---

[7] Johan Ludwig Jensen (1859 – 1925) was a Danish mathematician.
[8] Joseph-Louis de Lagrange (1736 – 1813) was an Italian mathematician and astronomer. Among other things, he is responsible for the Lagrange formalism of classical mechanics.

Transformation to Solve Recurrences. There are recurrences which can be transformed by a variable transformation into a difference equation (remark after Corollary 1.27, proof of Proposition 2.31 and of Proposition 5.31). From a closed solution of the difference equation – if we can continue the solution to $\mathbb{R}_{\geq 0}$ – we can compute a closed solution of the recurrence by applying the inverse transformation. In our applications, the solution is usually defined by functions whose domain consists of the positive real numbers and is restricted to $\mathbb{N}$. Therefore, in these cases the continuation is canonically given.

Let $f : \mathbb{N} \times \mathbb{R}_{\geq 0} \longrightarrow \mathbb{R}_{\geq 0}$ be a function and

$$y_k = y(k) = f(k, y(k-1)) \text{ for } k > 1, \ y(1) = b,$$

a first-order difference equation.[9] Let L_y be a closed solution for $y(k)$, i.e., $y(k) = L_y(k)$ for $k \in \mathbb{N}$. Suppose that the function L_y has a continuation on $\mathbb{R}_{\geq 0}$, which we again call L_y.

Lemma B.23. *Let* $t : \mathbb{R}_{\geq 0} \longrightarrow \mathbb{R}_{\geq 0}$ *be invertible, and let* $x : \mathbb{R}_{\geq 0} \longrightarrow \mathbb{R}_{\geq 0}$ *be a function such that for all* $k \in \mathbb{N}$

$$y(k) = x(t(k))$$

holds. Let L_y *be a continuation of the closed solution for* $y(k)$ *with* $y(k) = L_y(k)$ *for* $k \in \mathbb{R}_{\geq 0}$*. Then* $L_x = L_y \circ t^{-1}$ *is a closed solution for* $x(n)$*, i.e.,* $x(n) = L_x(n)$ *for* $n \in \mathbb{R}_{\geq 0}$*.*

Let t *be an increasing transformation and* $L_y = O(g)$ *for a function* g*. More exactly we require* $L_y(n) \leq cg(n)$ *for all* $n \in \mathbb{R}_{\geq 0}$ *and* $n \geq n_0$ *for constants* c *and* n_0*. Then* $L_x = O(g \circ t^{-1})$ *for all solutions* L_x*.*

Proof.

$$x(n) = x(t(t^{-1}(n))) = L_y(t^{-1}(n)) = L_y \circ t^{-1}(n) = L_x(n)$$

for $n \in \mathbb{R}_{\geq 0}$.

The statement about the order follows from

$$L_x(n) = L_x(t(t^{-1}(n))) = L_y(t^{-1}(n)) \leq cg(t^{-1}(n)) = c(g \circ t^{-1})(n)$$

for $n \in \mathbb{N}$ with $n \geq t(n_0)$. $\qquad\qquad\qquad\qquad\qquad\qquad\qquad\square$

Remark. The formula for L_x depends on the choice of the extension L_y. Regardless of the choice of L_y, the following applies: $x(t(n)) = L_y(n)$ for $n \in \mathbb{N}$. The statement about the order of L_x does not depend on the choice of the continuation L_y.

---

[9] To get the definition of a first-order linear difference equation (see Section 1.3.1), which is a special case of this notation, we set $f(k, y(k-1)) = a_k y_{k-1} + b_k$.

Metric Spaces. In a Euclidean vector space, such as the $\mathbb{R}^n$, the distance between two points can be calculated using the scalar product and the Theorem of Pythagoras[10]. The distance function defined in this way has values in the positive real numbers, it is symmetrical and the triangle inequality holds. For three points in the plane that form a triangle, this means that the sum of the lengths of two sides of the triangle is always greater than the length of the third side of the triangle. If you take these properties as axioms of a map on $X \times X$, for a set X, then you get the definition of a metric and a metric space.

Definition B.24 *(metric space).* Let X be a set. A map

$$d : X \times X \longrightarrow \mathbb{R}$$

is called a *metric* or *distance function* on X if for arbitrary elements x, y and $z \in X$ the following axioms are fulfilled:

1. $d(x, y) \geq 0$, and $d(x, y) = 0$ exactly if $x = y$ (positive definite).
2. $d(x, y) = d(y, x)$ (symmetry).
3. $d(x, y) \leq d(x, z) + d(z, y)$ (triangle inequality).

X is called a *metric space* if a metric is defined on X.

Examples of (finite) metric spaces are connected graphs (Chapters 5 and 6). Conversely, every finite metric space has a representation by a positively weighted graph.

---

[10] Pythagoras of Samos (c. 570 B.C. – after 510 B.C.) was an ancient Greek philosopher. There are no reliable sources about his life.

References

Textbooks

[AhoHopUll83] A. V. Aho, J. E. Hopcroft, J. D. Ullman: Data Structures and Algorithms. Reading, MA: Addison-Wesley Publishing Company, 1983.

[AhoHopUll74] A. V. Aho, J. E. Hopcroft, J. D. Ullman: The Design and Analysis of Computer Algorithms. Reading, MA: Addison-Wesley Publishing Company, 1974.

[AmannEscher05] H. Amann, J. Escher: Analysis 1. Basel, Boston, Berlin: Birkhäuser Verlag, 2005.

[Backhouse86] R. C. Backhouse: Program Construction and Verification. Englewood Cliffs, New Jersey: Prentice Hall, 1986.

[Bellman57] R. Bellman: Dynamic Programming. Princeton, NJ: Princeton University Press, 1957.

[CorLeiRiv89] T. H. Cormen, C. E. Leiserson, R. L. Rivest: Introduction to Algorithms. Cambridge, London: The MIT Press, 1989.

[CorLeiRivSte09] T. H. Cormen, C. E. Leiserson, R. L. Rivest, C. Stein: Introduction to Algorithms, 3rd ed. Cambridge, London: The MIT Press, 2009.

[DelfsKnebl15] H. Delfs, H. Knebl: Introduction to Cryptography, 3rd ed. Berlin, Heidelberg, New York: Springer-Verlag, 2015.

[MehSan08] K. Mehlhorn, P. Sanders: Algorithms and Data Structures. Berlin, Heidelberg, New York: Springer-Verlag, 2008.

[Elaydi03] S. Elaydi: An Introduction to Difference Equations. Berlin, Heidelberg, New York: Springer-Verlag, 2003.

[Feller68] W. Feller: An Introduction to Probability Theory and its Applications. 3rd ed. New York: John Wiley & Sons, 1968.

[Fischer14] G. Fischer: Lineare Algebra. 18. ed. Wiesbaden: Springer Spektrum, 2014.

[GarJoh79] M. R. Garey, D. S. Johnson: Computers and Intractability: A Guide to the Theory of NP-Completeness. San Francisco: W. H. Freeman, 1979.

[Gould88] R. Gould: Graph Theory. Menlo Park, California: The Benjamin/Cummings Publishing Company, 1988.

[GraKnuPat94] R. L. Graham, D. E. Knuth, O. Patashnik: Concrete Mathematics, 2nd ed. Reading, MA: Addison-Wesley Publishing Company, 1994.

[Gries81] D. Gries: The Science of Programming. Berlin, Heidelberg, New York: Springer-Verlag, 1981.

[HanHarJoh98] D. Hankerson, G. Harris, P. Johnson, Jr.: Introduction to Information Theory and Data Compression. Boca Raton, Boston, New York: CRC Press, 1998.

[Havil07] J. Havil: Gamma. Berlin, Heidelberg, New York: Springer-Verlag, 2007.

[Herrmann16] D. Herrmann: Mathematik im Mittelalter. Berlin, Heidelberg: Springer-Verlag, 2016.

© Springer Nature Switzerland AG 2020
H. Knebl, *Algorithms and Data Structures*, https://doi.org/10.1007/978-3-030-59758-0

[HopMotUll07] J. Hopcroft, R. Motwani, J. Ullman: Introduction to Automata Theory, Languages, and Computation, 3rd ed. Reading, MA: Addison-Wesley Publishing Company, 2007.

[Jungnickel13] D. Jungnickel: Graphs, Networks and Algorithms, 4th ed. Berlin, Heidelberg, New York: Springer-Verlag, 2013.

[Kao16] M. Kao (ed.): Encyclopedia of Algorithms. New York: Springer Science and Business Media, 2016.

[KelPisPfe04] H. Kellerer, D. Pisinger, U. Pferschy: Knapsack problems. Berlin, Heidelberg, New York: Springer-Verlag, 2004.

[KerRit78] B. W. Kernighan, D. M. Ritchie: The C Programming Language. Englewood Cliffs, New Jersey: Prentice Hall, 1978.

[KelPet91] W. G. Kelley, A. C. Peterson: Difference Equations. San Diego: Academic Press, 1991.

[Knebl19] H. Knebl: Algorithmen und Datenstrukturen, Grundlagen und probabilistische Methoden für den Entwurf und die Analyse. Wiesbaden: Springer Vieweg, 2019.

[Knuth97] D. E. Knuth: The Art of Computer Programming, Volume 1/ Fundamental Algorithms. Reading, MA: Addison-Wesley Publishing Company, 1998.

[Knuth98] D. E. Knuth: The Art of Computer Programming, Volume 2/ Seminumerical Algorithms. Reading, MA: Addison-Wesley Publishing Company, 1998.

[Knuth98a] D. E. Knuth: The Art of Computer Programming, Volume 3/ Sorting and Searching. Reading, MA: Addison-Wesley Publishing Company, 1998.

[Knuth11] D. E. Knuth: The Art of Computer Programming, Volume 4A/ Combinatorial Algorithms Part 1. Boston: Pearson Education, Inc., 2011.

[MartToth90] S. Martello, P. Toth P: Knapsack Problems: Algorithms and Computer Implementations. Chichester: Wiley, 1990.

[MotRag95] R. Motwani, P. Raghavan: Randomized Algorithms. Cambridge: Cambridge University Press, 1995.

[RemUll08] R. Remmert, P. Ullrich: Elementare Zahlentheorie, 3. ed. Basel: Birkhäuser Verlag, 2008.

[Sedgewick88] R. Sedgewick: Algorithms, 2nd ed. Reading, MA: Addison-Wesley Publishing Company, 1988.

[SedWay11] R. Sedgewick, K. Wayne: Algorithms, 4th ed. Reading, MA: Addison-Wesley Publishing Company, 2011.

[Schrijver03] A. Schrijver: Combinatorial Optimization. Berlin, Heidelberg, New York: Springer-Verlag, 2003..

[Wirth83] N. Wirth: Algorithmen und Datenstrukturen. Stuttgart: B. G. Teubner, 1983.

Papers

[Ackermann28] W. Ackermann: Zum Hilbertschen Aufbau der reellen Zahlen. Math. Ann. 99: 118-133, 1928.

[AdeLan62] G. M. Adel'son-Vel'skiĭ, E. M. Landis: An algorithm for the organization of information. Doklady Akademia Nauk USSR 146: 263 – 266, 1962 (English translation in Soviet Math. 3: 1259 – 1263, 1962).

[AragSeid89] C. R. Aragon, R. G. Seidel: Randomized search trees. Proceedings of the 30th Annual IEEE Symposium on Foundations of Computer Science: 540–545, 1989.

[BayMcC72] R. Bayer, E. McCreight: Organization and maintenance of large ordered indices. Acta Informatica, 1: 173–189, 1972.

[BeFa00] M. Bender, M. Farach-Colton: The LCA problem revisited. Theoretical Informatics. LATIN 2000. Lecture Notes in Computer Science, 1776: 88 – 94, Springer-Verlag, 2000.

[Borůvka26] O. Borůvka: O jistém problému minimálním. Práca Moravské Přírodovědecké Společnosti, 3: 37–58, 1926.

[Carlson87] S. Carlson: A variant of heapsort with almost optimal number of comparisons. Information Processing Letters, 24: 247-250, 1987.

[CarWeg79] J. L. Carter, M. N. Wegman: Universal classes of hash functions. Journal of Computer and System Sciences, 18: 143–154, 1979.

[CopWin90] D. Coppersmith, S. Winograd: Matrix multiplication via arithmetic progressions. Journal of Symbolic Computation, 9(3): 251–280, 1990.

[Dijkstra59] E. W. Dijkstra: A note on two problems in connexion with graphs. Numerische Mathematik, 1(1): 269–271, 1959.

[Ďurian86] B. Ďurian: Quicksort without a stack. Proc. Math. Foundations of Computer Science, Lecture Notes in Computer Science, 233: 283 – 289, Springer-Verlag, 1986.

[EdmoKarp72] J. Edmonds, R. M. Karp: Theoretical improvements in algorithmic efficiency for network flow problems. Journal of the ACM, 19(2): 248 – 264, 1972.

[Faller73] N. Faller: An adaptive system for data compression. Record of the 7th Asilomar Conference on Circuits, Systems and Computers (IEEE): 593-597, 1973.

[FordFulk56] L. R. Ford Jr., D. R. Fulkerson: Maximal flow through a network. Canadian Journal of Mathematics 8: 399-404, 1956.

[FordFulk62] L. R. Ford Jr., D. R. Fulkerson: Flows in Networks. RAND Corporation Report R-375-PR, 1962.

[Floyd62] R.W. Floyd : Algorithm 97: Shortest path. Communications of the ACM, 5(6): 345, 1962.

[Floyd64] R. W. Floyd: Algorithm 245: Treesort. Communications of the ACM, 7(12): 701, 1964.

[Hoare62] C. A. R. Hoare: Quicksort. Computer Journal, 5: 10–15, 1962.

[HopUll73] J. E. Hopcroft, J. D. Ullman: Set merging algorithms. SIAM Journal on Computing 2(4): 294–303, 1973.

[Huffman52] D. A. Huffman: A method for the construction of minimum-redundancy codes. Proceedings of the IRE: 1098–1101, 1952.

[IliPen10] V. Iliopoulos, P. Penman: Variance of the number of comparisons of randomised Quicksort. http://arXiv.org/abs/1006.4063v1, 2010.

[KarOfm62] A. Karatsuba, Yu. Ofman: Multiplication of multidigit numbers on automata. Doklady Akademia Nauk USSR 145: 293 – 294, 1962 (English translation in Soviet Physics Doklady 7: 595 – 596, 1963).

[Karger93] D. R. Karger: Global min-cuts in RNC, and other ramifications of a simple min-cut algorithm. Proc. 4th ACM-SIAM SODA: 21-30, 1993.

[KarSte96] D. R. Karger, C. Stein: A new approach to the minimum cut problem. Journal of the ACM, 43(4): 601-640, 1996.

[KarKleTar95] D. R. Karger, P. N. Klein, R. E. Tarjan: A randomized linear-time algorithm to find minimum spanning trees. Journal of the ACM, 42(2): 321-328, 1995.

[King97] V. King: A simpler minimum spanning tree verification algorithm. Algorithmica 18: 263–270, 1997.

[Komlós85] J. Komlós: Linear verification for spanning trees. Combinatorica, 5: 57–65, 1985.

[Kruskal56] J. Kruskal: On the shortest spanning sub-tree and the traveling salesman problem. Proceedings of the American Mathematical Society 7: 48–50, 1956.

[Leven65] V. Levenshtein: Binary codes capable of correcting deletions, insertions, and reversals. Sov. Phys. Dokl. 10(8):707–710 (English translation), 1966

[Newman80] D. J. Newman: Simple analytic proof of the prime number theorem. Am. Math. Monthly 87: 693–696, 1980.

[Pasco76] R. Pasco: Source Coding Algorithms for Fast Data Compression. Ph. D. Thesis, Dept. of Electrical Engineering, Stanford University, 1976.

[Prim57] R. C. Prim: Shortest connection networks and some generalizations. Bell System Technical Journal, 36(6): 1389–1401, 1957.

[Rissanen76] J. J. Rissanen: Generalized Kraft inequality and arithmetic coding. IBM Journal of Research and Development, 20(3): 198–203, 1976.

[RobSanSeyTho97] N. Robertson, D. Sanders, P. D. Seymour, R. Thomas: The four-colour theorem. J. Combin. Theory B70: 2–44, 1997.

[SarPat53] A. A. Sardinas, G. W. Patterson: A necessary and sufficient condition for the unique decomposition of coded messages. IRE Internat. Conv. Rec. 8: 104–108, 1953.

[SchStr71] A. Schönhage, V. Strassen: Schnelle Multiplikation großer Zahlen. Computing 7: 281–292, 1971.

[Shannon48] C. E. Shannon: A mathematical theory of communication. Bell Systems Journal, 27: 379–423, 623–656, 1948.

[Shannon49] C. E. Shannon: Communication theory of secrecy systems. Bell Systems Journal, 28: 656–715, 1949.

[Sharir81] M. Sharir: A strong-connectivity algorithm and its applications in data flow analysis. Computers and Mathematics with Applications 7(1): 67–72, 1981.

[SieSch95] A. Siegel, J. P. Schmidt: Closed hashing is computable and optimally randomizable with universal hash functions. Computer Science Tech. Report 687. New York: Courant Institute, 1995.

[Strassen69] V. Strassen: Gaussian Elimination is not optimal. Numerische Mathematik 13: 354-356, 1969.

[Tarjan79] R. E. Tarjan: Applications of path compression on balanced trees. Journal of the ACM, 26(4): 690–715, 1979.

[Tarjan99] R. E. Tarjan: Class notes: Disjoint set union. COS 423, Princeton University, 1999

[WagFis74] R. Wagner, M. Fischer: The string-to-string correction problem. Journal of the ACM, 21(1): 168–173, 1974.

[Warshall62] S. Warshall: A theorem on boolean matrices. Journal of the ACM, 9(1): 11-12, 1962.

[Wegener93] I. Wegener: Bottom-up-heapsort, a new variant of heapsort beating, on an average, quicksort. Theoretical Computer Science 118:81–98, 1993.

[Whitney35] H. Whitney: On the abstract properties of linear dependence. American Journal of Mathematics 57: 509–533, 1935.

[Williams64] J. W. J. Williams: Algorithm 232: Heapsort. Communications of the ACM, 7(6): 347–348, 1964.

[Yao85] A. C. Yao: Uniform hashing is optimal. Journal of the ACM, 32(3): 687–693, 1985.

[ZivLem77] J. Ziv, A. Lempel: A universal algorithm for sequential data compression. IEEE Transactions on Information Theory, 23(3): 337–343, 1977.

[ZivLem78] J. Ziv, A. Lempel: Compression of individual sequences via variable-rate encoding. IEEE Transactions on Information Theory, 24(5): 530–536, 1978.

Internet

[Queens@TUD-Team16] TU Dresden: News, 2016. https://tu-dresden.de/tu-dresden/newsportal/news/neuer-weltrekord-fuer-queens-tud-team, 2016.

Symbols

© Springer Nature Switzerland AG 2020

H. Knebl, *Algorithms and Data Structures*, https://doi.org/10.1007/978-3-030-59758-0

		page
$H(X)$	entropy of a source X	174
$l(C)$	average word length of a code C	174
$\{0,1\}^*$	bit strings of any length	
$a\|b$	concatenation of strings a and b	
$\mathbb{Z}_n$	residue class ring modulo n	328
a div n	integer quotient of a by n	325
a mod n	remainder of a modulo n	325
$\mathbb{F}_q$	finite field with q elements	
$\prod_{i=1}^n a_i$	product $a_1 \cdot \ldots \cdot a_n$	
$\sum_{i=1}^n a_i$	sum $a_1 + \ldots + a_n$	
$[a,b],]a,b], [a,b[,]a,b[$	intervals (closed, half-open and open)	
i..j	sequence $i, i+1, \ldots, j$	
a[i..j]	partial array $a[i..j]$	65
min $a[i..j]$	minimum in partial array $a[i..j]$	
$a.b$	structure member operator "."	65
$\lfloor x \rfloor$	biggest integer $\leq x$	
$\lceil x \rceil$	smallest integer $\geq x$	
$O(f(n))$	O notation	10
$p(\mathcal{E})$	probability of an event $\mathcal{E}$	307
$p(x)$	probability of an elementary event $x \in \mathcal{X}$	307
$p(\mathcal{E} \mid \mathcal{F})$	conditional probability of $\mathcal{E}$ assuming $\mathcal{F}$	308
$E(X)$	expected value of a random variable X	309
$\text{Var}(X)$	variance of a random variable X	309
$\sigma(X)$	standard deviation of a random variable X	309
$G_X(z)$	generating function of a random variable X	312

Index

algorithm
- algorithm design 31
-- branch and bound with backtracking 47
-- divide and conquer 33
-- dynamic programming 39
-- greedy 36
-- recursion 32
- breadth-first search 217
- computing the nth Fibonacci number 20
- correctness 2
-- postcondition 2
-- precondition 2
- depth-first search 131, 221
- efficient algorithm 13
- fast exponentiation 20
- LZ77 194
- LZ78 196
- LZW 198
- randomized algorithms 54
-- binary search trees 148
-- Las Vegas algorithm 58
-- min-cut algorithm 232
-- Monte Carlo algorithm 58
-- MST algorithm 284
-- quicksort 83
-- quickselect 99
algorithm of
- Borůvka 271
- Dijkstra 262
- Edmonds-Karp 300
- Faller, Gallager and Knuth 178
- Floyd, maximal flow 290
- Ford-Fulkerson 296
- Huffman 175
- Karger, Klein, Tarjan 284
- Kosaraju-Sharir 230
- Kruskal 270
- Prim 264
- Strassen 30
- Tarjan, LCA 254

- Tarjan, strongly connected components 227
- Warshall/Floyd 289

backtracking 47
Bellman's optimality equation 39
binary search, see searching in arrays
binomial coefficient, see formulas
binomial series, see formulas

Catalan numbers 203
codes 168
- alphabet 168
- arithmetic codes 184
-- adaptive arithmetic coding 192
-- calculation of the representative 186
-- coding the length of the message 192
-- decoding 191
-- decoding with rescaling 192
-- interval assignment 184
-- rescaling 188
-- underflow treatment 189
- average code length 174
- code tree, see tree
- compact or minimal 174
- criterion for unique decodability 169
- dictionary methods 193
- Elias delta code 173
- Elias gamma code 173
- encoding of X over Y 168
- entropy 174
- Huffman codes 174
-- adaptive procedure 178
-- encoding and decoding 178
-- Huffman algorithm 175
-- Huffman tree 179
-- weight list 183
- immediate codes, see prefix codes
- information content 174
- Lempel-Ziv codes 193
- lossless coding 168

Printed in the United States
by Baker & Taylor Publisher Services